Labor Laws
of the
Republic *of* Korea

Labor Laws
of the
Republic *of* Korea

Ji-Hyung Kim *et al.*

[] Hollym

Labor Laws of the Republic of Korea

Copyright © 2015
by JIPYONG

All rights reserved.

First published in 2015
by Hollym International Corp., USA
Phone 908 353 1655   **Fax** 908 353 0255
http://www.hollym.com   **e-Mail** contact@hollym.com

⌷ Hollym

Published simultaneously in Korea
by Hollym Corp., Publishers, Seoul, Korea
Phone +82 2 734 5087   **Fax** +82 2 730 5149
http://www.hollym.co.kr   **e-Mail** info@hollym.co.kr

ISBN: 978-1-56591-478-0
Library of Congress Control Number: 2015942403

Printed in Korea

CONTENTS

Chapter 2. Working Hours and Recess

Chapter 5. Retirement Benefit System

Chapter 6. Transfer of Labor Relations

Chapter 7. Rules of Employment

Chapter 8. Dismissals

Chapter 9. Personnel Movement

Chapter 10. The Equal Employment Opportunity and Work-Family Balance Assistance Act

UNION ACT

Chapter 1. Trade Unions

Chapter 2. Collective Bargaining and Collective Agreements

Part 1. Collective Bargaining

Chapter 3. Industrial Action

Chapter 4. Adjustment of Industrial Disputes

Chapter 5. Unfair Labor Practices

Appendix

PREFACE

This book is an introduction in English to the labor laws of the Republic of Korea. My co-authors and I wrote this book to help non-Korean-speaking people and foreign corporations understand how Korean labor law is interpreted and applied in practice.

Before the release of this book, there was a dearth of publications that addressed the basics of Korean labor law in a comprehensive manner. Of course, one could always refer to *The Statues of the Republic of Korea*, a book published by the Korea Legislation Research Institute that contains English translations of certain portions of Korean labor law. Up until now, however, it has been difficult to find any one book in English that renders interpretations of Korean labor law and provides careful analysis of how it is applied in practice.

The Labor & Employment Practice Group at JIPYONG has long represented and advised a wide range of clients, including many foreign clients, on various labor matters. Through our representation of foreign clients, we became aware that there was no reference book on Korean labor laws in English, and this made us explore the idea of publishing this book.

Today, the so-called "legal relations which contain foreign factors" (Article 1 of the Conflict of Law Act) are quite commonly created. Given this, it becomes obvious that no law, regardless of jurisdiction, can be applied separately to natives and foreigners. The same goes for labor relationships, and it becomes clear that Korean labor laws are not just for Koreans but are also for foreigners and foreign corporations.

The literature on laws of a nation, written in languages commonly understood such as English, is an invaluable resource for foreigners in understanding such laws. The premise for publishing this book started from this core assumption, and we wanted to write a reference book about Korean labor laws in English to facilitate the proper understanding of them by foreigners and foreign corporations.

However, no idea materializes by itself. Many people worked hard to publish this book. The Labor & Employment Practice Group attorneys and the U.S. attorneys at JIPYONG as well as a U.S. attorney who specializes in labor law gladly participated in writing this book. My heartfelt appreciation goes to them more than anyone else. Without their dedicated participation and affectionate efforts, this book could not have come into being.

I have maintained my interest in labor law for three decades as a judge, Supreme Court Justice and member of the Labor & Employment Practice Group at JIPYONG. As a jurist and legal professional who has engaged in the study of labor law throughout my entire career, I am overjoyed by the publication of this book.

Now I sincerely hope that on behalf of all the contributors to this book that it will realize our original intentions to assist foreigners and foreign corporations to better understand Korean labor laws by providing them practical, useful information.

Since this book is intended to introduce the basics of Korean labor laws, it may be limited in extensive coverage of specific legal provisions or issues. It is my wish, however, that the publication of this book will trigger others to publish more in-depth examinations of Korean labor laws in English. It would indeed be a great honor if this book can serve as a means by which people can increase their awareness of Korean labor law and how it is used in everyday, real-life situations.

I would like to take this opportunity to express my gratitude to Mr. Kong-hyun Lee and Mr. Young-tae Yang, managing partners of JIPYONG, for their great interest in and unwavering support for this book and to Hollym Publishers for gladly agreeing to publish this book and creating its beautiful design.

I believe that publishing a book is like giving birth to a new life. Our efforts should not stop there, however, and we must resolve ourselves to further efforts to continue the growth and development of its purpose.

Ji-hyung Kim
June, 2015

Reference Materials

The abbreviations used to refer to the statutes referenced in this book are as follows:

Title	Abbreviation
Labor Standards Act	LSA
Trade Union and Labor Relations Adjustment Act	Union Act
Equal Employment Opportunity and Work-Family Balance Assistance Act	EEO Act

Full translations of the Labor Standards Act and the Trade Union and Labor Relations Adjustment Act are attached as an appendix. Other Korean laws can be found at the Korea Legislation Research Institute's website. (http://elaw.klri.re.kr)

INTRODUCTION

I. The Structure of Labor Law

The term "labor law" generally describes the legal system regulating labor relations. The statute regulating labor relations in the Republic of Korea was enacted only in 1953 (five years after the founding of the Republic in 1948), and was generally modeled after post-war Japan's labor relations legislation. This Japanese system, in turn, is known to have been influenced by the labor policies of the military government led by General MacArthur. Such origins explain why labor relations laws of the Republic of Korea have elements of the U.S. labor system (e.g. laws establishing labor relations commissions and regulating unfair labor practices) despite having their foundations in the civil law system.

Similar to labor laws in other countries, the Republic of Korea's labor laws also consist of diverse regulatory systems to protect the status of workers in their legal relations with employers.

Labor relations, which are governed by labor laws, may be broadly divided into two categories: individual and collective labor relations. As such, the labor law system may also be classified into two corresponding groups: individual labor relations law and collective labor relations law.

Individual labor relations may be defined as the legal relationship between individual workers and their employers regarding duties and rights concerning working conditions, including its substance (e.g. content and validity) as well its procedure (e.g. the establishment, modification, and termination of the relationship). This relationship is determined by individual labor relations laws.

Collective labor relations may be defined as the legal relationship between workers and employers concerning activities related to collective action, such as organizing worker organizations (e.g. unions), engaging in collective bargaining with employers or employer organizations to agree upon (among other issues) working conditions, engaging in collective action such as industrial actions (e.g. strikes). This relationship is determined by collective labor relations laws.

The primary positive laws comprising labor law are the Labor Standards Act (hereinafter the "LSA") and the Trade Union and Labor Relations Adjustment Act (hereinafter referred as the "Union Act").

The LSA lays out the minimum standard of working conditions that must be met by employers. The LSA also provides the basis of the enforcement of working conditions. Working conditions violating the LSA are invalid. In many cases, violation of the LSA results in sanctions such as criminal prosecution and/or monetary fines.

The Union Act guarantees the worker's right of assembly, and on this basis stipulates regulations that make it possible to exercise rights in collective bargaining and collective action. Specifically, the Union Act guarantees the status of the worker by legislating on issue areas related to labor disputes such as trade unions, collective bargaining, collective agreement, and industrial action.

In analyzing the Korean labor law system as a whole, there is one conspicuous characteristic that most commentators take note of. This is the fact that while working conditions are relatively well protected under individual labor relations laws, protection of working conditions are relatively weak under the collective labor relation legal scheme.

Take the Statutory Severance Payment System, for example. This labor legislation, unique to the Korean system compared to that of other countries, mandates employers to pay severance amounts equal to or above the minimum level designated by the law. Protection of the employment relationship is also relatively strong, so once an employment relationship has been established employers may not terminate the relationship without just cause. Dismissal for managerial reasons is only possible upon the satisfaction of specific (and relatively difficult to satisfy) conditions.

Contrary to individual labor relations, the degree of legislative control over collective labor relations is relatively strict. This is due to the historical backdrop of the political, economic, and social context of the pre-1980s era, when collective labor action was subject to many restrictions by an authoritarian political system promoting the policy of concentrating resources for the sake of high economic growth. The political climate shifted since the late 1980s, however, and societal requests to alleviate such strict controls on collective labor started to be strongly advanced.

The tide shifted again during the late 1990s when the Asian Financial Crisis struck and neoliberalism came into practice, which resulted in calls for increased "flexibility of the labor market," meaning lower protections for individual labor relations. To meet these demands, recently there were revisions to the LSA as well as the enactment of new labor and employment statutes (e.g. The Act on the Protection of Fixed-Term and Part-Time Workers, and the Act on the Protection of Temporary Agency Workers) to relax protections regarding working conditions such as term of contract and working hours along with employment type such as irregular employment.

In this respect, it is appropriate to say that the labor law system of the Republic of Korea is quite complex.

II. The Sources of Labor Law

The term "source of law" may be used in many different ways. Here it will be used to indicate in what form legal norms exist.

Sources of labor law can be largely classified into positive law, local statute, customary (or consuetudinary) law, and international labor law.

A. Types of Legal Sources

1) Positive Law

i) Constitutional Law

The highest law of the land in the Korean legal system is the constitution. Any subordinate legal norm that is inconsistent with the constitution is considered invalid. If the constitutional court determines that a particular law violates the constitution, that law becomes nullified. The constitution also serves as the standard of interpretation for subordinate legal norms.

The representative constitutional provisions most related to the labor laws of Korea are Articles 32 and 33 of the Constitution. Article 32 is mostly related to individual labor relations, and Article 33 mostly with collective labor relations.

> Article 32 (Right and duty to work, minimum wage, protection of women and children, preferential opportunity for those who have given distinguished service to the state)
> (1) All citizens shall have the right to work. The State shall endeavor to promote the employment of workers and to guarantee optimum wages through social and economic means and shall enforce a minimum wage system under the conditions as prescribed by Act.
> (2) All citizens shall have the duty to work. The State shall prescribe by Act the extent and conditions of the duty to work in conformity

with democratic principles.

(3) Standards of working conditions shall be determined by Act in such a way as to guarantee human dignity.

(4) Special protection shall be accorded to working women, and they shall not be subjected to unjust discrimination in terms of employment, wages and working conditions.

(5) Special protection shall be accorded to working children.

(6) The opportunity to work shall be accorded preferentially, under the conditions as prescribed by Act, to those who have given distinguished service to the State, wounded veterans and police officers, and members of the bereaved families of military servicemen and police officers killed in action.

Article 33 (Right to association and collective action)

(1) To enhance working conditions, workers shall have the right to independent association, collective bargaining and collective action.

(2) Only those public officials who are designated by Act shall have the right to association, collective bargaining and collective action.

(3) The right to collective action of workers employed by important defense industries may be either restricted or denied under the conditions as prescribed by Act.

ii) Statutes

Statutes concerning individual labor relations include the LSA mentioned above, as well as the "Guarantee of Workers' Retirement Benefits Act," the "Minimum Wage Act," the "Wage Claim Guarantee Act," the "Act on the Protection of Fixed-Term and Part-Time Workers," the "Act on the Protection of Temporary Agency Workers," the "Equal Employment Opportunity and Work-Family Balance Assistance Act," the "Occupational Safety and Health Act," and the "Industrial Accident Compensation Insurance Act."

Statutes concerning collective labor relations include the "Trade

Union and Labor Relations Adjustment Act," as well the "Labor Relations Commission Act," and the "Act on the Promotion of Workers' Participation and Cooperation."

Statutes related to the field of labor law are by principle legally enforceable for the purpose of protecting workers. As such, should any collective agreement, rules of employment, or a labor contract contain provisions that disadvantage workers in violation of the labor laws outlined above, such instrument would be invalid.

iii) Enforcement Ordinances, Directives and Regulations

Enforcement ordinances, directives and regulations are established by administrative agencies within the boundary of their mandate as stipulated by the enabling law. The purpose of these regulations is to supplement statutory content and lay out provisions necessary to enforce the law that it supports. These regulations typically come in the form of executive orders, ordinances of the prime minister, and ministerial ordinances. Examples of the same would be the "Enforcement Decree of the Labor Standards Act" (an executive order) and the "Enforcement Regulation of the Labor Standards Act" (a ministerial ordinance) that supplements the LSA, as well as the "Enforcement Decree of the Trade Union and Labor Relations Adjustment Act" and the "Enforcement Regulation of the Trade Union and Labor Relations Adjustment Act" that supplements the Union Act.

Unlike legal orders, administrative regulations stipulate internal operational standards without specific statutory basis in the parent statute. Typically these come in the form of bulletins, instructions, standard operating procedures, and notifications. These regulations do not have a legally binding effect. An illustrative example of this would be the "Guideline on Ordinary Wages for Workers and Employers," which has been established by the Ministry of Employment and Labor.

2) Local Statutes

Labor relations are often compared to other legal relationships in that the constitution guarantees to the worker the right to freedom of independent association and collective bargaining. The courts acknowledge this special status by recognizing the following local statutes:

i) Union Bylaws

Labor/trade unions establish bylaws in order to self-regulate the organization and operation of the union as well as to manage its budget and determine the rights and duties of union members. Unions must submit bylaws when they notify their establishment to the labor administration office. Bylaws must contain information regarding matters designated by the subparagraphs in Article 11 (Bylaws) of the Union Act. Such bylaws, and other local regulations decided based on the authority of these bylaws, have legal authority over union members in the form of self-regulating norms.[1] However, bylaws become invalid if it is determined that they violate the spirit of the constitution by failing to uphold fundamental rights or are inconsistent with superior, imperative laws.[2]

ii) Rules of Employment

An employer may establish Rules of Employment and regulate working conditions as well as other matters related to the employment of its workers affiliated with its establishment. Employers that employ 10 or more full-time workers must develop Rules of Employment that deal with matters as required by Article 93 (Preparation and Reporting of Rules of Employment) of the LSA and notify this to the Minister of

---

1 Supreme Court 2000Da65086 (2002. 2. 22.), Supreme Court 2001Du10264 (2003. 12. 26.)
2 Supreme Court 91Da42128 (1992. 6. 9.), Supreme Court 96Da55457 (1997. 3. 25.), Supreme Court 97Da41349 (2000. 1. 14.), Supreme Court 2000Da65086 (2002. 2. 22.)

Employment and Labor. These Rules are unilaterally developed by the employer,[3] but the courts deem the Rules to have legally binding authority over workers.[4]

As such, should employment conditions determined in an employment contract fall short of the standards found in the Rules of Employment, the applicable section becomes void and its contents are substituted by the standards set forth in the Rules of Employment.[5]

iii) Collective Agreements

Labor/trade unions and employers (including employers' associations) enter into collective agreements that are valid for one or two years.[6] Collective agreements set forth the standard of employee working conditions and other treatment of workers who are union members. This is what is known as the "normative section" of the agreement. Collective agreements also include the rights and obligations between the parties to the agreement (i.e. the union and the employer). This is what is known as the "contractual section" of the agreement. Insofar the collective agreement remains valid, the normative section applies to existing and new union members, and may even apply to non-union employees, subject to certain conditions.[7]

Should any part of the Rules of Employment or an individual employment contract contradict the standards laid out by the normative part of the collective agreement (i.e. regarding working conditions and other treatment of workers), that part shall be determined invalid and replaced with the corresponding provisions of the collective agreement.[8]

---

3 However, should the Rules of Employment be modified to the detriment of the worker, the consent of the worker is required. See Article 94(1) of the LSA.

4 Supreme Court 77Da355 (1977. 7. 26.)

5 LSA, Article 97

6 Union Act, Article 32

7 Ibid., Articles 35 and 36

8 Ibid., Article 33

3) Customary Law – Common Law and Customary Practice

Common law arises when a certain social norm is created and that norm is practiced by society with the conviction that the conduct is required by law (*or, in other words, with opinio juris*).[9] Common law acquires binding legal force as long as it does not conflict with the overall legal order of the society.

On the other hand, if a social norm fails to assume *opinio juris* yet continues to be practiced as custom, this norm becomes "de facto custom"[10] and becomes the basis of interpreting expressions of intent. Labor practices may or may not become norms that regulate the employment relationship for a particular instance, depending how they are assessed in light of the totality of the circumstances.[11]

4) International Labor Law – ILO Conventions and Recommendations

The International Labour Organization (hereinafter "ILO"), a specialized agency of the United Nations, adopts Conventions and Recommendations to define the minimum international standards of protection for workers around the world through its International Labour Conventions. As of the end of 2013, the ILO had adopted a total of 189 Conventions. Among these, the following eight are deemed to be fundamental:

Freedom of Association
C87: Freedom of Association and Protection of the Right to Organize Convention
C98: Right to Organize and Collective Bargaining Convention

---

9 Supreme Court 2002Da1178 (2005. 7. 21.)

10 Civil Act, Article 106

11 For cases where labor practices have been recognized as norms that regulate employment relations, *see, e.g.* Supreme Court 2001Da41384 (2002. 4. 12.), Supreme Court 2000Da18127 (2002. 5. 31). For cases where labor practices failed to do so, *see, e.g.* Supreme Court 92Da11695 (1993. 1. 26.), Supreme Court 2000Da50701 (2002. 4. 23.).

The Abolition of Forced Labor
C29: Forced Labour Convention
C105: Abolition of Forced Labour Convention

Equality
C100: Equal Remuneration Convention
C111: Discrimination (Employment and Occupation) Convention

The Elimination of Child Labor
C138: Minimum Age Convention
C182: Worst Forms of Child Labour Convention

The Republic of Korea became a member state of the ILO when it joined on December 9, 1991, and to date has ratified 28 of the 189 conventions. Among the eight fundamental conventions, Korea has only ratified four (C100, C111, C138, C182), and is under strong pressure from the ILO, OECD, the international society in general, and the domestic labor industry to ratify the remaining four.

Ratified conventions have the same binding force as domestic laws, as per Article 6(1) of the Korean constitution. Unratified conventions do not have such authority, but the fundamental spirit of said conventions may be considered when interpreting domestic laws.

5) Individual Employment Contracts
The matter of whether individual employment contracts entered into between workers and employers may be considered as a source of law is as of yet unsettled amongst labor law scholars in Korea.

This matter is important (and will be dealt with in more detail below) because the question of whether the principle of "placing priority on better conditions" (i.e. the principle that rulings of subordinate courts may take precedence over that of superior courts if the former would result in better protection of working conditions) could be applied in determining the order of authority between sources of law would be answered differently depending on which side of the fence a person stands with regards to the validity of individual employment contracts as a source of law.

B. The Order of Authority between Sources of Law

1) The Principle of Placing Priority on Higher/Superior Laws

Among the sources of labor law in Korea, the Constitution assumes the highest authority, followed by statutes, ordinances directives, collective agreements, rules of employment, and union bylaws, in that respective order. Customary law and ratified international treaties and conventions are given equal authority as statutes.

Should there be conflict between legal sources that may simultaneously be applied to a particular issue, the higher/superior law takes priority over the subordinate law.

An interesting wrinkle to this principle is the hotly debated argument that legal norms from a subordinate source of law should take precedence over that of superior sources if the former would result in better protection of workers (the so-called "principle of placing priority on better working conditions"). As of date, however, case law[12] indicates that the Korean courts are rejecting the validity of the principle placing priority on better working conditions.

2) Principle of Placing Priority on Recent Regulations

If there are multiple legal regulations that may be applied to a given issue, and the sources of conflicting laws occupy the same level of authority and differ only by the date in which they were enacted or

---

12 Supreme Court 92Da51341 (1993. 3. 23.), Supreme Court 95Da34316 (1997. 6. 10.), Supreme Court 96Da6967 (1997. 8. 22.), Supreme Court 2003Da27429 (2005. 3. 11.)

determined, priority will be given to the regulation that has been most recently promulgated and/or decided.

3) Principle of Placing Priority on Special Regulations
In instances where multiple conflicting laws occupy the same level of authority yet differ in the fact that some are general laws and others are special laws, the latter sources take priority over the former.

III. Types of Labor Disputes

A. The Significance of Labor Disputes

Labor disputes are conflicts between workers (or unions) and employers (or employers' organizations). The legal relationship between workers and employers is a regular and periodic one, and is regulated in a collective and uniform manner. As such, an individual labor dispute often causes great repercussions to this relationship as a whole. Adding to this, should the labor/trade union present itself as a party to labor relations (relying on its authority as the association of workers), a labor dispute may quickly become complex and involve higher stakes.

Depending on whom the parties are, and what the characteristics of the dispute are, labor disputes may be classified as follows:

B. The Classification of Labor Disputes

1) Individual Labor Disputes
The first type of labor disputes are individual labor disputes, which are disputes regarding rights and duties surrounding employment conditions between individual workers and employers in an independent contractual relationship.

Scenarios representative of such disputes include: a) the employee disputing the validity of the employer's unfavorable personnel action (e.g. discharge) and calling for its nullification, b) the employee requesting the disbursement of unpaid wages, benefits, and severance pay from the part of the employer, c) the employee requesting compensation from the employer for injuries suffered from an industrial accident, d) one party disputing whether it is in an employment relationship with the other party.

Such individual labor disputes are generally resolved via the adjudicative process (which will be dealt with in more detail below). This is not to say that consensual or meditative processes are not used as well, but they are employed on a much less frequent basis.

2) Collective Labor Disputes

The second type of labor disputes are collective labor disputes. These are disputes that arise when unions and employers (including employers' associations) negotiate collective agreements, and usually involve disagreements regarding working conditions as well as duties and rights surrounding the employment relationship.

Scenarios representative of such disputes include: a) unions and employers failing to agree on a collective agreement due to discrepancies in demands regarding working conditions such as wages, working hours, welfare, termination and other treatment of workers;[13] b) workers and unions arguing that the employer has engaged in unfair labor practices by dominating and/or intervening in the activities of the union or during its formation process, and that the consequences of such actions must be declared void; c) employers arguing that industrial actions undertaken by unions or union members are illegal and requesting damages for losses resulting from such actions.

---

13 This scenario is identical to the concept of "industrial disputes" as defined in Article 2(5) of the Trade Union and Labor Relations Adjustment Act.

In resolving these different types of collective labor disputes, the consensual process is deemed to be appropriate methods to resolve the first type (a), whereas the adjudicative process is most frequently used to resolve disputes in scenarios b) and c).

C. The Process of Resolving Labor Disputes

1) The Adjudicative Process

The adjudicative process includes judicial proceedings via the court system as well as administrative proceedings via the Labor Relations Commission.

Let's say, for example, that an employer commenced an unfavorable personnel action (e.g. termination) against its employee. The employee now has the option to bring suit against the employer by going directly to the court system to dispute the action's validity. The resulting lawsuit will be adjudicated by the courts according to the regulations of the Civil Procedure Act.

Instead of going through the court system, however, the employee may also file for relief with the Labor Relations Commission. The Local/Regional and Central Labor Relations Commissions would then make judgments regarding this allegation of unfair termination in turn, and if the losing party wants to contest the decision it may file an administrative suit with the court.

Another example would be when the employer argues that the actions of employees or trade unions (e.g. organizing, strikes, etc.) constitute unfair labor practice and is hence invalid. In such a case, similar to the above example, the Labor Relations Commission deliberates this allegation of unfair labor practice and determines whether relief should be granted. The losing party then has the option of filing an administrative suit with the courts should they wish to appeal the decision of the Commission.

2) The Consensual Process

The objective of the consensual process is to have conflicting parties mediate in order to arrive at an amicable settlement. This process would be used when it is necessary to reconcile parties engaged in the collective bargaining process as they attempt to reconcile differences in demands regarding working conditions such as wages, working hours, welfare, termination and other treatments. In the current legal system there are two methods of promoting the consensual process: mediation and arbitration.

i) Mediation

Mediation may be subdivided into private and public mediation depending on the identity of the mediator. Private mediation is conducted when the parties to the dispute designate a mediator, who then presides over the mediation process.[14] Public mediation is conducted when the mediation process is led by a judicial or semi-judicial entity such as the Labor Relations Commission.[15]

Private mediation is rarely used, and most industrial actions are mediated by the Labor Relations Commission. This is due to the fact that the current law stipulates that all industrial actions cannot take place before completing adjustment procedures with the Labor Relations Commission.[16] This is the so-called "conciliation-prepositive principle," or the principle of prefixing conciliation.

Mediation can also be distinguished between voluntary or compulsory mediation, depending on whether or not the process is initiated by the parties' own volition. Public mediation provided by the Labor Relations Commission is by principle initiated voluntarily by the parties. An exception to this principle would be emergency mediation,[17]

---

14 Union Act, Article 52
15 Ibid., Article 53
16 Ibid., Article 45(2)
17 Ibid., Article 76

which is invoked when the Minister of Labor and Employment decides to exercise his authority to start the mediation process on a compulsory basis.

ii) Arbitration

Arbitration is a process where the arbitrator seeks to resolve a dispute between parties by proposing an arbitration plan. Like mediation, arbitration can also be divided into private arbitration[18] and public arbitration[19] depending on the identity of the arbitrator.

In principle, the parties to the dispute may voluntarily agree on whether to initiate arbitration proceedings, and whether to accept the arbitration plan presented by the arbitrator. However, arbitration carried out by the Labor Relations Commission deviates somewhat from this principle in that while the parties may voluntarily agree to initiate arbitration proceedings[20] (actually in many cases the proceedings are mandated under the collective agreement), once the arbitrator has proposed his/her arbitration plan the parties are legally bound to such plan.[21] Also, when the Minister of Labor and Employment deems it appropriate to commence emergency arbitration,[22] both the initiation of the proceedings and the binding legal effect of the resulting arbitration plan becomes compulsory.

iii) Labor Inspector Scheme

The labor inspector scheme is an administrative supervisory measure stipulated in the LSA[23] devised to proactively ensure compliance with the LSA and other related labor legislation, as well as to facilitate timely

18 Ibid., Article 52
19 Ibid., Article 62
20 Ibid.
21 Ibid., Article 70
22 Ibid., Articles 79 and 70
23 LSA, Articles 101 through 106

follow-up measures for incidences of non-compliance.

Labor inspectors are placed within the Ministry of Employment and Labor and affiliated institutions. Inspectors are bestowed with judicial as well as administrative authority.

Specifically, labor inspectors have administrative authority in that they may enter into and inspect business establishments, gain access to ledgers and business records, and interview employers and workers for necessary information to determine whether there have been violations to the LSA.

Labor inspectors also have judicial authority in that they conduct the duties of a judicial police officer as an agent of law enforcement when it comes to violations of the LSA. This authority is usually invoked when a worker files a complaint alleging that the employer has violated the LSA or related labor laws. At this point the labor inspector conducts the necessary investigations, and either commences an investigation when s/he concludes that an illegal act has taken place or (depending on the situation) sets a certain period of time during which the employer may remedy the cause of the complaint. In the latter case the investigator concludes the investigation if the employer implements the proposed remedial measures within the given timeframe, but if the employer fails to do so the investigator proceeds to recognize the act being illegal and commences a formal investigation.

The significance of the labor inspector scheme in resolving labor disputes is quite high, as the role and function of labor inspectors have steadily expanded in the field throughout the years.

D. The Process of Litigating Labor Disputes

There are nine typical methods used when the adjudicative process is employed to resolve labor disputes: Remedial procedures for wrongful terminations; Remedial procedures for unfair labor practices; Litigation procedures for payment of wages, benefits, and severance payments; Litigation procedures for payment of damages resulting from industrial actions; Remedial procedures for industrial accidents; Remedial procedures for the interpretation of collective agreements; Labor injunctions; Criminal litigation; Constitutional litigation.

1) Remedial Procedures for Wrongful Terminations
i) Procedures for Civil Litigation

When an employer implements an adverse action against its worker such as termination, suspension, transfer, pay reduction, or other measures of punishment, the worker may bring civil suit to the court and request the action be held as invalid.

An employer may implement an adverse action against its worker such as dismissal or discharge when it has just cause.[24] Therefore the burden of proof is on the employer to show that it had just cause in terminating the worker when s/he initiates a suit to affirm the invalidity of his/her discharge.

The terminated worker may also petition for unpaid salaries and wages for the period after the termination at the time s/he petitions for its invalidity.

Should it be determined the termination amounts to an unlawful act (tort), the worker may also sue for damages. Adverse action such as the following constitutes an unlawful act (tort): when the employer terminates a worker without just cause via disciplinary measures that merely serves as a pretext to conceal its illegal purpose and for the sole purpose of inducing the worker to leave the workplace; when the employer terminates a worker citing a disciplinary incident that, with minimal investigation, may be objectively and clearly determined to not warrant such a disposition. In such cases, the worker may sue the employer for damages arising from unlawfully causing mental harm.

---

24 Ibid., Article 23(1)

ii) Order of Remedy by the Labor Relations Commission

A worker that has suffered from an adverse action such as termination may petition the Labor Relations Commission for an order of remedy instead of utilizing the civil court system.[25]

This petition must be made within three months of the date the worker has suffered from the alleged wrongful termination[26] and the worker is prohibited from making this petition once this window has closed. The fact that the worker was unable to make timely petition due to factors beyond his/her control does not change this determination.

The Local/Regional Labor Relations Commission rejects requests for remedies that fail to meet such term limitations. After this administrative hurdle is cleared, orders for dismissal are issued if it is determined that the employer had just cause in terminating the worker, while orders for remedies are issued to the worker if the employer is determined to not have had just cause.[27]

Orders for remedies consist of "reinstatement to his/her former office" or "payment of amount of money or other valuable equivalent to or higher than the amount of wages which s/he would have been paid if s/he had been offered work during the period of dismissal."[28]

Should the Local/Regional Labor Relations Commission reject or dismiss a request for remedy, the worker petitioner may apply for the determination's reexamination by the Central Labor Relations Commission. Likewise, the employer may also appeal orders for remedies issued by the Local or Regional commissions with the said Commission. The timeframe within which applications for reexamination may be made is ten (10) calendar days from the date the party receives written notice of the order or decision made by the Local/

---

25 Ibid., Article 28(1)
26 Ibid., Article 28(2)
27 Ibid., Article 30(1)
28 Ibid., Article 30(3)

Regional commissions.[29]

The Central Labor Relations Commission rejects an application for reexamination if it is made inappropriately. The application is dismissed if it lacks cause. If the worker's application is held by the Central Labor Relations Commission to have cause, said Commission overturns the decision of the lower commissions and issues orders for remedies. If the employer's application is held by the Central Labor Relations Commission to have cause, the decision of the local and regional labor commission (i.e. order for remedy) is overturned.

Should the employer fail to implement the order of relief issued by the Local/Regional/Central labor commissions within the timeframe designated by the order, the relevant commissions shall impose compulsory performance money not exceeding twenty million won.[30]

iii) Administrative Litigation Procedure

Should the worker or employer be dissatisfied with the Central Labor Relations Commission's determination regarding the reexamination process, they may file an administrative lawsuit designating the Central Labor Relations Commission as the defendant. Such filing must be made within fifteen (15) days from the date when s/he is served with the written decision of the results of the reexamination.[31]

A point to keep in mind is that for the worker, there is the potential that this administrative litigation process may sometimes conflict with the civil litigation process. As reviewed above, the worker may commence a lawsuit with the civil court to affirm that an employer's action (e.g. termination) be held as invalid. There are two scenarios in which this may happen.

In the first scenario, a worker has filed for relief with the Labor

---

29 Ibid., Article 31(1)
30 Ibid., Article 33
31 Ibid., Article 31(2)

Relations Commission and has received notice that his/her petition has been denied. At this point the worker's termination has not yet been determined as being valid. As such, the worker still holds the ability to commence a separate lawsuit through the civil court system.[32]

Another scenario would be when a worker has filed a lawsuit with the civil court to affirm that his/her termination is invalid either before having filed for relief with the Labor Relations Commission, or before the proceedings have concluded at the time of filing for the lawsuit. Should the worker be unsuccessful in this civil suit, at that point the final legal determination has been made that the worker's termination is valid. This will result in the worker's petition with the Labor Relations Commission becoming moot, as no more benefits may be derived from the remedial, reexamination, or administrative litigation processes.[33]

2) Remedial Procedures for Unfair Labor Practices

There are remedial measures where a worker may file for relief when an employer allegedly engages in unfair labor practice such as dominating and/or intervening in the activities of the union or during its formation process. In the case a worker has been subject to an adverse action (e.g. termination) by the employer, the worker may file for relief from unfair labor practices in general and at the same time separately file for relief from the unfair termination (see 1(ii) above).

According to Article 82(1) of the Union Act, unions, as well as individual workers, have the capacity to file for relief from unfair labor practices.

The procedural requirements of these remedial measures such as statute of limitations, the procedural rules of local/regional and central labor relations commissions, the process of contesting the Central Labor Relations Commission's reexamination results via the administrative

---

32 Supreme Court 91Da22100 (1992. 5. 22.)

33 Supreme Court 92Nu6099 (1992. 7. 28.)

litigation process is identical to that of the process when petitioning for relief from unfair discharge (see 1(ii) above) or the process of initiating an administrative litigation (see 1(iii) above).

3) Litigation Procedures for Payment of Wages, Benefits, and Severance Payments

The worker may initiate civil litigation for payment of wages, benefits, and severance payments. The employer must pay wages and allowances due to the worker upon his/her death or retirement, and must do so within fourteen (14) days from the date the cause of the payment occurred. If this is not done within the designated period, the employer shall pay interest accrued for the delayed days from the following day to the day of the payment at a rate of a twenty percent per annum.[34]

When the employer fails to observe the terms and conditions of employment (e.g. failing to pay designated wages) as agreed upon in the employment contract, the worker is entitled to claim damages through the Labor Relations Commission or the court.[35]

4) Litigation Procedures for Payment of Damages Resulting from Industrial Actions

There are instances where the employer sues for damages for the economic harm caused by worker's industrial actions such as strikes, arguing that such actions are illegal.

In such incidences, case law suggests that "trade unions attributable for illegal industrial actions" or "union executive officials that play a leading role in an illegal industrial action by planning the industrial action and instructing or guiding the participants" are liable for damages that are caused by illegal industrial action.[36] For

---

34 LSA, Article 37(1); Enforcement Decree of the Labor Standards Act, Article 17

35 Ibid., Article 19

36 Supreme Court 93Da32828 (1994. 3. 25.), Supreme Court 93Da32835, Supreme Court 2005Da30610 (2006. 9. 22.)

"individual union members," however, mere participation in an illegal industrial action does not impose liability for damages, absent special circumstances.[37]

5) Remedial Procedures for Industrial Accidents

Should a worker suffer injury, death, or illness due to activities related to his/her employment during work, s/he may petition the Labor Welfare Corporation to collect payment from the Industrial Accident Compensation Insurance (IACI) scheme that the employer must be a part of. If a party wishes to contest the determination of insurance payment by the IACI, s/he may request an examination by the headquarters of the Labor Welfare Corporation. Should s/he wish to further contest the determination made by the Labor Welfare Corporation headquarters, a petition can be made to the IACI Examination Committee for further review. Further appeals challenging the decision of the IACI Examination Committee may be made through the court system via administrative litigation.[38] On the other hand, it is possible to proceed with the appeal directly through administrative litigation and bypass having to go through the review and examination process by the Labor Welfare Corporation and the IACI Examination Committee.[39]

If it is determined that an industrial accident is a result of illegal actions by the employer, the worker may proceed to sue the employer for damages.[40] In this case, should the worker receive separate insurance payments from the IACI scheme the employer may be relieved of its liability to compensate for damages up to the amount of the IACI payment.[41]

---

37 Supreme Court 2005Da30610 (2006. 9. 22.)
38 Industrial Accident Compensation Insurance Act, from Article 103 onwards
39 Administrative Litigation Act, Article 18(1)
40 Supreme Court 70Da2144 (1970. 11. 24.)
41 Industrial Accident Compensation Insurance Act, Article 80(2)

6) Remedial Procedures for the Interpretation of Collective Agreements

Should there be discrepancies in the interpretation or the implementation methodology of a collective agreement between the union and the employer, the parties may jointly request the Labor Relations Commission for its opinion on the issue. Should the collective agreement stipulate that any party may unilaterally make such a request, a request made by only one party is acceptable.[42] The purpose of this policy is to facilitate resolution of disputes related to the interpretation or the implementation of collective agreements with expedience.

The Labor Relations Commission must, upon receiving a request for its opinion on the above matters, give its clear-cut view within thirty (30) days from the date of receipt of the request.[43] The views on such interpretation and implementation methods which are given by the Labor Relations Commission shall have the same effect as that of an arbitration award.[44]

Should a party wish to contest the effectiveness of the views given by the Labor Relations Commission, as per Article 69 (which deals with disputing the effectiveness of arbitration awards) the party may apply for review of the arbitration award by the National Labor Relations Commission or directly commence administrative litigation proceedings, arguing that the view given by the Labor Relations Commission is inconsistent with the Union Act or ultra vires.

7) Labor Injunctions

In practice, injunctions are frequently used to resolve labor disputes. Typical injunctions requested by the worker include: injunction for payment of wages, injunction to maintain employment (or make-whole

---

42 Union Act, Article 34(1)

43 Ibid., Article 34(2)

44 Ibid., Article 34(3)

orders), injunction to suspend effect of unfavorable personnel actions such as discharge, injunction to prohibit obstruction of employment seeking activities, injunction to suspend the effect of employment rules, injunction to prohibit obstruction of union activities, injunction to compel compliance to collective bargaining, and injunction to prohibit closing the workplace.

Typical injunctions requested by the employer include: injunction to prohibit entry into the workplace, injunction to suspend the effect of collective agreements, injunction to prohibit disruptions to work activities, and injunction to prohibit industrial actions.

8) Criminal Litigation Procedure

There are many provisions related to criminal prosecution within both the LSA and the Union Act. As such, there are instances where industrial disputes are subject to litigation in the criminal court system.

A representative provision in the LSA that entail criminal prosecution is outlined in Articles 109(1), 36, and 43. Under these provisions, an employer is subject to criminal prosecution if it fails to pay wages or other valuables owed to a worker within fourteen (14) days from the date of the worker's death or retirement. The employer is also subject to such liability if it fails to pay its workers their due compensation every month. However, if the injured party does not wish to pursue prosecution an indictment against the employer cannot be made.[45] Also, the employer is relieved from its liability if the employer is recognized to have engaged in good faith efforts to pay the required wages and other valuables, but has been unable to do so due to unavoidable circumstances.

The Union Act regulates the purpose, subject, method and procedure of industrial action in Articles 37 and 46, and has penalty provisions in

---

45 LSA, Article 109(2)

Articles 88 and 91 to penalize the violation of such regulations. Article 81 defines unfair labor practices on the part of the employer, and Article 90 outlines the penalties to be given should they be committed by the employer.

A topic under dispute these days is whether strikes may be considered "interference with business through the use or threat of force" under the Criminal Act, as a separate cause of action distinct from the penalty provisions within labor laws. Case law suggests that strikes do not always fall under the category of "interference with business," and that in order to do so the strike must be conducted (from the perspective of the totality of the circumstances) in a sudden manner that could not have been foreseen by the employer, and result in serious confusion or significant harm to the extent that it oppresses or perturbs the employer's free will to continue conducting its business.[46]

9) Constitutional Litigation

As reviewed above, the Korean constitution is the highest law of the land, and hence is the highest source of law when it comes to interpreting labor law. The constitution serves as the interpretive standard of all subordinate laws, and any subordinate law that comes into conflict with the constitution does not have any effect.

As such, constitutional litigation through the Korean Constitutional Court may be used to determine whether particular labor laws (which regulate legal relations in labor disputes) violate the constitution. The law in question becomes invalid once declared unconstitutional by the Constitutional Court. To date, there exist several cases where the Court has reviewed the constitutionality of labor laws.[47]

---

46 Supreme Court 2007Do482 (2011. 3. 17.), unanimous decision

47 Regarding laws governing individual labor relations, see Constitutional Court 94HunBa19 (1997. 8. 21.), Constitutional Court 96HunBa27 (1998. 6. 25.), Constitutional Court 2000HunBa707 (2002. 7. 18.), Constitutional Court 2002HunBa11 (2005. 9. 29.), Constitutional Court 2007HunBa36 (2008. 11. 27.), Constitutional Court 2010HunBa209 (2013. 10. 24.).

Regarding laws governing collective labor relations, *see* Constitutional Court 89HunGa103 (1990. 1. 15.), Constitutional Court 89HunGa106 (1991. 7. 22.), Constitutional Court 90HunBa27 (1992. 4. 28.), Constitutional Court 88HunMa5 (1993. 3. 11.), Constitutional Court 92HunBa33 (1993. 3. 11.), Constitutional Court 92HunGa14 (1995. 3. 23.), Constitutional Court 90HunBa19 (1996. 12. 26.), Constitutional Court 94HunBa13 (1998. 2. 27.), Constitutional Court 95HunBa10 (1998. 2. 27.), Constitutional Court 96HunGa20 (1998. 3. 26.), Constitutional Court 97HunBa23 (1998. 7. 16.), Constitutional Court 95HunBa154 (1999. 11. 25.), Constitutional Court 98HunMa141 (1999. 11. 25.), Constitutional Court 2002HunBa12 (2002. 12. 18.), Constitutional Court 2001HunGa31 (2003. 5. 15.), Constitutional Court 2003HunBa50 (2005. 10. 27.), Constitutional Court 2002HunBa95 (2005. 11. 24.), Constitutional Court 2004HunBa67 (2006. 12. 28.), Constitutional Court 2003HunBa51 (2007. 8. 30.), Constitutional Court 2004HunBa9 (2008. 7. 31.), Constitutional Court 2005HunMa971 (2008. 12. 26.), Constitutional Court 2006HunMa358 (2009. 7. 30.), Constitutional Court 2007HunMa1359 (2009. 10. 29.), Constitutional Court 2009HunBa168 (2010. 4. 29.), Constitutional Court 2010HunBa385 (2011. 12. 29.), Constitutional Court 2011HunMa338 (2012. 4. 24.), Constitutional Court 2012HunBa169 (2013. 6. 27.).

Regarding cases dealing with other labor laws, *see* Constitutional Court 2011HunBa271 (2013. 9. 26.), Constitutional Court 2012HunGa16 (2013. 9. 26.).

Labor Standards Act

Chapter 1

The Worker
and the Employer

I. The Scope of "Worker" under the Labor Standards Act

A. General Principles

The LSA[1] defines the worker as "a person, regardless of being engaged in whatever occupation, who offers work to a business or workplace for the purpose of earning wages."[2] Therefore, whether a person can be considered a worker for the purpose of the Act turns on whether that person may be considered to have offered work to a business or workplace for the purpose of earning wages under a subordinate employment relationship.

B. Whether Work Is Provided under a "Subordinate Employment Relationship"

1) Significance
The decisive standard that differentiates the employment relationship

---

1 Labor Standards Act
2 LSA, Article 2(1)1

from other contractual relationships entered into, under which labor is provided in exchange for compensation, is whether the provider of the labor has entered into a subordinate employment relationship with the recipient. The term "subordinate employment relationship" is used when a worker conducts his/her labor under the detailed instructions and/or work orders of the entity receiving the labor.

To illustrate, the following scenarios would make it unlikely for laborer (A) to be considered a worker for the purpose of the LSA: should (A) provide labor for (B)'s factory yet has also provide the same labor (i.e. using the same methods of work) to another factory during the same timeframe and at the same time; should (A) not receive direction nor supervision by (B) during the times (A) works in (B)'s factory; and should (A) receive compensation solely for the amount of work done in independently completing products.[3]

A person that is free from external directions or supervision and exerts his/her free will in conducting work (like worker (A) in the above illustration) cannot be said to be under a "subordinate employment relationship." Such a working relationship should be classified not as one of "employment," but as one of delegation, subcontracting, or another form of contractual relationship.

The determination of subordinate employment relationships turns on substance rather than form. Even if a contract indicates that it is a delegation contract or a subcontract (or any other non-employment contract) on its face, if the substantive relationship between the worker and employer suggests a subordinate employment relationship, that relationship is deemed an employment relationship under the purviews of the LSA.

---

3 Supreme Court 84Do2534 (1984. 12. 26.)

2) Standard of Determination

Whether an employment relationship is that of subordinate employment depends on various factors. The following are the standards that may be derived from court precedents.[4]

① Whether the content of the work is determined by the employer; whether the worker is subject to the employer's Rules of Employment; whether the worker receives significant direction and supervision from the employer in carrying out his/her work;

② Whether the worker's working hours, working days and workplaces are designated and restricted by the employer;

③ Whether the worker owns the equipment, raw materials, or working tools that he/she uses; whether the worker may conduct his/her own business through independent business judgment (such as by subcontracting his/her work to a third party); and whether the worker assumes the risk of loss or profit resulting from his/her labor;

④ Whether payment may be considered remuneration for the work itself;

⑤ Whether a base wage or fixed wage is determined in advance;

⑥ Whether earned income tax is withheld upon payment, and other factors related to wages;

⑦ Whether the work providing relationship has been a continuous one;

⑧ Whether the worker provides his/her labor exclusively to the employer;

⑨ Whether the person is recognized as an employee under the Social Security Insurance Act or other related laws;

⑩ The economic and social status of both parties.

---

4 Supreme Court 2004Da29736 (2006. 12. 7.), 2005Du13018, 13025 (2007. 3. 29.), 2006Do777 (2007. 9. 7.), 2010Da50601 (2012. 1 12.)

Each of these standards holds differing weight in the ultimate determination process. For instance, the satisfaction of factors ⑤, ⑥, and ⑨ may be prevented due to the unequal power exerted by the employer. Therefore the courts do not easily dismiss the possibility that a worker is an employee/worker for the purpose of the LSA merely based on the fact that such factors are absent.[5]

3) Specific Examples

i) Chief Executive Officers, Directors, Auditors, and Other Officers of a Corporation

Having the authority to conduct the business of a corporation, CEOs, directors, and auditors are entrusted with the task of performing the affairs of the corporation despite not being shareholders themselves.[6] As such, barring the existence of special circumstances, these individuals cannot be considered workers under the LSA.[7] As a result, CEOs, directors, and auditors do not have the right to request severance pay upon resignation; they can only receive such payments if there are provisions within the articles of incorporation that allow it, or through resolutions adopted by a general meeting of shareholders.[8]

Of course, if a corporation is given an order to commence reorganization proceedings under the Debtor Rehabilitation and Bankruptcy Act, the authority of corporate officers to perform the affairs of the corporation is transferred exclusively to the appointed receiver/administrator. However, this does not mean officers suddenly become workers under the direction and supervision of the receiver.[9]

However, there are instances where an individual may be considered a worker under the LSA, even if s/he is given the title of

---

5 Supreme Court 2004Da29736 (2006. 12. 7.), 2011Da78804 (2014. 2. 13.)
6 Commercial Act, Articles 382(2) and 415
7 Supreme Court 92Da28228 (1992. 12. 22.), 93Nu12770 (1994. 9. 23.)
8 Commercial Act, Articles 338 and 415
9 Supreme Court 93Nu12770 (1994. 9. 23.)

director or auditor. Such is the case when the individual is required to report to work every day and work under the direction and supervision of the CEO or employer who has the authority to perform the affairs of the corporation, and receives compensation for the work. Here, the LSA would consider the title "director/auditor" to be nominal and meaningless, and treat the individual as a worker.[10]

In the Korean corporate taxonomy, directors or executive employees have as their titles the following: chairman (회장 *hoe-jang*), president/CEO (사장 *sa-jang*), vice-president (부사장 *bu-sajang*), executive director (전무이사 *jeonmu-isa*), managing director (상무이사 *sangmu-isa*), director (이사 *isa*), auditor/finance manager (감사 *gamsa*), team director (실장 *siljang*), department head (부장 *bujang*), assistant/deputy department head (차장 *chajang*), section chief (과장 *gwajang*), plant manager (공장장 *gongjang-jang*), site manager (현장소장 *hyeonjang-sojang*). If an individual is legally considered within the category of executive officers (e.g. CEO, director, auditor), then they are not workers as defined under the LSA.

However, if an individual primarily engages in technical work such as research and development as an engineer or other technical roles for the purpose of earning compensation, that person would be considered a worker even if his/her title within the corporation is that of plant manager, managing director or head of the planning department.[11] Also, if a director has consistently received payment for non-executive work (i.e. work separate from conducting the affairs of the corporation), s/he would be considered a worker under the LSA.[12] If an individual is registered as a director in the corporate registration form but is working as administrative manager of a motel, sauna, or restaurant run by a corporation, that individual is also considered as a

---

10 Supreme Court 2002Da64681 (2003. 9. 26.)

11 Supreme Court 73Da80 (1973. 3. 13.), 9Dda44393 (1997. 12. 23.)

12 Supreme Court 91Nu11490 (1992. 5. 12.)

worker under the LSA.[13]

ii) Salespeople for a Life Insurance Corporation

There are instances where a salesperson conducts his/her work under a delegation/commission contract with an employer, subject to a separate set of regulations developed for salespeople. In such cases, the Supreme Court determined that salespeople cannot be considered workers after taking the relationship between the salespeople and the employer regarding direction and supervision, method of remuneration, and method of work in to account, in particular, the following facts: ① there exists a compensation scheme that is separate from that for regular employees; ② the salespeople do not receive a base/regular pay from the employer but receive a fixed commission for solicitation of insurance; ③ there are no particular limits imposed by the employer on to how the salespeople use their hours and where they conduct their business, nor does the employer supply specific directions or supervision to the salespeople in conducting insurance solicitation and collection services.[14]

iii) Foreign Industrial Trainees

Foreign industrial trainees are placed in domestic corporations as per the Industrial Training System administered by the Korean government, and enter into a training contract with the corporation using a government approved form. The Supreme Court determined that these foreign workers are workers as per the LSA due to the following considerations:

① Trainees provide their labor under the direction of the corporation and receive money and valuable in return;

② Trainees receive overtime pay for work done after hours;

---

13 Supreme Court 2002Da4429 (2002. 9. 4.)

14 Supreme Court 77Da972 (1977. 10. 11.), 88DaKa28112 (1990. 5. 22.)

③ Trainees receive direction and supervision while working in the corporation's workplace.[15]

iv) Golf & Country Club Caddies

The Supreme Court determined that caddies that work at golf & country clubs are not considered workers as per the LSA, due to the following considerations:

① Non-existence of a contract to supply work between the caddies and the country club facility operator;

② Game assistance services provided by caddies are not considered essential to the operation of country club facilities;

③ Caddies receive a service charge directly from club visitors and do not receive any monies or valuables from the country club itself;

④ While there is a designated order as to who works among caddies, the exact time in which they must work is not designated;

⑤ Caddies are not given direction and supervision when carrying out their duties;

⑥ Even when a caddy provides game assistance services in an idle and inadequate manner, the golf & country club operator does not reprimand the caddy or cite a violation of the company's service policy.[16]

v) "Little President" (소사장 sosajang)

The term "little president" is used to indicate a person who has entered into a subcontract with an employer to do the same or similar work that s/he used to do as an employee, albeit this time with the appearance as being a manager of a business entity. In such cases, the following factors are considered when determining that the person could be considered a worker under the LSA: whether the

---

15 Supreme Court 95Nu2050 (1995. 12. 22.)

16 Supreme Court 2011Da78804 (2014. 2. 13.)

employee-turned-manager has terminated the previous employer-
worker relationship on his/her own volition or s/he has been forced
to assume this role as a mere formality; whether the little president
retains independence in running the business entity with regards to
business planning, making profits or losses, and assuming risks; the
degree of intervention from the parent corporation on work processes
and labor/personnel management; whether there is a difference in the
type and amount of remuneration between the little president and an
employee of the parent corporation doing the same work.[17]

vi) Preparatory Academy Instructors

Many preparatory academy instructors do not enter into a specific
employment contract that outlines working conditions (e.g. working
hours) with the academy they teach in, agreeing instead to an
arrangement where the academy and the instructor each takes 50% of
the tuition paid by students. Because of this arrangement, the amount
that the instructor earns fluctuates depending on the specific class
and times s/he teaches, which often results in significant discrepancy
in total remuneration between individual instructors. In cases where
there are no students enrolling in a course, the instructor in charge of
that course does not get paid at all. The Supreme Court, considering
this fact along with the fact that while academies may adjust course
schedules and locations to coordinate usage of facilitates with other
instructors, they do not specifically direct or supervise the content
of the lecture, determined that these instructors working with
preparatory academies are not workers under the LSA.[18]

In contrast, instructors who teach general classes in preparatory
academies get paid for teaching a predetermined number of classroom
hours; the number of students who actually sign up to take those

---

17 Supreme Court 94Do2122 (1995. 6. 30.)
18 Supreme Court 96Do732 (1996. 7. 30.)

classes do not affect the amount of remuneration these instructors receive. The Supreme Court determined that these instructors are workers under the LSA, noting that the employer academies designate work hours and location of classroom instruction, place de facto limitations on the possibility to work with other worksites, and require the instructors to work on tasks other than classroom instruction.[19]

vii) Education Counselors Working for Corporations Selling Study Materials
Educational counselors enter into consignment contracts with corporations that sell study materials, and do not receive directions or supervision from the corporation in conducting their work (i.e. work methods, work hours). The commission paid by the corporations is determined by objective indicators (i.e. number of new members, amount of fees collected) that demonstrate the success of the assigned work. As such, these educational counselors working for corporations selling studying materials cannot be considered workers.[20]

viii) Sales Representative for Door-to-Door Sales Corporations
A sales representative who sells household appliances using his/her own judgment and capacity, and receives a commission for the number of items s/he actually sells. The content of the sale representative's work is not determined by the corporation, nor is the representative subject to the latter's personnel policy. The sale representative also does not receive the direction or supervision of the corporation; this is still the case even if s/he cannot determine the retail price of the product that s/he is selling. The sale representative does not even have to sell the products him/herself, and may hold other jobs simultaneously. The remuneration the sales representative receives does not entail base or regular pay and only consists of commission for products sold. As

---

19 Supreme Court 2004Da29736 (2006. 12. 7.)
20 Supreme Court 95Da20348 (1996. 4. 26.)

such, it is difficult to consider this sales representative as a worker under the LSA.[21]

ix) Outsourcing Contractors

An outsourcing contractor working in a parent corporation enters into a outsourcing contract that outlines this relationship, and is free to adjust working hours unlike a regular employee. The corporation also does not require the outsourcing contractor to observe rules of employment or office regulations, and does not keep a timesheet. The corporation does not provide specific directions nor supervision regarding the outsourcing contractor's work, provides compensation (contract commissions) for work products completed and not for working hours, and does not pay benefits such as bonuses and vacation expenses (unlike its treatment of regular employees). As such, it is difficult to consider this outsourcing contractor as a worker under the LSA.

x) Owners and Drivers of Vehicles Registered with a Corporation

There are cases where a driver and owner of a vehicle registers his/her vehicle under the name of a corporation that has a transportation business permit and engages in a driving business at the corporation's workplace on his/her own account. The Supreme Court held that in these cases the driver/owner cannot be considered a worker under the LSA, considering that: the driver/owner has entered into a "management of entrusted vehicle" contract with the corporation and pays for the maintenance of the vehicle; the driver/owner (if need be) may be replaced with another vehicle or personnel (hence working under a high degree of freedom); and the driver/owner receives freight charges per tonnage moved.[22]

---

21 Supreme Court 2001Do5995 (2002. 7. 12.)
22 Supreme Court 2000Do4901 (2001. 4. 13.), 2002Da44915 (2002. 11. 8.), 2009Du9062 (2011. 6. 9.)

C. Whether Work Is Provided for the Purpose of "Earning Wages"

Wages are monies and valuables that a worker receives from an employer as compensation for working while under a subordinate employment relationship. As such, the provision of wages should not be used as a distinguishing indicator of whether an individual is a worker under the LSA or not, but as a conceptual counterpart to the provision of labor.

Under the Civil Law, employment is a contract in which an employer provides remuneration for labor provided by the worker. Therefore, remuneration constitutes a fundamental portion of an employment contract (which cannot exist without assuming remuneration will take place). In an employment contract there are no limitations on the method of remuneration; there is no requirement that the agreement be in writing either. It is assumed that an unspoken agreement of remuneration has been made between the parties if it is common practice in society that payments are made for the provision of labor. Yet, in such cases the type and scope of the agreed upon remuneration is determined based on custom due to the lack of an explicit contract.[23]

D. Whether Labor Is Provided in a "Business or Workplace"

1) Significance
The worker-employer relationship that is subject to the LSA assumes that labor is provided within a "business or workplace."[24] A "business or workplace" is defined as a business organization that is operated

---

23 Supreme Court 97Da58767 (1999. 7. 9.)
24 LSA, Article 11(1)

by a cohesive management in a continuous and organic manner (e.g. private business or an incorporated company).[25]

2) Standards

Under the category of "business or workplace," private businesses, businesses run by national or local governmental organizations,[26] government-run corporations, and government-funded organizations. For instance, the executive officers (i.e. directors or auditors) of a government-funded institution (e.g. The Korea Coal Corporation, Korea Housing Corporation, Korea Expressway Corporation, Korea Oil Development Corporation, the Bank of Korea) are considered workers under the LSA, and not civil servants.[27]

In addition to the above for-profit businesses, the definition of "business or workplace" includes non-profit businesses as well, such as public/social or religious businesses. For example, a teacher who teaches preschool children employed by a church-run preschool/ missionary school (which would qualify as a religious business) would still be a worker under the LSA as s/he receives wages from the church for the labor s/he provided.[28]

Finally, businesses that are limited or forbidden due to administrative purposes yet are run illegally (including those that have failed to operate under a valid permit) are also considered to be within the definition of "business or workplace." There are limits to this expanded definition however; in cases where the employer and worker are co-conspirers/accomplices in committing an illegal act such as drug dealing, that business would not be considered to fall under the definition of "business or workplace."

---

25 Supreme Court 93Da18365 (1993. 10. 12.), 97Da24511 (1997. 11. 28.), 98Da765 (1999. 8. 20.)
26 LSA, Article 12
27 Supreme Court 92Da32357 (1992. 11. 27.), 92Da923 (1993. 8. 24.)
28 Supreme Court 91Nu8098 (1992. 2. 14.)

3) Scope

The LSA does not apply to "businesses or workplaces in which four or fewer workers are ordinarily employed."[29] Also, the Act "shall neither apply to any business or workplace in which only the employer's blood relatives living together are engaged."[30] As such, by principle the employment relationship in business or workplaces that fall under the above conditions does not receive the protection of the LSA. However, the Act does provide that "with respect to a business or workplace in which not more than four workers are ordinarily employed, some provisions of this Act may apply as prescribed by Presidential Decree."[31]

E. Whether the Underlying Employment Contract Is Valid

As reviewed above, an employment relationship must be established for an individual to become a worker under the protection of the LSA. In order to establish an employment relationship, an agreement must be made that the worker will provide labor in the employer's business or workplace for the purpose of receiving remuneration. Therefore, it is clear that entering into a valid employment contract is a prerequisite to the establishment of an employment relationship.

An issue that arises related to this point is how to consider the case of "foreign workers that are employed in violation of the regulations that limit the employment of foreigners." Specifically, such cases arise when a foreigner who entered the country under an Industrial Trainee visa (not under an employment visa) works at a business or workplace and receives remuneration that is not the pre-authorized

---

29 LSA, Article 11(1)

30 LSA, Article 11(1)

31 LSA, Article 11(2); Enforcement Decree of the Labor Standards Act, Article 7, Asterisk 1

site of industrial training. Although these foreign trainees do not possess the right to employment under the Immigration Control Act, the employment contract is not considered invalid. As such, these foreigners would be considered workers under the LSA.[32]

F. Instances Where the LSA Assumes a Supplemental Role to Superseding Legislation Regulating Working Conditions

There are classifications of individuals that are fundamentally workers under the LSA in that they provide labor for remuneration under a subordinate employment relationship, but whose working conditions are regulated by other Acts. In such cases, the LSA assumes a supplemental role, filling in the gaps when the governing legislation fails to determine certain conditions.

1) Public Officials
The State Public Official Act and the Local Public Officials Act each regulates matters of personnel, remuneration, and service regulation related to state or local public officials.

The Public Official Pension Act regulates the pension payments made to regular state and local public officials as well as other employees of local governments that fit relevant conditions.[33] Therefore, the Pension Act governs the payment of pensions to the above workers barring special circumstances.[34]

However, as state or local public officials are fundamentally workers protected by the LSA, areas that have not been legislated on by special laws such as the Pension Act are subject to the regulation

---

32 Supreme Court 97Nu10352 (1997. 10. 10.)
33 Public Official Pension Act, Article 3(1)1; LSA, Article 2
34 Supreme Court 86DaKa1355 (1987. 2. 24.)

of the LSA. For example, the regulation on non-duty allowance as per Article 46 of the LSA applies even to public officials.[35]

2) Teaching Staff of Private Schools

Like other state public officials, the State Public Officials Act and the Public Educational Officials Act apply to public educational officials and the LSA does not apply.

Teaching staff working in private schools are different from public educational officials in that the Private School Act regulates their credentialing, appointment, service regulation, guarantee of status, social security, and discipline. The Pension for Private School Teachers and Staff Act regulates how pension payments will be made in the case of retirement, death, and career related illness. The LSA does not apply to these areas, although it does apply to any other areas not mentioned above.

In the meanwhile, the Private School Act does not have specific provisions regarding the appointment, remuneration, service regulation, and guarantee of status of administrative staff working in private schools. Jurisdictionally, these labor relations are fundamentally employment contract relations; therefore the working conditions of administrative staff (e.g. remuneration and service regulation) are regulated by the LSA.[36]

Also, the Private School Act does not have provisions regulating workers other than teaching and administrative staff. Therefore, such workers are regulated by the LSA.[37]

3) Seafarers

The Seafarers Act and the Ship Act primarily regulate the working

---

35 Supreme Court 78Da163 (1978. 3. 28.), 91Da45653 (1992. 4. 14.), 85DaKa2473 (1987. 6. 9.), 94Da446 (1996. 4. 23.)

36 Supreme Court 96Da38995 (1997. 7. 22.), 2002Da51555 (2004. 6. 25.), 2006Da48229 (2006. 12. 8.)

37 Supreme Court 2007Da87061 (2008. 3. 27.)

conditions of sailors. The LSA supplements what is not dealt with in the Seafarers Act.

II. The Scope of "Employer" under the Labor Standards Act

A. General Principles

1) Significance

Employers as defined under the LSA must comply with the Act's provisions regarding working conditions that have been established in order to protect workers. Employers are subject to civil and criminal liability should they violate such provisions.

The LSA considers not only business owners but also entities equivalent to business owners to be subject to legal duties. Under the Act, an employer is ① a business owner, ② or a person responsible for the management of a business, ③ a person who acts on behalf of a business owner with respect to matters relating to workers.[38]

2) Standard of Determination

Whether an entity is an employer under the LSA is (similar to determining whether an individual is a worker) dependent not on the form of the contract or on the content of relevant regulatory laws, but on the nature of the actual employment relationship. In determining which parties are actually engaged in a subordinate employment relationship, numerous factors must be considered in its entirety.[39]

To illustrate, the following scenario would make it unlikely that (A) would be considered the employer of (B) despite outward

---

38 LSA, Article 2(1)2

39 Supreme Court 2006Do300 (2006. 12. 7.)

appearances; (B) would instead be considered a worker employed by (C), providing (C) with his/her labor while working in (C)'s workplace: ① (B) lacks autonomy/identity and/or independence as a business owner and hence its existence is a mere formality; ② (A) has a de facto subordinate employment relationship under (C); and ③ in fact (A) provides labor to (C) and receive remuneration from the latter, which suggests that the two parties have entered into an unspoken employment contract.[40]

This standard of determination must be applied to determine whether workers have an employment relationship with the owner of the workplace that they provide labor in, even if those workers are formally employed by service companies. For instance, the Supreme Court has ruled that workers that become "little presidents" still maintain their employment relationship with their former employer. In the specific case, an employer established a separate corporation composed with a subsection of its employees, along with a CEO (i.e. the little president) and other officers. Said employer paid the wages of the workers in this new corporation directly, and directed and supervised the work method and personnel decisions in a specific and direct manner. The Supreme Court ruled that the workers of this new corporation have maintained their employment relationship with the original corporation.[41]

For vehicles owned by the driver yet registered with a corporation for business licensing purposes, the owner of the vehicle is still considered to have an employment relationship with the corporation as defined under the Labor Standard Act even if s/he outsources the driving to another driver and assumes liability.[42]

40 Supreme Court 97Nu19946 (1999. 11. 12.), 2002Do649 (2002. 11. 26.)
41 Supreme Court 2002Do649 (2002. 11. 26.)
42 Supreme Court 86Do2475 (1987. 2. 24.), Supreme Court 90Do1214 (1990. 9. 25.)

3) Relationship with Vicarious Liability under Civil Law

The concept of "employer" under the LSA and the term "employer" as used in "employer's liability for damages" under Article 756 of the Civil Act must be distinguished.

Article 756 stipulates that "a person who employs another to carry out an undertaking shall be bound to make compensation for damages done to a third person by the employee in the course of the execution of the undertaking: provided, that this shall not be the case, if the employer has exercised due care in the appointment of the employee, and the supervision of the undertaking, or if the damage would have resulted even if due care had been exercised."

The employer-employee relationship determined by Article 756 does not necessitate a valid employment relationship as defined under the LSA. It is sufficient that an individual has a relationship with another individual in which the former provides labor according to the latter's will, direction and supervision.[43] Let's say, for instance, the actual owner of a vehicle that is registered with a corporation for business licensing purposes has personally operated the vehicle. In this case, it is difficult to argue that the corporation is an employer as per the LSA. Under Article 756 of the Civil Act, however, as the corporation objectively has the status of an employer that provides direction and supervision to the owner/driver of the vehicle registered to it, the corporation is liable for damages incurred to a third party as a result of an intentional or negligent act by the owner/driver.[44]

B. Business Owners

The term "business owner" indicates the managing entity of a business

---

43 Supreme Court 97Da 13702 (1998. 8. 21.), 98Da62671 (1999. 10. 12.)

44 Supreme Court 90Da7616 (1990. 12. 11.), 97Da44676 (1998. 1. 23.)

or workplace. "Managing entity" is an individual in the case of private businesses, and a corporate body in the case of corporations or other corporate bodies.

The concept of business owner is not limited to owners of private corporations; national and local governments, public enterprises may also become business owners. Business owners may be owners of both for-profit and non-profit businesses.

Like the concept of "worker," under the LSA whether an entity is considered a business owner is determined by examining the actual employment relationship rather than the form of the contract and the content of related regulations.

In the case of temporary agency worker businesses as outlined under the Act on the Protection of Temporary Agency Workers, a worker employed by a temporary work agency provides work for a user company under the direction and instruction of the user company in accordance with the terms and conditions of a contract on temporary placement of workers, while maintaining his/her employment relationship with the temporary work agency.[45] For the duration of the contract, both the temporary work agency and the user company are considered employers under the LSA. However, in applying specific provisions of the LSA, Article 34 of the Act on the Protection of Temporary Agency Workers designates whether the agency or the user company would be considered as the employer.

C. Business Management Representatives

1) Business Management Representatives

Business management representatives are individuals that assume general responsibility for the management of the business. Business

---

45 Act on the Protection of Temporary Agency Workers, Article 2

owners entrust representatives with all or part of their authority to comprehensively manage business. These individuals serve as an agent or represent the business they manage.[46] Examples of business management representatives include CEOs of a corporation, administrators of debtors in reorganization proceedings, and managers as defined by the Commercial Act.

Unlike CEOs, a director of a corporation is not in the position to serve as an agent or represent the corporation in its operations. Directors merely partake in the decision making process on how operations should be conducted, and hence cannot be said to be business management representatives.

2) People Who Work on Behalf of a Business Owner with Respect to Matters Relating to Employees

An individual who works on behalf of a business owner with respect to matters relating to employees has authority to conduct on his/her responsibility: personnel actions (e.g. employ and dismiss workers), direct and supervise the worker's operations, determine and implement working conditions such as work hours and wages.

The formal title (and the relative level of authority that the title represents) of this individual within the corporation is largely irrelevant. As long as s/he has the independent authority decide on personnel actions, direct and supervise workers' operations, and determine and implement working conditions for certain workers, s/he is an employer to those workers "within the scope of his/her authority and responsibility." However, at the same time the same individual may be considered a worker vis-à-vis the business owner or the business management representative.

---

46 Supreme Court 2007Do1807 (2007. 5. 10.), 2007Do1199 (2008. 4. 10.)

3) Specific Examples

i) Chief Executive Officers, Directors, and Other Officers of a Corporation

As examined above, the LSA does not limit the definition of "employer" to just the business owner, but expands its scope to include business management representatives. The legislative motive behind this expansion is the policy objective to ensure that the effectiveness of each Article of the Act is secured when it is applied in the workplace.

In principle, if an individual assumes general responsibility for the management of the business and is bestowed the authority and responsibility to implement the various provisions of the LSA through related labor regulations, that individual would be considered a business management representative. It is not necessary for the individual to actually exercise this authority in practice.[47]

For an individual appointed as CEO, it is assumed that s/he institutionally possesses the authority and responsibility to implement the various provisions of the LSA. Even if in fact the de facto business owner excludes the CEO from functions such as issuing payments to workers, the CEO nevertheless retains liability for violations to the Labor Standard Act (e.g. non-settlement of payments due after a worker's retirement).

An exception to this rule would be when an individual is registered as a CEO but is merely a figurehead, being excluded from the operation of the corporation. In this case this individual cannot be said to serve as an agent or representative to the business owner, and hence is not considered an employer in charge of management of the business.[48]

Conversely, an individual who has formally resigned his/her position as corporate CEO on paper (i.e. the corporate registry) yet continues de facto management of the corporation (i.e. approves or

47 Supreme Court 97Do813 (1997. 11. 11.)
48 Supreme Court 99Do2910 (2000. 1. 18.)

presides over issuing wage payment to workers, and conducting personnel action), that individual is considered an employer as defined in the LSA.[49]

Directors and auditors of a corporation are by law part of the board of directors, and are entrusted with the authority to partake in making business decisions and auditing the operations of the corporation.[50] These individuals are not in the position to independently serve as an agent or represent the corporation in its operations; essentially, they are not people responsible for the management of business. However, if directors or auditors are given the authority and responsibility with respect to matters relating to employees by the business owner or other people responsible for the management of business, the director or auditor would be considered an employer up to the extent of this scope of authority.

A caveat to be aware of in making this determination is the fact that even if a director of a corporation has temporarily employed workers under the direction of the CEO, if it is determined that the director has generally limited his/her work within his/her prescribed scope of authority and that the director did not conduct the work of the corporation regarding its internal and external relations on an independent basis, that director would not be held liable as an employer under the LSA.[51]

ii) Factory Managers, Construction Managers, Mining Managers
Next is the case of factory managers, construction managers, mining managers. These individuals are considered as people who work on behalf of the business owner (i.e. the corporation) with respect to

---

49 Supreme Court 2001Do3889 (2002. 11. 22.)
50 Commercial Act, Articles 415 and 382(2)
51 Supreme Court 83Do2272 (1983. 10. 11.)

matters relating to employees that work within their scope of given authority and responsibility regarding a specific workplace (i.e. factories, construction sites, and mining sites), given the following: the managers employ workers to work at the sites; provide direction and supervision regarding the work; and pay wages to the workers from funds provided by the corporation. Under the LSA, these individuals are subject to criminal liability should they fail to pay wages in a timely manner.[52]

However, in the case of a construction manager for a shopping complex that was not able to conduct the above functions due to the fact that the direction and supervision of work was done by the relative of the CEO and the payment of wages was done by the CEO himself, that manager was determined not be an employer as defined by the LSA.[53]

Also, in the case of an individual that had the title of vice-president yet did not function as a director, did not participate in the management of the corporation, did not have the capacity to employ workers, and merely provided assistance to the CEO without remuneration, it has been determined that s/he was not an employer as defined by the LSA.[54]

iii) Partners
A hypothetical would be useful to illustrate the relationship between partners. Let's say A and B are partners. A is only in charge of internally managing finances despite having the title of executive or managing director. B, with the title of president, has her name listed as the representative in the corporate registry and conducts the de facto business of the corporation (e.g. conducts external billing transactions).

---

52 Supreme Court 99Do2910 (2000. 1. 18.)
53 Supreme Court 2001Do3889 (2002. 11. 22.)
54 Commercial Act, Articles 415 and 382(2)

In this scenario, only B would be considered an employer under the LSA.[55]

---

55 Supreme Court 96Da14838, 14845 (1997. 9. 26.)

Chapter 2

Working Hours and Recess

I. Working Hours and Recess

A. Standard Working Hours

According to the LSA,[1] working hours are 40 hours a week and eight hours a day, excluding hours of recess.[2] Generally a week is considered to be the period from Monday through Sunday, but this standard may be modified through employment contracts, employment rules, or collective agreements. The 40-hour work week is also generally understood to comprise of five working days per week. However, since the employer is only legally required to provide its workers with one day of break per week,[3] working 40 hours over six days per week is not illegal.

"Work-hours of a person at the age of not less than 15 and less than 18 shall not exceed seven hours per day and 40 hours per week."[4]

Requiring workers to work beyond legal working hours is an act

---

1 Labor Standards Act

2 LSA, Article 50

3 Ibid., Article 55

4 Ibid., Article 69

punishable by imprisonment for not more than two years or by a fine not exceeding ten million won.[5]

B. Actual Working Hours and Recess

Standard working hours are calculated while excluding times spent in "recess." The employer is required to provide the worker with 30 minutes of recess for four hours of working time, and an hour if the work time exceeds eight hours. Generally, an hour of recess between 12pm and 1pm is the norm for a worker who works between 9am and 6pm. Of course, it is permissible to provide longer recesses than is legally required.

Case law considers labor provided by workers under the direction and supervision of the employer per the employment contract as working time. In calculating work hours, "any waiting time spent by workers under the direction and supervision of their employers that is necessary for the relevant work shall be deemed work hours."[6]

In practice, however, it is often difficult to distinguish between recess and waiting time. This is because the worker is not doing actual work in both cases.

Case law suggests that recess as defined by the LSA is the period during working hours when a worker becomes free from the direction and supervision of the employer and is guaranteed the freedom to use that time as s/he sees fit.[7] In other words, case law interprets that any time when the worker is under de facto direction and supervision of the employer and hence cannot use the time as s/he sees fit should be included in working hours, regardless of the fact that the worker has

5 Ibid., Article 11(1)

6 Ibid., Article 50(3)

7 Supreme Court 91Da20548 (1992. 4. 14.)

not done actual work (e.g. waiting and break periods, sleeping hours).[8]

C. Special Provisions

If working hours are strictly enforced, circumstances may arise where public life becomes severely hampered. To prevent this from happening, in the case of certain industries the LSA allows for the employer to enter into written agreement with the workers' representative to have workers work beyond 12 hours or make modifications to recess arrangements.[9] The workers' representative, which functions as the agent of this agreement, is either an organized labor union that represents more than half of the workers at the business or workplace, or (where there is no such organized labor union) a person who represents more than half of the workers at that workplace.[10]

Industries where special provisions may be applied are: (i) transportation business, goods sales and storage business, finance and insurance business; (ii) movie production and entertainment business, communications business, educational study and research business, advertisement business; (iii) medical and sanitation business, hotel and restaurant business, incineration and cleaning business, barber and beauty parlor business; and (iv) public welfare business.

If a workplace falls within the above categories, the employer may have workers provide extended work beyond 12 hours a week. However, a workplace that has implemented a flexible work schedule or selective working hours cannot be subject to this provision. Also, while this provision does raise the limit of allowed extended work,

---

8 Supreme Court 92Da24509 (1993. 5. 27.), Supreme Court 2006Da41990 (2006. 11. 23.)
9 LSA, Article 59; Enforcement Decree of the LSA, Article 32
10 Ibid., Article 24(3)

it cannot be used to absolve the employer of its responsibility to pay premium rate wages for the extra work done.

II. Extended, Night, and Holiday Work

A. Extended Work

1) Limitations on Extended Work

By principle, the employer must receive labor from its workers within the working hour limitations as designated by the LSA. However, in the case of unavoidable circumstances (e.g. an increase in business), it becomes necessary to have workers provide labor that exceeds this limitation. This is called extended work (or overtime work). From the perspective of the employer, there will likely be circumstances where extended work becomes necessary. However, the LSA places limits on how much extended work would be allowed, as such work decreases the predictability of the worker's livelihood and may be detrimental to his/her normal life cycle and mental well-being.

2) Ordinary Extended Work

Where there exists an agreement between the parties, work hours may be extended up to 12 hours per week.[11] As the original limit on standard working hours is 40 hours per week, as a result a maximum working hours of 52 hours per week is possible. For workers 18 years and younger, work hours may be extended only for one more hour per day and six more hours per week by an agreement between the parties concerned.[12] Also, an employer is forbidden to have women for whom one year has not passed after childbirth carry out overtime

---

11 Ibid., Article 53(1)
12 Ibid., Article 69

work exceeding two hours per day, six hours per week, or 150 hours per year, even if provided for in a collective agreement.[13]

The law designates "agreement" as a condition for the provisions above, yet does not provide regulations regarding how that agreement may be reached. Therefore, it is acceptable to affix such agreement in writing. The Supreme Court states that "an agreement, which is the condition of permitting extended work designated by the LSA, is by principle an individual agreement between the employer and the worker. Such agreement does not need to take place whenever extended work is done, and may be provided a priori via means such as employment contracts, etc."[14]

On the flipside, the employer is not obligated to allow extended work because a worker wishes for it to take place. However, if an employer does not grant extended work due to the fact that a particular worker has participated in a strike or is an active participant to union activities, this would be considered a criminally liable act of unfair labor practice as the employer is deemed to be inflicting economic and work-related detriment to the worker.[15]

The amount of extended work that is possible via agreement between parties is 12 hours per week. Except workers younger than 18 or women who have given birth less than a year prior, there are no legal limitations as to how many hours of extended work may be given in a single day. Therefore, it is possible to have a worker conduct 12 hours of extended work in a single day per week.

There is debate as to whether working during holidays should be considered extended work. One position argues that work during holidays that stays within 8 hours per day is not extended work. According to this position, a worker who works during a Sunday (at a

13 Ibid., Article 71

14 Supreme Court 94Da19228 (1995. 2. 10.), Supreme Court 98Da54960 (2000. 6. 23.)

15 Supreme Court 2006Do388 (2006. 9. 8.)

workplace that designates Sundays as holidays) for 8 hours has engaged only in holiday work and not extended work. However, recent lower court precedent indicates that holiday work constitutes extended work regardless of how many hours of labor was provided that day to the extent that the total number of hours worked that week exceeds 40 hours.

The question is whether holiday work allowance and extended work allowance should be allowed to overlap for holiday work done beyond 40 hours. Article 50(1) of the LSA states "work hours shall not exceed 40 hours a week, excluding hours of recess," while Article 56 states "An employer shall, in addition to the ordinary wages, pay 50 percent or more thereof for extended work, night work, or holiday work. . ." Considering that the LSA only stipulates that a week's worth of work hours cannot exceed 40 hours and it would be difficult to interpret it to also mean that holiday work hours should be deducted, and considering that the system of premium wage rates is focused on reducing the number of work hours, this court rules that if the total work hours provided during non-holidays in a single week exceeds 40 hours, all work done during holidays should be considered to be at once holiday work hours and extended work hours, and hence both holiday work allowance and extended work allowances should be paid to the worker.[16]

While there is no Supreme Court decision on this issue as of yet, if the above ruling holds up at the highest court of the land both holiday and extended work allowance must be paid for holiday work done beyond the 40th hour in a work week.

An employer may be allowed to request extended work over 12 hours per week from the worker under special circumstance, provided that it has received the approval of the Ministry of Employment and Labor as well as the worker's consent. Where a situation is so urgent

---

16 Daegu District Court 2012Na61504 (2013. 9. 4.); see also Uijeongbu District Court 2012GaHap50704 (2013. 4. 19.).

that the employer does not have time enough to obtain authorization from the Ministry, s/he shall immediately obtain ex post facto approval from the Minister of Employment and Labor.[17] According to the Enforcement Decree of the LSA, the special circumstance mentioned above include situations such as natural disasters where extended work becomes necessary for recovery purposes.

B. Night Work

The term night work means work done between 10:00 p.m. and 6:00 a.m.[18] If night work also happens to be extended work, the necessary consent is needed to go ahead with the extended work. If the night work is not also extended work, there is no need to obtain separate consent.

Where an employer intends to have a woman of 18 years or over do night work, it must obtain the worker's consent.[19] An employer shall not have pregnant women and nursing mothers and those under 18 years old do night work, with the exception of those circumstances where it has obtained the consent of the worker and the approval from the Ministry of Employment and Labor.[20]

For workers that fall under LSA Article 63 (e.g. workers engaged in surveillance or intermittent work, whose employer has obtained the approval of the Minister of Employment and Labor), or workers engaged in directing and supervising or workers dealing with confidential information, provisions regarding working hours or holidays do not apply, and as a result, extended work or holiday work need not be

---

17 LSA, Article 53(3)
18 Ibid., Article 56
19 Ibid., Article 70(1)
20 Ibid., Article 70(2)

considered. Therefore, the payment of additional pay (which assumes the existence of extended or holiday work) is not necessary, nor is there need to pay premium rates for extended or holiday work (i.e. 100% of ordinary wages) for these types of workers. One caveat would be that provision regarding night work (LSA Article 56 regarding additional pay for night work) applies even to these workers, and hence the premium rate for night work must be applied and paid.

If night work provided also turns out to be extended work, the premium rates for both must be applied and paid.

C. Holiday Work

Article 55 of the LSA provides that "An employer shall allow workers at least one paid holiday per week on average." The 40-hour work week must be divided appropriately between six days, within the scope of the standard work-hours allowed per one day. For the remaining day of the week where no work is scheduled, the worker is assumed to have provided a day's worth of labor even if no such work has been provided, and shall be provided with a day's wages. Such paid holidays are called "weekly holidays." The only holidays that the law mandates are weekly holidays and Labor Day (the first day of May). As Labor Day is considered a paid holiday, the worker is paid wages even if s/he did not work that day. The term for such weekly holidays and Labor Day is "legal holiday." Other holidays may be specified in employment rules, collective agreements, or employment contracts. Holidays may be determined by labor relations custom.

Article 30 of the Enforcement Decree of the LSA stipulates "paid holidays under Article 55 of the Act shall be granted to a person who has had perfect attendance of the contractual working days during one week." However, there is no mention of the requirement of "perfect attendance" within the LSA. The Supreme Court ruled "the employer must provide the worker who has had perfect attendance of the contractual working days with one day of paid leave per week, and at least one day of nonpaid leave per week if the worker did not show perfect attendance."[21] In other words, weekly holidays are paid for workers who have had perfect attendance and non-paid for workers who had not. There is no obligation to designate the weekly holiday on a Saturday or Sunday.

In order to have workers work during holidays, their agreement is required. Here, "agreement" is defined in the same manner as when it is used in the context of extended work. Additional pay must be given for holiday work.[22] Regarding the scope of holiday work for which additional pay must be given, the majority opinion is that it must be given for weekly holidays, Labor Day, and other holidays as designated through employment rules, collective agreements, employment contracts, and industry custom. The minority opinion is that additional pay must be given only during weekly holidays and Labor Day.

Is there a way to work during a holiday and rest during a day that is not a holiday? If the substitution is done legally, the original holiday becomes a workday and hence there is no need to pay holiday allowance. While there is no regulation regarding substituting holidays in the LSA, the Supreme Court generally approves this practice, ruling "If there is a provision within the collective agreement that provides for the designation of specific holidays as workdays and substitute normal workdays as holidays, or even without such provision the consent of the worker is obtained and advance notice is given as to which holidays will be substituted, without the existence of special circumstance this becomes a legal holiday substitution (i.e. the original holiday becomes a normal workday, and the work provided during this

21 Supreme Court 2002Du2857 (2004. 6. 25.)

22 Ibid., Article 56

day becomes normal work, not holiday work). Therefore, the employer does not have the duty to provide holiday allowance for work done during substituted holidays."[23]

An employer that does not provide weekly holidays to its workers shall be punished by imprisonment for not more than two years or by a fine not exceeding ten million won.[24]

III. Special Provision Regarding Calculation of Work Hours

Work hours must be calculated by accumulating the actual hours worked by the worker. There are exceptions to this rule, however. According to the LSA, when it is difficult to calculate work hours provided by a worker because s/he carries out his/her duty in whole or in part outside the workplace owing to a business trip or any other reason, it shall be deemed that s/he has worked for the contractual working hours.[25] This is called the "acknowledged (deemed) working hour system." Examples of this would be workers who conduct marketing activities, installation and repair activities, and investigative/intelligence activities outside of the workplace. In order to apply this provision, calculation of work hours must be difficult to calculate due to the fact that all or part of the work is done outside of the workplace.

"Where it is ordinarily necessary for the worker to work in excess of contractual working hours in order to carry out the said duty, it shall be deemed that s/he has worked for the hours ordinarily required to carry out that duty.[26] The problem lies with the fact that calculating

23 Supreme Court 2007Da590 (2008. 11. 13.)
24 Ibid., Article 110(1)
25 Ibid., Article 58(1)
26 Ibid., Article 58(1) proviso

"hours ordinarily required" is often not straightforward. For example, an employer may assert that the "hours ordinarily required" for a given task would be 9 hours, whereas the worker would argue that it is in fact 10 hours.

Envisioning such conflicts, the LSA stipulates "in case where there exists a written agreement between an employer and the labor representative in regard to the work concerned, the hours as determined by such a written agreement shall be regarded as those ordinarily required to carry out the relevant duty."[27] If such a written agreement exists, even if a worker is able to prove that the completion of a particular task would take longer than the hours agreed upon, the employer would not be obligated to pay extra wages.

> "In case of . . . work which, in the light of its circumstances, requires leaving the methods of performance to a worker's discretion, it shall be deemed that the work be provided for such work hours as determined by a written agreement between the employer and the labor representative."[28] This is called the discretionary working system. This provision applies to professional occupations where the degree of capacity has a large impact on the work. The following jobs are eligible for the discretionary working system:[29]

1. Research on and developing new products or new technology, or research on the humanities, social sciences, or natural sciences;
2. Designing and analyzing data processing systems;
3. Gathering, compiling, or editing materials for a newspaper, broadcasting, or publishing business;
4. Designing or devising clothes, interior decorations, industrial products, advertisements, etc.;

---

27 Ibid., Article 58(2)
28 Ibid., Article 58(3)
29 Enforcement Decree of the Labor Standards Act

5. Working as a producer or director for production of broadcasting programs, motion pictures, etc.;

6. Other jobs specified further by the Minister of Employment and Labor.

If such a written agreement exists, even if a worker is able to prove that the completion of a particular task would take longer than the hours agreed upon, the employer would not be obligated to pay extra wages.

IV. Special Work Hour System Arrangements

Article 50 of the LSA stipulates standard working hours (40 hours per week, 8 hours per day). However, the LSA also allows for flexible distribution of these standard working hours under certain conditions. This is called the Flexible Work Hour System and the Selective Work-hours System.

A. Flexible Work Hour System

Under the flexible work hour system, an employer may extend work hours for a particular week or day in excess of the standard hours per week (40 hours), or per day (8 hours), by averaging total work hours with a certain period of time. This system allows for the employer to order work in excess of standard work hours for a given day or week without having to pay extended work allowance nor be subject to criminal liability.[30] The flexible work hours system shall not apply to workers who are between 15 and 18 years of age and to pregnant female workers.[31]

---

30 LSA, Article 51
31 Ibid., Article 51(3)

When an employer needs to have a worker work under the flexible work hour system, the employer shall take measures to supplement his/her wages so that the existing level of wages may not be lowered.[32] This clause was added to protect the livelihood of workers, due to the possibility that the extended work allowance a worker used to receive prior to the implementation of the flexible work hour system would no longer be provided, resulting in a lower total wage. This provision may be considered an "instruction without penalty," as no specific directions are provided as to how the wages of workers will be preserved, nor are there punitive measures introduced for when the provision is violated.

There are two types of flexible work hour systems: where the unit period is averaged across "within two weeks," or "within three months."

1) The "Two-Week Unit Period" Flexible Work Hour System

"An employer may, as prescribed by the rules of employment (including other rules equivalent thereto), extend work hours in excess of those as referred to in Article 50(1) in a particular week [i.e. 40 hours], or extend work hours in excess of those as referred to in Article 50(2) in a particular day [i.e. 8 hours], to the extent that average work hours per week during a certain unit period of not more than two weeks do not exceed the work hours as referred to in Article 50(1) [i.e. 40 hours]; provided, That work hours in any particular week shall not exceed 48 hours."[33] Whether modifying employment rules to incorporate provisions implementing the flexible work hour system would be considered a modification disadvantageous to the worker, and hence would require the consent of the worker's representative, is still an ongoing dispute.

---

32 Ibid., Article 51(4)
33 Ibid., Article 51(1)

The basic unit of averaging hours does not need to be exactly two weeks; it only needs to be longer than a week and within two weeks (e.g. 10 days). Unlike the "three-month flexible work hour system," the LSA does not require the "two-week flexible work hour system" to designate valid periods. Therefore, as per the employment rules the system may be implemented without limitations on its valid periods. While a week's maximum work hours is limited to 48, an extra 12 hours of extended work may be implemented during this same week. It is also possible to designate long working hours for a particular day without limitations under the "two-week flexible work hour system" (unlike the three-month flexible work hour system), although many point out that this is the result of a flaw in the statute.

2) The "Three-Month Unit Period" Flexible Work Hour System

The employer may agree in writing with the worker's representative the following: (1) scope of workers subject to the flexible work hour system; (2) unit period (determined to be a certain period of time not exceeding three months); (3) working days in the unit period, and work hours for each working day; (4) the written agreement's term of validity. Under this agreement, a worker may work during designated weeks and days beyond 40 hours per week and 8 hours per day, so long as the total number of hours averaged out across three months does not exceed 40 hours per week. However, even during the designated period the workweek may not exceed 52 hours and the workday may not exceed 12 hours.[34] Also, according to Article 53(2) of the LSA, where there exists an agreement between the parties weekly work-hours may be extended up to 12 hours per week while at the same time flexible work hours may also be extended up to 12 hours per week, which takes the maximum number of hours a worker may work per week to 64 hours.[35]

---

34 Ibid., Article 51(2); Enforcement Decree of the LSA, Article 28(1)
35 Ibid., Article 53(2)

B. Selective Work Hour System

The selective work hours system leaves the decision regarding the start and end point of the work period up to the worker, and averages the number of hours worked for a designated period up to one month. This system allows a worker to work beyond 40 hours a week, 8 hours a day so long as the averaged hours do not exceed 40 hours per week. If the flexible work hours system is a work hour modification arrangement that caters to the convenience of the employer, the selective work hours system caters to the convenience of the worker. While workers under the age of 18 cannot be subject to this system, workers who are pregnant are allowed to be.

In order to implement the selective work hours system, the employment rules must contain provisions that provide for its basis, and a written agreement of the worker's representative is required.[36] The content of the agreement must include the following: (1) scope of workers that will be subject to the system; (2) adjustment period (determined to be a specified period of not exceeding one month); (3) total work hours during the adjustment period; (4) beginning and finishing time of work hours during which work must be provided, if so required; (5) starting and ending time of work hours which workers are allowed to determine; and (6) Standard Work hours. Here, the term "Standard Work Hours" means daily work-hours that form the standard of calculating paid holidays, as well as the payment for unused annual leave allowance and weekly holiday allowance.

The calculation period may be set freely so long as it stays within one month. The total number of hours a worker may work within a calculation period is the sum of the fixed number of hours that may be worked during this period. For example, if a worker that works 40 hours of fixed hours per week designates four weeks (28 days) as the

---

36 Ibid., Article 52(1)

calculation period, the total number of hours that may be worked within the calculation period is 160. Hence, this worker may flexibly adjust his/her daily work schedule (i.e. start and end times) within this 160-hour period.

If the selective work hours system is implemented, there is no need to pay extended work allowances for work hours that go beyond 40 hours per week and 8 hours per day. However, should the total number of hours worked exceed that designated hours for the respective calculation period, the appropriate extended work allowance must be paid.

V. Leaves

A. Definition of Leaves

Article 60 of the LSA lays out the annual paid leave system. A leave is a relatively prolonged period during which the duty of the worker to provide labor is waived, and is distinguished from holidays or recesses. A recess is given during the workday, but a leave is given in days, often multiple days. A holiday is a designated day where provision of labor is not expected in the first place, whereas a leave takes place during a period when labor is supposed to be provided but that duty is subsequently waived.

B. The Leave System

Under current law, the leave system is comprised of annual paid leave,[37] monthly physiologic leave,[38] and leave for pregnant women

---

37 Ibid., Article 60
38 Ibid., Article 73

and nursing mothers.[39] Other leave periods may be designated via collective agreements, employment rules, and employment contracts. Leaves must be stated clearly when entering into the employment contract,[40] and employment rules must include provisions regarding leaves.[41]

C. Annual Paid Leave

1) Requirements for Annual Paid Leave

An employer must grant any worker who has worked not less than 80 percent of a one year paid leave of 15 days, and must grant any worker who has continuously worked for not less than three years paid-leave days that are calculated by adding one day for every two continuously working years not including the first year to the 15 paid-leave days; provided, that the total number of paid-leave days, including the additional paid-leave days, shall not exceed 25 days.[42]

Employers must grant any worker who has continuously worked for not less than one year or who has worked not less than 80 percent of one year one paid-leave day for each month during which s/he has continuously worked. Where an employer grants a worker a paid leave for the latter's first year of work, the former shall grant the latter a paid leave of 15 days; if the latter has already taken the paid-leave, the employer may deduct the number of days of such paid-leave from the said 15 days.[43]

In order to receive annual paid leave in the next year, the previous

39 Ibid., Article 74
40 Ibid., Article 17
41 Ibid., Article 93(1)
42 Ibid., Article 60(1) and (4)
43 Ibid., Article 60(2) and (3)

year's rate of work attendance must exceed 80 percent. This rate of work attendance is calculated based on the number of days in which the worker is obligated to report to work (i.e. contractual working days). Therefore, holidays or leaves are not factored in. Also, periods during which a worker takes time off due to any injury or sickness arising out of duty or for pregnancy and nursing purposes are considered as time where the worker has reported for duty.[44] Periods in which a worker has requested time to participate in Homeland Reserve Forces training, exercise his/her rights as a citizen or conduct pubic deeds are be deemed as time where the worker has reported for duty.

Whether the period during which legitimate strikes were held should be considered part of the contractual working days is a subject of debate. A recent Supreme Court decision ruled: "In cases where a worker engaged in valid industrial action or did not provide actual labor due to taking maternity leave under the 'Equal Employment Opportunity and Work-Family Balance Assistance Act,' the time that the worker has engaged in both acts must be deducted when calculating contractual working days."[45] The same ruling stated that a proportional approach would be reasonable in calculating annual paid leave in such cases. For example, let's say the number of annual paid leave days would be 20 days under normal labor relationship conditions (i.e. the worker satisfies the 80 percent work attendance rate). If the difference between the number of contractual working days under ordinary conditions and that impacted by non-working periods (i.e. industrial actions, maternity leave) results in only 90% of the original contractual working days being worked, the number of annual paid leave days under normal conditions (20 days) would be multiplied by 0.9, resulting in 18 days of annual paid leave.

---

44 Ibid., Article 60(6)
45 Supreme Court 2011Da4629 (2013. 12. 26.)

2) Calculating Annual Paid Leave

Often, workers in the same workplace have different starting dates. It is difficult to calculate annual paid leave based on the exact starting date of each individual worker while factoring in that worker's rate of work attendance; so the employer may calculate annual paid leave based on a designated period (usually January 1st through December 31st). In such cases, however, the employer must make sure there is no detriment to the worker. For example, if a worker started work on April 1st, 2013, the employer should provide the worker with nine months of annual paid leave in 2014 (15 days × 9/12), and provide 15 days for the years thereafter. If such a method is utilized, the employer may calculate the accurate annual paid leave dates owed to the worker upon the latter's retirement and compensate in the form of allowances if there are any that were not already provided.

3) Using Annual Paid Leave

There is nothing in the law that regulates how annual paid leaves are to be used. Normally, this is neither regulated through employment rules nor collective agreements. This is because leaves are by definition something that the worker has the freedom to use as s/he sees fit. A caveat to this would be that the Supreme Court has ruled the collective use of annual paid leave as a result of instigation would be considered a form of industrial action.[46]

In order to use annual paid leave, the worker must exercise his/her right to designate leave periods. In principle, the worker may exercise this right without limit. However, "in the event that granting the worker a paid leave at the time when such worker wants to take the paid leave greatly impedes the business operation, the relevant employer may change the time of the paid leave."[47] A mere increase

---

46 Supreme Court 96Nu587 (1996. 7. 30.)

47 LSA, Article 60(5) proviso

in workload experienced by other workers due to the leave is not interpreted to rise to the level of "great impediment" to business operations. If the employer validly exercises its right to modify the designated leave period, the worker must work in accordance to such designation.

There are cases, however, where an employer would have employment rules that require workers to obtain permission from the former in order to use annual paid leave. Some argue that such rules limit the right of the worker to annual leave without justifiable basis. However, the Supreme Court ruled on this matter that: "the employment rule that requires a worker who wishes to take leave to obtain permission from the CEO of the workplace does not purport to deprive the worker of his right to designate leave period but is in fact a method through which the employer may appropriately exercise its right to modify the designated leave period."[48] In other words, the Supreme Court ruled that the above employment rule is not illegal.

Annual paid leave is terminated if not exercised within one year. However, this is not the case where the paid leave is not taken for reasons attributable to the employer.[49] Case law also suggests that even though the right to request the use of annual paid leave terminates upon one year of non-use, the right to request additional allowance (ordinary or average wages) for the days worked instead of taking leave does not.[50]

4) System of Encouraging the Use of Annual Paid Leave

Often, the annual leave system is not used for its original purpose of providing rest for workers, but as a means to obtain allowance for work done during annual leave. Payment of allowances for work done

48 Supreme Court 92Da7542 (1992. 6. 23.)

49 LSA, Article 60(7)

50 Supreme Court 90DaKa14758 (1991. 6. 28.), Supreme Court 95Da36695 (1996. 11. 22.), Supreme Court 99Da10806 (2000. 12. 22.)

during annual leave becomes a significant burden to employers. An attempt to remedy this issue is the system of encouraging the use of annual paid leave.

"Where any worker's paid leave is terminated by time limitation after the worker fails to take his/her paid leave although the relevant employer has taken the measures . . . to urge workers to take their respective annual leave, the relevant employer is not liable to indemnify the worker for his/her failure to take the paid leave and his/her failure to take the paid leave shall be deemed not to fall under the reasons attributable to the employer."[51] Measures to urge workers to take annual leave are as follows: (i) notify in writing every worker of the number of days of his/her paid leave that has not been taken and to urge every worker to notify the employer of a period during which s/he intends to take his/her paid leave after deciding on such period within ten days as of six months before the right to take leave expires. (ii) if a worker does not set a period during which s/he will be taking leave within 10 days of receiving the above notice and notify the employer of this, the employer may notify in writing a period which the worker may take his/her paid leave (this must be done prior to two months before the worker's right to leave expires).

If the employer has taken the above steps to encourage the worker to take annual leave but the worker still does not do so, the former is not obligated to pay allowance for work done during annual leave.

"An employer may, by a written agreement with the labor representative, get workers to take a paid leave on a particular working day in substitution of an annual paid leave."[52]

An employer who does not provide annual paid leave to his/her workers "shall be punished by imprisonment for not more than two years or by a fine of not exceeding ten million won."[53] This criminal

---

51 LSA, Article 61
52 Ibid., Article 62
53 Ibid., Article 110(1)

liability applies when the employer does not provide the worker with annual leave upon the worker's request, and when the employer suppresses the worker's use of his/her right to use annual leaves in the first place.

D. Compensatory Leaves

The employer may grant workers leaves in lieu of wage payments for extended work, night work, or holiday work according to a written agreement that is concluded between him/her and the worker's representative.[54] For example, for 12 hours of extended work a total of 18 hours of leave may be given (i.e. with an addition of 50%). This system is called the compensatory leave system, but is hardly used in practice.

E. Monthly Physiological Leave

"Every employer shall, when any female worker files a claim for a physiological leave, grant her one day of physiological leave per month."[55] This system is very unique, and it is virtually impossible to find equivalent legislation in the employment laws of other countries.

Monthly physiological leaves are given on a non-paid basis. Wages owed for the day that the leave is used are not paid. An employer does not need to pay additional wages if s/he does not accept the request for monthly physiological leave and orders the worker to continue working. However, the employer may be fined by an amount not exceeding five million won for violations thereof.[56]

---

54 Ibid., Article 57
55 Ibid., Article 73
56 Ibid., Article 114(1)

F. Maternity Leave

An employer must grant a pregnant woman a 90-day maternity leave before and after childbirth (or 120 days if more than one child is gestating). Where a pregnant female worker requests maternity leave due to the following reasons, the employer must allow her to use leave multiple times any time before her childbirth: (i) when the pregnant worker experiences a miscarriage or a stillbirth; (ii) the pregnant worker is at least 40 years of age at the time of the request for leave; and (ii) the pregnant worker submits a diagnosis from a medical institution that she has a high risk of miscarriage or stillbirth. In such cases, the period of leave after the childbirth shall be at least 45 days (or 60 days if more than one child is gestating).[57]

This period is calculated reverse chronologically. Even if there are holidays during this period, only 90 (or 120) calendar days are guaranteed. This period must be ensured and cannot be shortened, even if it is the wish of the worker.

In principle, maternity leave is used consecutively. If there is a high risk for miscarriage or stillbirth, however, it may be used at multiple times throughout the pregnancy.

Where a pregnant woman has a miscarriage or a stillbirth, an employer shall, upon the relevant worker's request, grant her a miscarriage/stillbirth leave.

The first 60 days (or 75 for multiple children) of maternity leave or miscarriage/stillbirth leave shall be paid. While not stipulated in the LSA, the general interpretation is that ordinary or average wages are paid for this period. However, as per Article 18 of the "Equal Employment Opportunity and Work-Family Balance Assistance Act," any amount paid by the employer as maternity leave benefits serves as a deduction from the above amount. Also, under Article 75 of the

---

57 Ibid., Article 74(1) and (2)

Employment Insurance Act, the Ministry of Employment and Labor must provide maternity leave benefits to certain qualifying workers according to designated standards. For workers working with priority employers under the Employment Insurance Act, 90 days' worth of maternity benefits are paid. For workers working for non-priority employers, maternity benefits of up to 90 days (i.e. first 60 days plus up to 30 days depending on the actual amount of maternity leave used thereafter) are paid. The employer only needs to pay the difference between ordinary or average wages and the above maternity benefits. In the case of priority employers, if the pregnant worker's ordinary or average wages exceed the amount supported by unemployment insurance, the employer must pay the difference for the first 60 days. For non-priority employers, the employer pays 60 days' worth of ordinary or average wages.

G. Overlapping Holidays and Leaves

1) When Multiple Holidays Overlap

If two or more holidays overlap, unless there is a provision in the collective agreement or employment rules that specifically deals with such situations (e.g. designating the next day as a holiday), only one holiday is recognized. For example, if Labor Day falls on a weekly holiday (Sunday), it would be considered to be only one holiday. As such, if a worker works that day holiday work allowance is provided for one day only.

2) When Holidays and Leaves Overlap

Paid holidays and paid leave cannot be applied for the same day. For instance, if a worker takes paid leave from Monday though the following Tuesday but his/her workplace designates Saturdays and Sundays to be paid holidays, the worker would only use seven days of paid leave. If, on the other hand, the worker's workplace considers Saturdays and Sundays to be non-paid holidays, the worker would have used nine days of paid leave.

VI. Suspension

A. Concept

A suspension is a measure taken by the employer in which a worker is forbidden to work for a certain period while preserving his/her position, due to circumstance that make the worker's continued provision of labor impossible or impracticable. Generally, suspensions are regulated via employment rules or collective agreements.[58] The Equal Employment Opportunity and Work-Family Balance Assistance Act both have provisions regarding maternity leave as well.[59]

Topics of discussion regarding this subject include whether the worker has the right to request suspensions and whether the employer's order to suspend the worker has validity.

B. Conditions for Valid Suspensions

The validity of an employer's suspension order needs to be assessed based on a reasonable interpretation of the relevant provisions within the business's employment rules and collective agreements.

According to Article 23(1) of the LSA, the employer is prohibited from suspending workers without justifiable cause. In order for an employer's suspension order to be justifiable, grounds for suspension

---

58 Supreme Court 92Da16690 (1992. 11. 13.)
59 LSA, Article 74(1) and (2)

designated by the collective agreement or employment rules must exist. Also, the purpose and actual function of the provision regulating suspensions, the degree of reasonableness of the order for suspension, and the degree of economic and positional detriment suffered by the worker must be comprehensively assessed. In light of the above assessments, if it is recognized that it is impossible for the worker to provide work for a significant amount of time, or that it will be significantly unsuitable for the worker to provide work, the employer's suspension order would be considered valid.[60]

Should a worker be arrested and detained for prosecution, the employer's suspension measure is valid in light of the fact that it is impracticable for the worker to provide labor (i.e. suspension due to prosecution). There is an illustrative Supreme Court case on this subject:[61] Here, a worker was imprisoned for professional malpractice but was subsequently released due to the prosecution's revocation of custody. The employer ordered the worker's suspension until proven not guilty, citing the regulation within personnel policy that states: "if a worker is prosecuted or held under custody for a criminal case, the employer may order his/her suspension until the January following the verdict." Here, the court ruled that the order of suspension was valid insofar as the worker was under imprisonment due to the fact that the worker cannot provide labor at that state, but the order became invalid after the worker was released from custody, as continuing the suspension goes against the reasonable expectation of society.

---

60 Supreme Court 92Da16690 (1992. 11. 13.)
61 Supreme Court 2003Da63029 (2005. 2. 18.)

C. The Legal Effect of Suspensions

1) Suspensions and Wages
Payment of wages for workers under suspension is by principle regulated by collective agreements and rules of employment.[62]

If a suspension is brought about by a shutdown caused by managerial reasons attributable to the employer, Article 46 of the LSA designates that workers receive 70% of their average wages as allowance. If a suspension is brought about by intentional acts or acts of negligence, or other causes attributable to the employer as defined in the Civil Act, the employer assumes the liability to provide 100% of the worker's wages.

Periods in which workers are in suspension are included when calculating years of continuous employment.

2) Duty of Good Faith during Suspensions
While the worker is relieved of his/her duty to provide labor during suspension periods, the contractual employment relationship remains intact. As such, the worker is bound to the duty of good faith even during suspensions. If the worker discloses confidential information or engages in acts of defamation or libel, s/he will be subject to disciplinary action even during suspension.

---

62 Supreme Court 90Da8763 (1992. 3. 31.)

Chapter 3

Average Wages and Ordinary Wages

I. The Concept of Wages

A. The Concept of the Dual Instrumentality of Wages

The LSA[1] classifies wages into "average wages"[2] and "ordinary wages."[3] The following are calculated based on the "average wages": severance pay; shutdown allowances, paid leave, compensation for medical treatment, and punitive wage cuts for workers under the LSA;[4] as well as medical care benefits, temporary disability compensation benefits, disability benefits, nursing benefits, survivors' benefits, injury-disease compensation annuities, funeral expenses, and vocational rehabilitation benefits under the Industrial Accident Compensation Insurance Act.[5]

The following statutory allowances are calculated based on the "ordinary wages" (time wages): benefits provided for failing to give advance notice of dismissal[6] and benefits provided for overtime, night

1 Labor Standards Act
2 LSA, Article 2(1)6
3 Ibid., Article 2(2)
4 Ibid., Articles 34, 46, 60(5), 78, 83, 95
5 Ibid., Articles 40, 52, 57, 61, 62, 66, 71, 72
6 Ibid., Article 26

or holiday work.[7]

Therefore, it is necessary to have a good understanding of the concept of average and ordinary wages and related regulatory schemes in order to properly navigate the laws governing wages in the Republic of Korea. But first, as the valuables paid by the employer to the worker must first be classified as wages before we can analyze whether it is average or ordinary, let's first examine these two concepts of wages in detail.

B. The Legal Concept of Wages

Article 2(1)5 of the LSA defines "wages" as "wages, salary and any other kind of money or valuables, regardless of their titles, which the employer pays to a worker as remuneration for work." According to this definition, we must distinguish which of the valuables given by the employer to the worker would be classified as wages and which would not. The determining criterion would be whether the valuable was paid as remuneration for work.

Regarding the legal characteristic of wages under the LSA, court precedents suggest that wages are compensation for work done by workers under the direction of employers, and hence so-called "wages to ensure livelihood," or wages provided solely on the basis of the worker's position without the actual provision of labor cannot exist.[8] All valuables paid as compensation for labor are considered wages, and there is no legal basis in conceptualizing wages having two separate functions (i.e. the exchange function to provide compensation for actual labor provided, and the function to provide a living to a worker solely on the basis of his/her position). Court precedents suggest two indicators

7 Ibid., Article 56
8 Supreme Court 94Da26721 (1995. 12. 21.), unanimous decision

in determining whether valuables have been paid to compensate for labor: ① the valuables are paid continuously, periodically, and uniformly; and ② the employer must have the duty to pay such valuables.[9]

C. Disputes over Whether Valuables Are Wages

1) Meal Allowance

The provision of actual meals, meal allowance, or meal coupons to workers who actually provide labor, and not providing such benefits if the worker did not actually have meals, are not considered to be wages. However, if meal allowances are provided to all workers as a continuous, periodic, and uniform item, or if actual meals are provided while the cash equivalent of any missed meals are paid to workers, this would be considered to be wages.[10]

2) Welfare Expenses

By principle, the use of company housing and welfare facilities (e.g. exercise facilities inside and outside the corporate premises, recreation and leisure facilities, simple refreshments or welfare supplies) are not considered as wages. In the case of company housing, however, if workers not living in the facility are paid a housing allowance that corresponds to the value of its use, this may be considered as wages.[11] Allowances provided under the description of fitness maintenance or vacation bonuses, if paid continuously, periodically, and uniformly, would also be considered as wages.[12] However, if this allowance is

---

9 Supreme Court 98Da34393 (1999. 9. 3.)

10 Supreme Court 81Da697 (1981. 10. 13.), Supreme Court 90Da15662 (1991. 2. 26.), Supreme Court 93Da4816 (1993. 5. 11.)

11 Supreme Court 90DaKa6948 (1990. 11. 9.)

12 Supreme Court 90DaKa19647 (1990. 12. 27.), Supreme Court 90Da6170 (1991. 1. 15.), Supreme Court 92Da20316 (1993. 5. 27.), Supreme Court 2003Da54322, 54339 (2006. 5. 26.)

provided only to those who have actually consumed the utilities (i.e. fitness maintenance allowance is paid only to those who have used such facilities, and vacation bonuses given only to those who have actually gone on vacation), this would not be considered as wages.

As for family allowance, educational allowances for dependents, and household finance support allowance, despite names that suggest otherwise, these funds are generally not unrelated to the compensation for labor provided by the worker and are usually considered to be wages so long as they satisfy standards ① and ②, as suggested by previous court precedent.[13]

Funds paid as incentives or tips, or as congratulatory, condolence, or compensation funds are either provided randomly or as the occasion arises, and are generally not considered to be wages.[14]

3) Special or Performance-Based Bonuses

As the rate of payment for these bonuses (or whether payment would be provided at all) depends on that year's production or management performance, these bonuses are not compensation for labor; hence are not considered as wages.[15] However, if certain funds are paid regularly and continuously and the amount of payment is fixed, even if named special or performance-based bonuses, these funds would be considered as wages.[16]

Meanwhile, some courts have ruled that incentives paid depending on the performance of individual workers should not be considered wages.[17] However, this opinion is not yet upheld by the Supreme

---

13 Supreme Court 2000Da18127 (2002. 5. 31.)

14 Supreme Court 93Da4649 (1994. 5. 24.)

15 Supreme Court 2001Da16722 (2002. 6. 11.), Supreme Court 2001Da76328 (2004. 5. 14.), Supreme Court 2004Da41217 (2005. 9. 9.), Supreme Court 2009Da86246 (2011. 10. 13.)

16 Supreme Court 2003Da54322, 54339 (2006. 5. 26.)

17 Supreme Court 2001Da76328 (2004. 5. 14.)

Court. Rulings that contradict the above principle have been made in recent years.[18]

4) Other Cost-Compensatory Payments

The provision of automotive transportation to use for commuting is not wages. However, whether commutation allowance, transportation fees, vehicle driving allowance, vehicle maintenance allowance, or self-driving assistance allowance should be considered wages often comes under dispute. Case law states that if there is a duty on the part of the employer to provide the above payments, all workers (or workers above a certain level) are given the above on a regular, continuous, and uniform basis, and workers who do not receive the above allowances are provided with a vehicle to commute with, such allowances are considered to be wages.[19]

II. Calculation of Average Wages

A. The Concept of Average Wages

The LSA defines average wages in Article 2(1)6. The term "average wages" means the amount calculated by dividing the total amount of wages paid to a relevant worker during three calendar months immediately before the day on which a cause for calculating his/her average wages occurred by the total number of calendar days during those three months. This calculation applies even if the worker has been employed for less than three months.

Average wages serve as the standard on which severance payments

---

18 Supreme Court 2010Da77514 (2011. 3. 10.), Supreme Court 2011Da23149 (2011. 7. 14.)

19 Supreme Court 81Da697 (1981. 10. 13.), Supreme Court 91Da37522 (1992. 4. 10.), Supreme Court 96Nu15084 (1997. 5. 28.), Supreme Court 2000Da18127 (2002. 5. 31.)

under the LSA and insurance payments under the Industrial Accident Compensation Insurance Act are calculated. The purpose of these payments is to ensure that the worker is able to maintain his/her ordinary livelihood. Therefore, as the standard indicator on which such payments are based, the basic principle behind the calculation of average wages is to reflect the ordinary, actual living wage earned of the worker.[20]

B. Calculation of Average Wages: The Principle

Under the LSA, ① the basic timeframe on which the calculation of average wages is made is "three calendar months immediately before the day on which a cause of calculating average wages occurred"; ② the "total amount of wages paid to the worker" during this period is calculated; then, ③ the total wages calculated in ② is divided by the total number of days in ①, which results in daily average wages. This calculation is expressed in the following expression.

Daily Average Wage =	Total amount of wages paid to the relevant worker for three calendar months immediately before the day on which the cause of calculating average wages occurred
	Total number of days in the average wage calculation period (i.e. the total number of calendar days in the last three calendar months)

As item ③ is calculated automatically once items ① and ② are determined, this item does not pose problems. Below, we examine in

---

20 Supreme Court 90Nu2772 (1991. 4. 26.)

more detail how items ① and ② are calculated.

1) Determining the Average Wage Calculation Period

First, the phrase "the day on which the cause of calculating average wages occurred" in the above equation refers to the day when the cause arises where various payments must be made or deducted, and the calculation of average wages becomes necessary to specify the amount of payments or deductions. For example, this day would be the day a worker retires in the case of "severance payments," the day a shutdown occurred due to causes attributable to the employer in the case of "shutdown allowances," or the day the industrial accident that gave rise to injury or death occurred or the day of diagnosis of illness in the case of "disaster compensation" or "industrial accident compensation insurance payments."

Next, the phrase "three calendar months" is by principle a unit that is calculated according to the calendar.[21] There are cases where following such calculation methods would be unreasonable, however. To avoid this result, the Enforcement Decree of the LSA exclusively enumerates periods that are excluded from the average wage calculation period.[22] The relevant provision reads as follows.

Article 2 (Period and Wages Excluded from Calculation of Average Wages)

(1) Where a period for the calculation of average wage under Article 2(1)6 of the Labor Standards Act (hereinafter referred to as the "Act") includes a period falling under any of the following subparagraphs, such period and wages paid during that period shall be subtracted respectively from the period and the total amount of wage which shall serve as the basis for the calculation of average wage:

---

21 Civil Act, Article 160
22 Supreme Court 2001Da12669 (2003. 7. 25.)

1. A probationary period under subparagraph 5 of Article 35 of the Act;
2. A period during which the employer's business is closed because of a cause attributable to the employer as provided for in Article 46 of the Act;
3. A period before and after maternity leave under Article 74 of the Act;
4. A period of temporary suspension for medical treatment due to occupational injury or disease as provided for in Article 78 of the Act;
5. A period of child-care leave under Article 19 of the Act on the Equal Employment Opportunity and Work-Family Balance Assistance Act;
6. A period of labor dispute under subparagraph 6 of Article 2 of the Trade Union and Labor Relations Adjustment Act;
7. A period of temporary retirement from office or of absence from office in order to perform a duty under the Military Service Act, the Establishment of Homeland Reserve Forces Act, or the Framework Act on Civil Defense: provided, that this shall not apply where the period for which wages have been paid;
8. A period of temporary retirement from office due to a non-occupational injury or disease, or any other cause with the employer's approval.

As mentioned above, the basic principle behind the calculation of average wages is to reflect the ordinary, actual living wage earned of the worker. However, including the periods enumerated above in the calculation of average wages runs contrary to this basic principle. This is why these periods are excluded from the three months used to calculate average wages.

Court precedent suggests that so long as the provisions in Article 2(1) of the Enforcement Decree of the LSA do not apply, the average wages of the worker in question would be calculated using the normal method (unless there exists special circumstance that would make it significantly inappropriate to do so), and if the resulting average wages is lower than the his/her ordinary wages, the amount of ordinary wages will be recognized as average wages.[23] However, even in situations where ordinary wages are deemed as average wages, if due to the special and coincidental circumstance of the worker his/her ordinary wages amounts to less than one thirds of his/her average wages right before the occurrence of this special circumstance, following the preceding calculation method is deemed by the courts to be markedly inappropriate.[24] In such cases, the three months preceding the occurrence of the above special and coincidental circumstance is used as the basis of calculating average wages.

Meanwhile, if a worker has worked for less than three months after commencing employment but an occasion has risen in which the calculation of average wages is required (such as resigning), all dates within the period of employment are included in the calculation of average wages.[25]

2) Total Wages Paid to the Worker

To calculate average wages, the sum total of valuables possessing the nature of "wages" must be identified from the total valuables provided to the worker during the calculation period.[26]

The scope of "wages" under the LSA has been examined above. It is important to keep in mind that wages paid during the periods enumerated in Article 2(1) of the Enforcement Decree of the LSA are not included in the total wages when calculating average wages, and neither are "wages and allowances paid on a temporary basis" and "wages paid by any means other than money," unless such valuables have been specified by the Minister of Employment and Labor.[27]

---

23 Supreme Court 92Da20309 (1994. 4. 12.); LSA, Article 2(2)
24 Supreme Court 98Da49357 (1999. 11. 12.)
25 LSA, Article 2(1)6, second sentence
26 Supreme Court 66Da2270 (1967. 1. 31.)
27 Enforcement Decree of the Labor Standards Act, Article 2(2)

Wages "paid" to workers refers to not only actual wages paid but also wages that should obviously have been paid but were not as of the day on which the cause of calculating average wages occurred. However, if the relevant worker has received lower pay due to a process agreed upon between labor union and management, such as being removed from his/her position or having his/her salary reduced, this lowered wage becomes the standard on which average wages are calculated.[28]

C. Calculation of Average Wages: The Exceptions

Where it is impossible to calculate average wage using the methods designated in the LSA, the average wage shall be determined by the method designated by the Minister of Employment and Labor.[29] Towards this, the Ministry of Employment and Labor Public Notice No. 2012-11 "Special Notice Regarding Calculation of Average Wages" (2012. 9. 25.) is currently enforced.

> Article 1 (When the Period Excluded from the Calculation of Average Wages Exceeds 3 Months)
> ① According to Article 2(1) of the Enforcement Decree of the Labor Standards Act(hereinafter referred as "Decree"), if the period excluded from the average wage calculation period exceeds three months, the first day of this excluded period is considered the day on which the cause of calculating average wages occurred. ② Article 5 of the Decree utilizes paragraph 1 when calculating average wages. Here, "certain month in which an injury or a disease was inflicted" in Article 5(1) is interpreted to mean "the month in which the first

---

28 Supreme Court 92Da20309 (1994. 4. 12.)
29 Enforcement Decree of the Labor Standards Act, Article 4

day of the period excluded from the average wage calculation period is included."

Article 2 (When the Day on Which the Cause of Calculating Average Wages Occurs Is on the First Day of the Provision of Labor)
If the day on which the cause of calculating average wages occurs on the first day of the provision of labor (including the first day after the conclusion of the probationary period as per Article 35(5) of the LSA), the average wage is calculated to be one day's worth of wages, averaged from the total wages promised to be paid to the worker.

Article 3 (When Wages are Paid to Two or More Workers as a Lump Sum)
When two or more workers constituting one unit are paid their wages in lump sum, and no previous agreements exist as to how this would be distributed among individual workers, the wage of an individual worker will be estimated based on the worker's experience, actual output, number of days actually worked, skills and functions, responsibility, custom regarding distribution. This estimated amount would be considered the average wage for that worker.

Article 4 (When a Portion of the Total Wages Is not Definite)
If there is a period within the average wage calculation period during which a portion of the wages paid cannot be confirmed, that period is excluded. As such, average wages would be the total amount of wages paid during the total period while excluding the above period, divided by the total number of days remaining after the exclusion.

Article 5 (When the Entirety of Total Wages Is Not Definite)
If average wages cannot be calculated based on Articles 1 through

4 of this Special Notice, the Head of the Local Office of the Employment and Labor Department determines an amount deemed appropriate after due consideration of the following paragraphs, which would be considered the average wage of the relevant worker.

III. Calculation of Ordinary Wages

A. Introduction

According to the LSA, ordinary wages not only function as the minimum to average wages,[30] but also function as the basic for calculation of various legal allowances such as extended, night, holiday, and advance notice of discharge allowances. An employer shall, in addition to the ordinary wages, pay 50 percent or more for extended work, night work, or holiday work.[31] When an employer intends to dismiss a worker, he/she shall give the worker a notice of dismissal at least 30 days in advance, or pay that worker ordinary wages for not less than 30 days as advance notice of discharge allowance.[32] Also, workers are paid ordinary or average wages during the period of paid leave.[33]

There are no definitional provisions regarding ordinary wages in the LSA. The only definition provided is in Article 6(1) of the Enforcement Decree of the LSA, which provides this definition: "the term 'ordinary wage' means hourly wage, daily wage, weekly wage, monthly wage, or contract amount to be paid to a worker for a specifically agreed work or entire works on a regular and consistent basis." As a result, there has been constant dispute regarding the

---

30 LSA, Article 2(1)
31 Ibid., Article 56
32 Ibid., Article 26
33 Ibid., Article 60(5)

concept and scope of ordinary wages. The Supreme Court finally dealt with this matter via unanimous decisions in two cases regarding this issue on December 18, 2013 (regarding regular bonuses and other fringe benefits), bringing this debate to a close.[34] The following examines the main disputes surrounding ordinary wages, with an analysis of what the Supreme Court has ruled on the respective issues.

B. The Standard of Determining Ordinary Wages: The Concept and Scope of Ordinary Wages

The Supreme Court's unanimous decision unequivocally affirmed its basic stance through the following ruling: "Whether certain wages are to be considered ordinary wages is to be determined by considering its objective characteristics, examining whether valuables are provided to the worker as compensation for his/her prescribed provision of labor in a regular, uniform, and stable manner. Formal indicators such as the name assigned to the payment or the cadence of the payment schedule are not appropriate standards to make such a determination." In other words, whether certain wages are to be considered ordinary wages do not hinge on their "names" or "payment schedules," but on whether the valuables are provided as "compensation for prescribed labor" in a "regular, uniform, and fixed manner."

1) Compensation for Prescribed Labor, Regularity, and Uniformity
"Compensation for prescribed labor" means "valuables that an employer has agreed to pay the worker for normal labor provided by the latter during prescribed work hours." Prescribed work hours are work hours agreed upon by labor union and management within the

---

34 Supreme Court 2012Da89399 (2013. 12. 18.), unanimous decision; Supreme Court 2012Da94643 (2013. 12. 18.), unanimous decision

bounds of the standard work hours prescribed by the LSA. As such, additional wages paid for special work not determined under the employment contract is excluded from ordinary wages.

"Regularity" means that wages are paid "in regular intervals on a continual basis." Prior to the Supreme Court ruling there was a dispute as to whether wages that were regularly paid in intervals that exceed "one wage calculation period" (or one calendar month) should be considered ordinary wages. On this topic, the unanimous court decision reaffirmed existing precedent by ruling "a wage cannot be considered to be not ordinary merely because its payment interval goes beyond one calendar month." Therefore, even if bonuses or other allowances are paid bimonthly, quarterly, semi-annually, or annually, as long as such payments have been provided "continuously," the condition of "regularity" is satisfied.

"Uniformity" means that wages are paid to "all workers" or "all workers that have satisfied certain conditions or standards." Here, "certain conditions or standards" means "conditions related to the assessment of the value of the prescribed work, such as details of work done, skills, and experience." For example, since the condition of payment for family allowance (which is provided only to those who have dependent family members) is unrelated to "quality of work (skills, experience, etc.)," uniformity is denied for family allowances. A caveat would be when a certain wage item is formally called "family allowance," but is paid to all workers indiscriminately, which would satisfy the "uniformity" condition, as it is paid as compensation for prescribed labor.

2) Predetermination

"Predetermination" means that certain wages "are predetermined to be paid at a specified moment in time, independent from additional conditions." Since ordinary wages serve as the "standard wage" used to calculate additional wages for extended, night, and holiday work, this "standard wage" must be "predetermined" at the point when additional wages are calculated. Here, the Supreme Court ruled firmly that "only the minimal amount of wages that a worker would definitely receive should s/he choose to resign the next day as compensation for the previous workday (during which s/he has provided labor during prescribed work hours normally)" would be considered as ordinary wages that satisfies the condition of predetermination. As such, "wages that would be paid only upon the satisfaction of additional conditions" or "wages that fluctuate in its amount depending on the satisfaction of additional conditions" would not be recognized to have satisfied the condition of predetermination.

In that case, future disputes would likely arise on the issue of what wages would be considered those "a worker would definitely receive" and what would be wages considered fluctuate according to "additional conditions." The important point here is that the assessment of whether a payment source is "determined" or "fluctuating" is made according to "any given day (=moment when the calculation of additional wages is conducted)" standard. In other words, the "predetermined" ordinary wage a worker would receive is the "minimal amount" that would "definitely" be paid when a random day is chosen among that worker's entire work period. Let's examine this in more detail by going through the six categories of wages that the unanimous Court decision has provided as illustrations.

i) Wages Coupled to the Period of Continuous Service: Whether bonuses that adjust its payment rate depending on "term of service" (e.g. employment for over 6 months) or continuous-service allowances that change depending on the "number of years of continuous service" could be considered determined wages has been under dispute. Whether such wages would be paid, and the amount that would be paid may be determined under the "any given day" standard. To illustrate, the amount that a worker would receive as bonus or continuous-service allowance is predetermined on the "moment in which additional wages are to be calculated (i.e. any given day)," regardless of whether the worker has been employed for four, eight, or 18 months. Therefore, these types of wages are ordinary wages.

ii) Wages Coupled with the Number of Days Worked: There are wages that are calculated per diem according to the actual number of days that the worker worked. The predetermined nature of such wages are recognized so long as the payment is made "in direct proportion to the number of days worked." To illustrate, if a particular allowance is paid in its entirety when the number of days worked that month is 15 days or more but is paid on a per diem basis if the worker worked less than 15 days, it is settled that the worker would at least be able to receive a "minimum" amount according to the per diem calculation in "any given day." Therefore, the portion of the above allowance that follows the "minimum amount of wages paid under the per diem calculation" would be recognized as ordinary wages.

iii) Wages Paid to Workers Working during Particular Periods: Among various welfare allowances (e.g. vacation bonus), there are wages paid only to workers who "worked during allowance paydays." Whether payment for such allowances will be made in "any given day" cannot be predetermined for these types of wages. For instance, a worker who resigned right before the payment of a holiday allowance cannot know whether s/he will be receiving the allowance at the point of his/ her resignation. Therefore, wages having the "additional condition" of "working at the moment of payment" satisfies the condition of predetermination.

This condition of "working at the moment of payment" does not necessarily have to be stipulated in the rules of employment or collective agreements. The unanimous court decision ruled that the predetermination requirement would be satisfied as long as "explicit or implicit agreement exists between the labor the union and management or is established as custom" that the above condition would be required when paying the relevant allowance.

However, even if a particular wage is paid only to workers "working at the moment of payment," if that wage has in fact been calculated based on the number of days left until retirement (e.g. due to labor practices), this wage would not satisfy the condition of predetermination. To illustrate, let's say that under the rules of employment "vacation bonuses" paid every February and September are only provided to workers "working at the moment of payment," and a worker resigned in May. If the company's labor practice has been that 90 days' (March-May) worth of vacation bonus is calculated per diem, this bonus is recognized to have satisfied the condition of predetermination due to the fact that it falls under the "ii) Wages Coupled with the Number of Days Worked" category.

iv) Wages Paid to Workers Who Satisfy Conditions of Special Skills and Experience: There are additional wages paid to workers who possess special skills or experience (e.g. technology allowance, license allowance). Such wages are definitely paid as long as the worker possesses the applicable skill or experience on "any given day." Therefore, the condition of predetermination is satisfied.

v) Wages Coupled with Work Performance: There are wages that classify work performance into grades and provide differentiated payments according to this grade (e.g. bonuses). These type of wages satisfy the condition of predetermination only up to the "minimum amount that would be definitely paid" regardless of grades. In other words, if the work performance of workers is classified into grades of A, B, C, and D, with those who have obtained the grade of A receiving 400% of his/her base pay, while those who have obtained the grade of D receiving 100%, the "minimum amount that would be definitely paid" would be up to 100% of the worker's base pay. Therefore, only monies of up to 100% of bonuses would be recognized as ordinary wages.

There are also wages that fluctuate according to the work performance achieved during the previous year. By principle, as the amount of wages to be paid "on any given day" has already been determined by the start of that year, these types of wages satisfy the condition of predetermination. However, if particular funds were to be paid during the "previous year," yet due to special circumstance were postponed and paid in the "current year," these funds would not be included in the ordinary wages of the current year. Also, among these postponed funds, only the "minimum amount that would definitely be paid" are recognized as ordinary wages for the previous year.

vi) Wages Where Amount to Be Paid Is Not Determined: There are incidences during the establishment of welfare allowances where "the exact payment amount would be determined through subsequent worker-employer consultation." For example, let's say that a corporation's rules of employment state that "The corporation will pay a Gimjang Bonus during the *gimjang* season, with the specific amount to be determined by consultation between the labor union and management," and that the corporation paid 220,000 KRW between the years 2007 and 2009, and 240,000 KRW in 2010. The unanimous court decision ruled that this Gimjang Bonus failed to satisfy the conditions of predetermination, as "it cannot be seen that the amount to be paid has been predetermined if the arrangement requires the labor union and management to determine the amount through consultation without an objective standard." As such, cases in which the employer determines that a welfare allowance would be "paid" without specifying the "amount to be paid" would be excluded from being calculated as ordinary wages.

3) Section Conclusion

The following chart summarizes the standard of calculating ordinary wages based on the unanimous ruling by the Supreme Court.

	Recognized as Ordinary Wages	Denied Recognition as Ordinary Wages
Bonuses	• "Regular bonuses" paid continuously on a bimonthly, quarterly, semi-annual, or annual basis. • Regular bonuses that may or may not be paid depending on the terms of service, and that differentiate the amount paid depending on the terms of service (e.g. 0% for workers who worked less than 6 months, 50% for workers who worked between 6 months up to one year, and 100% for workers who worked more than one year).	• Bonuses that are paid temporarily or irregularly depending on the company performance (e.g. incentives)
Continuous-Service Allowances	• Allowances that may or may not be paid depending on "number of years of continuous service," with the amount paid also changing depending on this figure.	
Technology Allowances, License Allowances	• Allowances paid automatically upon possession of specific skills or licenses.	

Performance–Based Allowances	• In an allowance system that classifies work performance into grades (A, B, C, D) and provides differentiated payments accordingly, the portion that is guaranteed to be paid to those achieving the lowest grade (D)	• The portion of the performance-based allowance that is not guaranteed to those achieving the lowest grade (D)
Welfare Allowances, Etc. (Summer Vacation Allowance, Allowance for Presents, Personal Pension Support Allowance)	• In the case of workers who resign mid-year, the portion that is paid proportionate to the number of days worked up to the day of resignation (if the company does this as a regular labor practice)	• The portion that is paid only to workers who were "working at the moment of payment" • The portion for which the amount of payment is to be determined through subsequent deliberations between the labor union and management (e.g. Gimjang Bonuses: payment shall be made during *gimjang* season, but the bonus amount is determined via deliberation immediately prior to the payment).
Family Allowances	• The portion paid uniformly to all workers irrespective of the number of dependents in the household	• The portion paid differently depending on the number of dependents in the household.

C. The Effect of Agreements between the Labor Union and Management Regarding Ordinary Wages

Any agreement between the labor union and management that deducts a portion of the wages that possess the characteristics of ordinary wages and classifying them as allowances paid for work done for extended, night, or holiday work is by principle invalid.[35] Therefore, in principle, the worker possesses the right to request additional legal allowances by arguing the invalidity of the above agreement. However, the unanimous court ruling started that this right is limited in "exceptional cases" where "the general requirements to apply the good faith principle" have been satisfied and there exists "special circumstance that justifies the priority application of the principle of good faith despite the mandatory nature of the provisions of the LSA"

These "special circumstances" suggested by the unanimous court ruling are comprised of largely three components: ① The invalidity argument must be made regarding "regular bonuses"; ② the labor union and management must have conducted wage negotiations based on "total wages," while not recognizing that "regular bonuses" are included in ordinary wages; and ③ the incorporation of regular bonuses in ordinary wages (despite the agreement between the labor union and management) would result in unexpected excess earnings by workers and vice-versa for employers, which results in significant management difficulties on the latter's part. In determining whether such "special circumstances" exist, the unanimous court ruling started that the following factors must be considered in their totality: "the actual conditions of wage negotiations," "the amount of additional legal allowances that the employer will take on," "the rate of increase in real wages compared to the previous year," "the fiscal and managerial status of the employer," and "the specific method that bonuses will be paid."

---

35 Supreme Court 91Da3802 (1991. 12. 10.)

D. Calculation of Ordinary Wages

1) Introduction

Ordinary wages serve as the basic unit in the calculation of various "legal allowances" such as extended, night, and holiday allowances, when the worker has conducted special work during times outside of regular work hours. In order to calculate "legal allowances," the number of hours the worker has engaged in extended, night, and holiday work must first be established. At the same time, the exact figure of the "hourly ordinary wage" (ordinary wages converted to an hourly basis) that is to be given to the worker must be determined. Finally, the number of extended, night, and holiday hours is multiplied by the hourly ordinary wage as well as the applicable premium rates as determined under the LSA in turn. As such, in order to calculate the amount of legal allowance, the hourly ordinary wage must first be derived.

If all items included in the scope of ordinary wages are in the form of hourly wages, there will be no problem in calculating the hourly ordinary wage as all that would be required is to add up all of these items. However, the structure and actual practice of wage payments tailored for use by different types of corporations becomes very varied. While most corporations use the monthly wage system, paying a certain amount on a monthly basis, depending on circumstance the wage assessment period unit may become one day or one week. The corporation may also use the subcontract wage system, as is the case for those employing tax drivers or miners.

Due to this situation, determining how to convert non-hourly wage items included in the ordinary wage into hourly ordinary wage rates becomes a subject of dispute.

As such, the remainder of this section examines how different types of wage items are calculated into hourly ordinary wage rates, basing the analysis on Article 6(2) of the LSA.

2) Method of Converting Daily Wage Rates into Hourly Ordinary Wage Rates

With respect to wages determined by the daily wage rate, this amount is calculated by dividing the daily wage rate by the "contractual work hours per day."[36]

If the daily wage rate is determined as wages for the "contractual work hours within the limit of the legal standard work hours," the equation to calculate hourly ordinary wage rate is as follows.

$$\text{Hourly Ordinary Wage Rate} = \frac{\text{Daily Wage Rate}}{\text{Contractual Work Hours Per Day}}$$

On the other hand, if the daily wage rate is determined as wages for "contractual work hours that exceed the limit of the legal standard work hours," only the portion of the daily wage that remains after deducting extended work allowances would be considered that day's ordinary wages. In this case, therefore, the hourly ordinary wage rate becomes the ordinary wage per day (i.e. the daily wage rate received excluding the extended work allowance received) divided by contractual work hours per day.

$$\text{Hourly Ordinary Wage Rate} = \frac{\text{Ordinary Wage Per Day (= Daily Wage Rate – Extended Work Allowance)}}{\text{Contractual Work Hours Per Day}}$$

---

36 Enforcement Decree of the Labor Standards Act, Article 6(2)2

3) Method of Converting Weekly Wage Rates into Hourly Ordinary Wage Rates

With respect to wages determined by weekly wage rates, the hourly ordinary wage rate is calculated by dividing this weekly wage rate by the standard hours for the calculation of weekly ordinary wage (i.e. the sum of the week's contractual work hours and other paid hours not included in the contractual work hours, as defined under Article 2(1)7 of the LSA.[37] However, as per Article 55 of the LSA, the "weekly holiday allowance" paid for the weekly holidays where no actual work is done is excluded from the hourly ordinary wage rate.

If the weekly wage rate is determined as wages for the "contractual work hours within the limit of the legal standard work hours," the difference between the weekly wage rate and the weekly holiday allowance paid for one day becomes the weekly ordinary wage rate. As such, the hourly ordinary wage rate is arrived at by dividing the weekly ordinary wage rate with the contractual work hours per week.

$$\text{Hourly Ordinary Wage Rate} = \frac{\text{Weekly Ordinary Wage Rate } (= \text{Weekly Wage Rate} - \text{Weekly Holiday Allowance for One Day})}{\text{Contractual Work Hours Per Week}}$$

However, if the weekly wage rate is determined as wages for "contractual work hours that exceed the limit of the legal standard work hours," any allowances paid for extended work must be subtracted from the weekly wage rate in addition to the weekly holiday allowance for the week, which would result in the weekly ordinary

---

37 Ibid., Article 6(2)3

wage rate. The hourly ordinary wage rate is, again, arrived by dividing this weekly ordinary wage rate with the contractual work hours per week.

Hourly **Ordinary Wage** = **Rate**	Weekly Ordinary Wage Rate (= Weekly Wage Rate – Weekly Holiday Allowance for One Day – Extended Work Allowance) ——————————————————————— Contractual Work Hours Per Week

4) Method of Converting Monthly Wage Rates into Hourly Ordinary Wage Rates

With respect to wages determined by the monthly wage rate, the amount is calculated by dividing the monthly wage rate by the contractual work hours per month (i.e. the contractual work hours per week multiplied by the average number of weeks per year, divided by 12).[38] Here, like weekly ordinary wages rates, the monthly ordinary wage rate is determined by subtracting weekly holiday allowances from the monthly wage rate. The hourly ordinary wage rate is derived by dividing the above amount with the contractual work hours per month.

Three things must be kept in mind when calculating contractual work hours per month. First is the fact that the number of days in a month varies depending on the month. To address this, the number of days of the month is calculated by averaging the total days in a year, which would be calculated by dividing 365 days by 12 months (365/12).[39] The second is to assume that the worker has worked eight

---

38 Enforcement Decree of the Labor Standards Act, Article 6(2)4

39 Supreme Court 90DaKa11636 (1991. 7. 26.)

hours during paid holidays such as weekly holidays and include this time into the contractual work hours. The third thing to keep in mind is that while some corporations may reduce the normal contractual work hours per day by one hour during the winter season (e.g. from November 1st through March 31st of the following year) during the weekdays (although usually Saturdays are left alone), this reason does not in itself justify the reduction of contractual work hours per month for the purposes of calculating hourly ordinary wage rates.[40]

If the monthly wage rate is determined as wages for the "contractual work hours within the limit of the legal standard work hours," the monthly ordinary wage rate is calculated by subtracting the amount received as weekly holiday allowance for one month from the monthly wage rate. The hourly ordinary wage rate is calculated by dividing the monthly ordinary wage rate derived above with the contractual work hours per month. The equation for the weekly holiday allowance for one month is "hourly ordinary wage rate × contractual work hours per day (8 hours) × average weekly holidays per month." The equation for the average weekly holidays per month is "number of average working days per month (365 days / 12 months), divided by the number of days in the week (7)," or "365 (12×7)." Also, the contractual work hours per month is "contractual work hours per week (40 hours) × average number of weekly holidays per month." This "average number of weekly holidays per month" is also calculated by "the number of average working days per month (365/12) divided by 7," or "365 / (12×7)." The following table summarizes these calculations.

---

40 Supreme Court 90DaKa14728 (1991. 6. 28.)

Hourly Ordinary Wage Rate	=	Monthly Ordinary Wage Rate (= Monthly Wage Rate – Weekly Holiday Allowance for One Month) / Contractual Work Hours Per Month
Hourly Ordinary Wage Rate	=	Monthly Wage Rate – Hourly Ordinary Wage Rate × 8 Hours × 365/(12×7) / 40 Hours × 365/(12×7)
Hourly Ordinary Wage Rate	=	Monthly Wage Rate / 209 Hours (Round up numbers below the decimal point)

However, if the monthly wage rate is determined as wages for "contractual work hours that exceed the limit of the legal standard work hours," the hourly ordinary wage rate is calculated by dividing the monthly wage rate by the number of hours derived by adding the denominator of the above equation and the "number of extended work hours per month × 1.5." The following expresses this in the form of an equation.

Hourly Ordinary Wage Rate	=	Monthly Wage Rate / 209 Hours + Number of Extended Work Hours Per Month × 1.5

5) Method of Converting Wages under the Subcontract Wage System into Hourly Ordinary Wage Rates

With respect to wages determined by the subcontract wage system, the hourly ordinary wage rate is calculated by dividing the total sum of wages under the subcontract wage system for the period of wage calculation (if there is no designated date where the payroll is closed, this would be the payroll closing period) by the total number of work hours during that period.[41]

Let's take the example of a coal mine worker, assuming that the worker conducts his/her mining work for eight hours a day (i.e. the contractual work hours per day), and receives wages in the form of the agreed subcontract rate of 1000 KRW per 1 kilogram of coal. If the worker is able to mine 10 kg of coal for eight hours of work, the hourly ordinary wage rate of that worker would be the subcontracted wage 10,000 KRW (=10 kg × 1000 KRW) divided by eight hours, which is 1,250 KRW. If the same worker manages to mine 20 kg of coal, his/her hourly ordinary wage rate would be the subcontracted wage of 20,000 KRW (=20 kg × 1,000 KRW) divided by eight hours, which is 2,500 KRW.

IV. The Protection of Claims for Wages

A. Protection Provided during Execution Proceedings

1) The Right to Preferential Payment for Claims for Wages

The right to preferential payment for claims for wages is established in the LSA as a measure to offer strong protection to workers, reflecting public policy priorities regarding this issue.

---

41 Enforcement Decree of the Labor Standards Act, Article 6(2)6

Article 38(1) stipulates the right to preferential payment for claims for wages: "Wages, accident compensations, and other claims arising from labor relations shall be paid in preference to taxes, public charges, or other claims except for claims secured by pledges, mortgages or the security rights under the Act on Security over Movable Property, Claims on the whole property of the employer concerned, provided that this shall not apply to taxes and public charges which take precedence over the said pledges, mortgages or the security rights under the Act on Security over Movable Property, Claims." The claims for wages recognized under this right to preferential payment are not limited to those exercised by the worker him/herself. This right is recognized even if a third party is to repay the wages that the worker has the claim to instead of the employer.[42] Also, the "whole property of the employer" in the above Article refers to the entire property of the employer who, as the party to the employment contract, is the primary entity liable for the claims for wages.[43] As such, if the employer is an incorporated entity, the right to preferential payment for claims for wages does not apply to the personal property of the CEO.

Article 38(2) designates the items that possess the highest priority in the right to preferential payment for claims for wages. According to this article, "the wages of the last three months" and "accident compensations" are to be paid in preference to any claims secured by pledges, mortgages or the security rights under the Act on Security over Movable Property, Claims on the whole property of the employer, taxes, public charges and other claims. Here, "the wages of the last three months" refers to the final three months of wages that the employer failed to provide to the worker irrespective of when the worker terminated his/her employment; as such, this item is not limited to claims for wages where the worker resigned within three

---

42 Supreme Court 94Da21160 (1996. 2. 23.)
43 Supreme Court 95Da719 (1996. 2. 9.)

months of the date the employer closed his/her business.[44]

In order for a worker to receive preferential payment for claims for wages during the execution proceedings, s/he must submit a request for distribution to the executing court. Without a legal request for distribution, the worker will not be a part of the distribution proceedings, even if s/he has the highest priority in the right to preferential payment, and hence the disbursement of a significant portion of valuables to a lower priority entity that should instead have been distributed to the worker had s/he submitted the request for distribution would not be without legal basis.[45]

The right to preferential payment for claims for wages under Article 38 of the LSA only extends to bestowing priority to the payment of wages vis-à-vis other mortgages and debts when processing the assets of the debtor. Therefore, the Article does not independently function to produce cash.[46] Therefore, the right to request foreclosure on the object based on the right to preferential payment for claims for wages is not recognized.

2) Limitations on Seizures

Amount equivalent to 1/2 of wages, a pension, salary, bonus, retirement pension, retirement allowances or other wage claims of similar nature shall not be seized.[47] As retirement bonuses and early voluntary retirement allowance possess the nature of compensation, these payments are included in the above list.[48]

According to the Guarantee of Workers' Retirement Benefits Act, seizure of receivables in retirement pensions is prohibited in its

---

44 Supreme Court 95Da48650 (1996. 2. 23.)

45 Supreme Court 95Da28304 (1996. 12. 20.)

46 Supreme Court 93Da61611 (1994. 12. 9.)

47 Civil Execution Act, Article 246(4) and (5)

48 Supreme Court 2000Ma1439 (2000. 6. 8.)

entirety.[49] Also, according to the Framework Act on the Construction Industry, an amount equivalent to wages to be paid to workers of the relevant works (including any works subcontracted) among the contract price of construction works for which a constructor is awarded a contract may not be seized.[50]

B. Protection Provided during Insolvency Procedures

There is great need to protect the worker's claim for wages when the corporation has filed for insolvency. To provide this protection, the Debtor Rehabilitation and Bankruptcy Act designates the following to be made be made public-interest claims: wages, severance pay and disaster compensation of the debtor's workers, as well as the right to claim reimbursement of the bailment moneys and the money spent to guarantee the identities of the debtor's workers, which accrue from causes arising before the commencement of rehabilitation procedures.[51] The Act also requires that "public-interest claims shall be reimbursed frequently without resorting to rehabilitation procedures,"[52] and that they "shall take precedence over rehabilitation claims and rehabilitation security rights in the repayment thereof."[53] The issue of whether a worker with a wage claim could request the initiation of insolvency procedures has been under dispute until recently, but a Supreme Court ruling on this matter opined that s/he has the ability to do so.[54]

---

49 Supreme Court 2013Da71180 (2014. 1. 23.)

50 Framework Act on the Construction Industry, Article 88; Enforcement Decree of the Framework Act on the Construction Industry, Article 84

51 Debtor Rehabilitation and Bankruptcy Act, Article 179(10) and (11)

52 Ibid., Article 180(1)

53 Ibid., Article 180(2)

54 Supreme Court 2014Ma244

"The wages, severance pay and disaster compensation for the debtor's workers shall be made into foundations claim" under the Debtor Rehabilitation and Bankruptcy Act.[55] Furthermore, "foundation claims shall be met frequently without resorting to bankruptcy procedures, and shall be treated with greater preference than bankruptcy claims."[56] Also, "foundation claims for wages, severance pay and disaster compensation shall take precedence over other foundation claims."[57] However, when it is evidently clear that the bankruptcy foundation is unable to fully repay the total amount of the foundation claims, the repayment of the foundation claims shall be made according to the ratio of the unrepaid claim amount.[58]

C. Protection Provided under Substantive Law

1) The Principle of Direct Payment of Wages

Article 43 of the LSA stipulates that the "payment of wages shall be directly made in full to workers in currency," and must be "paid at least once per month on a fixed day" in order to ensure that the worker receive wages, the primary means of his/her livelihood, in a secure and expedient manner (the principles of currency payment, direct payment, full payment, and periodic payment at least once a month).

Regarding the principle of direct payment of wages, whether wage claims may be transferred, becomes an issue. Court precedent suggests that while wage claims of a worker may indeed be transferred, even if such a transfer has occurred the employer must still pay to the worker the latter's wages directly as per the principle of direct payment, and

---

55 Debtor Rehabilitation and Bankruptcy Act, Article 473(10)
56 Ibid., Articles 475 and 476
57 Ibid., Article 477(2)
58 Ibid., Article 477(1)

that the transferee of the wage claim may not request the disbursement of wages from the employer directly.[59] Court precedent also suggests that transferees of wage claims or those entrusted with the collection of wage claims may not submit a request for distribution regarding the employer's assets during execution proceedings.[60]

2) The Principle of Full Payment of Wages

The principle of full payment of wages as stipulated under Article 43 of the LSA requires that the employer must provide full payment of wages to his/her workers. Therefore, by principle the employer may not offset the worker's wage claims with claims that the former has against the latter.

An exception to this principle would be when excess wages have been paid due to causes such as miscalculations. In such cases, should a retired worker advance a claim for wages that hasn't been paid during his/her employment, or should a worker who is not yet retired do so, the employer may convert his/her claim to the reimbursement of excess wages paid to the worker into automatic receivables and offset that amount from the worker's claim, so long as the following circumstances exist: the moment the excessive payment of wage has been made by the employer is close enough to the moment the employer seeks to exercise his/her right to use this amount to offset the worker's wage claim so that the substance of the calculation and adjustment of the wages is not lost, and the worker's economic stability is not at risk to be harmed due to measures taken by the employer, such as notifying the worker in advance the amount and method of the offset.

If the employer has already paid the worker certain valuables as severance pay but this payment is determined to be invalid for

---

59 Supreme Court 87DaKa2803 (1988. 12. 3.)
60 Supreme Court 95Da2630 (1996. 3. 22.)

the purpose of severance pay and as a result the employer gains a reimbursement claim for the amount of excessive profits gained by the worker, the employer may (again) convert his/her claim to the reimbursement of excess wages paid to the worker into automatic receivables and offset that amount from the worker's claim. However, the exact amount allowed to be offset is limited to funds that exceed one-half of the worker's claim to severance pay.[61]

Meanwhile, even if offsetting is prohibited due to the principle of full payment of wages, this still does not prohibit the employer from requesting the seizure or assignment of up to one half of the worker's wage claims to supplement repayment when executing his/her title of debt against the worker.[62]

The question of whether "settlements to offset wage claims" agreed upon by the worker and employer (verses the employer unilaterally expressing the intent to do so) should be permitted is in dispute. Case law regarding this matter suggests that such settlements would be permitted so long as reasonable grounds to assume that the worker's expression of agreement to the offset was voluntary objectively exist, but the determination that the agreement was voluntary should only be made after rigorous and cautious assessment.[63]

The question of whether a worker possesses the ability to waive his/her right to wage claims *a priori* or *ex post* is also in dispute. The majority of courts rule that wage claims (excluding those regarding severance pay) may be waived via valid agreements between the labor union and management as long as the agreement does not substantially lack rationality.[64] As for wage claims against severance pay, any waivers prior to the generation the right to severance pay

---

61 Supreme Court 2007Da90760 (2010. 5. 20.), unanimous decision
62 Supreme Court 93Ma1822, 1823 (1994. 3. 16.)
63 Supreme Court 2001Da25184 (2001. 10. 23.)
64 Supreme Court 99Da67536 (2000. 9. 29.)

would be a violation of the LSA's mandatory provisions regulating this system and is therefore invalid. However, the court recognized that waiving the right after it has been generated (i.e. after resignation) through a valid agreement should be allowed as long as the agreement does not substantially lack rationality.[65]

3) Negative Prescription (Statute of Limitations) for Wage Claims

According to the LSA, claims for wages shall be extinguished by prescription, unless exercised within three years.[66] Claims for all payments such as wages, bonuses, extended work allowances, annual paid leave allowances, severance pay fall under this provision. Case law suggests that the statute of limitations (the period of prescription) begins to run the day after retirement for claims against severance payments, and the date of the interim payment of retirement has been made for claims against unpaid interim severance payments.[67]

---

65 Supreme Court 95Da3350 (1996. 6. 14.)

66 LSA, Article 49

67 Supreme Court 2001Da24051 (2001. 10. 30.), Supreme Court 2003Da54322, 54339 (2006. 5. 26.)

Chapter 4

Statutory Allowances

I. Allowances for Extended, Nighttime, and Holiday Work

A. Extended Work Allowances

1) The Concept of Extended Work

Extended work occurs when a worker provides labor beyond standard working hours under approval of the Ministry of Employment and Labor or by agreement between the union and the employer (for more detailed overview of this subject, see "Chapter 3: Working Hours and Breaks").

2) The Calculation of Number Extended Work Hours

The number of extended work hours is based on the actual work time that the worker has provided. Therefore, the number of actual hours worked overtime to comply with invalid directions from management to engage in such extended work must be calculated into the number of extended work hours. Of course, legally executed extended work hours are included in this calculation, such as those done as part of agreements entered between the labor union and management,[1] or

---

1 LSA, Article 53(1), (2)

those done under special circumstances (provided that the approval from the Minister of Employment and Labor and the consent of the workers has been secured.[2]

Meanwhile, shift work arrangements such as working 24-hour days every other day is subject to regulations of the LSA regarding allowances for extended, nighttime, and holiday work. In the case of such alternate day work, there is no basis for the employer to recognize only half of the extended and night hours worked when calculating extended work hours.[3] In the case of day-and-night shifts, however, courts generally recognize that since the work actually done during such shifts comprise mostly of low intensity labor such as surveillance and guard duties (e.g. conducting regular rounds, receiving phone calls and documents, and responding to other emergency situations while remaining on standby), day-and-night shifts are not customarily treated as normal work. As such, day-and-night shift work is interpreted to be a duty conducted in addition to the main obligations of the employment contract, and hence there is no need to compensate for such work to the same degree as regular work, nor is there a need to provide the worker night, extended, or holiday work allowances (although it *is* industry practice to provide for actual expenses incurred). However, if the day-and-night shift does not consist of surveillance and guard work and instead the worker actually engages in operations that s/he normally conducts during regular work hours in terms of both content and quality, the court generally rules that the worker is due his/her night, extended, and holiday allowance for the hours worked during day-and-night shifts.[4]

3) Premium Rates
"An employer shall, in addition to ordinary wages, pay 50 percent or

---

2 Ibid., Article 53(3)

3 Supreme Court 96Da38995 (1997. 7. 22.)

4 Supreme Court 93Da46254 (1995. 1. 12.)

more thereof for extended work, night work, or holiday work."[5]

Under a compensation scheme that utilizes the contract wage system, even if a worker engages in extended work hours this would be considered to be included in the worker's basic work, which compensated at 100% of ordinary wages.[6] Therefore, only payments that are made in addition to the worker's ordinary wages (at 50%) would be considered as an application of the premium rate.

If extended work coincides with night or holiday work, the premium rates for each item must be combined when calculating the total premium rate.[7]

B. Night Work Allowances

1) The Concept of Night Work
Work provided by a worker between the hours of 10:00 p.m. and 6:00 a.m. is considered as night work under the LSA.[8]

2) Premium Rates
The premium rate to calculate night work allowances is 50% of ordinary wages. If night work overlaps with extended and holiday work, the premium rates of each item must be combined.

C. Holiday Work Allowances

1) The Concept of Holiday Work

5 LSA, Article 56
6 Supreme Court 91Da11391 (1992. 3. 10.)
7 Supreme Court 90Da6545 (1991. 3. 22.)
8 LSA, Article 56; see "Chapter 3: Working Hours and Breaks" for a more detailed overview.

If a worker worked during a holiday (as defined under Article 55 of the LSA), during paid or unpaid holidays designated by the collective bargaining agreement, or during Labor Day, this would be considered "holiday work."[9]

2) Premium Rates

For work done during holidays, the remuneration would be 100% of the worker's ordinary wages plus an allowance of 50% of his/her ordinary wages (which is the rate stipulated in Article 56 of the LSA). As such, the worker would receive a total of "150% of ordinary wages" for work done during holidays.

For work done during paid holidays, a worker is recognized to have provided labor when s/he was not required to do so, and is compensated with 100% of his/her ordinary wages plus an additional 100% to compensate for the actual work done during that period, which is topped off with another 50% for holiday work done as stipulated under the LSA. As a result, the worker receives a combined total of 250% of his/her ordinary wages for work done during paid holidays.[10]

There is some debate as to whether the premium rates for holiday work and extended work should be combined when the holiday work pushes the total number of working hours over that designated for the standard working week. While there are no Supreme Court rulings on this issue, recent decisions in the lower courts ruled that the premium rates should indeed be combined.

When a worker conducts night work during holidays, the premium rates for night and holiday work are combined when calculating the total allowance.

---

9 *See* "Chapter 3: Working Hours and Breaks" for a more detailed overview.
10 Supreme Court 89DaKa1145 (1989. 11. 28.)

D. Special Issues Regarding the Form of Payment

1) The Validity of Blanket Wage Systems Such as Fixed Legal Allowance

In principle, the total amount an employer must pay the worker in extended, night, and holiday work allowance is derived by multiplying actual hours worked overtime and during nights and holidays with their respective premium rates as stipulated by the LSA, or as otherwise agreed upon by relevant parties.

However, there are recognized circumstances where it is difficult to calculate the number of hours worked due to the nature of the work (i.e. the time, type and characteristic of the labor entailed), such as surveillance and guard work. In such instances, case law suggests that blanket wage contracts are valid so long as they do not place workers at a disadvantage and is determined to be fair in light of the totality of the circumstances.[11] Here, the blanket wage system is an arrangement between the worker and employer that designates a certain amount as monthly or daily remuneration that would include base pay as well as legally mandated allowances (without actually calculating what the base pay would be). Another blanket wage arrangement would be when the base pay is determined, but all legally mandated allowances are lumped together (i.e. not distinguished) and paid as a fixed amount regardless of the actual time worked. Here, the requirement that court precedent identifies which would make blanket wage systems valid is: "workers must not be placed at a disadvantage." This means that the blanket wage system must not be disadvantageous in light of specific remuneration standards as defined under the collective bargaining agreement or employment rules, if such standards exist.[12]

In circumstances other than the above (i.e. when it is difficult to

---

11 Supreme Court 2003Da66523 (2005. 8. 19.)

12 Supreme Court 96Da24699 (1998. 3. 24.)

calculate working hours), the principles of remuneration based on working time designated under the LSA must be applied (assuming special circumstance making it difficult to strictly apply the provisions of the Act concerning working hours do not exist). Even in such cases, however, entering into blanket wage payment arrangements that pay a fixed amount as legal allowances regardless of the number of hours worked is prohibited if the arrangement conflicts with the provisions regarding working hours within the LSA.[13]

2) When Including Legal Allowances in Total Remuneration Is Permissible

Circumstances do exist where legal allowances are considered included in the remuneration package, even if the corporation does not specify in its payment rules a fixed amount to be paid as legal allowances and the total remuneration package consist of a single item (i.e. wages).

The following are some examples: ① For drivers at freight companies or security guards in apartment complexes who enter into contracts to work in 24-hour shifts every other day (i.e. alternate day work shifts), it is recognized that their monthly remuneration includes legal allowances such as extended, holiday and night work in addition to compensation for standard work hours as defined under the LSA. This is because the special nature of the work makes it reasonable to assume that the labor would entail extended, night and holiday work.[14] ② For so-called daily contract wage systems which arranges for taxi cab drivers to retain the remainder of their total earnings as daily income after paying a designated sum to their employers, legal allowances under the LSA are considered to be included within the taxi drivers' daily income.[15]

---

13 Supreme Court 2008Da6052 (2010. 5. 13.)
14 Supreme Court 2002Da16958 (2002. 6. 14.)
15 Supreme Court 87DaKa570 (1988. 3. 22)

3) Compensatory Leave System

The LSA stipulates that "an employer may grant workers leaves in lieu of wage payments for extended work, night work, or holiday work . . . according to a written agreement that is concluded between him/her and the representative of labor union."[16]

II. Annual Allowances and Maternity Leave Allowances before and after Birth

A. The Annual Allowance

1) The Concept and Types of Annual Allowances

There are two types of annual allowances: the "annual leave allowance" and the "payment for unused annual leave allowance." Ordinary or average wages to be provided during the period of paid leave are called "annual leave allowance."[17] However, if a worker does not take a break and works during annual paid leave days, the worker shall be given a corresponding allowance for this extra time worked. Such remuneration given to compensate work done during annual leaves are called "payment for unused annual leave allowance" (for more detailed overview of this subject, see "Chapter 3: Working Hours and Breaks").

2) Requisite Conditions, Timing, and Calculation of Annual Allowances

To illustrate how annual allowances work, let's examine the hypothetical case of a worker (let's call him Mr. Kim) who has worked for his company for 22 years as of December 31, 2013 (starting January

1, 1992).

i) Annual Leave Allowance

If Mr. Kim was able to work for the entirety of his 22nd year with his company without absences, according to Article 60 of the LSA he becomes eligible for 25 days of annual leave (= 15 days that come from a year's worth of work, plus an extra day accrued for every two years worked for the company after the first three years, up to 25 days per year). This annual leave of 25 days may be used in Mr. Kim's 23rd working year (January 1 through December 31 of 2014).

① Mr. Kim gains the right to request annual leave allowance on his 23rd working year once he requests that he will be using part of his 25 days of annual leave during a particular period. Timing wise, the annual leave allowance must be paid "on the pay day immediately before or after a paid leave is granted."[18] As annual leave allowances are based on the ordinary or average wage of the worker,[19] the standard on which annual leaves are calculated are on ordinary or average wages of the worker at the time of payment.

② If Mr. Kim uses only ten of the 25 days of annual leave that he is entitled to during his 23rd year with the company, and does not take the remaining 15 days of annual paid leave, he is able to request the payment of unused annual leave allowance (equivalent to withheld wages) for these unspent days on the first day of the following year, which is January 1, 2015.[20]

③ In the above situation, even if Mr. Kim retired during the middle of his 23rd year with the company on September 1, 2014, he is still eligible to request the payment of unused annual leave allowance (i.e. the 15 days left over after taking ten days off) after his

---

retirement.[21] Mr. Kim does not retain the right to request payment for unused annual leave allowance for the period worked from January 1st through September 1st in 2014, however; this is because Mr. Kim did not work the entire year, which is a requirement to receive annual leave allowances.[22]

ii) Allowance for Work Done during Annual Leave

Let's continue with the story of Mr. Kim. If Mr. Kim specified when he would be using his 25 days of annual leave accrued from the past work year but then proceeded to work during those days, Mr. Kim must be provided not only with his "annual leave allowance" but also "allowance for work done during annual leave." In other words, Mr. Kim gains the right to request allowances for work he has done during a date he has exercised his right to take a leave of absence. This request and subsequent payment of the allowance for work done during annual leave must then be made by the timeline examined above.

While there are no explicit regulations in the LSA, it is largely agreed upon in the literature that annual leave allowance is calculated based on the ordinary wages of the worker at the time his/her right to request payment is generated. A point to note, however, is that there is no need to add premium rates (50% of ordinary wages) when calculating annual leave allowances.[23]

3) Urging Workers to Take Annual Paid Leave

"Where any worker's paid leave is terminated by time limitation after the worker fails to take his/her paid leave although the relevant employer has taken the measures to urge workers to take their respective annual leave, the relevant employer is not liable to

21 Supreme Court 99Da10806 (2000. 12. 22.)

22 Supreme Court 99Da10806 (2000. 12. 22.)

23 Supreme Court 90DaKa11636 (1991. 7. 26.)

compensate the worker for his/her failure to take the paid leave and his/her failure to take the paid leave shall be deemed not to fall under the reasons attributable to the employer."[24] This special provision has been adopted due to the consideration that a worker avoiding the use of annual paid leave in order to receive additional wages is contradictory to the legislative intent of the annual leave system.

4) Substitution of Paid Leave
An employer may, through written agreement with a representative of the labor union, get workers to take paid leaves on a particular working day as a substitution to annual paid leaves.[25]

B. Maternity Leave Allowances before and after Birth

"An employer shall grant a pregnant woman a 90-day maternity leave before and after childbirth. In such case, after the childbirth, 45 days or more of the leave period shall be allotted" (LSA, Article 74). The first 60 of these days must be in the form of paid leave.

III. Business Shutdown Allowances

A. The Concept of Business Shutdown Allowances

Business shutdowns are defined as situations where a worker (who is maintaining his/her status as an employee) finds it impossible to provide work as specified in the employment contract due to impracticality or the employer's intervention, and hence is not

24 LSA, Article 61
25 Ibid., Article 62

working temporarily. If the cause of the shutdown is attributable to the employer, it must pay "business shutdown allowance" to workers even if no work has been done. Towards this, Article 46(1) of the LSA stipulates that: "When a business shuts down due to a cause attributable to the employer, he/she shall pay the workers concerned allowances of not less than 70 percent of their average wages during the period of shutdown: provided the amount equivalent to the 70 percent of their average wages exceeds that of their ordinary wages, at which time their ordinary wages may be paid as their shutdown allowance."

B. Why Employers Are Liable for Business Shutdown Allowances

According to Article 46(1) of the LSA, business shutdowns "due to causes attributable to the employer" are what make employers liable for payment of business shutdown allowances. In light of Article 538(1) of the Civil Act, the employer assumes liability if the shutdown (i.e. the environment where the employee cannot supply his/her labor) was brought about due to a cause attributable to the employer.

C. The Calculation of Business Shutdown Allowances

By principle, business shutdown allowances are "not less than 70 percent of [the worker's] average wages during the period of shutdown."[26] If, however, a worker whose work day consists of eight hours of labor works for four and is shut down for four, that worker must be paid the applicable wage rate for the hours actually worked

---

26 Ibid., Article 46(1)

and be additionally paid 70% of average wages for the hours that were shut down from conducting his/her work.

D. Exclusions from Business Shutdown Allowances

If the business shutdown is a result of *force majeure* (extraordinary events or circumstances like war or a natural disaster) that is beyond the control of the employer, the worker is not entitled to wages under the employment contract nor business shutdown allowance. While there are circumstances where business shutdown allowances may be paid at a lower rate than is prescribed above, to make such payments the employer must receive the approval of the relevant Labor Relations Commission.[27]

27 Ibid., Article 46(2)

Chapter 5

Retirement Benefit System

I. Introduction to the Retirement Benefit System

The retirement benefit system is regulated by the GWRBA,[1] and was enacted on December 1, 2005. The retirement benefit system is the general term representing the severance pay system and the retirement pension system in Korea. The latter is subdivided into the defined benefit type and the defined contribution type.

A workplace that employs more than five workers may establish and operate one or more retirement benefit systems (choosing among different severance and retirement pension schemes). However, if an employer is ready to decide on a retirement benefit scheme or seeks to transition from one scheme to another, the employer must obtain the consent of the worker's representative.[2] The employer must also listen to the feedback from the worker's representative when modifying the details of an established retirement benefit scheme, and must gain the consent of the representative if the scheme is to be modified in a

---

1 Guarantee of Workers' Retirement Benefits Act

2 This would be the labor union in businesses or workplaces that have organized unions representing more than half of the workers; if the business or workplace does not have such an organized labor union, the workers' representative would be a person who represents more than half of the location's workers.

manner detrimental to the worker.[3]

If an employer fails to establish a retirement benefit scheme, it shall be deemed to have established a retirement allowance system following the standards outlined under the GWRBA.[4]

II. Severance Pay System

A. Introduction to the Severance Pay System

Severance pay is an ad hoc form of remuneration to workers provided by the employer after the labor relationship has been terminated. Severance pay is provided based on the fact that the worker had an established labor relationship with the employer.[5] Severance pay is based on wages, as defined under Article 2(1)5 of the LSA.[6] Therefore, principles governing various facets of wages apply to severance pay as well.[7] These principles include those governing the method of payment;[8] those surrounding the regulation and protection of wages;[9] and those governing the time frame of payment as well as the conditions of execution.[10]

The present severance pay system is applied to all businesses and workplaces that employ workers. However, this system is not applicable for businesses and workplaces that only employ family

---

3 GWRBA, Article 4

4 GWRBA, Article 11

5 Supreme Court 2004Da8333 (2007. 3. 30.)

6 Supreme Court 75Da1768 (1976. 9. 28.)

7 GWRBA, Articles 8, 11

8 Principles of payment in currency, direct payment to workers, and full payment as found in LSA, Article 43(1)

9 Prohibition of offsetting wages, prohibition of seizure, prohibition of transfer, and the right to preferential payment found in LSA, Article 38

10 LSA, Articles 43 and 49

members of the same household, and for domestic workers.[11]

B. The Establishment and Modification of the Severance Pay System

1) Establishing the Severance Pay System

An employer who wants to establish a severance pay system may do so by including a provision within the employment rules that clearly designates the condition of payment, how and when the payment will be disbursed, and how payment calculations would be done.[12] Severance pay systems may be established through designating such a provision in employment contracts or collective bargaining agreements as well.

Even if a severance pay system has not been established through the above vehicles (i.e. employment contract, employment rules, collective bargaining agreement), the worker is still entitled to severance pay as calculated under the disbursement standards of the GWRBA.[13]

2) Requirements to Establish a Severance Pay System

Regardless of what it is actually called, severance pay must be provided entirely by the employer and the employer only.[14] Also, when a severance pay system is established, "differentiated schemes" must not be set up within the "same business."[15] This principle of "prohibiting differentiated severance pay systems" has given rise to numerous disputes, such as the following:

---

11 GWRBA, Article 3
12 LSA, Article 93(5)
13 Supreme Court 91Da27730 (1991. 11. 8.)
14 Supreme Court 98Da18568 (1999. 4. 23.)
15 GWRBA, Article 4(2)

① The principle of prohibiting differentiated severance pay systems apply to "workers that are employed in the same business," and hence is not applied to relationships between workers that work in different businesses. Here, the term "business" means a company organization that is organically and continuously operated while maintaining an independent management unit (e.g. a private business or independent corporate entity).[16] The Supreme Court ruled that since a corporation's domestic and overseas business is considered to be a single business, the corporation's policy of differentiating severance pay between domestic workers and that of overseas technician workers is a violation of the principle of prohibiting differentiated severance pay systems.[17] The Supreme Court also ruled that if a private university established under an educational foundation and its affiliated hospital is managed organically as a single unit by the same president and the board of directors when resolving to make accounting and managing decisions, the university and the hospital is considered a single business and hence may not implement differentiated severance pay systems between the two organizations.[18]

② Differentiating the severance pay rate between workers based on when they joined the company is a violation of the principle of prohibiting differentiated severance pay systems.[19] However, this principle is deemed not to have been violated if the use of the progressive stage system is agreed upon via collective bargaining agreement or employment rules, where currently employed workers maintain their severance pay rate while new recruits are given a lower rate.[20]

---

16 Supreme Court 98Da765 (1999. 8. 20.)
17 Supreme Court 97Da24511 (1997. 11. 28.)
18 Supreme Court 98Da765 (1999. 8. 20.)
19 Supreme Court 2001Da77970 (2002. 6. 28.)
20 Supreme Court 91Da45165 (1992. 12. 22.), unanimous decision

③ If there exists a reasonable basis for differentiating severance pay, the principle of prohibiting differentiated severance pay systems is not violated. For example, if the severance pay given to workers discharged due to disciplinary reasons is different from that given to workers resigning for other reasons, a reasonable basis is deemed to exist. This is assuming, of course, that the standard of calculation does not fall below the legally designated minimum as designated under the GWRBA.[21]

④ In the case of honorary resignation pay systems, which is a scheme used to induce early retirement of long-time employees by offering higher payments the higher the number of years remaining until retirement is, the principle of prohibiting differentiated severance pay systems is considered not to apply because it is different in nature from severance pay systems where years of service and average wages are used as bases of calculation.[22]

⑤ When labor relations are inclusively succeeded due to corporate mergers or business transfers, the worker's status under his/her previous employment contract is also succeeded. Therefore, if the severance pay scheme after the succession is disadvantageous to the worker than it was before, the former may not be applied unless consent has been provided by the relevant worker's organization's collective decision making process (as per LSA Article 94(1)).

The principle of prohibiting differentiated severance pay systems is considered not to be violated in cases like the above, as not differentiating severance pay would mean that the interests of the succeeded workers would be infringed (i.e. the workers would be forced to agree to an arrangement that is inferior to what they used to have). Hence, the new severance pay system would not be applied to these

21 Supreme Court 2002Da29442 (2002. 9. 6.)
22 Supreme Court 2005Da28358 (2007. 11. 29.)

workers, even if it means there will be multiple severance pay systems existing in a single business.[23]

3) Procedures to Modify Severance Pay Systems
If the severance pay system is established through collective bargaining agreements or employment contracts, its content may be modified through agreement by workers and management. On the other hand, if the system is established through stipulation within the employment rules, any modification to the system must abide by the requirements governing the employment rule modification process imposed by the LSA.

C. Conditions for the Payment of Severance Funds

1) Retirement of the Worker
Severance pay is given when a "worker" has "retired." Here, a "worker" is the party to an individual labor relationship, which is consistent with the concept of worker under the LSA.[24] Therefore, even temporary workers, irregular workers, day laborers are eligible to receive severance pay if they have provided continual labor,[25] which is also the case for workers from other countries.[26]

"Retirement" is used to indicate all situations in which a worker has terminated his/her labor relations with the employer. The cause of the retirement (whether the worker has quit, the employment contract has expired, or the worker has reached retirement age) is not relevant and is not inquired after.[27] The following issues have been brought

---

23 Supreme Court 99Da9370 (2001. 4. 24.); GWRBA, Article 2(1)
24 Supreme Court 91Da24250 (1991. 12. 13.)
25 Supreme Court 79Da1561 (1979. 10. 30.)
26 Supreme Court 2006Da53627 (2006. 12. 7.)
27 Supreme Court 71Da1033 (1972. 4. 11.)

forth regarding the "retirement" of the worker.

① The employer's duty to provide severance pay is generated at the point of the worker's retirement.[28] The employer must calculate the amount of severance pay based on the ordinary wages of the worker at the time of retirement (which in turn is assessed based on the method designated by the LSA).[29] As it is impossible for the employer to assume the duty to provide severance pay so long as the labor relationship is maintained, any payment of funds (often as part of regular wages) to the worker under the auspice of severance payment is not legally recognized as such.[30]

② Since a worker's right to request severance pay is generated only at the point of retirement (i.e. termination of the labor relationship), any agreement where the worker waives all or part of this right is invalid and is deemed to be in violation of binding regulations governing severance pay.[31] However, if a worker waives his/her right to request severance pay *after* retirement (i.e. when the right to request severance pay has been generated), this waiver is deemed valid as long as the expression of the waiver was an effective one.[32]

③ The GWRBA recognizes an exception to the principle that the right to request for severance pay is generated at the time of retirement: the interim severance adjustment pay. While originally the GWRBA allowed the employer to provide interim severance adjustment pay upon such request from the worker, after the Act's July 26, 2012 revision only requests made by the worker for reasons designated by the presidential decree (such as purchasing homes) would interim severance adjustments be permissible.[33]

---

28 Supreme Court 2001Da24051 (2001. 10. 30.)

29 Supreme Court 90Da14560 (1991. 6. 28.)

30 Supreme Court 2007Do1186 (2007. 4. 12.)

31 Supreme Court 97Da49732 (1998. 3. 27.)

32 Supreme Court 97Da11133 (1997. 11. 28.)

33 GWRBA, Article 8(2) and Addendum Article 3, Revised by Public Act No. 10967 on July 15, 2011

2) Continuous Employment for Over One Year

An employer is required to establish at least one severance scheme in order to pay benefits to retiring workers, provided that these workers have provided a "continuous" service period for "more than one year," or the workers worked an average of 15 working hours per week (when averaged out over a four-week period).[34] In other words, the employer does not have the legal duty to provide severance pay to retiring workers who work less than one year or work less than 15 hours per week when averaging the total number of hours worked every four weeks.

D. Standards and Methods of Calculating Severance Pay

Under Article 8(1) of the GWRBA, the minimum amount of severance pay that may be lawfully given by the employer to the retiring worker is "the number of years of continuous service" multiplied by "the average wage earned for 30 days of work." As such, the three factors relevant in calculating severance pay are "years of continuous service," "average wages," and "severance pay rate." Barring special circumstance, the figures for each factor is taken from how things stood at the time of the worker's retirement.[35]

1) Number of Years of Continuous Service

As a principle, the "number of years of continuous service" indicates the amount of time that the worker has been employed.[36] If the number of years of continuous service exceeds one year but includes months and days that do not amount to a full year, this period must be

---

34 Ibid., Article 4(1)

35 Supreme Court 97Da18936 (1998. 1. 20.)

36 Supreme Court 2005Da28358 (2007. 11. 29.)

converted so that it is expressed in terms of years.[37] For example, for a retiring worker who has continually worked for x years (here, x needs to be equal to or more than 1), y months and z days, his/her severance pay calculation is expressed in the following equation.

$$\text{Legal Severance Pay} = (\text{x years} + \text{y months}/12 + \text{z days}/365) \times 30 \text{ days} \times 1 \text{ day average wage}$$

Instances where "continuity of labor" has come into dispute when determining the number of years of continuous service are as follows:

① Day-to-Day Workers: Even if a worker is formally employed as a day-to-day worker, if this relationship has been continuous without break, this period must be incorporated when calculating the number of years of continuous service and hence reflected in the amount the worker receives as severance pay.[38] A case where this continuous service has been interrupted is when a worker has been repeatedly employed as a day-to-day worker by a corporation whenever there has been a construction project and subsequently let go after the project was concluded, which lasted for 11 years and 11 months. The court determined that if the total number of months where the worker did not engage in any work during this period amounted to 15 months, the continuity of labor has been severed barring special circumstance.[39]

② Modification of Employment Type: If a worker has initially worked as a temporary day-to-day worker but has been promoted to a regular employee without a break in his/her work during

---

37 Supreme Court 71Da485 (1971. 5. 11.)

38 Supreme Court 2000Da27672 (2002. 7. 26.)

39 Supreme Court 81DaKa571 (1982. 7. 13.)

the transition, the period s/he worked as a day-to-day worker is included in the total number of years served when calculating the amount of severance pay.[40]

③ The Renewal or Repeating of the Labor Contract Period: Even if an employment contract period has been set, a worker is not considered to have retired his/her employment upon the end of that period if the contract is renewed or a new contract with the same working conditions is entered into (i.e. repeated) at that point. It is only when the worker has definitely and finally resigned would the retirement become valid. Therefore, periods during which contracts were renewed or repeated are included when determining the number of years of continuous service.[41] Also, even should there be gaps between the renewed or repeated employment contracts, if the total period of such unemployment is not long in light of the entire period of employment, the gap is due to the nature of the employment (e.g. seasonal factors, school break periods), or there exists other justifiable causes for not paying wages for that period of time, the continuity of employment is maintained throughout this period.[42]

④ Reemployment after Retiring from the Same Workplace: Should a worker submit his/her resignation not of his own volition but as a result of the unilateral request from management as part of the latter's management policy (or the employer knows that the worker does not have the intent to retire when submitting his/her resignation) and the employer formally accepts the worker's resignation and processes the retirement, if the employer immediately re-employs the worker with no change in the work description and title (i.e. no de facto break in the labor relationship) and hence there is a

40 Supreme Court 93Da26168 (1995. 7. 11.)
41 Supreme Court 93Da26168 (1995. 7. 11.), unanimous decision
42 Supreme Court 2004Da29736 (2006. 12. 7.)

continuity in the provision of labor, such expression of intent to resign would be considered a form of non-bone fide statement or false representation and hence would not be legally effective.[43] A representative example would be when an employer forces its employees to retire and get reemployed as a way to control its severance pay burden brought on by the progressive stage system (i.e. by paying severance pay due to its employees before the system significantly kicks in).[44] However, there are certain situations where this method of rehiring employees immediately after retiring them would be considered valid for the purpose of resetting the number of continuous service: the first is when, irrespective of the management policy of the employer, the worker submitted his/her resignation voluntarily in order to secure a lump sum of cash in the form of severance pay (to pay off debts, or secure a down payment for mortgages, etc.).[45] The second is when the option of interim retirement is given freely and entirely to the worker, and the worker exercised this option of his/her own volition to receive the interim severance adjustment payment.[46]

⑤ Merger, Separation, Business Transfer, and Reorganization of the Business: In the case of "corporate mergers," the labor relationship between the extinguished corporation and its worker is succeeded in its entirety to the surviving or newly formed corporation, as the latter inclusively succeeds the rights and obligations of the extinguished corporation as a matter of law.[47] As for "corporate reorganizations,"[48] labor relations are preserved as well as there is no change regarding the identity of the corporation. Labor relations

43 Supreme Court 91Da40931 (1992. 9. 22.)
44 Supreme Court 92Da37673 1993. 1. 15.)
45 Supreme Court 2000Da60630 (2001. 9. 18.)
46 Supreme Court 92Da17754 (1992. 9. 14.)
47 Commercial Act, Articles 235, 530(2), 603; Supreme Court 93Da1589 (1994. 3. 8.)
48 Ibid., Articles 242, 269, 604, 607

are preserved in the case of "corporate separations" as well, as the separated business inclusively succeeds the rights and obligations of the originating corporation as a matter of law.[49] As for "business transfers," case law suggests that so long as the personnel and asset of the business maintains their identity and is transferred as a whole, the labor relationship between the transferor business and its workers is inclusively transferred to the transferee-business (so long as no special agreements to the contrary has been made).[50] For cases like the above where the labor relationship is succeeded, as a principle the work period with the previous corporation must be included when calculating the number of years of continuous employment for the purpose of giving severance pay. However, if a worker reentered the post-merger/separation/reorganization/ business transfer corporation with his/her own will in order to interrupt continuous employment, his/her labor relationship with the previous corporation is deemed severed; the worker would hence receive severance pay only for the period s/he worked from the point of reemployment.[51]

⑥ Outbound Transfers between Affiliated Corporations: "Outbound transfers" occur when a worker maintains his/her employment relationship with one company but works under the direction and supervision of another (often affiliated) company due to being dispatched (or other via other forms of personnel action). Court precedent suggests that if the submission of resignation and the subsequent receipt of severance pay is not due to the worker's own will but is due to the unilateral management policy or decision of the parent corporation, such expression would be a non-bona fide expression of intent and is therefore invalid, and the labor

---

49 Ibid., Article 530(2) and (12)
50 Supreme Court 93Da33173 (1994. 6. 28.)
51 Supreme Court 96Da38511 (1997. 6. 27.)

relationship between the parent corporation and the transferred employee is preserved.[52]

Whether certain items should be included when determining the number of years of continuous service also needs to be considered, as follows:

① Break Periods: As a principle, all break periods taken during a worker's employment are included in the number of years of continuous service. Administrative interpretations suggest that such breaks that do not interrupt continuous service include those taken: due to personal illness, due to detention resulting from illegal activity, due to suspension of one's driver's license as a result of a driver's violation of traffic laws.

② Periods of Full-time Work for a Trade Union: Even if a corporation's worker has worked full-time in conducting union business as part of the collective bargaining agreement, so long as the labor relationship has been maintained this period must be calculated as part of the number of years of continuous service.

③ Periods of Training and Education Abroad: The time spent on training recruits is included in the number of years of continuous service. If a worker's education abroad conducted for a purpose related to his/her job function, this period of education is also included. However, if the study abroad was conducted for personal reasons unrelated to the worker's job and the worker has taken a leave of absence or has been suspended during the education, this period is not included as part of the number of years of continuous service.[53]

---

52 Supreme Court 98Da36924 (1998. 12. 11.)

53 Supreme Court 75Da872 (1976. 3. 9.)

2) Average Wages

The legal severance pay is calculated by multiplying the worker's number of years of continuous service with 30 days' worth of the worker's "average wages at the time of retirement." Regarding this, case law dictates that among the total income earned by the worker, average wages are limited to funds that the employer can manage or supervise. The rationale is that since severance pay is always given entirely by the employer, and employers must be given the ability to predict how much would be expended as severance pay by assuming control of average wages.[54] Take taxi drivers who take home as personal income any funds left over after paying their employer a designated amount of their daily income, for example. As the employer of these drivers is unable to manage or control the funds that the drivers take as personal income, such income is not included when calculating average wages for the purpose of providing severance pay.[55] On the other hand, in the case of taxi drivers who submit the entirety of their earnings to their company (which then deducts the amount owed to the company and returns any funds left back to the driver), court precedent suggests that even the personal income of taxi drivers are included in average wages. This is because taxi companies have the possibility to control these funds and hence would be able to predict how much would be expended as severance pay.[56]

3) Rate of Severance Pay

Since statutory severance pay is calculated by multiplying the worker's number of years of continuous service with "30-days' worth" of the worker's average wages, the rate of severance pay is proportional. This does not always have to be the case, however, as a progressive

---

54 Supreme Court 95Da55733 (1998. 3. 13.)

55 Supreme Court 98Da18568 (1999. 4. 23.)

56 Supreme Court 2005Da25113 (2007. 7. 12.)

severance pay rate may be employed through designations in employment rules or collective bargaining agreements, so long as such an arrangement does not violate the GWRBA.

If the rate of severance pay is modified via a change in the employment rules or collective bargaining agreements during the employment of a worker, how the severance pay of this worker would be calculated (i.e. which rate would be applied) is put to question. If the modified rate is determined to be more advantageous to the worker than the previous rate, this modified rate should be applied to the entirety of the worker's employment period when calculating his/her severance pay, so long as there are no transitional provisions that regulate such scenarios.[57] There are cases, however, where the severance pay rate is modified in a manner disadvantageous to the worker. In such cases, there are two scenarios: the first is when the collective bargaining agreement or employment rule contains a provision that retroactively applies the new severance pay rate to periods worked prior to the modification. In such cases the modified rate is used when calculating the severance pay of the employee for the entire period worked.[58] However, if there is no such provision, only the work period after the modification is subject to the new severance pay rate while the old rate would apply to periods prior to the modification when calculating severance payments.[59]

In the meanwhile, there are cases where there haven't been changes in the severance pay rate within the collective bargaining agreement or employment rules, but a worker has transitioned between two job types or classifications that apply different severance pay rates. Here, which rate to apply when calculating severance payments is put to question. If the situation is determined to violate the principle

---

57 Supreme Court 96Da45399 (1997. 7. 11.)

58 Supreme Court 2000Da65239 (2001. 6. 26.)

59 Supreme Court 89DaKa15939 (1990. 11. 27.)

of prohibiting differentiated severance pay systems by establishing different severance pay rates within the same business or workplace depending on type of work done by the worker,[60] the severance pay rate that is not disadvantageous to the worker must be applied for the entirety of his/her work period. On the other hand, if the principle is deemed not to have been violated, the severance pay rate at the point of retirement must be applied in calculating severance pay as per Article 4(1) of the GWRBA. Of course, if there is a provision in the collective bargaining agreement or employment rules that regulates the method of severance pay calculation and this does not violate Article 4(1) of the GWRBA, the severance pay calculation would follow the method outlined in this provision.[61]

E. Interim Severance Adjustment Pay

The GWRBA allows for employers to give interim severance adjustment pay to workers for the period that they have worked up to that point upon their request, even if the request is made prior to their actual retirement.[62] Yet after the GWRBA's July 26, 2012 revision, only requests made by the worker for reasons designated by presidential decree (such as purchasing homes) would such interim severance adjustment payments be made possible.

The employer is not obliged to grant the worker an interim severance adjustment payment towards a part or the whole of the worker's time with the employer upon the worker's request. The agreement to do so is made only when the employer approves such a request.[63] When supplying its agreement to provide the interim

60 GWRBA, Article 4(2)
61 Supreme Court 93Da26168 (1995. 7. 11.), unanimous decision
62 GWRBA, Article 8(2)
63 Supreme Court 93Da26168 (1995. 7. 11.), unanimous decision

severance adjustment payment, the employer may not unilaterally grant payment for only a portion of the total period requested by the worker. However, should the unilateral grant of a portion of total period request be viewed as a new offer made by the employer with the addition of a new condition or modification,[64] the worker's subsequent acceptance of this offer without dispute would indicate that a valid agreement to provide interim severance adjustment payment towards a part of the worker's time has been made, at least within the scope of the new time period proposed by the employer.[65]

Meanwhile, agreements between the employer and the worker that allow set amounts of severance payments to be made along with monthly wages are not recognized as valid forms of severance payments or interim severance adjustment payments. The Supreme Court ruled that purported severance payments made under the above invalid schemes are considered unjust enrichment, and that the employer constructively possesses a "restitution of unjust enrichment bond" that is automatically enforceable. This bond may be used to offset the employer's obligation to the worker in the form of severance payment, only if done to the latter's portions exceeding 50%.[66]

F. The Effect of Severance Pay Regulations that Do Not Satisfy Legal Standards

If a severance pay regulation designated by collective bargaining agreements or employment rules does not satisfy the standard stipulated under Article 8(1) of the GWRBA, that portion becomes invalid and the worker receives a severance pay package that satisfies

---

64 Civil Act, Article 534

65 Supreme Court 2006Da20542 (2008. 2. 1.)

66 Supreme Court 2007Da90760 (2010. 5. 20.), unanimous decision

the minimum standard determined under Article 8(1). This is also the case should there be no such regulations in place at all.

The standard outlined under Article 8(1) of the GWRBA functions to mark the minimum amount that a worker may receive as severance pay. Even if a completely different standard of calculating severance payment is agreed upon via collective bargaining agreements or employment rules, the resulting amount of payment received by a given worker must exceed the amount that the worker would receive under the standard employed by Article 8(1) in order to be valid.[67] If it does not, that standard would be deemed invalid under the GWRBA.[68]

III. Retirement Pension System

A. The Drafting of the Retirement Pension Regulation

An employer who wishes to establish a retirement pension system must draft a "Retirement Pension Regulation," obtain the consent of the worker's representative, and register the document with the Ministry of Employment and Labor. The "Regulation" must include all legally required standards governing retirement pensions; beyond this, the labor union and management may freely agree on standards that go beyond legislatively determined minimums or on other matters not regulated by the GWRBA.[69]

---

67 Supreme Court 97Da21086 (1998. 1. 20.)

68 Supreme Court 2005Da25113 (2007. 7. 12.)

69 GWRBA, Articles 13 and 19

B. The Defined Benefit Retirement Pension System

The defined benefit retirement pension is a system where the amount of pension to be received by the worker is predetermined, and the amount that the employer ends up contributing fluctuates depending on how well the pension fund is managed. In other words, the pension payment that the worker will ultimately receive is set to match the amount of severance payment s/he will receive if paid as a lump sum today, which is disbursed across the remainder the of the worker's life or across a finite period exceeding 5 years. To secure the funds necessary to pay this pension, the employer must deposit an amount agreed with the workers (which is greater than the minimum statutory standard) to a financial institution, which independently manages the fund according to its contract with the employer.[70]

C. The Defined Contribution Retirement Pension System

The defined contribution retirement pension is a system where the amount of the employer's pension contribution is predetermined, and the amount that the worker ends up receiving fluctuates depending on how well the pension fund is managed. In other words, the employer deposits 1/12 or more (as agreed upon by the labor union and management) of a worker's total annual wage under the worker's individual account (the financial institution(s) where these accounts would be set up is determined by the Retirement Pension Regulation). The worker then decides among fund management options that the financial institution makes available, and the institution manages the funds according to the worker's direction, disbursing the amount either in pension or lump-sum format.[71]

---

70 Ibid., Articles 13 and 18
71 Ibid., Articles 19 and 23

Chapter 6

Transfer of Labor Relations

I. Introduction

When the owner of a business changes due to a business transfer or corporate merger, questions arise as to whether the labor relations established between the previous employer and his/her workers would succeed to the new owner. This chapter explores the nuances of the legal terrain surrounding this question.

II. Succession of Labor Relationships Due to Business Transfers

A. Business Transfers and Whether Labor Relationships Are Succeeded

1) Succession during the Contracting Phase

In most cases, the disposition of workers employed by the transferor is a central issue deliberated on during business transfer contract negotiations. Rarely does a business transfer succeed without adequate consent from the workers and unions of both transferor and transferee regarding this issue.

If the contracting parties to the business transfer agree to comprehensively succeed the labor relationship of the previous employer, and the workers affected by the transfer consent to this agreement, there is no question that this succession has in fact taken place.

2) No Explicit Agreements Regarding Succession during the Contracting Phase

Generally, both legal literature and case law recognizes the principle (i.e. the theory of succession as a matter of principle) that the transferee comprehensively succeeds the labor relationships of the transferor's business should a comprehensive transfer of a business take place, unless special provisions limiting such comprehensive succession have been agreed upon. In such cases, case law recognizes the worker's right to either remain as the transferor's employee by expressing his/her opposition to being transferred or resign from both transferor and transferee.

3) Exclusion of Part of the Labor Relationship from Being Succeeded

In this case, it is possible for the labor relationship to not be succeeded. However, application of this special provision in effect means that the worker being excluded from the transfer would be terminated from his/her employment. Therefore, such special provisions must have a justifiable cause as defined under Article 23(1) of the LSA[1] in order to be valid. A business transfer in and of itself cannot be a justifiable cause of termination.[2] An exception to this would be when an urgent managerial necessity (as defined in the second clause of Article 24(1) in the LSA) arises as a result of the business transfer, providing justifiable

---

1 Labor Standards Act
2 Supreme Court 93Da33173 (1994. 6. 28.), Supreme Court 2000Du8455 (2002. 3. 29.)

cause for the so-called "dismissal for managerial reasons." Of course, such a dismissal is possible only if other requirements for a valid dismissal for managerial reasons are met.

4) Succession Resulting from Business Transfers

Where labor relationships are succeeded, in principle all workers who have a legally valid labor relationship with their former employer would have their labor relationship succeeded irrespective of whether they were actually working at the business at the time of the business transfer.[3]

In the case of transfers where only part of the business is affected, it is possible to consider that only those employees working with the transferred division would have their labor relationship succeeded.[4] However, this issue is essentially a matter of contract interpretation, looking at the explicit or implicit agreement between the parties regarding the scope of the labor relationship succession at the time of the contract.

B. Requirements to Succeed Labor Relationships

1) The Business Transfer Contract and the Agreement to Succeed

i) The Business Transfer Contract

For business transfer contracts entered into for the purpose of changing the business owner (i.e. managing entity) but maintaining the identity of the business itself, the labor relationship is succeeded.

---

3 Supreme Court 93Da33173 (1994. 6. 28.)
4 Supreme Court 91Da41750 (1993. 5. 25.)

(1) "Business"

A business is defined as an organic organization that conducts operations in accordance with the business purpose of the owner, utilizing personnel (i.e. workers) and property (i.e. capital). Business operations conducted by the owner, the physical facilities owned by the organization (capital), and personnel resources (labor) make up the three components of business.[5]

Parts of the business that are smaller than the whole (i.e. the business division) may become subjects of business transfers. In this case, the transferred business division must independently maintain organizational coherence sufficient to achieve certain business objectives.

Without the transfer of business operations, transferring business facilities (e.g. machinery or trade names) do not in and of themselves result in business transfers.[6] In other words, as transferring business property (and not operations) does not result in a change in management, there is very low chance that the issue of labor relations succession would arise. If the transfer of business property results in the transferor closing its operations, the business owner may validly terminate his/her workers citing business closure so long as the transfer is not determined to be an unfair labor practice (i.e. disguised closure for the purpose of interfering with union activities) or a pre-textual transfer (i.e. a facility transfer made to implement the original intention of a business transfer).[7]

(2) "Transfer"

The following scenarios are not business transfers under the strict definition of the term, but are considered to be constructively so:

5 Supreme Court 88DaKa10128 (1989. 12. 26.), Supreme Court 91Da15225 (1991. 8. 9.)
6 Supreme Court 68Da185 (1968. 4. 2.)
7 Supreme Court 90Nu9421 (1992. 5. 12.)

when a business in whole or in part is invested in kind to establish a corporation;[8] and when a company makes an investment in kind of all or part of its business at the time shares are issued upon incorporation.[9]

As the above scenarios illustrate, whether a business transfer in fact occurs cannot be determined solely by examining the type and quantity of business property that has been transferred. For an accurate determination, one must also examine whether the transferred business operation has maintained its organization, and functions as a whole or at least an important part of the transferee's business. If it is generally accepted that the transferred division has maintained its organization, the transfer of business facility will be considered a business transfer despite the fact that part of the business property was withheld from the transfer. On the other hand, even if the entire business property is transferred, the transaction would still not be considered a business transfer if the original business organization is dissolved in the process.[10]

(3) "Contract"

As long as a contract is entered into for the purpose of transferring business, the exact form of the contract (whether it be sales, trade, gift, or trust) is not significant. If a party to the contract is a corporation, however, special decision-making procedures must be observed as mandated by the Commercial Act before a contract can be validated. Furthermore, insurance companies must obtain approval from the Financial Services Commission in order to transfer business operations,[11] and in certain business transfers are prohibited if it is

---

8 Commercial Act, Article 290(2)

9 Supreme Court 88DaKa12100 (1989. 3. 28.); Commercial Act, Article 416(4)

10 Supreme Court 88DaKa10128 (1989. 12. 26.), Supreme Court 2002Da23836 (2003. 5. 30.), Supreme Court 99Du2680 (2001. 7. 27.)

11 Insurance Business Act, Article 150

determined that such transfers would substantially limit competition.[12]

ii) The Agreement to Succeed Labor Relationships
    (1) Comprehensive Succession
Even if there is no explicit agreement (or ambiguity exists) regarding the content of the business transfer contract, should the business maintain its identity and operations before and after the contract, it is generally assumed that an agreement has been made for the transferee to comprehensively succeed the transferor's labor relations.[13]

Another instance where the comprehensive succession of labor relations is recognized is when a worker who was terminated by the transferor (or has resigned) prior to the business transfer disputes the validity of the termination or resignation and argues that his labor relationship still exists. If the termination or resignation that took place before the business transfer is determined to have had justifiable cause under Article 23(1) of the LSA and is therefore valid, the labor relationship between the grieved worker and the employer is considered to have been resolved prior to the transfer; hence the question of whether his/her labor relationship is succeeded becomes moot. However, if it is determined that the termination or resignation that took place before the transfer is invalid, and that a labor relationship exists between the worker and the employer (despite the fact that the worker is not providing actual labor after the termination), this relationship is recognized to have succeeded to the transferee in case the owner has changed as part of a business transfer.[14]

    (2) Exclusion of All or Part of Labor Relations from Being Succeeded
Parties to a business transfer contract may specifically agree on a

---

12 Monopoly Regulation and Fair Trade Act, Article 7(1)4
13 Supreme Court 91Da15225 (1991. 8. 9.)
14 Supreme Court 93Da33173 (1994. 6. 28.), Supreme Court 95Nu1972 (1996. 4. 26.)

special provision that excludes the succession of a part of the labor relations of the transferor. However, this special provision comes under the scrutiny of Article 23(1) of the LSA (which imposes limitations on discharge without justifiable cause), and its validity may be limited.

For instance, issues regarding whether labor relations have been duly succeeded would not arise in the following cases (i.e. non-succession would be fully recognized): the transferor legitimately discharged the worker prior to the transfer, the labor relationship is validly concluded through means such as the mutual termination of the employment contract, or the worker is transferred to another business division in a legitimate manner prior to the business transfer.

On the other hand, the following scenarios would be problematic: (i) when a worker's termination or resignation is expected to be caused by the transferor shortly before a business transfer and the transferor obtains the consent of the transferee in doing so; (ii) when the parties of the business transfer agree to take on a certain number of the transferor's workers, or to exclude the succession of specific workers due to the fact that they have proactively engaged in union activities (and hence poses a potential encumbrance to the operation of the corporation), and as a result the transferor lays off these workers.

The purpose of a business transfer is to change the business's managing entity. Therefore, a party to a business transfer may not take advantage of the situation and impute the risk resulting from the transfer to its workers. Therefore, scenario (i) in the preceding paragraph would be a violation of Article 23(1) of the LSA (which prohibits termination without justifiable cause), and scenario (ii) would also be a violation of the Union Act[15] regulations that prohibit unfair labor practice. Both scenarios would therefore become invalid.

Another common scenario is when the transferor lays off all of its

---

15 Trade Union and Labor Relations Adjustment Act

workers in light of the business transfer, after which the transferee re-hires either a selection or most of these workers, offering them the same working condition as before to do the same work they did under the transferor.

In such a scenario, the issue of whether labor relations will be succeeded at the time of the transfer becomes significant when determining the number of years of continuous employment of a worker when the time comes for the worker to retire. The validity of the layoff at the time of the business transfer impacts the amount of severance pay the worker will receive. The answer to this question hinges on whether the agreement between the transferor and the workers to have them resign should be recognized as being lawful and valid or not.

If the worker first resigned from his/her employment with the transferor freely with the intention of discontinuing his/her labor relationship (and accepted severance payment in the process), and then subsequently proceeded to gain employment with the transferee, the worker should be considered to have severed his/her labor relationship with the transferor. Here, the worker would calculate his/her severance payment based on the number of continuous years s/he has worked from the moment s/he joined the transferee and not include the period s/he worked with the transferor.[16]

However, if the worker did not resign and regain employment due to his/her own volition and merely followed the direction of the management plan mutually agreed upon by the parties to the business transfer, even if the worker has received severance pay under this scheme, the worker cannot be seen to have possessed the intention to discontinue his/her labor relationship with the transferor. Therefore, should the worker decide to retire from his/her position at a later date, the transferee has the obligation to include the number of continuous

---

16 Supreme Court 90Da16801 (1991. 5. 28.), Supreme Court 91Da12035 (1991. 12. 10.)

years the above worker worked with the transferor when calculating the severance payment to be disbursed (here, the severance payment the worker has already received from the transferor is deducted from the total amount ultimately paid).[17]

2) De Facto Transfer of the Business Organization
The moment that the succession of labor relations is given legal effect is not when the business transfer contract is entered into. That moment is when the transferee is in fact given the ability to manage the organization transferred by the transferor. Therefore it is incorrect to say that labor relations have been succeeded by the mere fact that the business transfer contract has been entered into. As such, the moment the obligations assumed by transferor and transferee regarding labor relations arise is when the transferee takes over de facto control over the transferor's business operations.

3) Whether Consent of the Worker Is Necessary
Article 657(1) of the Civil Act stipulates that "the employer may not assign his rights to a third person without the consent of the employee." Whether this provision applies to the succession of labor relations during business transfers or not is a question not settled at this point. However, the discrepancy between the two opposing camps is not much; the main point of contention is that in the case of partial business transfers, the workers are entitled to choose for their labor relations to be succeeded to the transferee.

As a practical matter, there is minimal chance that workers would refuse to consent to the succession of their labor relations if the entirety of the business is transferred, as it would effectively mean the termination of their employment. Also, if the worker does not

---

17 Supreme Court 84DaKa1409 (1987. 2. 24.), Supreme Court 90Da-6545 (1991. 3. 22.), Supreme Court 91Da12806 (1991. 11. 12.), Supreme Court 91Da40276 (1992. 7. 14.).

communicate special objection or rejection to this arrangement and continues to provide labor to the transferee, it may be deemed as implicit consent to the succession.

The picture becomes a bit more complicated in the case of partial business transfers. The transferor must not discharge its worker for reasons of cessation of business operations just because the worker remains at the transferor's workplace while objecting to his/her labor relationship succeeding to the transferee business. The transferor must make good faith efforts to allow this worker to continue his/her employment with it through means such as relocating to different business divisions within the corporation. However, if the case turns out that as a result of the business transfer there is an inevitable managerial need to downsize the transferor's business, laying off the worker mentioned above becomes a legitimate option. However, the issue then becomes that of layoffs rather than that of business transfers.

C. The Legal Effect of the Succession of Labor Relations

1) The Legal Relationship between the Transferee Business and the Worker

i) The Content and Nature of the Obligations Held by the Transferee Business
The transferee takes over from the transferor the latter's status vis-à-vis its workers. In other words, the content of the labor relationship (e.g. working conditions) for the worker remains unchanged, as the labor relationship between the transferor and its workers is merely substituted with the transferee business.

It should not be seen that the worker establishes a new labor relationship with the transferee by being incorporated into the new organization. The proper understanding would be that the labor relationship that workers from the transferor had remains unchanged, independent from the relationship that existing workers in the transferee business maintain with the transferee.

As a result, a situation may occur in which two or more groups of workers are working in the same business or workplace under different working conditions. However, this situation is not considered problematic in light of the principle of equal treatment[18] nor the principle of the prohibition against differentiation of pension benefits within the same business.[19]

ii) The Scope of Responsibility of the Transferee Business
(1) Responsibilities under the Employment Contract
The transferee business must honor its obligation as an employer by fulfilling its responsibility regarding the labor relationship established between the workers and the transferor (i.e. pay wages, designate work schedules, etc. according to individual labor contracts, employment rules, collective agreements).[20]

A transferee may not amend the rules of employment unfavorably to workers without first obtaining their consent, if the rules were in effect at the time of the transfer.[21] The transfer in itself is not a sufficient cause that legitimizes such an amendment, and whether the modification should be allowed would depend on the totality of the circumstances, with a comprehensive examination of the details of each case.

Collective agreements between unions and the transferor remain in force between the union and the transferee business as long as it was valid at the time of the business transfer, as collective agreements

---

18 LSA, Article 6
19 Guarantee of Workers' Retirement Benefits Act, Article 4(2)
20 Supreme Court 91Da15225 (1991. 8. 9.)
21 Supreme Court 93Da58714 (1994. 8. 26.)

are also an aspect of labor relations.

However, sorting out the relationship between the unions in the transferee and transferor may become an issue if there is a union already established in the transferee business's workplace at the time of the transfer. As trade unions exist independently from corporations and are established with the workers as main subjects, business transfers do not impact the viability of unions nor impose organizational changes in them. Therefore, unions in the transferor maintain their existence unless they disburse or merge with the transferee business's union, and as a result multiple unions may co-exist in the same workplace.[22]

So long as this co-existence of unions is maintained, the transferee business has no choice but to enter into collective bargaining and collective agreements with the union representing the workers it succeeded from the transferor. As a result, the working conditions of workers from the transferor are determined through the collective agreement entered into with their respective union whether or not personnel movement takes place.

However, in reality the chance of this scenario occurring is very low. Usually one union will agree to disperse and join the other union, or the two unions will merge. In the latter case (i.e. the unions of the two transferring businesses merging without communicating with the transferee business), how the previous collective agreements would be applied becomes an issue (unless an agreement is struck between the remaining union and the transferee business on how to apply the collective agreements). There are conflicting viewpoints on how to resolve this issue; one argues that the collective agreement entered into with the union remaining after the merger is the only one in effect, as agreements entered into with a union generally become unenforceable

---

22 Supreme Court 90Nu9421 (1992. 5. 12.)

once that union is dispersed. The other viewpoint argues that collective agreements existing before the transfer remain effective due to the fact that unions of both sides succeed the legal status of being parties of the agreement. Under this logic, it is only after preexisting agreements have lost their validity (e.g. through expiration) that labor relations may be regulated under a unified collective agreement.

(2) Accident Compensation Liability under the LSA and Unlawful Acts/Tort Liability Arising from the Labor Relationship

It should be interpreted that the transferee business succeeds not only the obligations assumed by the transferor in its employment contracts with the latter's workers, but also the transferor's accident compensation liability (outlined in the LSA) and the tort liability that arises from the labor relationship (e.g. obligation to pay compensation for wrongful dismissal).

In the case of liabilities assumed by the transferor prior to the transfer as part of the succession of labor relations, whether the period of compliance has been satisfied at the time of the transfer is not examined. However, a caveat would be when a worker has resigned or is justly discharged and has ceased his/her labor relationship with the transferor prior to the transfer. In such cases the worker is not a part of the business transfer in the first place; hence the transferee business does not take on the liability that the transferor has assumed (e.g. unpaid wages, severance payments, and advance notice of discharge pay).

(3) The Cancellation or Nullification of the Business Transfer Contract

While it is natural that the transferee would honor any liability that may result from its relations with its new workers after a business transfer, questions may be raised as to whether this is still the case if the business transfer contract is cancelled or nullified and as a consequence the labor relationship established between the transferee and its transferred workers is severed.

According to the "legal principle of de facto labor relations," the transferee business cannot evade liability that results from work performed by workers during the period where it was the de facto management entity (i.e. after it has assumed control over the business).

The legal principle of de facto labor relations is an interpretive theory that posits that labor relations maintains its validity despite there being a cause for revocation of an employment contract or the contract being invalid if there has been a provision of labor by the worker. The rationale behind this principle is that the invalidity of the contract should not be retroactively applied and should only impact work to take place in the future. As such, under this principle a labor relation is valid until a party expresses his/her intention to terminate the relationship. This is a principle that has been established under German precedent and common wisdom.

However, there is a case which ruled that in order to file for severance pay under the LSA there must be a legal and valid labor relationship between the employer and the worker established at the time of termination.[23] This ruling may seem to suggest that the principle of de facto labor relations has been rejected. However, the case must be understood to be a case primarily about whether the right to request pensions under the Public Officials Pension Act exists, hence making it inappropriate to apply to the context of civil law dealing with labor relations.

iii) Limiting the Transferee Business from Discharging Due to Business Transfers

Business transfers are merely the changing of business owners, and it is unreasonable to impute the risk of the transfer to workers. Therefore, it is invalid for a transferee business to terminate workers for reasons

---

23 Supreme Court 86Nu459 (1987. 4. 14.)

of the business transfer alone, as such an act lacks just cause.[24]

2) The Legal Relationship between the Transferor and the Worker

The labor relationship between the transferor and the worker is concluded at the time of the business transfer. However, the debt that the transferor has towards the worker is not necessarily exempted due to the transfer. In other words, liabilities assumed by the transferor prior to the transfer remain, whether or not the period of compliance has been satisfied at the time of the transfer. However, if an indemnification agreement has been made by the parties of the transfer so that the transferee assumes the liability of the transferor (and the workers have agreed to this arrangement), the transferor no longer retains this liability. Therefore, the transferor mentioned above will bear joint and several liability with the transferee.

It is certain that the transferee does not assume liability for debts that have not been accrued as of the business transfer. From the Supreme Court's ruling[25] that the employer's obligation to provide severance pay arises at the point the employment contract ends, the onus to provide severance pay for workers who resign from a corporation after a business transfer seems to be on the transferee. In calculating the severance payment, the time the worker has worked with the transferor must be included.

In the case that the business transfer contract becomes invalid or cancelled and consequently the transferor regains control of the business, the liability assumed by the transferee after the transfer and before the reacquisition by the transferor is subject to a joint and several liability with the transferee.

---

24 Supreme Court 93Da33173 (1994. 6. 28.)
25 Supreme Court 73Da278 (1973. 10. 10.), Supreme Court 74Da1840 (1975. 7. 22.), Supreme Court 77Da1137 (1977. 9. 28.), Consensus Decision, Supreme Court 90Da1 4560 (1991. 6. 28.)

III. The Succession of Labor Relations Due to Corporate Mergers

A. Corporate Mergers & Acquisitions and the Succession of Labor Relations

1) Mergers

A corporate merger is a combination of two or more companies via a contract (which complies with statutory guidelines and is determined by Commercial Law) where one corporation is extinguished in whole or in part without undergoing liquidation, while the other survives (or an entirely new company is formed). Depending on the method, merges may be classified as mergers or consolidations. A merger occurs when a party to the merger is extinguished, with the other party absorbing the former corporation's resources while maintaining its identity. A consolidation occurs when all parties to the merger are dispersed, and a new corporation that embodies the previous entities is formed.

2) Labor Relations with Workers from the Extinct Corporation

The Commercial Act stipulates that "a surviving company or a company newly incorporated in consequence of a merger shall succeed to the rights and obligations of the company which disappeared."[26] Both literature and case law interpret this provision to mean that the labor relationship between the worker and the extinct corporation should be legally and comprehensively succeeded by the surviving or newly incorporated company.[27]

3) Consent from the Worker

Article 657(1) of the Civil Act states: "The employer may not assign his

---

26 Commercial Act, Articles 235, 530(2), 603
27 Supreme Court 93Da1589 (1994. 3. 8.)

rights to a third person without the consent of the employee." However, in light of the regulations of the Commercial Act cited above, plus the consensus in both literature and case law that labor relations between workers and extinct corporations are comprehensively succeeded by the surviving company, it is appropriate to assume that Article 657(1) does not apply to cases of corporate mergers.

4) Exclusion of All or Part of the Workers from Being Succeeded

Agreements or resolutions between parties of a merger to exclude all or part of the workers of the extinct corporation from succession should be deemed invalid. The labor relations of these workers survive the merger, regardless of the existence of such agreements between the merging parties. Extinct, surviving, or consolidated corporations may not discharge workers during the period leading to and right after a merger when only citing the merger as justification for the discharge.

However, this does not preclude scenarios where labor relations are concluded via valid expressions of intention on the part of both pre-merger corporations and their workers. For example, if a worker expresses the intention to discontinue labor relations with the pre-merger corporation of his/her own volition and submits a letter of resignation, and subsequently gains employment with the surviving or consolidated corporation, it is appropriate to consider that this worker has severed his/her labor relations with the extinct corporation before the merger occurred.[28]

However, if it is determined that the resignation by the worker was not due to his/her own volition but merely an act of compliance to the merging parties' unilateral management policy to have the worker resign before reemploying him/her in the surviving corporation, seeming mutual agreements (i.e. resignation, etc.) between the pre-merger corporation and its worker to conclude their labor relations

---

28 Supreme Court 91Da12035 (1991. 12. 10.)

would be considered invalid, and the worker's expressions of his/her intent to resign becomes void as ungenuine expressions of intent or false representation. In such cases the worker cannot be seen to have possessed the intent to sever labor relations, and hence the continuity of his/her labor relation with the corporation is maintained. This is true even if the worker has received severance pay as part of the imposed process.

B. The Legal Effect of Corporate Mergers on Succession

In principle, the labor relations between a worker and an extinct corporation (i.e. working conditions such as wages, working hours, content of work, severance pay) that have been established prior to a merger is maintained as-is to the surviving or consolidated corporation. Therefore, there is little dispute regarding the interpretation that the workers above must not be seen as having gained new employment (and hence established new labor relations) with the surviving or consolidated corporation. This is also consistent with case law.[29]

Especially in the case of mergers, while it would seem that the operations of the extinct corporation have become absorbed to become part of the surviving corporation's operation, legally it is inaccurate to conceptualize that the workers from the extinct corporation's workplace have been newly incorporated into the surviving corporation's operations and hence has established a new labor relationship. Instead, the labor relationship these workers established with the extinct corporation is seen to have continued, independent from the labor relationship between the surviving

---

29 Supreme Court 93Da1589 (1994. 3. 8.), Supreme Court 99Da9370 (2001. 4. 24.), Supreme Court 2002Da23185, 23192 (2004. 5. 14.)

corporation and its workers.

As a consequence, the working conditions of workers from the extinct corporation (as outlined in the employment rules or as agreed upon through collective agreements from their previous workplace) may be different from the working conditions of workers in the surviving corporation. This does not place the surviving or consolidated corporations in violation of the principle of equal treatment under Article 6 of the LSA nor the principle of the prohibition against differentiation in retirement benefit schemes under Article 4(2) of the Guarantee of Workers' Retirement Benefits Act. However, like the aforementioned case of business transfers, it is possible to unify working conditions through means such as validly amending the employment rules or by concluding a new collective agreement with the trade union.[30]

The issues of applying and modifying employment rules and implementing collective agreements are dealt with in the same manner as business transfers that this chapter has examined above.

---

30 Supreme Court 93Da58714 (1994. 8. 26.), Supreme Court 99Da9370 (2001. 4. 24.), Supreme Court 2001Da24051 (2001. 10. 30.)

Chapter 7

Rules of Employment

I. The Rules of Employment and Their Legal Regulations

A. The Concept of the Rules of Employment

The rules of employment are regulations unilaterally devised by the employer that determine the service code and working conditions that workers are subject to within the workplace.[1] Here, "working conditions" refer to conditions relating to the treatment of the worker in the labor relationship, such as wages, working hours, welfare, discharge, etc.[2]

Rules of employment are distinguished from individual labor contracts (which are agreements individually entered into by individual workers and employers) or collective agreements (which are agreements made between unions and employers) in that they are unilaterally prepared by the employer. In addition to this unilateral drafting authority, the employer also possesses the ability to modify the rules of employment as s/he sees fit.

If a certain regulation is unilaterally prepared by the employer and

---

1 Labor Standards Act, Article 93
2 Supreme Court 91Da19210 (1992. 6. 23.)

concerns codes of service or working conditions, that regulation has the nature of a rules of employment regardless of what it is actually called. It is possible to prepare multiple rules of employment that apply to subsets of workers according to job positions in the same workplace. However, the employer must make sure that s/he is not violating laws that prohibit unjustified disparate treatment in working conditions[3] as well as differentiated severance pay systems within the same workplace.[4]

B. Legal Regulations Concerning the Rules of Employment

As rules of employment are prepared unilaterally by the employer, there is a risk that s/he will draft the content of working conditions in a manner that is advantageous only to the employer. Considering the reality that workers are subordinate to their employers, the following limits exist to protect workers.

First, when preparing a list of the rules of employment for the first time, or when modifying an existing list, the employer must receive the administrative supervision of the state, and must take steps to sufficiently incorporate the opinion of his/her workers.[5]

Also, while a rules of employment list that has been devised or modified through legal means is considered a legal regulation and hence takes precedence over individual labor contracts,[6] any provisions that come into conflict with the collective agreement, or any part of the Act related to labor relations, are considered invalid.[7]

---

3 LSA, Article 6
4 Guarantee of Workers' Retirement Benefits Act, Article 4(2)
5 Ibid., Articles 93 and 94
6 Ibid., Article 97
7 Ibid., Article 96(1)

II. The Preparation and Modification of the Rules of Employment

A. General Procedure of Preparation or Modification

1) The Entry or Modification of Requisite Items by the Employer

i) Entities that Must Prepare the Rules of Employment

An employer who ordinarily employs ten or more workers is obligated to prepare the rules of employment.[8] The requirement of "employing ten or more workers" includes those employers who, according to socially accepted norms, employ ten or more employees, even if the exact number of individuals employed sometimes falls below this number. Here, daily workers are included in addition to regular workers. Whether an employer ordinarily employs ten or more workers is determined independently, on a workplace by workplace basis.

ii) The Substance of the Duty to Prepare the Rules of Employment

Article 93 of the LSA stipulates items that must be included in the rules of employment. The employer must prepare the rules of employment that contain these items in writing at the moment s/he ordinarily employs ten or more employees without delay.

If it is difficult to include in one document all matters that must be determined under the rules of employment, separate documents may be prepared by subject matter (e.g. wages, retirement, human resource management, occupational accidents), or by job type. In this case, the sum of these prepared documents would be considered to be parts of a single rules of employment document.

---

8 Ibid., Article 93

As the rules of employment must be prepared so that all workers within the workplace are subject to them, the employer is not considered to have satisfied his/her duty to prepare the rules if s/he devises one set of rules for certain workers but does not do so for the rest.

iii) Effect of Violating the Duty to Prepare the Rules of Employment
The rules of employment are valid to the extent that they have been prepared, even if the employer partially omitted items that must be included in the document or failed to prepare the rules some of his/her workers. However, the employer is subject to a fine for violating the LSA.[9]

2) Listening to the Opinions and Gaining the Consent of Worker Organizations

"An employer shall, with regard to the preparation or alteration of the rules of employment, take into account the opinions of a trade union if there is such a trade union composed of the majority of the workers in the business or workplace concerned, or otherwise listen to the opinion of the majority of said workers if there is no trade union composed of the majority of workers."[10] However, when "amending the rules of employment unfavorably to workers, the employer must obtain the above workers' consent."[11] Such 'unfavorable modification to the rules of employment,' being the most important section regarding the preparation and modification of the rules of employment, will be dealt with in more detail below under a separate heading.

If a regional or local office of a craft or industrial union is installed in the workplace and has registered its establishment and been issued its registration document, and if that union is composed of the

---

9 Ibid., Article 116(2)

10 Ibid., Article 94(1)

11 Ibid., Article 94(1) proviso

majority of the workers in the business or workplace concerned, the employer must listen to its opinion.

If there are no unions organized in a workplace, or the number of union members does not rise to the majority of the total workers in a workplace, the employer must take into account the opinion of the majority of its workers. Here, "majority of workers" means the majority of those workers who were subject to the previous rules of employment.[12]

Employers may listen to the opinions of workers' organizations, but are not bound to their contents. In principle, even if the employer violates the process of listening to opinions, so long as the working conditions were not modified in a manner disadvantageous to the workers, the modification stands as valid.[13] However, the employer does still assume criminal liability.[14]

3) Reporting to the Ministry of Employment and Labor and Acquainting Workers with the Rules of Employment

An employer who ordinarily employs ten or more workers must prepare the rules of employment, conduct an opinion-gathering process, and report the results together with the rules of employment to the Minister of Employment and Labor without delay.[15] If the reporting requirement is violated, the non-reported rules of employment do not become invalid,[16] but the employer will be fined as a result.[17]

Furthermore, the employer must acquaint workers with the rules of employment by posting or keeping them in a readily accessible

---

12 Supreme Court 2007Da85997 (2008. 2. 29.)

13 Supreme Court 88DaKa4277 (1989. 5. 9.), Supreme Court 90Da16245 (1991. 4. 9.), Supreme Court 94Nu3001 (1994. 12. 23.), Supreme Court 98Du6647 (1999. 6. 22.)

14 LSA, Article 114(1)

15 Ibid., Article 93

16 Supreme Court 2001Da63599 (2004. 2. 12.)

17 LSA, Article 116(2)

place for workers at all times.[18] According to the majority view, if the employer fails to acquaint workers with the rules of employment and as a result his/her workers remain ignorant of their content, this would not only subject the employer to fines,[19] it would also result in the rules becoming invalid.

B. Special Provisions Regarding Unfavorable Modifications to the Rules of Employment (The Procedure of Obtaining a Worker's Consent)

1) The Concept of Unfavorable Modifications and Grounds for Exceptions

i) Unfavorable modifications to the rules of employment refers to situations where the rules of employment are to be prepared from scratch or existing rules are to be modified by the employer, with the new provisions resulting in a detriment of the vested rights or interests of the workers regarding working conditions or service regulations, or resulting in a unilateral worsening of working conditions or strengthening of service regulations.[20]

One case concluded by the Supreme Court dealt with a situation where a corporation modified its rules of employment without obtaining the consent of the workers' group, revising its severance pay scheme so that the rate of severance pay was generally lower (i.e. the corporation extended the period where the scheme would have control over the payment rate to 30 years, which is up from the 15 years before the revision). In this case, as the progressive rate of severance payments after the modification is drastically lower than what workers

---

18 Ibid., Article 14(1)

19 Ibid., Article 116(2)

20 Supreme Court 88DaKa4277 (1989. 5. 9.), Supreme Court 2001Da16722 (2002. 6. 11.), Supreme Court 2002Da23185 and 23192 (2004. 5. 14.)

were entitled to prior to the modification, the employer has to obtain the consent of the workers regarding this matter. However, as the severance pay scheme for the period of employment that exceeds 15 years should be considered as a new regulation that had not existed prior to the modification, and as this portion of the scheme does not disadvantage the working conditions of workers vis-à-vis that the workers enjoyed prior to the modification, the court ruled that this portion of the modification to the rules of employment was valid, despite the lack of consent by the workers' organization.[21]

Another Supreme Court case ruled that not touching a set of provisions in the old personnel regulation that stipulated, in an abstract manner, the causes and types of disciplinary actions, and instead newly designating specified and detailed regulations that elaborate the above abstract concepts should not be interpreted as being an unfavorable modification against the worker.[22]

Also, if a corporation establishes a new benefit and modifies the severance payment regulations to exclude this new benefit from being calculated as a base wage (i.e. prevent the benefit from being incorporated into the final severance payment amount), the vested rights of workers cannot be said to have been derogated so long as the total amount of payment did not change, and hence the modification is not an unfavorable one against workers.[23]

ii) If multiple components impacting the working conditions of workers are modified at once, even if only a part is unfavorably modified against the worker and other modified parts are in fact advantageous, whether the modification would be considered as unfavorable to workers is assessed by considering all modifications as

21 Supreme Court 92Da28556 (1994. 6. 24.)
22 Supreme Court 98Du6647 (1999. 6. 22.)
23 Supreme Court 96Da1726 (1997. 8. 26.)

a whole.[24] For example, even if the rate of severance pay is generally decreased and is in itself an unfavorable modification, other factors related to the severance payment scheme may have been favorably modified; hence, the determination of whether the modification to the provisions governing severance payments is unfavorable or not needs to consider the totality of the circumstances.

If it is difficult to assess whether a modification to the rules of employment is generally favorable to workers, and if interests between workers clash as a result of the modification, this modification will be deemed as being unfavorable to workers; whether the modification will be valid or not is determined according to the will of the entire workers' population.[25]

As the determination of whether a modification to the rules of employment is valid should be made at of the time of modification;[26] changed circumstances that arise after the modification are not taken into consideration.

For example, if the rules of employment are modified so that the rate of severance pay is lowered but the scope of wages that would be calculated in the calculation of the total severance pay (i.e. base wages) is expanded, and as a result at the moment of modification employees with shorter years of service are advantaged while those with longer years of service are relatively disadvantaged, this modification should be considered to be unfavorable to the workers as a whole. This determination remains the same even if a new category of wages is established to supplement base wages, resulting in higher severance payments to retirees than prior to the modification.[27] However, case

---

24 Supreme Court 84DaKa414 (1984. 11. 13.), Supreme Court 94Da18072 (1995. 3. 10.), Supreme Court 96Da1726 (1997. 8. 26.), Supreme Court 99Da45376 (2000. 9. 29.), Supreme Court 99Da9370 (2001. 4. 24.)

25 Supreme Court 93Da1893 (1993. 5. 14.)

26 Supreme Court 96Da1726 (1997. 8. 26.)

27 Supreme Court 96Da1726 (1997. 8. 26.)

law suggests that even if a modification to severance pay regulations is enforced due to change in circumstances without first obtaining the consent of workers, so long as the modified provisions do not violate the vested rights that workers enjoyed prior to the modification they would be considered as valid. Thus, the newly enforced severance pay regulation should be enforced against retiring workers who served the company prior to the modification.[28]

iii) Even if the rules of employment are unfavorably modified, if the relevant modified provisions are reasonable to socially accepted norms to the extent that their legal normality is recognized, the exception is made so that the consent of workers' organizations would not be required.[29]

To determine whether a modification to the rules of employment is reasonable to socially accepted norms, the following factors must be considered in their totality: the extent of disadvantage suffered by the worker due to the modification; the extent of the need by the employer to modify the rules; the reasonability of the content of the modified the rules of employment; the degree to which other working conditions have been improved; the process of negotiations with the union; the response from unions or other workers; and the general circumstances within the country.[30] A strong caveat would be that, as a principle, the recognition of the existence of reasonability to social accepted norms is given only if strict conditions are satisfied.

If there were previously no regulations regarding retirement age and such a regulation is to be established, the employer does not need to obtain the consent of his/her workers so long as the content of the

---

28 Supreme Court 96Da1726 (1997. 8. 26.)

29 Supreme Court 2002Da57362 (2004. 7. 22.), Supreme Court 2007Do3037 (2009. 6. 11.), Supreme Court 2009Da32362 (2010. 1. 28.)

30 Supreme Court 87DaKa2853 (1988. 5. 10.), Supreme Court 99Da45376 (2000. 9. 29.), Supreme Court 99Da70846 (2001. 1. 5.), Supreme Court 2002Da23185, 23192 (2004. 5. 14.)

provision (nature, type of work done in the workplace, etc.) is seen as being reasonable to socially accepted norms. In general, designating a retirement age between 55 and 60 would likely be recognized as being reasonable to socially accepted norms.[31] However, if the situation before the establishment of the retirement age in the rules of employment was that workers were free to work beyond this age, and this became limited post-establishment in that the same workers would now have to undergo evaluation in order to continue working, the employer would need the consent from the workers via a collective decision-making process.[32]

Another situation where a modification would be considered as being reasonable to socially accepted norms is when a reason for dismissal is newly established where it was previously not stipulated in the rules of employment, if the new reason for dismissal is one that, considering the regulatory system in the rules of employment, would have been justified to be included in the original list of reasons for dismissal in the first place yet has been omitted until that point. As such, the new reason for dismissal would be recognized as supplementing the original list.[33]

A situation where a modification without the consent of the workers' organization would not be considered as being reasonable to socially accepted norms is when an employer attempts to unfavorably modify provisions regarding severance pay (i.e. subtract certain categories from being included when calculating base pay), even if the resulting severance payment amount would significantly exceed the amount mandated in the LSA and the new provisions would be consistent with industry standards.[34]

---

31 Supreme Court 78Da1046 (1978. 9. 12.)
32 Supreme Court 96Da2507 (1997. 5. 16.)
33 Supreme Court 87DaKa2853 (1988. 5. 10.)
34 Supreme Court 99Da45376 (2000. 9. 29.)

A final example of a situation where a modification would be considered as being reasonable to socially accepted norms is when the retirement age and base wages are both increased but the rate of severance payment is lowered at the time of a corporate merger. This modification was justified due to the fact that there was significant need for a unified severance payment regulation and other working conditions were improved, such as the retirement age being extended by ten years, thereby mitigating the negative effects brought about by the lowering in the rate of severance pay.[35]

2) The Subject of Consent

The employer must obtain the consent of a trade union if there is such a trade union composed of the majority of the workers in his/her workplace, or otherwise obtain the consent of the majority of workers if there is no such trade union.[36] The consent that must be supplied by the trade union representative cannot be substituted by individual union members, unless there is a recognized special circumstance that would limit the former's capacity to represent the union.

Here, "workers" indicates workers' organizations that have been subject to pre-existing working conditions or rules of employment. In other words, "workers" means workers or trade unions composed of the majority of workers who have established labor relations with the employer prior to the modification of the rules. However, if an employer attempts to impose additional modifications to a set of rules of employment that has already been effectively modified without the consent of workers or trade unions, workers or trade unions working for the employer at the point of the additional modification become the "workers" for the purpose of the LSA and hence the subjects from whom consent must be garnered (not the workers who have been

---

35 Supreme Court 99Da70846 (2001. 1. 5.)

36 LSA, Article 94(1) proviso

working at the time of the initial modification).[37]

If workers in a workplace are divided into multiple groups and there exists separate rules of employment for each (or the working conditions for each group are different), only those workers affected by a particular modification to the rules becomes subjects from which consent must be obtained. In other words, workers in groups that are not affected by a particular modification in working conditions do not become subjects of consent; hence consent from all workers in a workplace is not required for modification.

For example, there was a case where the severance pay regulation for a corporation was divided into two parts—one for regular employees and one for service employees—and the employer attempted to modify this regulation unfavorably to both regular and service employees. Even if the corporation was successful in obtaining the consent of over 85% of its service employees, if it was not able to obtain the consent from the majority of its regular employees the modification would only be valid as applied to service employees (and not against regular employees who had been working at the time of the modification).[38]

In cases where a modification to the rules of employment is directly unfavorable only to certain workers' organizations yet it is anticipated that the unfavorable rules will be implemented against other workers' groups in the future, the groups that may potentially be affected by the modification also become subjects from which consent must be obtained.[39]

3) The Procedure of Obtaining Consent

In order to unfavorably modify the rules of employment, the employer must obtain the consent of a trade union, if there is such a trade

---

37 Supreme Court 93Da8870 (1995. 4. 21.)

38 Supreme Court 90DaKa19647 (1990. 12. 7.), Supreme Court 90Da6170 (1991. 1. 15.), Supreme Court 90Da15952, 15969, 15976 (1991. 2. 12.)

39 Supreme Court 2009Du2238 (2009. 5. 28.), Supreme Court 2009Da49377 (2009. 11. 12.)

union composed of the majority of the workers in his/her workplace, or otherwise obtain the consent of the majority of workers if there is no such trade union. In the latter case, the non-represented workers must provide this consent via a "conference method." So long as such consent is provided, there is no need to obtain consent from individual workers to have the modification to the rules of employment be considered valid.[40]

This "conference method" does not necessarily have to take the form in which all union members (in the case of trade unions) or all workers in a business or workplace (in the case of non-represented businesses) gather at a single place in a single time frame. The method may also include arrangements where workers or union members of separate organizations or units in a single business or workplace gather separately and exchange opinions while being free from the intervention or interference of the employer. The conference method may also include arrangements where individuals who were chosen to be workers' representatives via general trade union meetings or Council of Delegates meetings are given the authority to provide such consent on their workers' behalf.[41]

Here, "intervention or interference of the employer" refers to situations where the employer pressures the workers via express or implied means to provide consent, to the extent that the capacity of the workers to make autonomous and collective decisions becomes inhibited. If the employer merely explains and advertises the contents of the proposed modification(s) to the rules of employment to his/her workers, it cannot be said that the employer has exerted unjust intervention or interference.[42] However, the following methods do

---

40 Supreme Court 91Da31753 (1992. 11. 24.), Supreme Court 93Da46841 (1994. 5. 24.), Supreme Court 2001Da18322 (2003. 11. 14.), Supreme Court 2009Da32362 (2010. 1. 28.)

41 Supreme Court 91Da25055 (1992. 2. 25.), Supreme Court 92Da39778 (1993. 1. 15.), Supreme Court 93Da17898 (1993. 8. 24.)

42 Supreme Court 2001Da18322 (2003. 11. 14.), Supreme Court 2009Da32362 (2010. 1. 28.)

not qualify as being valid provisions of worker consent: the employer explaining the purpose and necessity of the modification to the rules of employment via writing and having workers sign consent forms;[43] or the employer having workers pass around the modification proposal and subsequently requesting them to provide written consent.

As consent needs to be obtained through active means that at least takes the form of a conference, implied consent cannot be assumed to have been provided from the mere fact that trade unions or workers failed to object after being notified of the changes to the rules of employment, or from the fact that a worker failed to object to or defer from receiving severance pay under a scheme that has been invalidly modified.[44]

4) The Timing of Consent

As a principle, a worker or trade union's consent to unfavorable modifications to the rules of employment must be obtained prior to the implementation of the modified rules. According to case law, however, it is permissible to obtain this consent after the implementation has occurred. Such consent provided after the fact is then applied retroactively to the moment that the unfavorable modification has been implemented, thereby confirming the modification.[45]

In such cases where consent is provided retroactively, an expression of consent to such a measure must be made by the subject of consent, which in this case would be workers employed at the time of consent, or the trade union that is comprised of the majority of these workers. Case law recognizes that the act of entering into collective agreements

43 Supreme Court 2001Da18322 (2003. 11. 14.)

44 Supreme Court 91Da17542 (1991. 9. 24.), Supreme Court 92Da49324 (1993. 1. 26.), Supreme Court 99Da45376 (2000. 9. 29.)

45 Supreme Court 91Da34073 (1992. 7. 24.), Supreme Court 91Da31753 (1992. 11. 24.), Supreme Court 92Da52115 (1993. 3. 23.), Supreme Court 96Da6967 (1997. 8. 22.)

provides such retroactive consent to unfavorable modifications to the rules of employment, irrespective of whether workers or unions were actually aware of the invalidity of the rules.[46]

Such expressions of retroactive consent, like prior consent, must be provided via a collective decision making process on the part of the workers.

5) The Effect of Consent

Prior consent has the effect of bestowing validity to unfavorably modified rules of employment, ensuring that they may be validly implemented and applied from that point onwards.

In case consent has been provided to the unfavorably modified rules of employment after the latter has been implemented, there are two possible ways this consent may take effect. The first is for the consent to be applied retroactively to the moment where the unfavorable modification has taken place initially. The second is for the consent to be effective at the moment that it is actually given, in which case the unfavorable modification will be valid only from the point that the consent has been provided. Case law recognizes that consent after modification has the former effect.[47] However, this retroactive consent does not apply to workers who have retired from the business before it has been provided.[48]

6) The Effect of Violating the Procedure of Obtaining Consent

i) The Relative Invalidity of Modifications to the Rules of Employment

If an employer fails to obtain consent from the workers via collective decision making process when modifying the rules of employment in a manner unfavorable to his/her workers, this modification is invalid

---

46 Supreme Court 95Da34316 (1997. 6. 10.)

47 Supreme Court 91Da25055 (1992. 2. 25.)

48 Supreme Court 91Da34073 (1992. 7. 24.), Supreme Court 92Da52115 (1993. 3. 23.)

unless it is reasonable to socially accepted norms. Therefore, workers who have been subject to the rules prior to the modification remain subject to the unmodified rules.

However, the modified rules of employment remain formally changed even if the unfavorable modification failed to receive the consent of workers. As such, workers who join the business after the modification are subject to the modified rules.[49] Furthermore, there are situations where a particular modification has been unfavorable to workers at the time of the revision, yet due to changing circumstances the modification no longer derogates the vested rights of workers. In such situations, the modified rules of employment become validly applicable to the workers who did not provide their consent and hence become the current, legally recognized rules of employment of that business.[50]

ii) Exclusion of Individual Consent
If an employer fails to obtain consent from the workers via collective decision making process when modifying the rules of employment in a manner unfavorable to his/her workers, this modification is not effective against all existing workers. Even if an individual worker has provided his/her consent to the modification, this does not mean that the unfavorable rules apply to him/her on an individual basis.[51]

iii) The Indivisibility of Invalid Employment Condition Items
Let us take a situation where a working condition (e.g. severance payment) is composed of several items that relate to or compensate for each other (e.g. severance pay rate and base wages). If one of these items

---

49 Supreme Court 92Da39778 (1993. 1. 15.), Supreme Court 94Da30638 (1996. 4. 26.), Supreme Court 96Da3241 (1996. 9. 10.), Supreme Court 95Da53188 (1996. 10. 15.), Supreme Court 95Da32631 (1996. 12. 23.), Supreme Court 96Da1726 (1997. 8. 26.), Supreme Court 99Da30473 (1999. 11. 12.)

50 Supreme Court 96Da1726 (1997. 8. 26.)

51 Supreme Court 91Da3031 (1991. 3. 27.), Supreme Court 91Da38174 (1992. 12. 8.)

(e.g. severance pay rate) is unfavorably modified while another item (e.g. base wages) is favorably modified, this modification, taken as a whole, would be considered as an unfavorable modification to the working conditions.

In this situation, when the courts say that the modification to the working condition in question (i.e. the severance payment) is invalid due to the employer's failure to obtain the consent of his/her workers' organizations, the courts do not mean that only the unfavorably modified item is invalid (i.e. the severance pay rate) while the favorably modified item remains valid (i.e. the base wage); they mean that all items that relate to or compensate for each other (i.e. both severance pay rate and base wages) are invalid.[52]

Also, if a modification to severance pay regulation is invalid due to the reasons outlined above, this would mean that the entire severance pay regulation has also become invalid. As such, any modifications to the severance pay regulation (including changes to severance pay rates or base wages) after this initial modification would also be deemed invalid, as long as the subsequent modification is not a confirmation that makes previously invalid modifications valid, or the subsequent modification changes the regulation on a level entirely separate from the original to the extent that it can be said that a new severance pay regulation has been established.[53]

iv) Criminal Liability for Violations
Employers who have unfavorably modified the rules of employment yet failed to obtain the consent of workers are subject to criminal liability.[54]

---

52 Supreme Court 94Da18072 (1995. 3. 10.)
53 Supreme Court 94Da18072 (1995. 3. 10.)
54 LSA, Article 114(1)

III. The Legal Effects of the Rules of Employment

A. The Legal Effects and Authority

All rules of employment that have been validly prepared or modified by the employer (this is not limited to rules made by employers who possess the duty to prepare and report the rules of employment) obtain the status of being an objective "legal norm" that determines the labor relations between the workers and employers.[55]

1) Relationship with Legislative Acts and Collective Agreements

"Rules of employment shall not conflict with any Acts and subordinate statutes, or a collective agreement applicable to the business or workplace concerned."[56] Any rules of employment that conflict with Acts or collective agreements are invalid. "The Minister of Employment and Labor may give an order to modify any part of the rules which conflict with any Acts and subordinate statutes or the collective agreement concerned."[57]

In addition, any part of the rules of employment or a labor contract that violates standards concerning working conditions and other treatment of workers as prescribed in a collective agreement shall be null and void, and such parts are supplemented by relevant standards in the collective agreement.[58]

It is not disputed that parts of rules of employment that are more unfavorable to workers than the corresponding provisions stipulated in the collective agreement are not applied, as per Article 33(2) of the Union Act.[59] However, whether parts of the rules of employment

---

55 Supreme Court 77Da355 (1977. 7. 26.), Supreme Court 77Da1378 (1977. 12. 27.)

56 LSA, Article 96(1); Trade Union and Labor Relations Adjustment Act, Article 33(1)

57 LSA, Article 114(2)

58 Trade Union and Labor Relations Adjustment Act, Article 33(2)

59 Trade Union and Labor Relations Adjustment Act

that are more favorable to workers than the corresponding provisions stipulated in the collective agreement would be applied is an unsettled topic. The literature is divided between those arguing that such favorable parts should not be applied just like the case with unfavorable parts, and those arguing that favorable parts should indeed be applied. Case law on this topic suggests that the former argument (i.e. the non-recognition of favorable provisions in the rules of employment) is acknowledged by the courts, at least in a case where the situation was that parts of the rules were more favorable to workers than in a collective agreement that was subsequently entered into.[60]

If matters determined by the rules of employment are not dealt with in any Acts or collective agreements, the rules determine the relevant working conditions on a supplemental basis.

2) Relationship with Employment Contracts

While there is no case law on this topic, academic literature generally agrees that rules of employment is a legal norm that generally applies to workers and employers, and while it does not precede Acts or collective agreements in authority, it does precede that of individual employment contracts. As such, if an employment contract includes any terms or conditions of employment which fail to meet the standards of labor as provided for in the rules of employment, such part shall be null and void. In this case, the invalidated part shall be governed by the standards provided for in the rules of employment.[61]

Should working conditions agreed upon in an employment contract be more advantageous to the worker than is designated by the rules of employment, the employment contract precedes the rules. If the employment contract makes determinations on

---

60 Supreme Court 92Da51341 (1993. 3. 23.), Supreme Court 2000Da30516 (2001. 1. 19.), Supreme Court 2002Du9063 (2002. 12. 27.), Supreme Court 2004Da4683 (2006. 4. 27.)

61 LSA, Article 97

matters not covered in the rules of employment, the details of that worker's working conditions are supplemented by the contents of the employment contract. However, the labor relationship between the worker and the employer is determined by rules of employment, unless special provisions have been agreed upon (e.g. when entering into the employment contract, both parties agree to enforce provisions that differ from the rules of employment).[62]

B. The Scope of Workers Affected by Modifications to the Rules of Employment

Any preparations or modifications to the rules of employment made validly by the employer are effective only as to workers who have already been working for the employer at the moment of implementation, or against workers who started to work after this point.[63] That being said, the modified rules do not affect workers who have already retired at the point of implementation.

If an unfavorable modification to the rules of employment has successfully been implemented with the consent of a majority of the workers, this modification will be effective even against those workers who did not provide their consent during the procedure.

C. When the Rules of Employment Become Effective

1) Timing the Enforcement of the Rules of Employment
If the employer embeds in the prepared or modified rules of employment a provision that designates a "date of enforcement,"

---

62 Supreme Court 97Da53496 (1999. 1. 26.)
63 Supreme Court 97Da53496 (1999. 1. 26.)

and succeeds in securing the conditions that would make such rules valid, the new rules obtain the status of a legal norm from that date onwards. If no such date has been designated, by principle the rules of employment gain the status of a legal norm from the moment that the entire process of validly preparing or modifying the rules is completed.

2) Timing the Application of the Rules of Employment

Matters determined by the rules of employment are in principle applicable from the moment the preparation or modification of the rules has been completed onwards. However, even if the worker or union has provided consent to unfavorable modifications to the rules of employment, the vested rights of workers cannot be recklessly infringed upon retroactively, and the unmodified version of the rules must be applied to the extent that the above vested rights are violated.[64]

In cases where certain provisions in the rules of employment are advantageous to workers, it is permissible to retroactively apply those provisions to a point in time prior to the enforcement date of the rules.[65] It is also possible to retroactively apply provisions in the prepared or modified rules of employment in a manner unfavorable to workers, given that workers or trade unions consisting of the majority of the workers provide valid consent to the employer to do so.

---

64 Supreme Court 89DaKa15939 (1990. 11. 27.), Supreme Court 90DaKa24311 (1990. 12. 26.), Supreme Court 95Da32631 (1996. 12. 23.), Supreme Court 96Da45399 (1997. 7. 11.)

65 Supreme Court 93Da30181 (1994. 5. 10.)

Chapter 8

Dismissals

I. The Legal Regulation of Dismissals and Disciplinary Measures

A. The Concept of Dismissals

1) The Concept and Legal Characteristic of Dismissals

Dismissals are unilateral expressions of intent by the employer notifying the worker that the labor relationship is to be terminated, thereby discontinuing the employment contract. The LSA[1] contains many provisions that places limitations on dismissals, in order to provide adequate protection to the worker's opportunity to work.[2]

The employer's expression of intent to dismiss becomes effective upon the receipt of the notification by the worker. The LSA requires the employer to notify the worker "in writing" of the reasons for and the time of the dismissal in order for the dismissal to become effective.[3] This is to prevent and resolve disputes regarding dismissals.

The written notice of dismissal must inform the worker of the specific reasons behind the disposition from the perspective of the

---

1 Labor Standards Act
2 LSA, Articles 23 and 27
3 Ibid., Article 27

worker. Especially in the case of disciplinary dismissals, the actual reason of the dismissal, including descriptions of specific facts or violations, must be included in the notification. In a related case, the Supreme Court ruled that even if the employer has provided the worker with a written notification containing the reason of the dismissal, merely "stating the provision of the rules of employment violated by the worker" is not enough to satisfy the written notification requirement contained in Article 27 of the LSA; the employer must also state the "specific facts of violations by the worker."[4]

2) Distinctions between Dismissals and Similar Dispositions

Dismissals subject to the regulations of the LSA limiting dismissals include all instances where the labor relationship is terminated by the unilateral expression of the employer's intention. Specifically, the following situations have been subjects of dispute.

i) Natural Retirements

Even if the employer has stipulated the grounds for natural retirement in the rules of employment or collective agreement and distinguished this from disciplinary dismissals, if this "retirement" is unilaterally imposed on the worker irrespective of his/her intention, this disposition will be recognized as a dismissal under Article 23(1) of the LSA. Therefore, the labor relationship is terminated only upon the expression of the intent to dismiss the worker by the employer. Exceptions to this rule would be when labor relations are automatically terminated due to death, reaching the retirement age, or the expiration of the employment contract; all of which would not be considered dismissals.[5]

For example, a worker is sometimes "naturally retired" if s/he fails

---

4 Supreme Court 2011Da42324 (2011. 10. 27.)
5 Supreme Court 92Da54210 (1993. 10. 26.), Supreme Court 2007Du2067 (2007. 10. 25.)

to secure a position for a certain period after being removed from his/ her previous position. Since natural retirement dispositions like this example terminates the labor relationship with the worker regardless of the latter's intent via unilateral intent of the employer, this would in effect be considered as a dismissal.[6]

ii) Voluntary Dismissals, Honorary Resignations
   (1) Resignation Due to Official Suggestion and Voluntary Dismissal
"Resignation due to official suggestion" refers to a situation where the employer suggests that the worker resign, and the worker voluntarily does so by submitting his/her letter of resignation. "Voluntary dismissals" refers to a situation where the worker voluntarily submits his/her letter of resignation and the employer accepts the resignation. Both these situations are distinguished from dismissals, as the employment contract is terminated by mutual agreement. In principle, provisions in the LSA regarding dismissals do not apply to mutually agreed terminations.[7]

   (2) Resignations
A voluntary resignation by the worker is a termination of the labor relationship by the unilateral communication of intent by the worker, and is distinguished from dismissals made by employers.[8] Therefore, the employment contract is effectively terminated if one month has passed since the receipt of the letter of resignation by the employer, or, if remuneration has been fixed on a set and regular periodical basis, after one full period has elapsed from the date of completion of the current period.[9]

---

6 Supreme Court 2003Du6665 (2004. 10. 28.)

7 Supreme Court 2002Da60528 (2003. 4. 11.), Supreme Court 2005Du7914 (2006. 2. 24.)

8 Supreme Court 99Du8657 (2000. 9. 5.), Supreme Court 2005Du7914 (2006. 2. 24.)

9 Civil Act, Article 660(2) and (3)

Once the notice of intent to resign has been received by the employer, the worker cannot retract this notice without the consent of the employer even if the time period stipulated in Articles 660(2) and (3) of the Civil Act has yet to expire.[10] The notice of rescission of the employment contract communicated by the employer after s/he has received the worker's notice of intent to resign (thereby making the termination of the employment contract effective) is only a constructive notification and is not recognized as a dismissal.[11] Rules of employment that designates the period after which the resignation becomes effective after the worker submits his/her letter of resignation to be shorter than is stipulated under Articles 660(2) and (3) of the Civil Act is valid. In other words, the employment contract is effectively terminated after the period designated in the rules of employment expires.[12]

However, in situations where the worker does not unilaterally resign like the above but the employment contract is terminated by mutual agreement, the termination becomes effective at the moment the employer approves the resignation and notifies the worker of this fact. Therefore, in principle, the worker may withdraw his/her intent to resign before s/he receives the above notification from the employer. However, if special circumstances are recognized where the withdrawal of the letter of resignation by the worker would violate the principle of good faith such as inflicting unexpected damage to the employer, this withdrawal is not permitted. Furthermore, once the worker is notified that his/her letter of resignation has been processed and approved, s/he can no longer retract the letter.[13]

---

10 Supreme Court 99Du8657 (2000. 9. 5.)

11 Supreme Court 95Nu7765 (1996. 7. 30.)

12 Supreme Court 96Nu5087 (1997. 7. 8.)

13 Supreme Court 94Da14629 (1994. 8. 9.), Supreme Court 99Du8657 (2000. 9. 5.)

(3) De Facto Dismissals

There are situations where workers involuntarily submit letters of resignation and the employers get it processed due to the employers saying something along the lines of "we will dismiss you if you do not submit a letter of resignation." These cases may take the form of a "resignation due to official suggestion" or a "voluntary dismissal," but they are in fact recognized as dismissals.[14] This is because the employer coerced the worker to submit the letter of resignation.

There are also situations where the employer receives a resignation en bloc from the worker, and resigns the latter through the process of "selectively processing" a part of the resignation. This is also a de facto dismissal.[15] This is because the employer forced the worker to draft and submit his/her letter of resignation.

(4) Honorary Resignations

Honorary resignations refer to when the worker files a request for honorary resignation, which the employer evaluates based on certain criteria and subsequently issues his/her approval. The labor relationship is terminated by mutual agreement through this process.[16] Once this agreement has been made, one party may not unilaterally withdraw his/her expression of intent. Honorary resignations only come into effect on the "date of the honorary resignation."[17]

iii) Conditional Dispositions of Dismissal

Conditional dispositions of dismissal refer to situations where a worker receives the disposition of disciplinary dismissal due to the

---

14 Supreme Court 87DaKa1280 (1988. 4. 25.), Supreme Court 92Da3809 (1992. 7. 10.), Supreme Court 93Nu16185 (1994. 4. 29.), Supreme Court 2001Du11076 (2002. 6. 14.), Supreme Court 2005Da38270 (2005. 11. 25.)

15 Supreme Court 90Da11554 (1991. 7. 12.), Supreme Court 92Da3670 (1992. 5. 26.)

16 Supreme Court 98Da42172 (2000. 7. 7.), Supreme Court 2003Da1632 (2003. 6. 27.)

17 Supreme Court 2000Da60890 (2002. 8. 23.)

fact that s/he did not submit his/her letter of resignation within a certain period after receiving a notice of disciplinary disposition. The Supreme Court ruled that once it is determined that the conditional disposition of dismissal is invalid on either substantial or procedural grounds, the disposition of voluntary dismissal due to the worker's submission of the letter of resignation also becomes invalid.[18]

iv) Refusing to Renew the Employment Contract

In principle, once the employment contract expires (for those that have designated periods), the employment contractual relationship ends as well. However, even for workers under a fixed-term contract, if the situation is that the renewal of the contract has been repeated for a long time to the extent that the term has become a mere formality, the employment contract is recognized to not be subject to a contract period. In such situations, the refusal to renew the employment contract is constructively recognized as a dismissal, and hence is invalid if no justifiable reason exists.[19]

B. Legal Regulations Regarding Dismissals

1) Legal Regulations Depending on the Nature of the Employment Contract

i) Non-Fixed Term Employment Contracts

(1) The Principle of Placing Restrictions on Dismissals

"If no period for the employment has been fixed by the parties in the employment contract, either party may give notice to the other party of his/her intention to voluntarily terminate the contract at any time. The notice of intention to terminate becomes effective after one

---

18 Supreme Court 95Nu1422 (1995. 11. 14.)
19 Supreme Court 98Du625 (1998. 5. 29.), Supreme Court 2005Du5673 (2006. 2. 24.)

month has elapsed from the date of receipt by the other party of such notice."[20] However, the LSA recognizes an exception to the above rule for when the employer terminates the employment contract, which is considered to be a dismissal. In such cases, the LSA limits dismissals by stipulating causes and procedures required for a valid dismissal, and by establishing the advance notice of dismissal procedure.

(2) Reasons and Procedures of Dismissal

An employer shall not, without justifiable cause, dismiss workers.[21] Both the cause and procedure of the dismissal must be justifiable.

(3) The Advance Notice of Dismissal Procedure

"When an employer intends to dismiss a worker, s/he shall give the worker a notice of dismissal at least 30 days in advance of such dismissal, and, if the employer fails to give such advance notice, s/he shall pay that worker ordinary wages for not less than 30 days."[22] "When an employer has provided advance notice of dismissal by notifying the worker in writing of the reasons for and the time of the dismissal, the written notice of the reasons for and the time of dismissal is deemed to have been communicated at the moment of dismissal."[23] A worker may be dismissed immediately without advance notice in the following situations: where a natural disaster, calamity or other unavoidable circumstances prevent the continuance of the business of the employer or where the worker has caused a considerable hindrance to the business or inflicted any damage to the property on purpose and it falls under any cause determined by the Ordinance of the Ministry of Employment and Labor.[24]

---

20 Civil Act, Article 660(1) and (2)

21 LSA, Article 23(1)

22 Ibid., Article 26

23 Ibid., Article 27(3)

24 Ibid., Article 26 proviso

A point to keep in mind is that even if the advance notice of dismissal has been given and 30 days' worth of ordinary wages have been paid, if there is no justifiable cause for the dismissal, the employer's disposition of dismissal does not become effective.

ii) Fixed-Term Employment Contracts
  (1) Principles Governing Fixed-Term Employment
The Act on the Protection of Fixed-Term and Part-Time Workers limits fixed-term employment contracts to a period not exceeding two years.[25] However, "where the period required to complete a project or a particular task is specified, the contract term may exceed two years."[26] "Where any employer hires a fixed-term worker for more than two years despite the fact that the exceptions described above do not exist or cease to exist, such fixed-term worker shall be deemed to have entered into a non-fixed term employment contract."[27]

---

25 Article 4 (Employment of Fixed-Term Workers)
  (1) Any employer may hire a fixed-term worker for a period not exceeding two years (where his/her fixed-term employment contract is repetitively renewed, the total period of his/her continuous employment shall not exceed two years). Provided that a fixed-term worker falls under any of the following subparagraphs, any employer may hire such worker for more than two years:
    1. Where the period required to complete a project or particular task is specified;
    2. Where a fixed-term worker is needed to fill a vacancy arising from a worker's temporary suspension from duty or dispatch until the worker returns to work;
    3. Where the period required for a worker to complete his/her schoolwork or vocational training is specified;
    4. Where an employer awards an employment contract with a senior citizen as defined in subparagraph 1 of Article 2 of the Employment Promotion for the Aged Act;
    5. Where the job requires professional knowledge and skills or is offered as part of the government's welfare or unemployment measures, as prescribed by Presidential Decree;
    6. Where any reasonable grounds exist equivalent to those mentioned in subparagraphs 1 through 5, as prescribed by Presidential Decree.
  (2) Where any employer hires a fixed-term worker for more than two years although those grounds under the proviso to paragraph (1) do not exist or cease to exist, such fixed-term worker shall be deemed a worker subject to a non-fixed-term employment contract.
26 Act on the Protection of Fixed-Term and Part-Time Workers, Article 4(1) proviso
27 Ibid., Article 4(2)

Also, "If the employee continues to render services after the expiration of the agreed period, and the employer has not raised any objection thereto within a reasonable period, their employment contract will be deemed to have been renewed on the same terms."[28]

Even if a particular employment contract sets forth a fixed term, if the situation is that the renewal of the contract has been repeated for a long period of time, to the extent that the term has become a mere formality, the employment contract is recognized as having no fixed term.[29] In order to have the courts recognize the above contract as having no fixed term that is contrary to the terms of the employment contract, various circumstances must be taken comprehensively into account. Such circumstances include the content of the employment contract, the motivation and process in entering into the contract, the purpose of stipulating a fixed term, the bona fide intentions of the parties, the industry practice when entering into the same type of contract, and regulations that protect workers.[30]

Among fixed-term employment contracts, there exist those that require the renewal process to be completed prior to the expiration of the contract. If the contract is not renewed by that point, the employment contract expires and the worker is automatically terminated. A Supreme Court case regarding such a contract ruled that just because a contract has been renewed repeatedly without having been rejected, and that the contract includes an automatic renewal provision, it does not mean that workers under this contract have the same status as workers under non-fixed-term contracts.[31]

If a worker has maintained his labor relations with an employer beyond the retirement age with the consent of the employer and

28 Supreme Court 97Nu14132 (1998. 11. 27.); Civil Act, Article 662(1)
29 Supreme Court 2004Da29736 (2006. 12. 7.)
30 Supreme Court 98Du625 (1998. 5. 29.)
31 Supreme Court 97Da42489 (1998. 1. 23.)

without a designated term, the employer must have justifiable cause as per Article 23(1) of the LSA in order to dismiss that worker.[32] In the absence of special circumstances, an employer may not dismiss a worker due solely to the fact that s/he has exceeded the retirement age or is of old age.

(2) The Causes and Procedures of Dismissal

According to the LSA, an employer shall not dismiss workers without justifiable cause, regardless of whether the employment is based on a fixed- or non-fixed-term contract.[33] Even if the term is fixed, the employer must possess "justifiable cause" in both grounds and procedure that goes beyond "unavoidable cause" in order to dismiss a worker during the contract term.[34] If the unavoidable cause arises out of the negligence of the employer, s/he is liable for damages incurred by the worker.[35]

(3) The Advance Notice of Dismissal Procedure

Even in the case of fixed-term employment contracts, in principle the employer must provide an advance notice of dismissal when dismissing a worker.

However, there are exceptions to this rule for workers in the following situations: a worker who is employed for a period not exceeding two months; a worker who has been employed for less than six months as a monthly paid worker; a worker who is employed for seasonal work for a period not exceeding six months.[36] An employer may immediately dismiss the above workers without providing

---

32 Supreme Court 2002Du12809 (2003. 12. 12.)

33 LSA, Article 23(1)

34 Regarding layoffs (or dismissal for managerial reasons, *see* Supreme Court 70Da523, 524 (1970. 5. 26.).

35 Civil Act, Article 661 proviso

36 LSA, Articles 35.2 through 4

advance notice of dismissal.

The requirement to provide advance notice of dismissal applies even to employers who manage a business or workplace that usually employs fewer than four workers.[37]

2) Regulations Depending on the Cause of the Dismissal (Ordinary Dismissal, Disciplinary Dismissal, Layoffs)

The employer may dismiss a worker for causes separate from disciplinary reasons (i.e. ordinary dismissal), or dismiss a worker for disciplinary reasons by going through disciplinary proceedings (i.e. disciplinary dismissal). Also, the employer may dismiss a worker as part of its policy of reducing personnel for managerial reasons (so-called "layoff" or "dismissal for managerial reasons").

Whatever the reason for the dismissal, there must be a justifiable cause as defined under Article 23(1) of the LSA, and dismissal for managerial reasons (i.e. layoffs) must especially satisfy the conditions laid out in Article 24 of the LSA.

C. Special Provisions Regarding Restrictions on Dismissals

1) Special Restrictions Regarding Timing of Dismissals (Restrictions on Dismissals during Leaves of Absence)

An employer shall not dismiss a worker during a period of suspension of work for medical treatment of an occupational injury or disease and within 30 days immediately thereafter, and any woman before and after childbirth shall not be dismissed during her 90-day maternity leave and for 30 days immediately thereafter.[38] Case law states, however, that the following suspension situations are not subject to

---

37 Supreme Court 2002Do1216 (2002. 5. 10.)

38 LSA, Articles 74(1) and 23(2)

this restriction stipulated by the LSA: "when the worker does not take leave and reports to work despite suffering from an industrial accident and is receiving treatment," and "when it is not recognized that the worker needs to take leave for the treatment of the industrial accident."[39]

However, the employer may dismiss the worker where s/he has paid a lump-sum compensation for occupational injuries, or where the employer is unable to continue to conduct his/her business.[40]

2) Special Restrictions from Other Acts Regarding Cause of Dismissal

Employers may not dismiss or impose other unfavorable treatment on a worker on grounds that s/he has joined or intends to join a trade union, attempted to organize a trade union, or performed any other lawful act for the operation of a trade union.[41] Employers may also not dismiss workers on the grounds that they have participated in justifiable collective activities, reported to or testified before the Labor Relations Commission, or presented evidence to a relevant administrative agency.[42] Also, the employer shall not dismiss or treat a worker unfairly for reporting to the Minister of Employment and Labor or a labor inspector of any violation of the LSA or the Enforcement Decree of the LSA in his/her business or workplace.[43]

According to the Equal Employment Opportunity and Work-Family Balance Assistance Act, an employer may not discriminate against a worker on grounds of gender in dismissing his/her workers, and cannot conclude employment contracts that stipulates marriage,

---

39 Supreme Court 2009Da63205 (2011. 11. 10.)

40 LSA, Article 23(2) proviso

41 Trade Union and Labor Relations Adjustment Act, Article 81(1)

42 Ibid., Article 81(5)

43 LSA, Article 104(2)

pregnancy or childbirth of female workers as grounds for retirement.[44] An employer also cannot dismiss or take any other disadvantageous measures against a worker on account of temporary retirement for childcare or dismiss the relevant worker during the period of temporary retirement for childcare.[45] The cause for dismissals is also indirectly limited in the LSA as it stipulates that "an employer shall neither discriminate against workers on the basis of gender, nor take discriminatory action in relation to terms and conditions of employment on the grounds of nationality, religion, or social status."[46]

In addition, a ship-owner shall not dismiss a seafarer worker during a period of suspension of work for medical treatment of an occupational injury or disease and within 30 days immediately thereafter.[47]

3) Penalties for Violations of the Dismissal Restriction Period and Unfair Dismissal

The LSA subjects employers to criminal liability for violating the dismissal restriction.[48] Such criminal liability is attached when the employer intentionally disregards procedural regulations in order to impose unjustified disciplinary action.

The Labor Relations Commission may impose compulsory performance money not exceeding 20 million won on an employer who fails to comply with an order for remedy (e.g. remedial measures for unjust dismissal) up to two times per year, and up to two years.[49] This is to secure the efficacy of the Labor Relations Commission's order for remedy. The LSA imposes upon people who have failed to comply with an order for remedy imprisonment for not more than one

---

44 Equal Employment Opportunity and Work-Family Balance Assistance Act, Article 11(1) and (2)
45 Ibid., Article 19(3)
46 LSA, Article 6
47 The Seafarers Act, Article 34(2)1
48 LSA, Articles 107 and 23(2)
49 Ibid., Article 33

year or by a fine not exceeding ten million won.[50]

II. Disciplinary Dismissals

A. Justifiable Cause for Disciplinary Dismissals

1) The Justification Requirement
i) The Rules of Employment
In order for an employer to disciplinarily dismiss a worker by citing cause [A] as the reason, [A] must be listed as one of the reasons for disciplinary dismissal in the employment contract, the rules of employment or the collective agreement.[51] If the worker is dismissed for cause [B] (a reason not enumerated in the above documents), the dismissal is invalid.[52]

Even if a particular cause is listed in the rules of employment as a reason for disciplinary dismissal, if the collective agreement determines that only its regulations govern dismissals, the above reason cannot be used as grounds for disciplinary dismissal if it is not also listed in the collective agreement.[53] Furthermore, in such cases where provisions regarding the same disciplinary cause or procedure differ between the collective agreement and the rules of employment, and they come into conflict, the provision in the collective agreement is given precedence. However, if the collective agreement does not specifically impose the above restraint, the rules of employment may define a new cause for disciplinary dismissal not listed in the collective agreement, and impose the measure accordingly.[54] This remains the

---

50 Ibid., Article 111
51 Supreme Court 89DaKa5451 (1990. 4. 27.)
52 Supreme Court 93Da37915 (1993. 11. 9.)
53 Supreme Court 93Da62126 (1994. 6. 14.)
54 Supreme Court 92Da48697 (1993. 4. 27.), Supreme Court 98Du4672 (1999. 3. 26.)

case where the collective agreement only states that its provisions are given priority in implementation vis-à-vis the rules of employment.[55]

If a worker is disciplinarily dismissed for cause [A], the determination of whether the disposition was justifiable or not should only be conducted based on cause [A]. In other words, causes [B] and [C] (which have different substance and characteristics from [A]) should not be factored in when determining the degree of justification in cause [A].[56]

Introducing a cause for disciplinary dismissal that has not been dealt with at the initial disciplinary hearing during the appeals process is not permitted, as this would effectively deprive the worker of the opportunity to appeal this new cause.[57] However, even if circumstances surrounding the disciplinary action cannot be used as direct cause of disciplinary dismissal, they may be introduced to be considered when determining the extent of the penalty to be imposed upon the worker during the original disciplinary hearing or during the appeals process.[58] Even violations that have been settled to be exempt from liability or have passed the date of prescription may be presented for consideration during the penalty calculation process.[59]

ii) Compliance with Relevant Acts

Even if cause [A] is determined by the rules of employment or other documents as being a reason for disciplinary dismissal, that regulation in itself must still be in compliance with relevant laws. Meanwhile, even conflicts within the trade union, if they inflict damages to the corporation, may be valid causes for disciplinary dismissal.[60]

---

55 Supreme Court 94Da37851 (1995. 1.20.)

56 Supreme Court 92Da34933 (1993. 11. 23.)

57 Supreme Court 95Nu6410 (1996. 6. 14.)

58 Supreme Court 2001Du10455 (2002. 5. 28.), Supreme Court 2008Du22211 (2009. 4. 9.)

59 Supreme Court 98Du10424 (1999. 11. 26.)

60 Supreme Court 2001Du10455 (2002. 5. 28.), Supreme Court 2008Du22211 (2009. 4. 9.)

iii) The Cause of Dismissal

Even if cause [A] is included among the causes of disciplinary dismissal enumerated in the rules of employment, which in turn is valid according to the relevant Acts, imposing the most serious form of disciplinary action (i.e. dismissal) may still not be justified. If the goal of the disciplinary action may be attained through softer penalties in light of "the specific circumstances surrounding the dismissal," then dismissing the worker would not be justified.

In order to justify the dismissal of a worker, the heaviest among disciplinary actions, the violation giving rise to the disposition must be "such that continuation of the employment contract would be impossible considering socially accepted norms." Whether a certain violation would satisfy this standard is determined while considering the totality of the circumstances. Factors to be considered are: the purpose and nature of the employer's business, workplace conditions, the position and job description of the relevant worker, the motivation and details of the violating act, the risk that the corporation's order of ranks would be disrupted due to the violating act (and other consideration regarding the potential impacts on the corporation's order), and past work conduct.[61]

If there are multiple causes of disciplinary dismissal, these are considered in relation to the overall cause.[62] The circumstances surrounding the disciplinary dismissal are also considered.[63]

iv) The Principle of Equity

If disciplinary dismissals are given in a manner inconsistent with the principle of equity when multiple workers are subjected to disciplinary measures during the disciplinary measure determination phase,

---

61 Supreme Court 2003Du11858 (2004. 5. 14.), Supreme Court 2005Du11630 (2006. 2. 24.)
62 Supreme Court 97Nu9161 (1997. 12. 9.)
63 Supreme Court 98Da2365 (1998. 5. 22.), Supreme Court 2005Du11630 (2006. 2. 24.)

this would be an abuse of the right to discipline on the part of the employer. However, case law permits an exception to this principle. If the number of workers who become eligible for disciplinary dismissal for the same reason is too large—and dismissing all of them would detriment the employer's conduct of his/her business— the employer can establish a standard of disciplinary action that reduces the disposition that workers with fewer violations would receive. In regard to this, the Supreme Court has ruled that unless there is no rational basis to this standard, or it is determined that this standard was established in order to dismiss a particular worker, the disciplinary action cannot be said to be invalid.[64]

2) Types of Causes of Disciplinary Dismissal
i) Misrepresentations and Omissions of Education and Experience
Previously, case law assessed the justification of dismissals from the perspective of "hypothetical causation." Specifically, if a worker misrepresented or omitted his/her education and experience when he first started with the employer but was later found out, the employer was considered justified in disciplinarily dismissing the worker if the former would not have employed the worker or at least not have employed the worker under the same conditions.

However, recent precedent is recognizing the legal theory that even dismissals for reasons of misrepresentation of experience would need to demonstrate "justifiable cause;"[65] the same standard as with other reasons for dismissal. Therefore, considerations other than hypothetical causation must be considered as a whole. In other words, the determination of whether a violation is such that continuation of the employment contract would be impossible considering socially accepted norms is not conducted by merely examining circumstances

---

64 Supreme Court 96Nu5780 (1997. 10. 28.)
65 LSA, Article 23(1)

surrounding a person's hiring, such as whether the employer would not have entered into the employment contract or not have employed the worker under the same conditions had s/he known of the misrepresentation or omission. Other considerations must be comprehensively examined as well, such as the total length and content of the work done by the worker from the beginning of his/her employment up to the dismissal whether the misrepresentation of education and experience impedes the normal performance of the labor provided by the worker; how the employer came to learn about the misrepresentation of education and experience; the attitude of the worker and the measures taken by the employer after the misrepresentation was disclosed; the impact that the misrepresentation or omission of education or experience had on the maintenance of mutual trust between labor and management and between workers, as well as on the stable management of the business and the maintenance of order.[66]

The fact that a worker has gained employment while concealing or exaggerating his/her educational credentials would be a valid cause for disciplinary dismissal, even if the work done by the worker up to that point has not been impacted due to this fact and s/he has faithfully worked for a significant amount of time.[67]

However, with the existence of special circumstance, such as the fact that the false entry has been made due to a composition error, the fact that the subject of misrepresentation is extremely trivial that to use this as a cause of disciplinary dismissal would not be appropriate considering socially accepted norms,[68] and/or the fact that the subject of misrepresentation was regarding an event or fact that occurred significantly prior to the worker's start with the company,[69]

---

66 Supreme Court 2009Du16763 (2012. 7. 5.)

67 Supreme Court 87DaKa3196 (1989. 3. 14.)

68 Supreme Court 98Du4672 (1999. 3. 26.), Supreme Court 98Da54960 (2000. 6. 23.)

69 Supreme Court 93Da30921 (1993. 10. 8.)

the concealing or exaggeration of educational credentials is not a valid cause for disciplinary dismissal. This is especially true in cases where an employer disciplinarily dismisses a worker who is actively engaged in union activities as retaliation, and the misrepresentation of educational credentials is used as a pretext, making it an unfair labor practice under the Union Act.[70]

If the employer has discovered the misrepresentation or omission, yet has continued to employ the worker after having the latter sign an agreement, the misrepresentation may no longer be a valid cause of disciplinary dismissal.[71]

ii) Undependable Work Conduct such as Absence Without Notice

In the rules of employment or other such documents, there are often provisions that stipulate as causes for disciplinary dismissal. This includes undependable work conduct or absence without notice through clauses such as "absence without notice for more than a certain number of days in a month," or "inadequate work performance or competence." Absent special circumstance, these terms are recognized as valid causes for disciplinary dismissal.[72]

(1) Absence without Notice

If the rules of employment or the code of conduct stipulates that "If a worker must be absent from work due to illness or other unavoidable reasons, the worker must obtain prior permission through the submission of a notice of absence, then even if the worker has received this permission by providing notice orally in person or over the phone, the worker must still submit a notice of absence attached with a statement of reasons." This is due to the fact that an absence is considered in principle an absence without notice if a "notice of

---

70 Trade Union and Labor Relations Adjustment Act; Supreme Court 85Nu851 (1986. 10. 28.)

71 Supreme Court 86Da204, 86DaKa1035 (1988. 12. 13.)

72 Supreme Court 91Da17931 (1992. 4. 24.)

absence has not been submitted."[73] This remains the case even if the illness or unavoidable circumstance has in fact occurred, or if the worker has received prior consent orally in person or over the phone.

Even if there are no special provisions regarding absences or early leaves due to illness or unavoidable circumstance in the rules of employment or other like documents, if the worker did not receive prior or post-event consent, such absences or early leaves would be considered an absence without notice.[74]

If a worker applies for annual or monthly paid leave but does not specify the period during which s/he will take this leave and subsequently does not report to work, this would be considered an absence without notice.[75]

If a worker applies for a leave of absence due to assault and duress from a superior or co-worker but the employer does not grant this application, resulting in the worker not reporting to work in order to protest this decision, this action would be considered an absence without notice. However, imposing the heaviest penalty of disciplinary dismissal due to this fact is considered an abuse of the right to discipline on the part of the employer.[76]

The following reasons are not justifiable causes for absence: refusing to conduct flight attendant duties due to trade union activities; going against the intent of the union and the latter's resolutions;[77] failure to report to work due to electoral activities to become a union delegate;[78] and working undependably due to the fact that the employer did not pay extended work allowance.[79]

---

73 Supreme Court 86DaKa1875 (1987. 4. 14.), Supreme Court 89DaKa5451 (1990. 4. 27.)

74 Supreme Court 91Da17931 (1992. 4. 24.)

75 Supreme Court 96Da4930 (1997. 3. 25.)

76 Supreme Court 95Da53096 (1997. 7. 22.)

77 Supreme Court 89Nu4666 (1990. 10. 23.), Supreme Court 92Da42974 (1993. 7. 13.)

78 Supreme Court 91Da5976 (1992. 2. 11.)

79 Supreme Court 91Da17931 (1992. 4. 24.)

If a full-time union staff member fails to report to work for a significant amount of time without prior notice or approval from the employer due to personal illegal activity unrelated to the work of the trade union in order to avoid the administration of a preliminary arrest warrant, this would be considered an absence without notice.[80] Also, a worker failing to report to his/her original workplace before being formally appointed as a full-time union staff member is also considered to be an absence without notice.[81]

(2) No Absence without Notice

If a worker is suddenly injured and needs to receive treatment, as long as s/he contacts the human resources officer or other personnel of like capacity within his/her corporation over the phone and requests the use of annual paid leave during the treatment period, this would not be considered an absence without notice (assuming that the corporation did not use its right to change the time of paid leave as provided for in the proviso in Article 60(5) of the LSA).[82]

In principle, if a worker fails to report to work for a few days due to his/her need for the treatment of injuries inflicted by a manager of the corporation in relation to work, this cannot be considered an absence without notice. However, if the period of treatment is prolonged and results in a long-term absence and the worker is responsible for not having submitted his/her notice of absence, this will be considered an absence without notice.

(3) Calculation of Number of Days of Absence without Notice

If the rules of employment stipulate that failing to report to work beyond a set number of days would constitute grounds of disciplinary dismissal, this provision must be interpreted to apply only to situations

---

80 Supreme Court 92Da34926 (1993. 8. 24.), Supreme Court 95Da46715 (1997. 3. 11.)

81 Supreme Court 97Da6926 (1997. 4. 25.)

82 Supreme Court 92Nu404 (1992. 4. 10)

where the worker has failed to report for a certain number of days within a "reasonable" and designated period of time. In other words, this provision should not be interpreted to mean that failing to report to work for a set number of days within an unlimited time frame would result in a valid disciplinary dismissal.[83]

iii) Refusal to Comply with Personnel Movement Orders

If a worker refuses to comply with personnel movement orders such as job, workplace or company transfers of the employer, and does not report to work, s/he is hence subject to disciplinary dismissal due to "absence without notice" or "noncompliance to work orders." Whether there is valid cause for disciplinary dismissal hinges on the degree of justification in the above orders.[84]

If a worker who has been dismissed is reinstated to his/her original job and refuses to work for a significant amount of time due to the non-acceptance of this disposition, then this represents a valid cause for disciplinary dismissal. This is true even if the job description differs somewhat from the original job, so long as this change is recognized to be within the scope of the employer's sole right to managerial discretion.[85]

iv) Noncompliance with Directions Regarding Work

In cases where the cause of disciplinary dismissal arises from the fact that a worker failed to comply with the directions of the employer regarding work, whether the cause retains justification (and hence would allow for a valid disciplinary dismissal) depends on whether the employer's direction is a valid one which does not violate any provisions in the employment contract, the rules of employment, the collective agreement, or any relevant Acts.

---

83 Supreme Court 94Da46596 (1995. 5. 26.)

84 Supreme Court 93Da47677 (1994. 5. 10.)

85 Supreme Court 94Da4295 (1994. 7. 29.), Supreme Court 96Da47074 (1997. 5. 16.)

Using provisions in the rules of employment or other documents, the non-submittal of written explanation/apology could be subject to disciplinary disposition as such act could be considered a form of noncompliance to valid directions of the employer regarding work. However, in the absence of exceptional circumstances, dismissing a worker due to the mere fact that the worker has failed to submit a written explanation/apology is considered to be beyond the scope of the employer's right to disciplinary action.[86] According to case law, if the written document produced by the worker goes beyond a mere report of the details of the incident but also requires the worker to self-reflect and apologize for his/her wrongdoings (i.e. a letter of apology), a direction to submit such a document cannot be seen as a valid direction regarding work.[87] This is because a provision in the rules of employment that requires the submittal of letters of explanation/apology is an imposition against the worker's internal ethical judgment, and is therefore an infringement on one's freedom of conscience as protected by the Constitution (which is made into substantive law in the form of Article 96(1) of the LSA).

v) Acts of Violence Against Co-workers or Superiors

Defining a worker's acts of violence against co-workers or superiors as causes for disciplinary dismissal in the rules of employment or the collective agreement is generally valid.[88] However, this validity is lost if it is determined that the employer has abused his/her right to disciplinary action.

vi) Incurrence of Loss Due to Grave Incidents Caused by the Worker

Disciplinary dismissals are valid if the causes are grave incidents

---

86 Supreme Court 94Nu11767 (1995. 3. 3.)

87 Supreme Court 2009Du6605 (2010. 1. 14.)

88 Supreme Court 91Da39339 (1992. 3. 13.)

or accidents caused by illegal acts (embezzlement, malpractice, theft, destruction/spoliation of property) or by negligence.[89]

vii) Wrongdoings in Personal Life
If an act of wrongdoing committed by a worker in his/her personal life may be objectively construed as having a serious detrimental effect on the societal reputation of the company (e.g. an employee of the Metropolitan Development Corporation making speculative real estate investments), this would be grounds for a valid disciplinary dismissal.[90]

viii) Violation of the Duty Not to Hold Concurrent Offices
Long-term concurrent employment to the extent that the provision of labor is impeded, or appointment as director of the employer's competitor may be prohibited, and constitute grounds for disciplinary dismissal.

ix) Violation of the Duty Not to Engage in Non-work Activities
There are instances where the rules of employment or other such documents generally prohibit workers from assembling, posting items on the bulletin board, and distributing flyers and pamphlets within the workplace, and only allow such activities to occur with permission from the employer. These rules would then stipulate the violation of the above as constituting valid cause for disciplinary dismissal. The Supreme Court recognizes the validity of such provisions under the LSA if they are used when the content of the information has the potential to disturb corporate order, or if there is concern that the free use of breaks by other employees would be disturbed.[91] However, the Court also ruled that if the above activities of the worker are those

---

89 Supreme Court 91Da4775 (1992. 4. 14.), Supreme Court 92Da19910 (1992. 8. 18.), Supreme Court 93Da22524 (1993. 9. 28.), Supreme Court 96Da33556 (1997. 4. 8.)

90 Supreme Court 93Nu23275 (1994. 12. 13.)

91 Supreme Court 94Da4042 (1994. 9. 30.)

protected under the Constitution and the Union Act as "justifiable activities of unions," the prohibition of such activities would be unjustified.[92]

According to case law, the following are the conditions that would allow an act to be recognized as a "justifiable activity of trade unions."[93]

First, the "Nature of the Union Activity": Even if an activity is not organized by the trade union *per se*, its nature must be construed as purporting to advance the work of the union, and as well as be construed to have received the implied authorization (approval) from the trade union.[94]

Second, the "Purpose of the Union Activity": The activity must be necessary for the purpose of maintaining and enhancing working conditions as well as advancing the economic status of workers, and must contribute to enhancing the solidarity of workers.

Third, the "Timing of the Union Activity": The activity must be conducted outside of work hours, unless there is a separate provision allowing the activity during work hours in the rules of employment or the collective agreement, a labor relations custom that allows for this, or the employer's consent.

Fourth, the "Method of the Union Activity": Union activities within the workplace must follow reasonable regulations or restrictions based on the employer's right to manage facilities, and must not employ "methods" of violence or destruction.

A matter especially prone to dispute in practice is the distribution of printed materials. Even if the rules of employment or other like documents stipulate that prior approval or permission from the employer is needed in order to distribute printed materials, the determination of whether such activity is justified or not cannot be

---

92 Supreme Court 91Nu4164 (1991. 11. 12.), Supreme Court 92Nu4253 (1992. 6. 23.)

93 Supreme Court 92Da18542 (1992. 9. 25.)

94 Supreme Court 89Nu8217 (1990. 8. 10.), Supreme Court 91Nu4164 (1991. 11. 12.)

made solely by examining whether such prior approval was given by the employer due to the fact that the employer may not forbid justified activities towards the maintenance and advancement of working conditions or the enhancement to welfare. In these situations, the content and the quantity of the printed material distributed; the timing, target, and method of distribution; the impact that the distribution activity has on the business and its work must be taken into consideration as a whole.[95] For distribution taking place during break hours (not work hours), considerations such as whether negative influence has been exerted to the work of non-union employees, whether the freedom to use break hours enjoyed by these employees is being impeded, and whether there exists specific instances of disruption to the workplace are examined when determining the action's degree of justification.

Even if printed material distributed to other union members during break hours contains somewhat exaggerated or partially incorrect facts, as long as the material does not contain content that could defame another person and the purpose of the distribution is to maintain or improve working conditions and enhance worker welfare and other economic and social status, and as a whole the printed material remains truthful, the act of distributing such material is recognized to possess justification.[96]

However, if a set of printed material contains false information that slanders the employer and may potentially instill resentment against the latter, the material was distributed inconspicuously in the employer's factory (thereby impinging on the right of the employer to manage his/her facilities), and poses a specific threat of disrupting order within the workplace, such distribution cannot be justified even

---

95 Supreme Court 91Nu5020 (1992. 3. 13.), Supreme Court 95Da11504 (1996. 9. 24.), Supreme Court 96Nu11778 (1997. 12. 23.)

96 Supreme Court 91Nu4164 (1991. 11. 12.), Supreme Court 93Da13544 (1993. 12. 28.), Supreme Court 96Nu11778 (1997. 12. 23.), Supreme Court 98Da2365 (1998. 5. 22.)

if the distribution was made during the trade union delegate election season.[97]

If a set of printed material composed and distributed by a worker contains information that defames an executive of the corporation, a part of the information is unfounded and concerns matters not directly related to the labor relationship, purports to incite other workers to collectively use their monthly paid leave, and actually results in multiple workers actually taking absence from the workplace without prior notice thereby impeding the normal operations of the corporation, this also cannot be said to be a valid form of union activity.[98]

x) Causes of Disciplinary Dismissal Related to Industrial Action

Even if a worker's activity is conducted as union activity, if it is considered to be an unjustified industrial activity such as an illegal strike, this activity may still be a direct or indirect cause of disciplinary dismissal. For example, a worker who has been unfairly dismissed and hence does not in fact provide labor is still considered a worker if s/he has requested relief from the Central Labor Relations Commission, at least until the latter concludes its review of the application.[99] In this case, if the dismissal is ultimately found to be invalid and the worker is reinstated his/her status as an employee, s/he may be subject to disciplinary action for illegal industrial actions conducted during the term s/he was dismissed.[100]

For dismissals due to industrial action, whether the cause of disciplinary dismissal is justified turns on whether the relevant industrial action is justified.[101] In order for a worker's industrial action

---

97 Supreme Court 92Nu4253 (1992. 6. 23.)

98 Supreme Court 91Nu5020 (1992. 3. 13.)

99 Union Act, Article 2.4.d

100 Supreme Court 93Da26496 (1994. 9. 30.)

101 Supreme Court 91Da4317 (1992. 9. 22.)

to obtain justification, conditions regarding the subject, purpose, timing, and method must all be satisfied.

xi) Guilty Verdict for a Criminal Offense

There are instances where the rules of employment or the collective agreement designate the receipt of a guilty verdict for a criminal offence as a "ground for disciplinary dismissal," or such a verdict is considered a "cause of natural retirement" or a "cause of retirement during suspension due to indictment."

The Supreme Court ruled that in cases where the collective agreement or the rules of employment determine "receipt of a guilty verdict for a criminal offence" to be a cause for disciplinary dismissal, the general purpose of such provision is as follows: ① the purpose of the employment contract cannot be fulfilled because of the prolonged inability of the worker to satisfy his/her duty to provide labor due to the guilty verdict; ② the maintenance of the employment contract becomes difficult because of the loss of the trust relationship between the worker and employer due to the verdict; or ③ the guilty verdict would seriously detriment the reputation or credibility of the employer or negatively impact the employer's business relationships.[102]

Depending on the facts, the definition of "guilty verdict" may be interpreted narrowly. An example would be when "receipt of a guilty verdict for a criminal offence" is stipulated as a cause of natural retirement or natural dismissal, along with other causes such as the explicit or implicit expression of the worker's lack of intention to provide labor, or the inability to provide labor due to the nature of the circumstance. In such cases, the receipt of a prison sentence in the first trial may be interpreted as satisfying the condition of "receipt of a guilty verdict for a criminal offence," as this would make the provision

---

102 Supreme Court 97Da9239 (1997. 5. 23.), Supreme Court 97Da7066 (1997. 7. 25.), Supreme Court 97Nu1600 (1997. 9. 26.)

of labor by the worker practically impossible. Once such a cause for natural retirement arises, this cause does not extinguish even in light of the subsequent release of the worker due to success in the appeals process (i.e. getting the sentence suspended).[103]

There are instances where the rules of employment or other like documents stipulate "where a worker receives a guilty verdict while under suspension due to indictment" as a cause of natural retirement. Here, the "guilty verdict" (designated as a cause of retirement due to suspension) refers to an "actual prison sentence," which would mean that the cause of the initial suspension (i.e. physical detention that renders the provision of labor impracticable) has not been resolved by the end of the suspension term, which is the day the verdict is handed down in the trial of first instance.[104]

However, without the existence of special circumstances that would necessitate restricted interpretations like the above, the term "guilty verdict" refers to when the decision of the court is made final and conclusive.[105] Therefore, in order for the disciplinary disposition using the above reason to be lawful, it must be enforced after the guilty verdict has been finalized. If the guilt of the worker has not been finalized at the time of the disciplinary action, this action remains unlawful even if the worker's guilt is indeed confirmed at a later date.[106]

xii) Refusal to Regularly Employ a Worker under the Provisional Contract Relationship

A provisionary contractual relationship is one where a worker's compatibility with the job (e.g. job performance, qualifications, character, integrity) is observed and assessed for a fixed provisional

---

103 Supreme Court 94Da42082 (1995. 3. 24.), Supreme Court 98Du18848 (1999. 9. 3.)

104 Supreme Court 92Nu6082 (1992. 11. 13.), Supreme Court 92Nu12452 (1993. 5. 25.)

105 Supreme Court 93Da28584 (1994. 6. 24.), Supreme Court 97Da7066 (1997. 7. 25.)

106 Supreme Court 97Da9239 (1997. 5. 23.)

term, and the worker is offered regular employment after this period if no grounds of disqualification are found during this period (this is a form of employment contract where the employer defers exercising his/her right to cancel the offer of employment).[107]

The provisionary contractual relationship should be seen as a form of continuous employment contractual relationship subject to the provisions of the LSA.[108] Therefore, in order to dismiss a worker during the provisional period, the employer must have a justifiable reason under the LSA, and the refusal to employ provisional workers as regular employees after the designated period would require justifiable cause.

However, the standard of determining whether justifiable cause exists should not be seen to be the same as that applied to the dismissal of regular workers. All that would be required is a cause reasonable to socially accepted norms in light of the purpose of the system of provisional contracts. Therefore, a somewhat more flexible standard is applied when determining the justifiability of the cause to dismiss provisional workers than other cases.[109]

xiii) Physical Disability of a Worker

It is common practice for the rules of employment to stipulate causes for ordinary dismissal such as natural retirement (in contrast to causes for disciplinary dismissals) to provide for situations where the worker can no longer perform his/her work due to physical disability or it becomes impracticable to do so.

In such cases, the justifiability of the cause of dismissal must be determined by reasonably considering the following relevant matters in their entirety: the details of how the worker acquired the physical

---

107 Supreme Court 2003Da50580 (2005. 7. 15.)

108 Supreme Court 92Da44695 (1994. 1. 11.)

109 Supreme Court 87DaKa555 (1987. 9. 8.), Supreme Court 92Da44695 (1994. 1. 11.), Supreme Court 2003Da5955 (2003. 7. 22.), Supreme Court 2003Da50580 (2005. 7. 15.), Supreme Court 2002Da62432 (2006. 2. 24.)

disability; whether this accident was caused due to reasons attributable to the employer or was an industrial accident; the length of time taken to treat the illness and the degree of loss of capacity to work after the treatment; the nature and content of the work that the worker was responsible for at the time of the accident; whether there are jobs that the worker can still handle with his/her remaining capacity to provide labor and their descriptions; whether the employer was considerate to the injured worker and assisted in his/her successful return to work by adjusting the tasks assigned to him/her; and the extent of the worker's effort to adapt to the new job that was provided through the employer's consideration.[110]

The standard in the above paragraph (i.e. determining the justifiability of the cause of dismissal by reasonably considering relevant matters in their entirety) applies to cases where the worker has suffered from an industrial accident and is left with a physical disability, or where the worker is naturally retired due to his/her inability to return to work after exhausting his/her sick leave.[111]

3) Immunity Agreements between Labor and Management, and the Justifiability of Causes of Disciplinary Dismissal

Even if a worker is subjected to one of the causes of disciplinary dismissal as defined in the rules of employment or the collective agreement due to actions attributable to him/her, the worker's liability is excepted if labor and management agree to bestow immunity to the worker regarding such actions. Hence, the disciplinary dismissal of this worker would become invalid as such a disposition would run contrary to the above agreement.[112] If the worker is subject to disciplinary action for a separate violation, the existence of a violation

---

110 Supreme Court 95Nu15728 (1996. 11. 12.), Supreme Court 95Da45934 (1996. 12. 6.)

111 Supreme Court 93Da3721 (1993. 7. 13.), Supreme Court 96Da21065 (1996. 10. 29.)

112 Supreme Court 90DaKa21176 (1991. 1. 11.), Supreme Court 91Ja1233 (1991. 8. 13.), Supreme Court 92Da14786 (1992. 7. 28.)

that has been immunized due to agreement between labor and management may be incorporated in the disciplinary sentencing phase.[113]

Meanwhile, substituting the phrase "employer will not discipline (a worker arrested due to industrial action)" with "the employer will offer maximum favorable treatment" does not constitute an immunity agreement.[114]

B. Legitimate Process for Disciplinary Dismissals

Expressions of the intent to dismiss a worker must be made by notifying the worker in writing of the reasons for and the time of the dismissal.[115] According to the recently revised LSA, however, when an employer has provided advance notice of dismissal by notifying the worker in writing of the reasons for and the time of the dismissal, the written notice of the reasons for and the time of dismissal is deemed to have been communicated at the moment of dismissal.[116] Other procedural requirements for legitimate disciplinary dismissals are as follows:

1) Regulations on Disciplinary Procedures
i) The Violation of Disciplinary Procedures and Its Effect
If the collective agreement or the rules of employment contain regulations on the disciplinary procedures (i.e. where the worker being disciplined is notified of this fact and is required to submit a report detailing the cause of the disciplinary action and testify in front of a

---

113 Supreme Court 94Da4042 (1994. 9. 30.)
114 Supreme Court 93Da1503 (1993. 5. 11.)
115 Supreme Court 67Nu162 (1968. 11. 26.); LSA, Article 27
116 LSA, Article 27(3)

disciplinary committee meeting), disciplinary dismissal in violation of these regulations is invalid as a matter of principle.[117]

The disciplinary procedure is still considered to have been violated when the disciplinary committee seemingly (formally) passes a resolution but this process does not conform to that defined in the rules of employment or other similar documents.[118]

ii) The Relationship between the Original Disciplinary Procedure and the Appeals Process

If an "appeals process" to disciplinary dispositions is included in the regulations, this process is combined with the original disciplinary procedure to constitute a "single" disciplinary disposition procedure. Therefore, a disciplinary disposition is legitimate only when there are no procedural violations throughout the entire disciplinary procedure. If the appeals process has not been undertaken to review the original disposition, or if a significant defect exists in its process, the entire disciplinary disposition becomes invalid.[119]

iii) Defects in the Composition of the Disciplinary Committee

If the collective agreement or the rules of employment contain regulations regarding the composition of the disciplinary committee, any decision to disciplinarily dismiss a worker by a committee that was formed not in compliance with the above regulations would be invalid as a violation of the disciplinary procedure.[120] For example, a disciplinary committee composed of only corporate managers

---

117 Supreme Court 90Da8077 (1991. 7. 9.), Supreme Court 92Da14786 (1992. 7. 28.), Supreme Court 94Da25889 (1994. 10. 25.)

118 Supreme Court 99Du2604 (1999. 10. 26.)

119 Supreme Court 80Da1769 (1981. 6. 9.), Supreme Court 87DaKa1187 (1987. 9. 22.), Supreme Court 93Da968 (1994. 1. 14.), Supreme Court 93Da29662 (1995. 1. 24.), Supreme Court 97Da10956, 10963 (1997. 9. 30.), Supreme Court 98Da31172 (1998. 12. 8.)

120 Supreme Court 94Da3612 (1994. 4. 12.), Supreme Court 94Da7553 (1994. 8. 23.)

is invalid if the disciplinary procedure in the rules of employment stipulates that the disciplinary committee must include the participation of workers. If such a regulation does not exist, however, composing disciplinary committees exclusively of managers from the corporation would be in compliance with the law.[121]

If the rules of employment or other like documents contain provisions that restrict the participation of interested parties when composing disciplinary committees, any disciplinary disposition from committees that violate these provisions are invalid.[122] This remains the case even if the quorum for voting has been met without the inclusion of the disqualified committee member.[123] However, in the face of necessity (e.g. preventing unfair outcomes), a new disciplinary committee may be appointed to pass necessary resolutions authorizing disciplinary action.[124]

iv) Prior Notification of the Grounds of Disciplinary Action and the
   Granting of the Opportunity to Defend One's Case

If the rules of employment or other like documents contain provisions regarding the disciplinary procedure of when to notify workers that they are subject to disciplinary action, these must be observed. Even if such provisions do not exist, the notification must provide for significant time towards the preparation of defensive arguments and explanatory materials.[125] The method of notification may either be oral or written, but either way the "grounds of disciplinary action and the date and the time the disciplinary committee will be meeting" must be specified.

If the notification of the fact that the worker is subject to

---

121 Supreme Court 93Da35384 (1993. 11. 9.)

122 Supreme Court 94Da7553 (1994. 8. 23.), Supreme Court 93Nu20214 (1994. 10. 7.)

123 Supreme Court 94Da53716 (1996. 6. 28.)

124 Supreme Court 97Nu3637 (1997. 12. 12.)

125 Supreme Court 90Da15884 (1991. 2. 8.), Supreme Court 2003Du15317 (2004. 6. 25.)

disciplinary action is mandated in the provisions of the above documents, this process must be observed.[126] The opportunity for the worker to defend his/her case must be given, but it is not necessary that a defensive argument actually be made.[127]

v) The Remedying of Defects in the Disciplinary Procedure
Even if the employer violates disciplinary procedure regulations and fails to provide advance notice to the worker of the fact that a disciplinary action will take place as well as its timing and method, or there is a defect in the composition of disciplinary committees, such defects do not pose a problem as long as there are grounds to complement or remedy them. For example, if the worker to be disciplined voluntarily partakes in the process and provides sufficient defensive arguments or submits explanatory material without raising objections to the disciplinary process itself, the legal effect of the disciplinary action is not affected by the defects.[128]

Even if the employer has failed to state the cause for the disciplinary action in its advance notification to the worker, if the worker subsequently becomes aware of the cause and does not appeal this fact within the prescribed period despite the fact that the employer has given such an opportunity to him/her, the worker is assumed to have waived his/her right to defend him/herself regarding this matter.[129] However, if the worker is not notified of the cause for the disciplinary action by the time the appeals process has been concluded, the worker cannot be assumed to have waived his/her right to defend him/herself just because the worker has submitted his/her written defense, yet was

126 Supreme Court 92Da14786 (1992. 7. 28.), Supreme Court 91Da36123 (1992. 9. 22.)
127 Supreme Court 2007Da51758 (2007. 12. 27.)
128 Supreme Court 78Nu123 (1979. 11. 27.), Supreme Court 80Da1769 (1981. 6. 9.), Supreme Court 90Da15884 (1991. 2. 8.), Supreme Court 92Da55251 (1993. 7. 16.), Supreme Court 95Da55900 (1997. 7. 11.), Supreme Court 98Du4672 (1999. 3. 26.)
129 Supreme Court 93Da27413 (1994. 3. 11.)

not present in the disciplinary appeals committee meeting.[130]

Even if there is a defect in the composition of the disciplinary committee, this defect is remedied once the disciplinary appeals committee (excluding the defective committee member) undergoes valid deliberation and resolution procedures.[131] However, if the appeal is dismissed even before the disciplinary appeals committee meeting is held, the complementing and remedying of the defect will not be recognized.[132]

vi) The Relationship between Ordinary Dismissals and Compliance of
   Disciplinary Procedure Regulations

The disciplinary procedure regulation is applied in the case of disciplinary dismissals, but is not automatically applied to cases of ordinary dismissals such as suspensions or natural retirements.[133]

If a particular incident may be a cause for disciplinary dismissal but not ordinary dismissal, the employer may ordinarily dismiss the relevant worker. This is because not being subject to disciplinary action is advantageous to the worker. However, the worker must still go through the disciplinary procedure.[134] If an incident may justify both disciplinary and ordinary dismissal, the employer can again ordinarily dismiss the worker, given that the disciplinary procedure is observed.[135] Case law forbids the worker's position to be destabilized by sidestepping the disciplinary procedure regulations.

However, if causes for disciplinary dismissal and ordinary dismissal are distinguished from each other, there is no need to go through the disciplinary procedure even if the employer ordinarily dismisses or

---

130 Supreme Court 92Da45230 (1994. 1. 28.)

131 Supreme Court 94Da7553 (1994. 8. 23.), Supreme Court 96Da23627 (1997. 11. 11.)

132 Supreme Court 96Da23627 (1997. 11. 11.)

133 Supreme Court 91Nu10480 (1992. 5. 8.), Supreme Court 98Da54960 (2000. 6. 23.)

134 Supreme Court 93Da57551 (1994. 5. 27.), Supreme Court 94Da25889 (1994. 10. 25.)

135 Supreme Court 92Da49935 (1993. 10. 22.)

naturally retires a worker.[136]

2) Prior Deliberation with the Union for Personnel Action of Union Executives

If the collective agreement contains a provision that requires prior deliberation with the union for personnel actions, this provision is activated in the case of disciplinary dismissals.[137] Provisions requiring prior deliberation are not mandatory, though, so the dismissal is not invalid just because the deliberation did not occur.[138] However, if the provision requires not only simple deliberation but also consultation with and agreement, approval, consent of the union, any dismissals that do not go through these processes are in principle invalid.[139] Here, the union may provide its consent by any external expression of intent. In other words, prior consent by the union representative, the participation and deliberation of union executives in disciplinary committee meetings, and resolution would be sufficient to satisfy the above provision. Whether there has been a formal process of converging opinions within the union is irrelevant.[140]

Even if the employer did not go through the process of soliciting consent from the union, the disciplinary dismissal is still valid in the face of special circumstances. Examples of such special circumstances would be when the relevant worker or the union waives his/her right to refuse providing consent, or when the exercising of this right would go against the principle of good faith.[141] An illustration of the waiver

---

136 Supreme Court 94Da42082 (1995. 3. 24.), Supreme Court 95Nu17571 (1996. 11. 26.), Supreme Court 97Da58750 (1998. 4. 24.), Supreme Court 99Du4235 (2000. 6. 23.)

137 Supreme Court 91Da22100 (1992. 5. 22.), Supreme Court 92Da13400 (1992. 9. 22.)

138 Supreme Court 91Da4775 (1992. 4. 14.), Supreme Court 93Da28553 (1994. 3. 22.), Supreme Court 95Da53102 (1996. 4. 23.)

139 Supreme Court 92Da32074 (1992. 12. 8.), Supreme Court 93Da50017 (1994. 9. 13.), Supreme Court 2005Du8788 (2007. 9. 6.)

140 Supreme Court 92Da42774 (1993. 7. 13.)

141 Supreme Court 92Da32074 (1992. 12. 8.), Supreme Court 93Da50017 (1994. 9. 13.), Supreme Court 94Da46763 (1995. 3. 28.)

or abuse of the right to provide consent would be when the worker or union refuses to participate in the disciplinary committee meeting despite the fact that the employer has provided prior consent multiple times, or when the worker refuses the disciplinary action despite the existence of evident and grave cause that resulted in this action.

However, if the employer does not recognize the legality of the trade union and did not provide the written notification or advance deliberation as provided for in the collective agreement, this is regarded as a rejection on the part of the employer and not an abandoning of the deliberation process by the union. Also, the worker cannot be seen to have waived or abused his/her right to provide consent merely because s/he was in a state of dispute.[142]

3) Non-existence of Disciplinary Procedure Regulations

If no disciplinary procedure regulations exist, there is no duty to notify the worker that s/he is the subject of disciplinary action. The disciplinary action is valid even without going through such a process.[143]

C. The Legitimacy of Secondary Disciplinary Dismissals after the First Disciplinary Dismissal

If the employer acknowledges defects in the disciplinary procedure, the process of assessing the disciplinary cause, or the determination of disciplinary disposition, the employer may cancel his/her previous disciplinary action and hand down a new disciplinary disposition that is compliant with relevant laws.[144]

---

142 Supreme Court 93Da50017 (1994. 9. 13.), Supreme Court 94Da46763 (1995. 3. 28.)

143 Supreme Court 78Da304 (1979. 1. 30.), Supreme Court 85Da375 (1986. 7. 8.), Supreme Court 92Da18542 (1992. 9. 25.), Supreme Court 97Nu14132 (1998. 11. 27.), Supreme Court 2001Da6800 (2004. 1. 29.)

144 Supreme Court 93Da26496 (1994. 9. 30.)

As such, it is possible to supplement new procedures and introduce new disciplinary causes to a preexisting disciplinary disposition (currently under dispute regarding its validity), while not cancelling the disposition itself. This would in essence make possible secondary disciplinary dismissals.[145]

Also, even if the first disciplinary dismissal is ultimately determined to be invalid due to procedural defects in the disciplinary action, it is permissible to undertake an entirely new disciplinary procedure concerning the same disciplinary cause, thereby resulting in a secondary disciplinary dismissal.[146]

III. Layoffs (Dismissals for Managerial Reasons)

A. Introduction

Dismissals for managerial reasons are the reduction of workers in light of urgent managerial necessity, or the dismissal of workers under certain conditions. A point to keep in mind is that absent urgent managerial necessity, such dismissals would not be considered layoffs but ordinary dismissals.[147]

B. Requirements for Legitimate Dismissals for Managerial Reasons

In earlier years, the Supreme Court ruled that in order for businesses to conduct legitimate dismissals for managerial reasons, the following four requirements must be strictly adhered to: ① urgent managerial

145 Supreme Court 95Da53102 (1996. 4. 23.)
146 Supreme Court 95Da36138 (1995. 12. 5.), Supreme Court 97Nu16084 (1998. 6. 12.)
147 Supreme Court 96Da22198 (1996. 10. 29.)

need; ② efforts to avoid dismissals; ③ reasonable and fair criteria for the selection of those persons subject to dismissal; and ④ advance notification and a consultation process.[148]

This ruling became relaxed in recent years, however, and as case law stands at the moment the satisfaction of all four requirements is not required for legitimate layoffs; instead, a dismissal for managerial reasons that did not undergo advance consultation processes or satisfy other requirements may still be recognized as valid if objective rationality and social reasonability exists after a comprehensive consideration of the relevant circumstances.[149] In other words, the courts have ruled that individual matters comprising each requirement must be considered as a whole.[150]

1) Urgent Managerial Need

i) Causes External to the Business

Causes external to the business include a decrease in sales, or difficulties in procuring energy or materials. The LSA recognizes that there is an urgent managerial necessity for the transfer, merger, or acquisition of the business in order to prevent managerial deterioration.[151]

ii) Managerial Measures Internal to the Business

Managerial measures internal to the business would include decreasing production, reorganizing, utilizing external subcontractors to alleviate financial difficulties, hiring of external service businesses to reduce excess personnel, developing or introducing new technology, or shutting down industry fields or units.

When shutting down industrial units, the employer may not dismiss all workers comprising the unit, but must expand the scope

---

148 Supreme Court 87DaKa2132 (1989. 5. 23.), Supreme Court 92Da14779 (1992. 12. 22.)
149 Supreme Court 94Nu15783 (1995. 12. 5.), Supreme Court 94Da52119 (1995. 12. 22.)
150 Supreme Court 2000Du9373 (2002. 7. 9.), Supreme Court 2003Da69393 (2006. 1. 26.)
151 LSA, Article 24(1)

of the layoff to the entire business and select workers to be dismissed from this expanded pool.[152]

On the other hand, it is important to keep in mind that so-called "dismissals due to business closure" (where the entire business is shut down and all its workers are laid off) are in principle ordinary dismissals.[153]

iii) Standards for Assessing "Urgent Business Necessity"
(1) The Degree of Urgency
In order to satisfy this requirement, the employer does not necessarily have to be placed in an urgent managerial crisis where bankruptcy is imminent.[154] Rather, if workforce reduction is objectively reasonable to prepare for future risks, the courts recognize the existence of urgent business necessity.[155]

However, if managerial actions that obviously contradict the employer's argument of managerial necessity follow the layoff (e.g. the wage of remaining workers is significantly increased after the layoffs, new workers are recruited in numbers similar to the number of workers laid off,[156] or high-yield dividends are distributed to shareholders), the court would not recognize the existence of urgent managerial necessity in this case.[157]

(2) Continuity of Necessity in Relation to Business
Urgent managerial necessity requires a continuous deterioration of

152 Supreme Court 90Nu9421 (1992. 5. 13.), Supreme Court 92Nu3076 (1993. 1. 26.)

153 Supreme Court 93Da7457 (1993. 6. 11.), Supreme Court 2001Da27975 (2001. 11. 13.), Supreme Court 2003Da7005 (2003. 4. 25.)

154 Supreme Court 87DaKa2132 (1989. 5. 23.), Supreme Court 89DaKa24445 (1990. 3. 13.)

155 Supreme Court 90Nu4433 (1991. 1. 29.), Supreme Court 91Da8647 (1991. 12. 10.), Supreme Court 90Nu9421 (1992. 5. 12.), Supreme Court 96Nu8031 (1997. 9. 5.), Supreme Court 2001Da29452 (2002. 7. 9.), Supreme Court 2004Du9616, 9623 (2004. 11. 12.)

156 Supreme Court 69Da135 (1969. 3. 31.), Supreme Court 86DaKa1873 (1987. 4. 28.), Supreme Court 87DaKa2132 (1989. 5. 23.)

157 Supreme Court 92Da34858 (1993. 12. 28.), Supreme Court 94Nu10931 (1995. 11. 24.)

the employer's business activities or financial health by which the employer is obliged to reduce a certain number of workers, and the probability that such difficulties will not be easily resolved going into the future.[158]

(3) Standards for Examining Business Necessity

In principle, even conglomerates must be analyzed at the level of the individual corporate entity when conducting an analysis regarding urgent business necessity.[159] Within this corporate entity, urgent necessity should not be estimated on the basis of the condition that certain partial business divisions are in, but should be estimated by evaluating the entire business as a whole.[160] Even if an entity is ensured a certain degree of managerial independence, it is only considered a business division if it does not possess a corporate personality.[161]

However, if a corporation's business division is separate and independent from other business divisions in terms of personnel, facilities, location, budgeting, and accounting; and if the business division possesses a trade union that is organized according to business divisions while the managerial conditions of each of these parts are discrete, the "urgent managerial necessity" requirement may be assessed for this business division separately.[162]

Continuing from the above perspective, if two specific business divisions from two separate corporate entities that manage the same business are in fact operated as a single corporate entity by maintaining close mutual relationship (i.e. respond to the economic environment simultaneously, personnel and facilities are not strictly divided, and share the same union), the "urgent business necessity"

158 Supreme Court 92Nu3076 (1993. 1. 26.)
159 Supreme Court 2005Da30580 (2006. 9. 22.)
160 Supreme Court 99Du202 (1999. 4. 27.)
161 Supreme Court 89DaKa24445 (1990. 3. 13.)
162 Supreme Court 2005Da30580 (2006. 9. 22.)

requirement for a layoff measure co-implemented by the two business divisions would be assessed by considering the situation of the two entities as a whole.[163]

(4) The Moment Urgency Is Assessed

The moment that urgency should be assessed is the point when the layoff actually took place. Any improvements in management conditions after the layoff are not put into consideration.[164]

2) Efforts to Avoid Layoffs

An employer will have made "efforts to avoid layoffs" by taking various managerial measures in order to cope with business difficulties facing the company and thereby minimizing the scope of dismissals, such as rationalizing management policy or work methods, restricting new hiring, utilizing temporary suspensions, voluntary resignations, and workplace transfers. The specific degree and methods required is not definite; this varies depending on the extent of the relevant employer's management crisis, the managerial reasons behind why layoffs must be conducted, the content and scale of the business, and the number of workers in each position.[165]

There is a Supreme Court precedent where the Court ruled that if the corporation is managed across multiple workplaces, a worker subject to layoffs must be job or workplace transferred if there is a position at a workplace where the employer manages that s/he may work in (i.e. the scope of examination is not limited to the workplace that the relevant worker is from but is expanded to all workplaces).[166] However, if the workplaces are entirely independent from each other,

163 Supreme Court 2005Da30580 (2006. 9. 22.)
164 Supreme Court 91Da19463 (1992. 11. 10.)
165 Supreme Court 2003Du11339 (2004. 1. 15.)
166 Supreme Court 92Nu3076 (1993. 1. 26.)

the employer is not unrecognized to have extended the necessary efforts to avoid layoffs despite not having transferred the worker as above.[167]

The employer must offer workplace or job transfers to a worker subject to dismissal for managerial reasons so that s/he may continue to work, even if that means deterioration in working conditions. However, if the worker clearly rejects such an offer, the employer may then proceed to immediately dismiss the worker.[168]

3) Reasonableness and Fairness in Selecting Workers Subject to Layoffs

i) The Scope of Workers Subject to Layoffs

While workers to dismiss for managerial reasons must be selected from among the entire business of the employer that has the urgent managerial need to reduce workers (horizontal scope), the specific workers to be laid off are those engaged with work directly targeted by the management rationalization effort that brought about the personnel reduction, or those who work on job functions that are interchangeable with the above targeted work considering the rank and nature of the job (vertical scope).

ii) Standard of Selecting Specific Workers to Dismiss

If the rules of employment or the collective agreement sets out the standards for selecting workers to lay off, this standard is observed unless special circumstance exists that demonstrate its unfairness or unreasonableness.

If there are no such standards stipulated, the subjective circumstance of workers should be considered, along with matters related to the employer's managerial interests.

---

167 Supreme Court 90Nu9421 (1992. 5. 12.), Supreme Court 92Da14779 (1992. 12. 22.)
168 Supreme Court 88DaKa11145 (1989. 2. 28.)

4) The Process of Advance Notice and Deliberation

i) Introduction

Even if all substantive conditions for a valid layoff are met, the employer must inform the person(s) in question at least 50 days before the intended date of dismissal and consult in good faith with the labor union (where there is no such organized labor union, with a person who represents more than half of the workers) regarding the methods for avoiding dismissals, the criteria for dismissal, etc.[169]

Also, when an employer intends to dismiss personnel above the fixed limit prescribed by the Presidential Decree,[170] s/he shall report to the Minister of Employment and Labor as determined by the Presidential Decree.[171]

The term "prior consultation" used here does not mean "consent," so it is different from the consent[172] required when modifying rules of employment which may be unfavorable to workers.

ii) Consultation with Trade Unions or Labor Representatives

Consultation with the labor representative is sufficient, and further consultation with other workers is not necessary.[173] As this requirement only mandates that the employer engage in the consultation process itself, the employer is not bound to act on the opinion of the workers.

The labor representative must be selected in a manner that would reflect the intent of the workers subject to the layoff. If there is no organized labor union that represents more than half of the workers at the business or workplace, the procedural requirement is deemed to be satisfied if circumstances exist that allow the recognition that the consulting person is in fact able to represent the intent of the

---

169 LSA, Article 24(3)

170 Enforcement Decree of the LSA, Article 10

171 LSA, Article 24(4)

172 Ibid., Article 94(1) proviso

173 Supreme Court 2001Da29452 (2002. 7. 9.)

workers (even if that person does not formally satisfy the requirement of representing more than half of the workers), and the employer engages in consultations with this person.[174]

iii) The Effects of Violation

Under current law, the effect of the dismissal is not recognized if the requirement of consultation is not satisfied at all.

However, the Supreme Court interprets the requirement concerning the consultation period as being an instructional regulation without penalty. As such, a layoff is considered to be valid as long as the facts of an individual case do not indicate that the period between the notification of the layoff and its implementation is unduly short, and if the other requirements are met.[175]

Recently, the Supreme Court ruled that if an employer has entered into a collective agreement that restricts layoffs as a result of negotiations with the trade union, conducting layoffs that contradict this agreement is in principle unjustified.

Yet if the circumstance from which the original collective agreement has been agreed upon has changed significantly—forcing the employer to implement a collective agreement that would objectively and obviously result in an unreasonable consequence—the employer may proceed with the layoff.[176]

---

174 Supreme Court 2001Du1154, 1161, 1178 (2004. 10. 15.), Supreme Court 2003Da69393 (2006. 1. 26.)
175 Supreme Court 2003Du4119 (2003. 11. 13.), Supreme Court 2001Du1154, 1161, 1178 (2004. 10. 15.)
176 Supreme Court 2011Du20406 (2014. 3. 27.)

IV. Issues Related to Dismissals

A. The Principle of Good Faith and Invalidation

When a worker exercises his/her right to argue the invalidity of his/her dismissal, s/he is subject to the principle of good faith. Any right that contradicts this principle becomes invalidated. Case law rules that there is need to actively apply the principle of invalidation when dealing with litigations to confirm the invalidity of dismissals.[177]

The principle of invalidation is applied when: ① the holder of a right does not exercise this right for a significant amount of time; ② or the duty bearer (i.e. the other party) must have justifiable cause to believe that the right will not be exercised. In both cases, the relevant right is not recognized.

Case law rules that if a worker receives severance pay without raising any conditions, objections or deferment upon his/her dismissal, contesting the validity of the dismissal once a significant period has passed would be a violation of the principle of good faith. Yet even if the worker receives severance pay without express objection, "if circumstance or other grounds exist that objectively suggest that the worker is contesting the validity of the dismissal," the court interprets the worker to not have acknowledged the validity of the dismissal.[178] In other words, the standard of determining whether the principle of good faith has been violated is whether "circumstances exist that objectively suggest that the worker is contesting the validity of the dismissal."

Other circumstances that the court takes into consideration are: the worker failed to protest for a long period of time after the dismissal; the worker did not exercise his/her right for a long period of time

---

177 Supreme Court 91Da30118 (1992. 1. 21.)
178 Supreme Court 95Da51847 (1996. 3. 8.), Supreme Court 99Da34475 (2000. 4. 25.)

despite knowing that the dismissal was invalid; or a long period of time has passed since the employer constituted a new personnel system.[179]

B. Wrongful Dismissal and Wages

1) The Wages Payable during the Wrongful Dismissal Period

Where the employer dismisses a worker and the dismissal is invalid due to a lack of justifiable cause or the dismissal is cancelled for any other reason, the worker may demand the payment of the wages that s/he would have received but for the wrongful dismissal (i.e. for the duration of the wrongful dismissal period).[180]

In this case, the "wages that a worker would have received from the employer" refers to the wages a worker has been promised to be paid by working the contractual working hours agreed upon between labor and management.[181] All wages to be included in the calculation of average wages as outlined under LSA Article 2(1)6 would be included in this amount. This amount is not limited to ordinary wages.[182]

If the worker has been promised bonuses or allowances for good attendance, their average would be included in the "wages that a worker would have received from the employer," but portions of various allowances that do not possess the nature of wages would not be included, nor would valuables paid irregularly upon the satisfaction of special conditions be included.[183]

As legal allowances (allowances paid for extended, night, and holiday work) are calculated and paid according to the actual number of

---

179 Supreme Court 91Da30118 (1992. 1. 21.), Supreme Court 92Da3670 (1992. 5. 26.), Supreme Court 92Da24462 (1992. 10. 13.), Supreme Court 92Da13080 (1992. 11. 13.), Supreme Court 92Da23285 (1992. 12. 11.), Supreme Court 99Du4662 (1999. 6. 25.)

180 Civil Act, Article 538(1)

181 Supreme Court 81Da626 (1981. 12. 22.), Supreme Court 87DaKa2132 (1989. 5. 23.)

182 Supreme Court 93Da11463 (1993. 12. 21.)

183 Supreme Court 90DaKa25277 (1991. 6. 28.)

hours worked by the worker, in principle these are not included when calculating wages. However, in cases where the collective agreement contains provisions regarding extended work, and based on these provisions extended work allowance has been paid continuously, uniformly and regularly for a relatively long time, it could be sufficiently expected that the worker would have received the same amount of legal allowance that s/he received prior to the dismissal. Consequently, this amount is included in his/her "wages that s/he would have received from the employer."[184] For workers in special wage systems such as those working in alternate day or rotation shifts, where a fixed amount is determined to be paid under the title of legal allowances in their employer's wage regulations, such wages are obviously included in the amount the worker would have received from the employer but for the dismissal.

Payment for work done during annual leave is also included in the wages that a worker would have received from the employer but for being dismissed. Therefore, the number of contractual working days and the number of days the worker reported to work (or should have reported to work but for the wrongful dismissal) are both considered, and if this satisfies the requirements laid out in Article 60(1) of the LSA, the appropriate payment must be made. Even if the wrongful dismissal period occupies the entirety of the worker's annual working days, the above standard is applied in the same manner.[185]

If the wrongfully dismissed worker was expected to get a promotion in salary class, or if coworkers working in the same job as the dismissed worker receive a salary raise due to a newly negotiated collective agreement, this raise is also assumed to have been applied to the wage of the dismissed worker.[186]

---

184 Supreme Court 92Da39860 (1992. 12. 8.)

185 Supreme Court 2011Da95519 (2014. 3. 13.)

186 Supreme Court 93Da21736 (1993. 9. 24.)

On the other hand, if the worker falls in a state where employment would be impossible even without the dismissal (e.g. illness, prison sentence, army service), or if the employer shuts down its business for valid reasons, the worker is unable to request wages for this period as the non-provision of labor is not due to reasons attributable to the employer.[187]

2) Deduction of Interim Earnings

Under Article 538(2) of the Civil Act, any interim earnings that a worker has reaped by working in another job during the wrongful dismissal period would be considered a benefit from being relieved of the obligation to provide labor to the employer. Therefore, the employer may deduct this amount from the total wages that s/he must pay the worker for the wrongful dismissal period.

Interim earnings by the worker are not fully deducted, however; only the amount that exceeds the scope allowed for shutdown allowances (as determined under the LSA) are subject to deduction. In other words, Article 46 of the LSA stipulates that "when a business shuts down due to a cause attributable to the employer, s/he shall pay the workers concerned allowances of not less than 70 percent of their average wages during the period of shutdown" in order to ensure the minimum livelihood of the worker. As the payment of shutdown allowances must be ensured during the wrongful dismissal period, the amount of interim earnings is not deducted from the total wages to be paid to the worker up to the limits ensured by shutdown allowance.[188]

Also, even if the worker has found interim employment, if this only functions as a side job sufficient to maintain the minimum livelihood of the worker, this amount may not be deducted from the total wages that the worker would have received from the employer

187 Supreme Court 93Da50017 (1994. 9. 13.), Supreme Court 94Da25889 (1994. 10. 25.)
188 Supreme Court 91Da2656 (1991. 5. 14.), Supreme Court 93Da37915 (1993. 11. 9.)

during the wrongful dismissal period.[189] Any subsidies that the worker receives from the funds of the trade union cannot be deducted as well.[190] Finally, any profits earned during periods where wages are not normally paid by the employer also may not be subject to deductions.[191]

3) The Start and End Dates of Payment of Wages

If wages during the wrongful dismissal period must be paid, this amount is calculated from the date of the wrongful dismissal (or the day following) up to the date of reinstatement (or the date the worker is secondarily dismissed). If applicable, the age of retirement or death functions as the end date.[192]

C. Wrongful Dismissal and Unfair Labor Practices

As the provisions within the Union Act that prohibit unfair labor practices are compulsory regulations, if the dismissal of a worker is determined to be unfair an labor practice, the legal effect of the disposition is denied as well. This is a separate issue from when dismissals become invalid due to lack of justifiable cause under the LSA.[193]

The worker bears the burden of proving that the dismissal is an unfair labor practice, or that the actual cause of the worker's dismissal by the employer is the fact that s/he has engaged in valid union activity.[194]

189 Supreme Court 92Da31125 (1993. 5. 25.)
190 Supreme Court 91Da2656 (1991. 5. 14.)
191 Supreme Court 90DaKa25277 (1991. 6. 28.)
192 Supreme Court 91Da36192 (1993. 12. 24.)
193 Supreme Court 93Da11463 (1993. 12. 21.)
194 Supreme Court 2007Du25695 (2009. 3. 26.)

D. Wrongful Dismissals and Illegal Acts

A dismissal does not automatically become an illegal act merely due to its invalidity. However, if the employer intentionally devises a cause for disciplinary dismissal despite there being none as pretext to remove the worker from the workplace; or if the reason for dismissal is not in fact one that would justify dismissal; or if the fact that the reason for dismissal cannot be one that would justify dismissal is objectively apparent (and nominal research would lead a reasonable person to this conclusion) yet the employer has gone ahead with the dismissal regardless; or if it is apparent that the employer's abuse of his/her right to disciplinary action cannot be tolerated by sound and accepted social norms (e.g. an employer who violates Article 81 of the Union Act, which is a mandatory regulation prohibiting the wrongful treatment of workers, and wrongfully dismisses a worker), such actions by the employer may constitute illegal acts against the worker, as the former has unlawfully subjected the latter to emotional pain and suffering.[195] If the employer's acts are indeed recognized as illegal, the direction of causation (i.e. to the employer) is constructively assumed.

If an employer wrongfully dismisses a worker and this is confirmed via litigation, yet the employer refuses to reinstate the worker for a prolonged period despite paying the worker his/her wages, this would be an infringement of the worker's personal rights and an illegal act subjecting the employer to providing compensation for damages.[196] This is also the case when the employer refuses to reinstate a worker despite receiving an order of relief for the wrongful dismissal.

---

195 Supreme Court 92Da43586 (1993. 10. 12.), Supreme Court 91Da36192 (1993. 12. 24.), Supreme Court 95Da6823 (1996. 4. 23.), Supreme Court 95Da24821 (1997. 1. 21.), Supreme Court 98Da12157 (1999. 2. 23.), Supreme Court 2006Da30730 (2008. 6. 26.)

196 Supreme Court 92Da893 (1994. 2. 8.), Supreme Court 95Da6823 (1996. 4. 23.)

E. Remedial Procedure for Wrongful Dismissals

1) Civil Litigation or Remedial Procedures Involving the Labor Relations Commission

A worker who has been wrongfully dismissed may move forward with confirmation litigation of the invalidity of the dismissal via the civil court system, or instead request relief from the Labor Relations Commission for the wrongful dismissal and other unfavorable acts of the employer.[197] The applicable procedure is initiated depending on the worker's selection, and starting one process does not mean the other option is then closed to the worker. The employer or worker may appeal the order of relief or decision to dismiss that is handed down by the Labor Relations Commission, and subsequently sue the Central Labor Relations Commissioner as the defendant in front of the administrative court in charge of their jurisdiction so that the appeals determination may be cancelled. The opposing employer or worker participates in this litigation as a supporting participant to the defendant.

However, an order of relief by the Labor Relations Commission only burdens the employer with obligations under public law, and does not generate or modify legal relations under private law. Therefore, if the employer refuses to comply with the order and reinstate the worker, the worker has no choice but to resort to private civil litigation such as suits to confirm the invalidity of dismissal in order to confirm his/her status as an employee and obtain a binding order from the court for the employer to pay due wages.[198]

If the employer protests the re-examined determination of the Central Labor Relations Commission and presents the case to an administrative court, and subsequently exhausts all three levels of

---

197 Supreme Court 90Da9353 (1991. 7. 12.)
198 Supreme Court 86Da204 (1988. 12. 13.), Supreme Court 91Da22100 (1992. 5. 22.)

appeal in the court system, this would result in the case having gone through five levels of review (including the two levels in the Labor Relations Commission system). In this case, the worker may end up expending more time and money than s/he would have if s/he went directly to the civil court litigation to obtain relief.

2) When Employers Fail to Comply with Orders for Remedy

The LSA stipulates the imposition of penalties and compulsory performance money to employers who fail to comply with orders for remedy by the Labor Relations Commission regarding wrongful dismissal and other issues for the purpose of ensuring the effectiveness of the orders.[199] The LSA also contains provisions that impose penalties against people who fail to comply with an order for remedy that has become final and conclusive.[200]

3) The Monetary Compensation System for Dismissals without Justifiable Cause

The LSA stipulates that it is possible to order the employer to pay a worker that s/he has dismissed without justifiable cause an amount of valuables worth not less than the wages the worker would have been paid during the period of dismissal instead of ordering reinstatement, if the worker refuses to return to his/her former job.

F. The Union Shop Agreement and Dismissals

If the employer dismisses a worker who has left the union as per the union shop agreement, the worker may sue the employer directly to confirm the invalidity of the dismissal without having to first request the confirmation of his/her status as a union member from

---

199 Ibid., Article 33
200 Ibid., Article 111

the union.[201] If the trade union refuses to grant the request to nullify the withdrawal of members to only a part of the total number of workers who submitted this request, and those workers are ultimately dismissed by the employer, such dismissals are invalid due to the violation of equity.[202]

G. The Status of the Worker Disputing the Validity of His/ Her Dismissal

The Union Act determines the status of a worker disputing the validity of his/her dismissal, stipulating that "a dismissed person shall not be regarded as a person who is not a worker, until a review decision in made by the National Labor Relations Commission when he has made an application to the Labor Relations Commission for remedies for unfair labor practices."[203] This regulation, however, merely determines the qualification of a worker who may be a union member in order to protect the establishment and maintenance of the trade union. Therefore, this regulation of the Union Act cannot be extended and applied generally to the individual employment contract between the worker and employer.[204]

A dismissed worker who is also a member of a union has the duty to comply with the employer's regulations or Acts regarding industrial action. Therefore, if the dismissed worker engages in illegal acts during industrial actions, the employer may impose disciplinary action against the worker for these acts after the dismissal is invalidated and s/he is reinstated.[205]

---

201 Supreme Court 94Da15363 (1992. 2. 28.)

202 Supreme Court 96Da28899 (1996. 10. 29.)

203 Union Act, Article 2.4(d)

204 Supreme Court 92Da42354 (1993. 6. 8.)

205 Supreme Court 93Da26496 (1994. 9. 30.)

Chapter 9

Personnel Movement

I. Job and Workplace Transfers

A. The Concept

Job transfers or workplace transfers are personnel movements within the same corporation that result in a long-term change in the type and substance of work of a worker as well as his/her workplace. A "job transfer" occurs if the type and substance of work (but not the workplace) changes, and a "workplace transfer" occurs if the transfer involves a changing of the workplace. As a whole, these are known generally as "relocations," and are classified as intra-corporate transfers.

B. Essential Conditions

1) Substantive Conditions

Personnel orders such as job and workplace transfers are the prerogative of the employer (who holds the right to personnel management) and therefore the employer has significant discretion within the scope of business necessity.[1] However, if a personnel order is determined to abuse the employer's rights or violate Articles 23(1) or 104(2) of the LSA,[2] the order loses its legitimacy.

If an employer's job or workplace transfer order satisfies the conditions outlined in the relevant labor regulations (the rules of employment or the collective agreement) or industry practice in light of the totality of the circumstances, the personnel order would be binding on the worker. The conditions for an order to hold such legitimacy are: first, the order must result in the worker providing the type and substance of labor that remain within the scope of the employment contract. Second, the type and substance of labor must be comparatively reasonable in light of the detriment or disadvantage the worker experiences in his/her living conditions. Finally, the process of the transfer (i.e. consultation with the worker, etc.) must include all steps as required in order to satisfy the principle of good faith.[3]

However, transfers that go beyond the scope of the employment contract by changing its substance are not binding on workers. So long as the worker does not consent to the transfer, any unfavorable personnel action such as dismissal for reason of noncompliance to personnel orders is determined invalid.[4]

Even if the personnel order has grounds in the employment contract, the order is still invalid if: it does not possess "justifiable cause"[5] in that the transfer is not necessary for the work and/or causes unforeseeable significant detriment to the worker; or the order

1 Supreme Court 86DaKa2567 (1989. 2. 28.), Supreme Court 90DaKa27389 (1991. 2. 22.), Supreme Court 90Da8046 (1991. 5. 28.), Supreme Court 90Da9353 (1991. 7. 12.), Supreme Court 91Da12752 (1991. 7.12.), Supreme Court 90Da12366 (1991. 9. 24.) Supreme Court 90Da20428 (1991. 10. 25.), Supreme Court 91Nu5204 (1992. 1. 21.), Supreme Court 91Nu11025 (1992. 12. 8.), Supreme Court 93Da10279 (1994. 4. 26.), Supreme Court 93Da47677 (1994. 5. 10.), Supreme Court 97Da36316 (1997. 12. 12.), Supreme Court 2007Du20157 (2009. 4. 23.)

2 Labor Standards Act

3 Supreme Court 90Da9353 (1991. 7. 12.), Supreme Court 91Da12752 (1991. 7. 12.), Supreme Court 90Da12366 (1991. 9. 24.)

4 Supreme Court 91Da22100 (1992. 5. 22.), Supreme Court 93Da10279 (1994. 4. 26.)

5 LSA, Article 23(1)

constitutes an "unfair labor practice" in that the outward rationale of business necessity serves as a mere pretext to disguise retaliatory measures against workers for their unionization and union activities.[6]

2) Procedural Conditions

Job and workplace transfers occur when employers unilaterally express such intent to their workers within the scope recognized by the employment contract. This expression of intent becomes effective the moment it is communicated to the worker; the specific medium of communication (written, oral, or by phone) does not impact the validity of the communication.

Even if a job or workplace transfer functions as a pretext that conceals the employer's intention to reprimand its worker, if the transfer does not fall within the list of negative personnel action (as designated by the collective agreement or the rules of employment) that requires the use of disciplinary proceedings, such proceedings are not mandatory.[7]

C. Specific Illustrations

If the validity of the job or workplace transfer is put to question, the determination analysis turns on the facts of each case.

1) Determining Validity via Interpretation of Employment Contracts

i) When the "Type or Substance of Work" Is Specified

Transfer orders made by an employer are not automatically binding on

---

6 Supreme Court 92Nu9425 (1992. 11. 13.), Supreme Court 91Nu11025 (1992. 12. 8.), Supreme Court 97Nu18035 (1998. 12. 23.)

7 Supreme Court 93Da26496 (1994. 9. 30.), Supreme Court 97Da58750 (1998. 4. 24.), Supreme Court 97Nu5435 (1998. 12. 22.)

workers who have their type and substance of labor specified in their employment contract. Workers who have gained employment under the condition that they possess special skills or professional licenses (e.g. doctors, nurses, drivers, boiler engineers, typists, operators of hotels) are assumed to have their type and substance of work specified within their employment contract, barring the existence of special circumstances.[8]

For workers who have acquired certain skills through vocational training or have worked as a skilled worker in the same capacity for a prolonged period of time, transfers to positions that have nothing to do with the skillset of the worker are considered to have exceeded the scope of the employment contract.[9] However, if the job that the worker is transferred to is similar to the worker's previous position and s/he would be able to use his/her acquired skills, such a transfer would be considered within the scope of the employment contract.

ii) When "Workplace" Is Specified
If the worker is based in a fixed location, and this is one of the assumptions underlying the employment contract that led to his/her employment, it is interpreted that the worker's workplace is specified even if there is no such stipulation within the rules of employment or other regulatory documents. As such, workplace transfer orders are not binding if the worker him/herself does not provide consent.[10]

However, this is not the case for workers employed in administrative positions of corporations that have workplaces in multiple locations. The general interpretation in such instances is that it cannot be deemed that there was an agreement between the worker and the employer to designate a specific workplace. The fact that the

8 Supreme Court 93Nu3837 (1993. 9. 28.), Supreme Court 92Da893 (1994. 2. 8.)

9 Supreme Court 90Da8046 (1991. 5. 28.)

10 Supreme Court 91Nu5204 (1992. 1 21.)

worker has filled out in his/her employment application form his/her preferred work locations does not mean that there has been an explicit or implicit agreement between the worker and the employer as to where the worker's workplace will ultimately be.[11]

iii) Modification of Working Conditions Due to the "Consent of the Worker"

An employer's personnel order (i.e. job or workplace transfer) is considered to be valid if the worker has provided consent, even if the order results in a modification of working conditions such as the type, subject, or place of work.[12]

Such consent may be obtained through two ways: the first is to obtain comprehensive consent from the worker during recruitment or employment to agree with all job or workplace transfers for the duration of the term of employment; the second is to obtain consent for each personnel order as the need arises. Consent may be given implicitly: for example, a worker is considered to have given implied consent if s/he complied with a job or workplace transfer order that significantly modified his/her working conditions for a period of time without raising objections or rejecting the order. However, such implied consent is invalid if compliance to the job or workplace transfer order is due to threat of reprisal (i.e. harsher penalties) from the employer.

2) Determining Validity via the Existence of "Justifiable Cause"

"An employer shall not, without justifiable cause, transfer or take other unfavorable measures against a worker."[13] Therefore, if a job or workplace transfer order is given for reasons not necessary for the

---

11 Supreme Court 92Nu18825 (1993. 9. 14.)

12 Ibid.

13 LSA, Article 23(1)

work itself,[14] or (if the order was indeed necessary but) the transfer results in a significant and reasonably unforeseeable detriment to the worker, the order is deemed invalid due to the lack of just cause.

"Work necessity" for the purpose of job and workplace transfers means the reasonable need for an employer to change the allotment of personnel within the business and to determine which workers will be involved in the new arrangement.[15] Therefore, should the degree of detriment to the transferred worker's living conditions remain within the socially accepted bounds of predictability and acceptability, and should the job or workplace transfer be ordered for the purpose of appropriately allotting the workforce, enhancing productivity, promoting work skill development, raising morale, facilitating operations, and maintaining or recovering workplace order/worker unity, the order in question is considered to possess "work necessity."[16]

Even if the detriment to a worker's living conditions resulting from a job or workplace transfer is significant and exceeds reasonable bounds of predictability, if there are special circumstances that make it difficult to find alternative workers that could be transferred in the former's stead, the transfer order is deemed to satisfy the requirements of justifiable cause. However, if there is another worker available, the job or workplace transfer is deemed to lack just cause.

3) Determining Validity via the Existence of "Unfair Labor Practices"

"Employers shall not take unfavorable measures against a worker on the grounds that s/he has joined or intends to join a trade union, or has

---

14 Supreme Court 90Da8046 (1991. 5. 28.), Supreme Court 93Da51263 (1995. 5. 9.), Supreme Court 97Da29417 (1998. 1. 20.)

15 Supreme Court 92Nu18825 (1993. 9. 14.) , Supreme Court 94Da52928 (1995. 10. 13.)

16 Supreme Court 86DaKa2567 (1989. 2. 28.), Supreme Court 91Da12752 (1991. 7. 12.), Supreme Court 90Da20428 (1991. 10. 25.), Supreme Court 91Da22100 (1992. 5. 22.), Supreme Court 92Nu18825 (1993. 9.14.), Supreme Court 93Da47677 (1994. 5. 10.), Supreme Court 94Da52928 (1995. 10. 13.), Supreme Court 95Nu7130 (1996. 4. 12.), Supreme Court 97Da18165, 18172 (1997. 7. 22.), Supreme Court 97Nu5435 (1998. 12. 22.), Supreme Court 97Nu2528, 2535 (1999. 9. 3.), Supreme Court 2007Du20157 (2009. 4. 23.)

attempted to organize a trade union, or has performed any other lawful act for the operation of a trade union."[17] Therefore, if the employer's job or workplace transfer order is determined to be an "unfair labor practice," that order becomes invalid. Likewise, disciplinary action or dismissal of a worker for reasons of disobedience to the above invalid transfer order is invalid due to the lack of just cause.[18]

The following factors are considered when determining whether personnel orders such as transfers should be considered unfavorable measures against a worker as retaliation against legitimate union activity: motivation; objective; the existence of rational reasons to necessitate the transfer; the detriment of living standards to the worker as a result of the transfer and comparative costs; the timing of the transfer; the relationship between the union and the employer; the existence of disparate treatment between union and non-union member workers in terms of penalties involved for similar actions; the legitimacy of the reasons given for the transfer; consistency with company custom; the process used by the employer in reaching the decision to transfer the worker; other external, objective circumstance that may be used to infer the existence of impermissible intent to engage in unfair labor practice; and whether the employer's measure results in a decrease of union activity.[19]

II. Out-Transfers/Position Transfers

A. The Concept

"Out-transfers" or "position transfers" are forms of personnel

---

17 Trade Union and Labor Relations Adjustment Act, Article 81(1)

18 Supreme Court 91Nu5204 (1992. 1. 21.), Supreme Court 92Nu11121 (1993. 2. 23.)

19 Supreme Court 91Nu5204 (1992. 1. 21.), Supreme Court 91Nu11025 (1992. 12. 8.), Supreme Court 92Nu11121 (1993. 2. 23.)

movement where a worker is transferred to work with a company that is different from the one that s/he is currently employed in. "Out-transfers"[20] occur when a worker maintains his employment with his/her employer and yet his/her duty to provide labor is waived due to dispositions such as suspensions, long-term business trips, dispatches, and telecommuting; in such cases, the worker provides his/her labor under the direction and supervision of the other company.

On the other hand, "position transfers" occur when a worker transfers his/her work position from the original employer to another employer, and hence becomes a worker of the latter corporation completely. While job and workplace transfers are intra-corporation transfers, out-transfers and position transfers are inter-corporation transfers.

B. Essential Conditions

1) Consent of the Worker

"Out-transfers" assume the existence of a contract between corporation (A), the worker's original employer, and corporation (B), which receives the out-transferred worker. The main substance of the contract between corporations (A) and (B) outlines the agreement that (A) transfers its right to direct work over the transferred worker to (B).

Article 657(1) of the Civil Act stipulates that "The employer may not assign his rights to a third person without the consent of the employee." Hence, corporation (A) must secure appropriate and legitimate consent from the worker regarding changes in the latter's working conditions prior to issuing out-transfer orders.[21] However,

---

20 Supreme Court 95Da51397 (1997. 3. 28.), Supreme Court 98Da36924 (1998. 12.11.)
21 Supreme Court 88DaKa4918 (1989. 5. 9.), Supreme Court 92Da11695 (1993. 1. 26.), Supreme Court 92Nu8200 (1993. 1. 26.)

for position transfers between affiliated corporations that have a wide range of business types and conditions, specific consent is not necessary for the transfer to be considered valid.[22]

2) Implied Consent

If there is implied consent from the worker, both "out-transfers" and "position transfers" are valid.

For example, a worker is considered to have provided implied consent if s/he complied with an "out-transfer" or "position transfer" order for a certain period of time without raising objections or rejecting the order and continued to provide his/her labor normally. However, such implied consent is invalid if compliance to the transfer order is due to threats of reprisal (i.e. harsher penalties) from the employer.[23]

3) Comprehensive Prior Consent

It is possible for a worker to provide his/her comprehensive prior consent to comply with all personnel orders within the same corporate group at the time of recruitment or during his/her employment. Such consent is applicable to "out-transfers" and "position transfers" as well.

That said, even if such a comprehensive prior consent is permitted, in order for this to be valid the employer must specify whether the worker would be "out-transferred" or "position transferred" to a single corporation or multiple corporations, as well as elaborate on basic working conditions after such a transfer.[24] In order to acknowledge that a worker has provided comprehensive prior consent to "out-transfers" or "position transfers," it is not enough for the employer to stipulate in the rules of employment or the collective agreement that personnel movement within affiliated companies are allowed, nor is

---

22 Supreme Court 95Da42270 (1996. 5. 10.)

23 Supreme Court 92Nu8200 (1993. 1. 26.)

24 Supreme Court 92Da11695 (1993. 1. 26.), Supreme Court 92Nu8200 (1993. 1. 26.)

it enough to inform all recruits that such is company policy during group-wide orientation sessions.[25]

4) Established Corporate Custom

"Out-transfers" or "position transfers" to affiliated companies are valid even without the specific consent of the worker if there is a corporate custom of transferring workers to affiliated companies without the consent of the worker, and that custom is clearly recognized as a general norm that regulates labor relations, or it has become a *de facto* institution due to general lack of objection from workers.[26]

C. Legal Effects

1) Legitimate Disposition Authority to Give "Out-transfers" Orders

The transferor corporation possesses the disposition authority for violations committed by its worker at the transferee corporation. The transferee corporation also possesses such authority independently from the transferor corporation.

2) "Position Transfers" and the Succession of Labor Relationships

Whether the labor relationship between the worker and the transferor corporation is succeeded to the transferee corporation is determined by the contract governing the position transfer entered into by the relevant parties.

Case law suggests the following:[27] Valid position transfers occur upon the successful conclusion of the agreement to terminate the labor

---

25 Supreme Court 92Nu8200 (1993. 1. 26.)

26 Supreme Court 95Da42270 (1996. 5. 10.)

27 Supreme Court 95Nu1972 (1996. 4. 26.), Supreme Court 95Da42270 (1996. 5. 10.), Supreme Court 95Da42270 (1996. 5. 10.), Supreme Court 95Da29970 (1996. 12. 23.), Supreme Court 96Da38438 (1997. 7. 8.), Supreme Court 97Da17575 (1997. 12. 26.), Supreme Court 98Da36924 (1998. 12. 11.), Supreme Court 97Nu5435 (1998.12. 22.), Supreme Court 2006Da34015 (2006. 10. 26.)

relationship with the transferor corporation and the establishment of a new relationship with the transferee corporation. Therefore, by principle, once a valid position transfer has been made the transferred worker would have severed his/her labor relationship with the transferor corporation and thus the labor relationship is not succeeded to the transferee corporation.

However, the labor relationship between the transferred worker and the transferor corporation is succeeded by the transferee corporation in the following special circumstances: i) when there exists between the parties a special agreement to do so, or ii) when the rules of employment or other regulations of the transferee corporation contain a provision that requires the inclusion of the time the worker was employed at the transferor corporation when calculating the total term of employment.

III. Suspensions and Leaves

A. The Concept

A suspension or leave are measures taken by the employer to prohibit a worker from working for a certain period of time, while his/her position is maintained. This measure is taken when it is impossible or impracticable to have the worker engage in that particular work. Generally, suspensions and leaves are governed by the rules of employment or the collective agreement.[28] In addition, the Equal Employment Opportunity and Work-Family Balance Assistance Act contain provisions that regulate the use of maternal/paternal leaves (Article 19).

The relevant issues regarding this concept are: whether the worker

---

28 Supreme Court 92Da16690 (1992. 11. 13.)

has the right to request suspensions/leaves, and whether an employer's order for suspension is legitimate in the first place.

B. Essential Conditions

The validity of an employer's order to suspend a worker needs to be assessed via a reasonable interpretation of the applicable provisions in the corporation's rules of employment or the collective agreement.

Article 23(1) of the LSA limits the employer's use of suspensions against workers without the existence of justifiable cause. Therefore, even if an employer is given the right to suspend a worker upon the occurrence of designated grounds for suspension, it is only when the circumstances indicate that the worker will be prevented from providing labor for a significant period or that it would be inappropriate for the worker to continue providing labor, the employer's suspension orders would be considered to possess validity. In making this determination, the following specific factors must be considered for each case: the purpose behind the relevant provision governing suspensions and leaves; the actual function of the provision; the degree of rationality should the right to suspend be exercised; the degree of detriment suffered by the worker to his/her livelihood and career.

To illustrate, one case[29] ruled the following: While a worker who has chronic persisting hepatitis (type B) satisfies the provision that makes it possible for an employer to suspend him (i.e. "a person who contracts a contagious disease or a disease that may potentially be contagious"), suspending a worker completely and prohibiting him from providing labor for up to six (6) months until the worker has completed treatment of the disease falls beyond the scope of the

---

29 Supreme Court 92Da16690 (1992. 11. 13.)

socially accepted bounds of rationality.

Should a worker be arrested and detained for prosecution, the employer's suspension measure would be valid in light of the fact that it is impracticable for the worker to provide labor (i.e. suspension due to prosecution). Furthermore, the validity of the employer to stipulate that "suspended workers who received guilty verdicts in the first trial in a criminal case" or "workers who have been detained for prosecution for more than six months" satisfy grounds for termination is in question. In order for an employer to validly terminate its contractual labor relationship with a worker through a unilateral expression of such intent, the employer must ultimately possess "justifiable cause."[30] Ultimately, the totality of the related matters (i.e. whether there is a chance for early release within the period of suspension, the impact the prosecution may have on the employee's work, the nature of the criminal trial) must be reasonably accounted for in order to determine the validity of the employer's suspension.[31] Should the worker be handed down a verdict of not-guilty with regard to the crime that s/he was prosecuted for, s/he must be reinstated to his/her position without delay.

C. Legal Effects

1) Wages
In principle, matters regarding payment of wages during suspension are determined by the collective agreement or the rules of employment.[32]

According to Article 46 of the LSA, the employer must provide

---

30 LSA, Article 23(1)

31 Supreme Court 92Nu12452 (1993. 5. 25.)

32 Supreme Court 90Da8763 (1992. 3. 31.)

70% of the suspended worker's average wages as suspension allowance if the suspension is a result of a shutdown due to causes relating to management of the corporation attributable to the employer. If the suspension is a result of an act attributable to the employer that is subject to civil liability (e.g. willful conduct or negligence), the employer must provide 100% of the suspended worker's wages as suspension allowance. Suspension periods are included when calculating years of continuous service.

2) Duty of Good Faith

While the worker's duty to provide labor is waived during the suspension period, as the labor contract relationship itself continues to be maintained the suspended worker retains his/her duty of good faith. Among other things, the worker must not disclose confidential information or commit defamatory acts. Should the worker violate this duty, s/he is subject to disciplinary action even during the suspension period.

Chapter 10

The Equal Employment Opportunity and Work-Family Balance Assistance Act

I. Introduction

The old Equal Employment Opportunity Act was established based on the principle of equality enshrined in the Korean Constitution, in December 4, 1987, and which was subsequently amended as the Equal Employment Opportunity and Work-Family Balance Assistance Act (hereinafter referred as the "EEO Act"). The EEO Act establishes systems that ensure equal opportunity and treatment for both genders, while also providing for the work-family balance of workers, and stipulating the obligations of both the state and the employer in this regard.

II. Prohibition of Discrimination

A. The Concept of Discrimination and the Prohibition of Discrimination

Sexual discrimination is generally classified as direct discrimination and indirect discrimination. Direct discrimination is directly discriminating against an individual for reasons due to sex. For example, if a corporate regulation reads "The retirement age for women is 50, while for men it is 60," this would be a form of direct discrimination. Indirect discrimination places the same formal standard to both sexes, but the resulting effects are disadvantageous to a particular sex.

The "discrimination" prohibited by the EEO Act are those acts in which the employer discriminates between his/her employees regarding hiring or employment conditions, or engages in other unfavorable acts without justifiable reasons on the grounds of gender, marriage, status within family, pregnancy or childbirth, etc. The "justifiable reason" requirement is not satisfied even if an employer applies employment or working conditions equally between male and female workers, should the number of men or women capable of satisfying such conditions is remarkably fewer in comparison with the opposite gender, and thus causes disadvantageous results to the opposite gender, in which case said conditions may not be attested to be justifiable. However, this shall not apply in the following cases: (1) cases where a specific gender is inevitably requested in view of the characteristics of duties; (2) cases where measures are taken for protecting motherhood, such as pregnancy, childbirth and lactation of female workers; or (3) other cases where positive employment improvement measures are taken under the EEO Act or other Acts.[1] The EEO Act stipulates as the standard of sexual discrimination on whether "justifiable reason" exists or not, and the Supreme Court cases follows suit. This practice is criticized by some groups, which argue that a stricter standard of review should replace this justifiable reason standard.

No employer shall discriminate on the grounds of gender in recruitment or employment of workers.[2] Additionally in recruiting or employing female workers, no employer shall exhibit or demand

---

1 EEO Act, Article 2(1)

2 Ibid., Article 7(1)

physical conditions, such as appearance, height, weight, etc., nor require someone to be married or unmarried to perform the relevant duties.[3] Also, the employer shall provide equal pay for work of equal value within the identical business,[4] and no employer shall discriminate on the grounds of gender in providing welfare, such as money, goods, loans, etc. in order to subsidize the living of his/her workers aside from wages.[5] No employer shall discriminate on the grounds of gender in education, assignment, age limit, retirement, and promotion or dismissal of his/her workers,[6] and no employer shall conclude an employment contract that stipulates marriage, pregnancy, or childbirth of female workers as grounds for retirement.[7]

The Ministry of Employment and Labor stipulates that in order to satisfy the "justifiable reason" requirement in treating workers differently according to sex, the purpose of the business and the nature, type, and conditions of the actual work carried out must be specifically and comprehensively considered, and the need to treat workers differently according to sex due to business management reasons must be recognized after this process. The method and duration of the disparate treatment must also be appropriate as well.[8]

---

3 Ibid., Article 7(2)

4 Ibid., Article 8(1)

5 Ibid., Article 9

6 Ibid., Articles 10 and 11(1)

7 Ibid., Article 11(2)

8 Operational Regulations to the Equal Employment Opportunity Act: Ministry of Employment and Labor Regulations, Article 2(1)

B. Supreme Court Decisions Regarding Prohibition of Discrimination

The Supreme Court ruled that a collective agreement that designates a higher retirement age of male union members than that of female union members is invalid due to the fact that it violates compulsory law.[9]

The Supreme Court also reviewed a case where the employer restructured the organization of the company and deprived the promotion opportunities of a specific position in an ad hoc basis, without justifiable reason. Considering the fact that the position in question comprises exclusively of female workers, the Supreme Court determined that this reorganization constituted discriminatory treatment against women workers (i.e. depriving them of promotional opportunities) that was not supported with justifiable reason.[10]

In contrast, the Supreme Court ruled in favor of a case where a company designated the retirement age of switchboard workers (a position comprised exclusively of female workers) to be 53 (versus age 58 for regular workers), saying the five years' difference in retirement age between switchboard workers and regular workers imposed by the employer cannot definitely be said to go against the sense of justifiable reason commonly possessed by society[11] after taking into account multiple factors (i.e. the surplus supply of workers, the composition of employees across age groups, the degree of difference in retirement age, the fact that labor and management had agreed to this arrangement, the period in which new recruitment had not taken place, and the general opinion among employees about the present retirement age).

---

9 Supreme Court 92Nu16765 (1993. 4. 9.)

10 Supreme Court 2006Du3476 (2006. 7. 28.)

11 Supreme Court 94Nu13589 (1996. 8. 23.)

C. Equal Remuneration for Work of Equal Value

Equal pay must be provided for work of equal value. The LSA[12] stipulates that an employer shall neither discriminate against workers on the basis of gender, nor take discriminatory treatment in relation to terms and conditions of employment on the ground of nationality, religion, or social status.[13] The EEO Act stipulates that an employer shall provide equal pay for work of equal value within identical businesses.[14] This provision of the EEO Act prohibits discriminatory wages based on the sex of the worker. In addition to the above, there are laws that prohibit wage discrimination against irregular workers (Act on the Protection of Fixed-Term and Part-Time Workers, Act on the Protection of Temporary Agency Workers).

According to the EEO Act, the standard to determine work of equal value is skill, labor, responsibility, working conditions, etc. required for the performance of duties.[15] According to case law,[16] "work of equal value" means "work in an identical business that is the same or essentially the same for both male and female workers, or, if the jobs are somewhat dissimilar, where an objective job assessment (or other such measures) would recognize that the labor provided by both jobs possess essentially the same value." In determining whether the work provided possesses equal value, skill, labor, responsibility, working conditions, etc. required for the performance of duties as per Article 8(2) of the EEO Act, as well as other standards such as the worker's education, career, number of years worked must be comprehensively considered. The case above also states that the term "skill" mentioned in Article 8(2) indicates objective indicators of work

---

12 Labor Standards Act
13 LSA, Article 6
14 EEO Act, Article 8(1)
15 Ibid., Article 8(2)
16 Supreme Court 2010Da101011 (2013. 3. 14.)

competency or ability such as licenses, degrees, and acquired skillsets; the term "labor" indicates physical or mental labor or the physical or mental tension required for performing the work (i.e. labor intensity); the term "responsibility" indicates the nature, scope, and complexity of duties inherent in the work and the degree the employer relies on the work in question; and the term "working conditions" indicates the physical working environment that the worker in the industry in question typically is exposed to, such as noise, heat, physical and chemical danger, isolation, cold or heat.

The above case also ruled the employer providing less wages to female workers vis-à-vis male workers despite the fact that both workers provide work of equal value in the same business without justifiable reason would constitute an illegal action and hence the business owner is liable to the injured female worker for the difference between the wages that the worker should have received but for the discrimination and the actual wages paid.

D. Effects of Violation

Where an employer discriminates on the grounds of gender in age limit, retirement and dismissal of his/her workers or concludes an employment contract that stipulates marriage, pregnancy, or childbirth of female workers as grounds for retirement in violation of the EEO Act, Article 11, s/he shall be punished by imprisonment for not more than five years or by a fine not exceeding thirty million won.[17] Where the employer fails to equally pay for work of equal value within the identical business, s/he shall be punished by imprisonment for not more than three years or by a fine not exceeding twenty million won.[18]

---

17 EEO Act, Article 37(1)
18 EEO Act, Article 37(2)

Where the employer discriminates on the grounds of gender in recruitment and employment of a worker, or exhibits or demands physical conditions in hiring female workers such as appearance, height or weight and unmarried status, which are not required for performing the relevant duties; or where the employer discriminates on the grounds of gender in providing welfare, such as money, goods or loans in order to support the livelihood of his/her workers except for wages; or where the employer discriminates on the grounds of gender in education, assignment, and promotion of his/her workers. In all of these cases, the employer shall be punished by a fine not exceeding five million won.[19]

III. Sexual Harassment in the Workplace

According to the EEO Act, "the term 'sexual harassment on the job' means that an employer, a superior or a worker causes another worker to feel sexual humiliation or a repulsive feeling by sexual words or actions by utilizing a position within a workplace or in relation with duties, or providing any disadvantages in employment on account of disregard to sexual words or actions or any other demands."[20]

The Supreme Court ruled that "sexual words or actions," which is a condition for sexual harassment in the workplace, is "a physical, verbal, visual action regarding the physical relationship between the sexes or physical characteristics of a particular sex that would objectively cause a normal layperson placed in the same situation to feel sexual humiliation or repulsiveness in light of the common sense and norms of society."[21]

---

19 Ibid., Article 37(4)
20 Ibid., Article 2(2)
21 Supreme Court 2007Du22498 (2008. 7. 10.)

In the above case, the Supreme Court opined that in order for sexual harassment to be recognized, "it is not strictly necessary for the person in question to possess sexual motivation or intent, but that in considering specific circumstances of the case (e.g. relationship of the parties, the location and circumstance of the action, the explicit or abstract response of the recipient of the action, the substance and degree of the action, whether the action was a one-off action or of short duration, or was continuous), there must exist an act that is recognized to objectively cause a normal layperson placed in the same situation to feel sexual humiliation or repulsiveness, and that such sexual humiliation or repulsiveness has in fact taken place."

According to the EEO Act, "no employer, superior or worker shall commit any sexual harassment on the job against another worker,"[22] and the employer shall conduct preventive education of sexual harassment on the job at least once a year.[23] Also, "the employer shall, where an occurrence of sexual harassment on the job has been verified, take without delay disciplinary measures or any other action corresponding thereto against the relevant person in question," and "the employer shall not dismiss, or take any other disadvantageous measures against, a worker who has been damaged with regard to sexual harassment on the job or claimed damage occurred from sexual harassment."[24] The employer must endeavor to take all possible measures should a worker be sexually harassed by a person closely related to the duties, such as a client.[25]

The Supreme Court also ruled that an employer's dismissal of a worker "due to disciplinary reasons for the latter's sexual harassment actions which, from the perspective of a normal layperson in the same

22 EEO Act, Article 12
23 Ibid., Article 13(1)
24 Ibid., Article 14
25 EEO Act, Article 14(2)

circumstance as the other party, is objectively severe to the extent that it would deteriorate the working environment or is conducted repeatedly" cannot easily be viewed as an abuse of the employer's right to discipline its workers (assuming that the disciplinary dismissal is not objectively unfair).[26] In the same case, the Supreme Court also ruled: "This is especially true when considering the fact that victims of sexual harassment in the workplace committed by employers or agents of employers (due to the latter's use of his/her superior position) is highly likely to stay silent and accept such actions for fear of explicit or implicit retaliation to his/her employment, such cases must be dealt with correspondingly stern measures."

Where the employer dismisses, or takes any other disadvantageous measures against, a worker who has been victimized by sexual harassment on the job or for a claim is brought against him/her for the occurrence of sexual harassment on the job, that employer shall be punished by imprisonment for not more than three years or by a fine not exceeding twenty million won.[27]

Where an employer commits sexual harassment on the job, s/he shall be punished by a fine for negligence in an amount not exceeding ten million won. Where the employer fails to take, without delay, any disciplinary measures or other actions corresponding thereto against the relevant person in question, although the occurrence of sexual harassment on the job has been verified, and where the employer dismisses, or takes any other disadvantageous measures against, a worker on the grounds of a claim for any damage from sexual harassment from the client, or of disregard for sexual demand from the client, the employer shall be punished by a fine for negligence not exceeding an amount of five million won. Finally, an employer who fails to provide preventive education of sexual harassment on the job

---

26 Supreme Court 2007Du22498 (2008. 7. 10.)

27 EEO Act Article 37(2)

shall be punished by a fine for negligence not exceeding an amount of three million won.[28]

IV. Protection of Motherhood and Assistance for Work-Family Balance

The LSA determines maternity leave and the obligation of employers to pay wages to pregnant and nursing workers. The EEO Act stipulates that the state may pay maternity leave benefits to persons meeting specific requirements.[29] As such, the Employment Insurance Act stipulates that maternity leave benefits may be paid to workers meeting certain criteria.[30] Also, where a male worker requests leave on the grounds of his spouse's childbirth, the employer shall grant leave for at least three and up to five days. In such cases, such workers shall be paid for the first three days out of the period of leave used.[31] In calculating annual paid leave, the maternity leave period shall be deemed as a period where the worker has attended work.[32]

"Where a worker parenting his/her pre-school children (including adopted children) less than six years old applies for temporary retirement (hereinafter referred to as "temporary retirement for childcare"), the employer shall grant permission."[33] The period allowed for temporary retirement extends up to twelve full months. "No employer shall dismiss or take any other disadvantageous measures against a worker on account of temporary retirement for childcare or dismiss the relevant worker during the period of temporary retirement

---

28 EEO Act, Article 39
29 Ibid., Article 18
30 Employment Insurance Act, Article 75
31 EEO Act, Article 18(2)
32 LSA, Article 60(6)2
33 EEO Act, Article 19(1)

for childcare. After completing temporary retirement for childcare, the employer shall reinstate the relevant worker in the same work as before temporary retirement, or any other work paying the same level of wages.[34]

There is no regulation which stipulates that the period of maternity leave must be considered a period where the worker has attended work when calculating annual paid leave. On this matter, the Supreme Court ruled that it is reasonable to first determine whether the worker has satisfied the required rate of attendance to qualify for annual paid leave based on the number of days worked after subtracting the period where maternity leave has been used. If the worker qualifies for annual paid leave based on the above calculation, the Supreme Court then presented the following equation to calculate the extent of annual paid leave that should be given to the worker:

[Annual Paid Leave Days, or the number of annual paid leave days that would have been given to the worker if s/he has satisfied the 80% attendance rate under normal labor relations] × [(Fixed Annual Work Days − Days Spent During Maternity Leave) / (Fixed Annual Work Days)].[35]

The worker may elect to reduce work hours instead of taking maternity leave. The resulting work hours must exceed 15 but be less than 30. In exceptional cases, such as when it is impossible to employ the worker's substitute, the employer may deny the reduction of work hours.[36] While it is possible to determine working conditions such as wages in proportion to the worker's reduced working hours, the employer is prohibited from applying unfavorable working conditions to a worker

---

34 Ibid., Article 19(3)

35 Supreme Court 2011Da4629 (2013. 12. 26.)

36 EEO Act, Article 19(2)

in other cases. Also, the employer may not request that the worker engage in overtime work, unless the worker specifically requests such overtime work.[37]

Where the employer dismisses, or takes any other disadvantageous measures against, a worker on the grounds of temporary retirement or reduction of work hours due to childcare, s/he shall be punished by imprisonment for not more than three years or by a fine not exceeding an amount of twenty million won.[38]

Where an employer requests his/her worker under the reduction of working hours for a period of childcare to do overtime work although such worker has not specifically requested such overtime work, s/he shall be punished by a fine not exceeding ten million won.[39]

Where an employer fails to reinstate his/her worker in the same work as before the reduction of working hours for a period of childcare, or any other work paying the same level of wages after the completion of a period for reduction of working hours for a period of childcare of a worker, s/he shall be punished by a fine not exceeding five million won.[40]

---

37 Ibid., Article 19(3)
38 Ibid., Article 37(2)
39 Ibid., Article 37(3)
40 Ibid., Article 37(4) and (5)

Union Act

Chapter 1

Trade Unions

I. The Concept of Trade Unions

The Union Act[1] defines trade unions as "an organization or associated organizations of workers, which is formed in a voluntary and collective manner upon the workers' initiative for the purpose of maintaining and improving their working conditions and enhancing their economic and social status."[2] This regulation mainly determines the positive requirements of the trade union. However, the proviso of Article 2(4) of the Union Act also lays out the passive requirements of the trade union, stipulating that "an organization shall not be regarded as a trade union [under certain conditions]."

Meanwhile, the Union Act stipulates that workers are free to establish a trade union or to join it,[3] and lays out the formal requirements in establishing a trade union, which is that when a trade union is established it must submit a report of establishment to the appropriate administrative agency, and only when the union subsequently receives the certificate of report will it be deemed to have

---

1 Trade Union and Labor Relations Adjustment Act
2 Union Act, Article 2(4)
3 Ibid., Article 5

been formed (which would be at the time the Minister of Employment
and Labor receives the report of establishment).[4]

As can be seen through these regulations, a workers' organization
may enjoy the special protection afforded by the Union Act only if it
has satisfied the substantive and formal requirements designated by
the Act.

II. The Requirements of Trade Unions

A. Substantive Requirements

1) Positive Requirements
i) Subject of Trade Unions
A trade union must be organized with workers being its main agents.
Here, "the term 'worker' means any person who lives on wages, a
salary, or any other income equivalent thereto, regardless of the
person's occupation."[5] Therefore, "workers" would include not only
those employed by a certain employer and are working in fact, but also
those temporarily unemployed or seeking employment, to the extent
that their three fundamental labor rights ensured by the Constitution
need to be protected.[6] For reference, recent case law suggests that the
concept of "worker" is interpreted differently depending on whether
the term is used in the Union Act or the LSA.[7]

ii) Independence of Trade Unions
A trade union is an organization organized by the independent

---

4 Ibid., Articles 10 and 12(4)
5 Ibid., Article 2(1)
6 Supreme Court 2001Du8568 (2004. 2. 27.)
7 Labor Standard Act; Supreme Court 2011Da78804 (2014. 2. 13.)

unification of workers. Independence means the act of organizing and managing the trade union without the domination or interference of external influences. External influences include employers, governmental authorities, political parties and religious organizations.[8]

iii) Purpose of Trade Unions
The trade union must purport to enhance or maintain working conditions and otherwise promote the social status of workers. Matters included in working conditions are wages, working hours, the location and substance of the work. As such, the trade union's primary purpose must not only be the enhancement of working conditions directly related to the provision of labor by the worker, but must also include the enhancement of economic and social status of workers (which are indirectly related to the determination of working conditions).[9]

iv) Collectiveness of Trade Unions
A trade union must possess organizational substance. As a trade union must be a corporate entity comprised of multiple workers, a trade union with only one worker member is not recognized. However, it will not lose its collectiveness just by the fact that there is only one worker remaining as a member if this has been caused by the employer's hindrance and there is a possibility that the trade union will grow in number.[10] Also, even if a union has satisfied the requirement of collectivity by being comprised of more than one worker in its establishment, if subsequently the member count reaches one without general prospect that this number will increase, this union loses its characteristic of collectiveness and hence cannot be the subject of rights and duties, unless they relate to the purpose of shutting down

---

8 Ha Gab-rae, *Collective Labor Relations Law*, p. 107 (Joongang Economy 2013)

9 The Judicial Research and Training Institute, *Trade Union and Labor Relations Mediation Law*, p. 57 (2014); Ha Gab-rae, *supra*, p. 107

10 Im Jong-ryul, *Labor Law*, p. 49 (Pakyoungsa 2014)

the organization.[11]

2) Passive Requirements

i) Employers or Other Persons Who Act in the Interest of the Employer Must Not Be Allowed to Join

The Union Act stipulates that an organization shall not be regarded as a trade union where an "employer" or "other persons who always act in the interest of the employer" is allowed to join it.[12]

Here, the term "employer" means a business owner, a person responsible for the management of a business or a person who acts on behalf of a business owner with regard to matters concerning workers in the business.[13] Specifically, the term "a person responsible for the management of a business" means a person who is generally responsible for the management of the business, acting on behalf of the business owner regarding all or part of the management of the business and acts as the representative of the business or its agent in external dealings.[14] Also, a "person who acts on behalf of a business owner with regard to matters concerning workers in the business" means a person who has received certain authority and duties from the business owner regarding determination of working conditions, such as personnel matters, wages, welfare, and labor management, or to provide operational orders, direction, and supervision regarding the operation of the business.[15]

A "person who always acts in the interest of the employer" (hereinafter referred to as "the representative of the employer's interest") is one whose job duties and responsibilities directly conflict with that of the trade union member. That is because these persons may directly

---

11 Supreme Court 97Nu19830 (1998. 3. 13.)

12 Union Act, Articles 2(4) proviso, 2(4)(a)

13 Ibid., Article 2.2

14 Supreme Court 2007Do1199 (2008. 4. 10.), Supreme Court 88Do1162 (1988. 11. 22.)

15 Supreme Court 2008Du13873 (2011. 9. 8.), Supreme Court 2005Do8364 (2006. 5. 11.)

participate in the determination of labor relations such as personnel matters, wages, disciplinary action, auditing, and labor management, and may also have the authority to deal with confidential information such as the employer's plans and policy regarding labor relations.[16]

ii) Most of the Trade Union's Expenditures Must Not Be Provided by the Employer

An organization will not be regarded as a trade union when most of its main expenditures are provided by the employer.[17] As this would indicate the organization failed to satisfy the substantive requirement of independence, this entity is not a trade union under the Union Act. The term "expenditures" refers to money and valuables required for the existence and activities of the trade union and other economic profits, while the term "main expenditures" considers whether a portion of the expenditures if provided by the employer would, in nature, subject the trade union to the risk of losing its independence.[18]

iii) The Trade Union Must Not Only Aim at Welfare Undertakings

The Union Act stipulates that an organization shall not be regarded as a trade union where its activities are only aimed at mutual benefits, moral culture and other welfare undertakings.[19] This aim would indicate the organization failed to satisfy the substantive requirement of purporting to enhance working conditions, meaning this entity would not be a trade union under the Union Act.

iv) The Trade Union Must Not Allow Non-Workers to Join

An organization will not be regarded as a trade union where those

---

16 Supreme Court 2008Du13873 (2011. 9. 8.)
17 Union Act, Article 2.4(b) proviso
18 Im Jong-ryul, *supra*, p. 55
19 Ibid., Article 2.4(c) proviso

who are not workers are allowed to join.[20] Yet, the proviso in Article 2.4(d) stipulates "a dismissed person shall not be regarded as a person who is not a worker, until a review decision is made by the National Labor Relations Commission when he has made an application to the Labor Relations Commission for remedies for unfair labor practices." Therefore, even if a worker is dismissed, if s/he has requested relief from the Labor Relations Commission, s/he must be treated the same as a worker who has direct labor relations with the employer until a review decision is made by the National Labor Relations Commission. As such, even if a trade union allows such dismissed workers to become members, this would not affect its status as a union under the Union Act.

Also, case law states that since Article 2.4's proviso and 2.4(d)'s proviso are provisions prepared for situations where a member of the enterprise union is dismissed by the employer and not recognized as a worker, the provisions will be limited in their application to only such situations. Consquently, these provisions are not applicable to craft, industrial, and regional unions, as these unions do not necessitate subordinate relationships with a particular employer in the first place.[21] In other words, case law has clarified that the proviso of Article 2.4(d)'s application is assumed to apply only to workers who are members of enterprise unions and are in fact employed by a specific employer.[22] Therefore, there are no problems in recognizing craft, industrial or regional unions that allow dismissed workers to enroll as members.

v) The Trade Union's Aims Must Not Be Mainly Directed at Political Movements

The Union Act stipulates that an organization shall not be regarded

20 Ibid., Article 2.4(d) proviso
21 Supreme Court 2011Du15404 (2013. 9. 27.), Supreme Court 2001Du8568 (2004. 2. 27.)
22 Supreme Court 2007Du4483 (2011. 3. 24.)

as a trade union where its aims are mainly directed at political movements.[23] Needless to say, the main purpose of the trade union must not be political movements as its purpose is to maintain and enhance working conditions.

B. Formal Requirements

1) Reporting the Establishment of a Trade Union
i) Reporting

Even if a worker's organization satisfies the substantive requirements of a trade union, in order for the organization to be recognized as a trade union under the Union Act the following formal requirements must be met. First, a report of establishment accompanied by the organization's bylaws must be submitted to the Minister of Employment and Labor, the Governor of a Special Self-Governing Province, or the head of a Si/Gun/Gu.[24] Next, the organization must receive the certificate of report issued by the relevant administrative agency.[25] Once the trade union receives the certificate of report, it is deemed to have been retroactively established at the time the Minister of Employment and Labor received the report of establishment.[26] In other words, a trade union under the Union Act is validly established only once it has submitted a report of establishment and is issued the certificate of report.

ii) Reporting Procedure

Any person who intends to establish a trade union shall submit a report ① to the Minister of Employment and Labor when the trade

---

23 Union Act, Article 2.4(e)
24 Ibid., Article 10(1)
25 Ibid., Article 12(1)
26 Ibid., Article 12(4)

union is in the form of an associated organization and when a unit trade union extends over no fewer than two Special Metropolitan Cities, Metropolitan Cities, Do or Special Self-Governing Province, ② to the Special Metropolitan City Mayor, Metropolitan City Mayor or Do Governor when the trade union extends over no fewer than two Si/Gun/Gu, and ③ to the Governor of a Special Self-Governing Province and the head of a Si/Gun/Gu for any other trade unions.[27] Here, information as stipulated under Article 11 of the Union Act must be attached, including the following: the title of the trade union; location of the main office; the number of union members; the name and addresses of union officers; and the title of an associated organization to which it belongs, if any. When the relevant administrative agency deems it necessary that a report on establishment or bylaws of a trade union needs to be supplemented because of any omission or other reasons, it must order a supplementation of such information within a specified period of up to 20 days.[28]

2) The Evaluation of the Establishment

The administrative agency that has received a report on the establishment of a trade union evaluates whether the petitioning union satisfies the positive and passive requirements of a trade union as stipulated under Article 2.4 of the Union Act. The agency also reviews if the report or the union's bylaws need supplementation due to omissions in required entries or any other reasons. A certificate of report will be issued within 3 days once all requirements are determined to have been met, but if the agency deems it necessary that a report on the establishment or bylaws of a trade union needs to be supplemented because of any omission or other reasons, it orders that such information be supplemented within a specified period of up

---

27 Ibid., Article 10(1)
28 Ibid., Article 12(2)

to 20 days. If the petitioning organization fails to supply the requested supplemental information within the specified period or if the agency determines that it does not satisfy the necessary requirements to become a legal trade union, the relevant agency must return the report of establishment it received.[29]

If the administrative agency receives the report on the establishment of a trade union but does not return or request supplemental information within 3 days, the trade union is not considered to have been formally established. There is also an old precedent which ruled that the administrative agency may request supplemental information or return the report after the stipulated period of 3 days.[30] However, if the agency does not return or request supplemental information after 3 days without any special or reasonable cause, it would be proper to say that the trade union has been established,[31] since Article 12(1) of the Union Act stipulates that the administrative agency shall issue a certificate of report within 3 days, except in certain cases.

What is the scope of the administrative agency's authority to evaluate whether a report on the establishment of trade unions has satisfied the necessary requirements? The Supreme Court opined on this matter, ruling that the relevant administrative agency must determine whether the petitioning organization has satisfied the substantive requirements outlined in Article 2.4 of the Union Act using generally expected appropriate methods to arrive at reasonable conclusions. In other words, the courts give administrative agencies considerable actual evaluative authority in making such determinations.[32]

---

29 Ibid., Article 12(1) and (3); Enforcement Decree of the Union Act, Article 9
30 Supreme Court 89Nu3243 (1990. 10. 23.)
31 Ha Gab-rae, *supra*, p. 119
32 Supreme Court 76Nu189 (1979. 12. 11.)

III. The Legal Status of Trade Unions

A. The Legal Status of Trade Unions under the Union Act

Trade unions that have been established while satisfying the substantive and formal requirements stipulated by the Union Act receive the legal protection of the three primary rights of labor ensured by the Constitution. These trade unions (hereinafter referred to as "legal unions") may exercise their proper rights to assembly and collective action, have immunity from civil and criminal liability for the exercise of these rights, and may request relief from the private law system against acts that infringe their rights to assembly and collective action by suing them as illegal acts, among other theories.[33]

Legal unions may apply for adjustment of industrial disputes and for the remedy of unfair labor practices to the Labor Relations Commission,[34] may use the title of trade unions,[35] may be formed as a juristic person,[36] and be exempt from taxes as per tax-related Acts.[37]

B. The Legal Status of Workers' Organizations Other than Legal Unions

Even when a workers' organization fails to be a legal union established in compliance with the requirements of the Union Act, if the organization possesses the characteristics of "subject," "independence," "purpose," and "collectiveness," under Article 33(1)

---

33 The Judicial Research and Training Institute, *supra*, p. 81
34 Union Act, Article 7(1)
35 Ibid., Article 7(3)
36 Ibid., Article 6
37 Ibid., Article 8

of the Constitution (and its interpretation) and Article 2.4 of the Union Act, this organization would receive the legal protection afforded by the Constitution regarding its three primary labor rights.[38]

As a result, such organizations (hereinafter referred to as "extralegal unions") may exercise proper rights to collective assembly and action, irrespective of individual subordinate legal regulations. Extralegal unions also gain immunity from civil and criminal liability when exercising their labor rights, and activities that infringe upon the labor rights of extralegal unions are subject to relief via private law through causes of action such as illegal acts. The Constitutional Court has determined that a workers' organization satisfying the substantive requirements of a trade union but not the formal requirements has the authority to bargain and conclude collective agreements.[39]

Extralegal unions are put under the following disadvantages under the Union Act: (i) the extralegal union may not make an application for adjustment of industrial disputes;[40] (ii) it cannot make an application for the remedy of unfair labor practices;[41] (iii) the extralegal union may not use the name "trade union;"[42] (iv) it cannot be formed as a juristic person;[43] and (v) it is not exempt from taxes.[44]

Finally, due to the fact that extralegal unions enjoy the three fundamental labor rights ensured by the Constitution, they may not only bargain and conclude collective agreements,[45] but also, according to the majority view,[46] be indemnified from civil and criminal liability

---

38 Kim Hyung-bae, *Labor Law*, p. 826 (Pakyoungsa 2014); Im Jong-ryul, *supra*, p. 65

39 Constitutional Court 2004HunBa9 (2008. 7. 31.)

40 Union Act, Article 7(1)

41 Ibid., Article 7(1)

42 Ibid., Article 7(3)

43 Ibid., Article 6(1) and (2)

44 Ibid., Article 8

45 Ibid., Article 29(1)

46 Kim Hyung-bae, *supra*, p. 827; Im Jong-ryul, *supra*, p. 65; Ha Gab-rae, *supra*, p. 122; The Judicial Research and Training Institute, *supra*, p. 84

that may arise from their justifiable industrial actions.[47]

IV. The Operation of Trade Unions

A. Basic Principles

Trade unions are organized in a voluntary and collective manner by the initiative of workers for the purpose of maintaining and improving working conditions as well as for improving their economic and social status. Therefore, the principle of self-government is applicable to the trade unions in making their internal decisions for operation, and the trade union must be operated democratically, as the union members have equal rights and duties to participate in all matters of the trade union.[48] For this purpose, the Union Act requires that material matters regarding the operation of the trade union be resolved at general meetings of the trade union, which is the highest decision-making institution, and regulates the methods of such resolutions.[49]

B. Trade Union Bylaws

When submitting a report on the establishment of a trade union, the report must be accompanied by a bylaw that stipulates matters related to the organization and operation of the union as designated by Article 11 of the Union Act (i.e. 15 items), such as the title of the trade union, its purpose and activities, and location of its principal office.[50]

---

47 Union Act, Article 3 and 4
48 Ibid., Article 22
49 Ibid., Article 16
50 Ibid., Article 10(1)

The bylaw is established and amended via a general meeting, with the attendance of a majority of all union members and with a concurrent vote of over two-thirds of the members present utilizing a direct, secret, and unsigned ballot.[51] As the provision in the Union Act that regulates the quorum necessary to establish or amend bylaws is compulsory, weakening the quorum than this standard is prohibited. However, it is permitted for an employer to have stronger quorums than is mandated in the Union Act.[52]

C. Acquiring and Losing Union Member Status

According to the Union Act, workers are free to establish a trade union or to join it.[53] However, the specific scope of union members (for trade unions, the form of associated organizations and their constituent organizations) is determined by the bylaws of the trade union.[54]

A worker may become a union member by freely joining a trade union in compliance with the union's bylaws. However, in practice, the collective bargaining agreements also stipulate the scope of eligibility of a union member, and in such case it becomes an issue where the eligibility requirements stated in the bylaws are different from those stipulated in the collective bargaining agreement. In this case, the Supreme Court has decided that the status of a union member should in principle be regulated by the provisions stipulated in the bylaws of the trade union, and where the eligibility requirement of the union member is also stated in the collective bargaining agreement, those matters stated in the agreement are only relevant as to whom such

51 Ibid., Articles 16(1)1, 16(2) proviso, 16(4)
52 The Judicial Research and Training Institute, *supra*, p. 88
53 Union Act, Article 5
54 Ibid., Article 11(4)

matters are applicable.[55]

The Union Act stipulates that a "person who is not a worker" or "an employer or other person who always acts in the interest of the employer" is not eligible to join the trade union.[56] The Union Act does not recognize an organization formed by such persons as a trade union.[57]

The Union Act stipulates that having the employer hire workers on the condition that they should join a particular trade union—and thereby imposing union enrollment—is a type of unfair labor practice and prohibits such practices.[58] However, "where a trade union represents two-thirds or more of the workers working in the workplace concerned, a conclusion of a collective agreement under which a person is employed on condition that he should join the trade union shall be allowed as an exceptional case,"[59] and will not be considered as an unfair labor practice. Such provisions in collective agreements are so-called "union shop" provisions, and are agreed upon for the purpose of allowing restrictions on the freedom of the worker to become part of a collective with trade unions that possess the organizational capacity to have over two-thirds of workers in a workplace as its members. However, as the Union Act has recently started to recognize multiple unions, it now also prohibits the employer from imposing disadvantageous measures to union members who withdraw their membership and organize a new trade union or join a pre-existing one despite the existence of the "union shop" provision.[60] In reality, the "union shop" provision has lost much of its significance under the multiple union system.

---

55 Supreme Court 2001Da5142 (2004. 1. 29.)

56 Union Act, Article 2(4)

57 Ibid., Article 2(4) proviso

58 Ibid., Article 81(2)

59 Ibid., Article 81(2) proviso

60 Ibid., Article 81(2) proviso

According to the Union Act, "all the union members shall have equal rights and duties to participate in all matters of the trade union."[61] Therefore, a union member may participate in the decision-making process of the general or council of delegates meeting regarding the operation of the trade union and exercise his/her right to vote, and also possesses the right to vote (or be voted for) during the election of council delegates or union officers.

On the other hand, a union member also assumes duties to the trade union as determined by union bylaws. A basic duty would be to pay union dues. A trade union may, under its bylaws, restrict the rights of those members who fail to pay union dues.[62]

A union member loses his/her membership upon death, dissolution of the union, or withdrawal of membership. Membership may also be lost when certain circumstances determined in the bylaws arise, such as expulsion, dismissal, promotion, or job transfer. The union member may also voluntarily withdraw his/her membership from the union. Therefore, going beyond formal procedures (e.g. requiring the submission of the application to withdraw) and imposing substantive restrictions on this freedom to withdraw through provisions in the union bylaws (e.g. requiring prior approval from the general or council of delegates meeting in order to withdraw membership) is not allowed.

D. Trade Union Institutions

1) General Meetings and the Council of Delegates
i) Meaning and Composition
A general meeting is the highest decision-making institution of the trade union, composed of all members of the union. A trade union

---

61 Ibid., Article 22
62 Ibid., Article 22 proviso

may, by its bylaws, establish a council of delegates, which may be substituted for a general meeting.[63] Delegates must be elected by members through direct, secret and unsigned ballots,[64] and the term of office of the delegates must be determined according to the bylaws, but not exceeding 3 years.[65] The rationale behind regulating council delegates to be elected via direct, secret and unsigned ballots is to allow the members of the trade union to participate in the decision-making process regarding the organization and management of the union, and thereby realize democracy within the organization, so this regulation is compulsory.[66] As such, a general meeting or council of delegates must be organized in order to fulfill the role as the highest decision-making apparatus of the trade union, and if a council of delegates is established, the provisions regarding a general meeting will apply *mutatis mutandis* to it.[67]

ii) Convocation and Opening

A trade union must hold general or council of delegates meetings at least once a year,[68] and the representative of the trade union must be the chairman of the general or council of delegates meetings.[69] The general meeting or council of delegates may (i) convene regular general meetings or council of delegates meetings as determined by the union's bylaw, and (ii) may, if deemed necessary by the representative of a trade union or one-third or more of the union members or delegates (for trade unions in the form of an associated organization, one-third or more of its constituent organizations) present the matters to

---

63 Ibid., Article 17(1)
64 Ibid., Article 17(2)
65 Ibid., Article 17(3)
66 Supreme Court 97Da41349 (2000. 1. 14.)
67 Union Act, Article 17(4)
68 Ibid., Articles 15(1) and 17(4)
69 Ibid., Articles 15(2) and 17(4)

be referred to a meeting and require the convocation of the meeting, convene an extraordinary general meeting or an extraordinary council of delegates, or convene an extraordinary general meeting or an extraordinary council of delegates.[70]

When the representative of a trade union intentionally avoids or neglects the convening of a general or council of delegates meeting, and then one-third or more of the union members or delegates submit a request for nomination of a person authorized to convene a meeting, the administrative agencies must request the Labor Relations Commission to make a resolution within 15 days and must, promptly upon the resolution of the Commission, nominate a person authorized to convene the meeting.[71] Also, when the trade union has no person authorized to convene a general meeting or a council of delegates, if one-third or more of the union members or delegates present the matters to be referred to a meeting and submit a request for the nomination of a person authorized to convene a meeting, the administrative agencies must nominate that person within 15 days.[72]

Bylaws may determine methods of convening general or council of delegate meetings that differ from the method mandated above by the Union Act. However, variations are only allowed to the extent that the rights of union members and council delegates that come from the method of convening in the Union Act are preserved. In other words, in order to convene a general meeting (or council of delegates meeting), at least 7 days prior to its commencement date of a meeting or council, a general meeting or council of delegates must give public notice of the matters to be referred to at the said meeting or council for deliberation, and must be convened in accordance with the methods as provided in the bylaws of the trade union. When the trade union is

---

70 Ibid., Articles 18(1) and (2)

71 Ibid., Article 18(3)

72 Ibid., Article 18(4)

composed of people working in the same workplace, the said period of public notification may be reduced in accordance with its bylaws.[73]

iii) Resolutions

In principle, the general meeting must make resolutions with the attendance of a majority of all union members (or council delegates) and with a concurrent vote of a majority of the members (or council delegates) present.[74] As an exception, however, if in an election of union officers, any candidate does not obtain the consent of a majority of the union members (or council delegates) that are present, a candidate with the highest votes in a run-off election may be elected in accordance with the bylaws.[75] Meanwhile, matters concerning the enactment and modification of bylaws, the discharge of union officers, the merger, division, dissolution and structural change of a trade union must be resolved with the attendance of a majority of all union members (or council delegates) and a concurrent vote of two-thirds majority of the members (or council delegates) present.[76]

While the method and process of resolutions may be determined freely, matters concerning the enactment or modification of the bylaws, the election and discharge of union officers must be decided by members through direct, secret, and unsigned ballots.[77] For example, if an individual union member or union members who are part of a particular social club vote in a particular way in response to a specific candidate and attempt to communicate to the candidate on how they have voted by intentionally folding the ballot bill in an agreed upon, identifiable manner, this vote becomes invalid due to the violation of

---

73 Ibid., Article 19

74 Ibid., Article 16(2)

75 Ibid., Article 16(3)

76 Ibid., Article 16(2) proviso

77 Ibid., Article 16(4)

the principle of anonymous and secret voting.[78]

Whether a resolution passed in the general meeting or council of delegates meeting is valid when there is a defect in the process of convening or the method of passing resolutions in light of the provisions stipulated in the bylaws of the Union Act sometimes arises as an issue. The Supreme Court ruled that even if such procedural defects exist, as long as they did not pose any obstacles to the union members in their reflecting their intent when passing the resolution in general or council of delegates meetings, the resolution should not be deemed invalid even if it suffers from procedural defects.[79]

iv) Relationship between General Meetings and the Council of Delegates

A general meeting is the highest decision-making institution of the trade union, and a general meeting can be substituted by the council of delegates, provided that the material matters of the trade union such as the bylaw or election of officers are resolved by the general meeting.[80] In this case, the issue of whether the general meeting cannot resolve matters that are delegated to the council of delegates arises due to such delegation.

Recently, the Supreme Court has decided that unless there are special circumstances involved, the general meeting cannot resolve matters that require the resolution of the council of delegates if the bylaw of the trade union clearly distinguishes and stipulates matters that require the resolution of the general meeting and matters that must be resolved by the council of delegates. However, as the general meeting has the authority to amend the bylaw, the provisions of the bylaw could be amended through a resolution made by the attendance of a majority of all union or council delegate members and

---

78 Supreme Court 97Da43567 (1998. 2. 27.)

79 Supreme Court 91Da29071 (1992. 3. 27.), Supreme Court 91Da14413 (1992. 3. 31.)

80 Union Act, Article 16

a concurrent vote of two-thirds majority of the members present.[81] Therefore, if the matters requiring the resolution of the council of delegates are stipulated in the bylaw, and the general meeting cannot resolve those matters. However, it may amend the bylaw to require the resolution of those matters be addressed at the general meeting.

2) Union Officers

The trade union must have officers as part of its administrative apparatus, such as a union representative. Matters concerning the enactment or modification of the bylaws, and the election and discharge of union officers must be decided in the general or council of delegates meeting by direct, secret, and unsigned ballots.[82] In addition, as we have reviewed above, the general or council of delegates meeting makes resolutions with the attendance of a majority of all union members or council delegates, with a concurrent vote of a majority of the members or delegates present.[83] However, if no candidate obtains the consent of a majority of the union or council delegate members present, a candidate with the highest votes in a run-off election may be elected in accordance with the bylaws.[84] Union officers elected in this manner may have a term of office determined by union bylaws, but not exceeding 3 years.[85]

In addition, matters concerning the discharge of union officers must be resolved with the attendance of a majority of all union or council delegate members and a concurrent vote of two-thirds majority of the members present.[86]

81 Supreme Court 2012Du6063 (2014. 8. 26.)
82 Union Act, Article 16(1)2 and (4)
83 Ibid., Article 16(2)
84 Ibid., Articles 16(3)
85 Ibid., Article 23(2)
86 Ibid., Article 16(2) proviso

3) Full-time Officer of the Trade Union

According to the Union Act, "if provided in a collective agreement or consented by employers, workers may be engaged exclusively in affairs of the trade union without providing the employer with work specified in their employment contracts."[87] Such workers are referred to as full-time officers of the trade union. A full-time officer may engage exclusively in the affairs of the trade union without providing all or part of the work specified in his/her employment contract.

Full-time officers of the trade union are exempt from the duty to provide labor, and in principle, the employer is exempt from the duty to pay them wages.[88] Full-time union officers are subject to the rules of employment such as regulations regarding working hours unless the collective agreement contains special provisions regarding the full-time union officer or a special practice exists in the relevant workplace. Therefore, full-time union officers have the duty to be present during designated work hours in the trade union office (in order to conduct the affairs of the union), and will be considered absent without leave if s/he fails to be present.[89]

The current Union Act stipulates, "A full-time union officer shall not be remunerated in any kind by the employer during the period of exclusive engagement."[90]

The Union Act also defines the payment of wages to the full-time union officer as being an unfair labor practice,[91] and subjects anyone who has violated this to criminal liability.[92]

---

87 Ibid., Article 24(1)

88 Supreme Court 97Da54727 (1998. 4. 24.)

89 Supreme Court 92Da34926 (1993. 8. 24.), Supreme Court 94Da58087 (1995. 4. 11.), Supreme Court 2003Du12790 (2005. 6. 23.)

90 Union Act, Article 24(2)

91 Ibid., Article 81(4)

92 Ibid., Article 90

4) Time-off Workers

Where it is prescribed by collective agreement or consented by an employer, a certain number of workers may conduct affairs of maintaining and managing a trade union for the healthy development of labor-management relations such as consultation or bargaining with an employer, grievance settlement, or industrial safety activities without loss of wages, within the "maximum time-off limit" (deliberated and resolved by the Time-Off System Deliberation Committee and proclaimed by the Minister of Employment and Labor) in consideration of the number of members, etc. of a trade union by business or by place of business.[93] This system is known as "time-off" and such workers are known as "time-off workers."

A time-off worker is similar to a full-time union officer in that their duty to provide labor is waived to the extent that they engage in the activities outlined above. They are also distinguished in that they receive wages from the employer for their activities.

Time-off workers are determined by agreement between labor and management via instruments such as collective agreements, within the "maximum time-off limit" as announced by the Minister of Employment and Labor. The following is the "maximum time-off limit" as designated under Ministry of Employment and Labor Announcement No. 2013-13 (2013. 6. 25.).

---

93 Ibid., Articles 24(4) and 24-2

Maximum Time-Off Limit by Scale of Trade Union Members

Scale of Trade Union Members	Time-Off Limit	Members That May Be Used
99 members and under	Max. within 2,000 hours	
100~199 members	Max. within 3,000 hours	
200~299 members	Max. within 4,000 hours	• Sections with under 300 union members: The number of members using time-off hours on a part-time basis cannot exceed three times the number of members that may use time-off hours.
300~499 members	Max. within 5,000 hours	
500~999 members	Max. within 6,000 hours	
1,000~2,999 members	Max. within 10,000 hours	• Sections with over 300 union members: The number of members using time-off hours on a part-time basis cannot exceed twice the number of members that may use time-off hours.
3,000~4,999 members	Max. within 14,000 hours	
5,000~9,999 members	Max. within 22,000 hours	
10,000~14,999 members	Max. within 28,000 hours	
15,000 members and over	Max. within 36,000 hours	

* "Scale of Trade Union Members" refers to the total number of union members in the "business of workplace" as stipulated under Article 24(4) of the Union Act, and is calculated based on the numbers of days the collective agreement has been entered into or the day the employer provided his/her consent.

Maximum Time-Off Limit by Regional Distribution

Subject	Maximum Time-Off Limit Added	
	Number of Metropolitan Councils	Hours
Business or workplace with more than 1,000 total union members	2~5	(Annual Time-Off Limit of the Business or Workplace)×10%
	6~9	(Annual Time-Off Limit of the Business or Workplace)×20%
	10 and over	(Annual Time-Off Limit of the Business or Workplace)×30%

* Standard of calculating the number of metropolitan councils: ① The term "metropolitan council" refers to Metropolitan Cities, Dos and Special Self-Governing Cities and Provinces as per Article 2(1)1 of the Local Autonomy Act. ② The number of metropolitan councils are calculated based on those where at least 5% of the total number of union members of the relevant business or workplace work.

A time-off worker may engage in collective bargaining and consultations with the employer "without loss of wages."[94] However, the trade union must not request the payment of wages for the time-off worker's work beyond the maximum time-off limit, and must not take any industrial action for the purpose of realizing of such intention.[95] In addition, an employer's act of paying time-off workers wages for their work beyond the maximum time-off limit constitutes an unfair labor practice[96] and will be subject to punishment.[97]

94 Ibid., Article 24(4)
95 Ibid., Article 24(5)
96 Ibid., Article 81(4)
97 Seoul High Court 2013Nu27762 (2014. 7. 23.)

V. Union Activities

A. The Meaning of Union Activities

"Union activity" means any acts by workers to achieve the purpose of the trade union, except for establishment, admission, collective bargaining, and industrial actions of the trade union.[98] Union activities generally include attending assemblies, wearing ribbons or bandannas, distributing leaflets, posting bills, and giving speeches.

Conducting activities to validly exercise the workers' or union's three fundamental labor rights constitute union activities. Thus, not only is a worker protected from civil or criminal liability for damages suffered by the employer,[99] the employer's dismissal or unfavorable treatment of a worker on grounds of such union activities is prohibited as an unfair labor practice that infringes upon the right of the worker to engage in union activity, making the employer subject to criminal prosecution.[100] In other words, the worker is ensured his/her right to engage in union activities within the scope of the legal protection provided by the Constitution and the Union Act.

B. Requirements for Justifiable Union Activity

The subject, purpose and means of a union activity must each be justified.[101]

1) Justification of the Subject
The worker's activities must be seen as an organized activity conducted

---

98 Im Jong-ryul, *supra*, p. 104; Ha Gab-rae, *supra*, p. 171

99 Ibid., Articles 3 and 4

100 Ibid., Articles 81(1) and 90

101 Supreme Court 91Do3044 (1992. 4. 10), Supreme Court 93Do613 (1994. 2. 22.)

by the trade union in that the worker followed the resolution or specific direction provided by the latter. If no such resolution or direction from the trade union exists and the act was done individually and voluntarily, it could also be considered that the act was done to advance the work of the union due to the nature of the act, or to consider that the act was done under the implied authorization or approval of the trade union.[102]

2) Justification of the Purpose

The purpose of the union activity must be to maintain and improve working conditions and to enhance the economic and social status of the worker, and to help strengthen the solidarity of workers.[103] Specifically, to say that a certain union activity possesses justifiable purpose is not only to say that the activity has the purpose stated in the previous sentence, but also to say that the activity includes various supportive and indirect activities towards the fulfillment of this purpose.[104]

However, even when the activity is taken against the employer, if the purpose of the activity is unrelated to the maintenance or enhancement of working conditions, such as changing management rights, for example, this activity is not recognized to possess justifiable purpose.[105]

3) Justification of Methods and Means
i) Union Activities during Work Hours

Union activities must be conducted outside of work hours, unless special provisions in the rules of employment or collective agreements,

---

102 Supreme Court 92Da18542 (1992. 9. 25.)
103 Supreme Court 91Do3044 (1992. 4. 10.)
104 The Judicial Research and Training Institute, *supra*, p. 123
105 Supreme Court 2004Da62597 (2006. 5. 26.)

labor relations customs, or employer consent permit otherwise.[106] Therefore, a worker's act of attending a trade union assembly during work hours is not justified.

However, some case precedents have acknowledged union activities during work hours in certain special circumstances. The Supreme Court decided that even when an extraordinary general meeting is held during work hours, if the employer is able to prepare for such activities as the union had notified the employer in writing a number of times of such a meeting, and it is necessary to hold the meeting during work hours for all union members to attend the meeting due to day and night shifts, the holding of the extraordinary general meeting during work hours is justified.[107] In another case, where workers could not complete their work at a specific time, such as with ready-mixed concrete truck drivers, and the collective bargaining agreement permitted union activities during work hours, the Supreme Court determined that there were special circumstances at play, and ruled that it cannot be said that the general meeting held during work hours is not justified merely for the reason that it was during work hours.[108]

Recently, another court ruled that the act of a worker who had brought printed materials to work and placed them in meeting rooms and lounges, even going so far as to hand out the material to one worker who was working, neither constituted a violation of the employer's right of facility management, nor an interference with the worker's duties, and held that it was not a cause for disciplinary action.[109]

---

106 Supreme Court 90Do357 (1990. 5. 15.)

107 Supreme Court 93Do613 (1994. 2. 22.)

108 Supreme Court 94Nu5496 (1995. 3. 14.)

109 Supreme Administrative Court 2012GuHap27541 (2014. 3. 6.). It is unclear whether this case explicitly permits union activities not approved by the employer during work hours. However, it is noteworthy as it relates to an act of distributing printed matter within the workplace during work hours.

ii) Union Activities within the Workplace

Union activities within the workplace must observe reasonable regulations and restrictions based on the employer's right to manage facilities and must not employ methods of violence and destruction. Generally, the following methods and means may be used by a union member to express and communicate his/her intention: (i) assemble, protest, or conduct a speech both inside and outside of the workplace; (ii) distribute or attach printed material; (iii) wear ribbons or bandanas; (iv) raise union flags or banners; or (v) refuse to comply with certain directions of the employer.

The Supreme Court decided that posting bills on a place other than the place designated for posting printed materials is not justified.[110] Recently, lower courts have tended to more broadly acknowledge the justification of distributing printed matter related to a trade union without the employer's permission for the reason that it is difficult to obtain the permission of the employer, it does not cause significant interference with one's work duties, the content of the printed matter is not clearly false or defamatory, and decide that although such act may be a cause for disciplinary action, it is justified as a union activity.[111] Other courts have also decided that the act of distributing printed matter during a work break, and without the employer's approval, is justified as a union activity.[112]

The Supreme Court has ruled that, if due to the nature of the business, such as hospitals, strict dress codes are stipulated in the rules of employment, the act of not wearing designated uniforms during work hours could be a cause for disciplinary action.[113] Conversely, for

110 Supreme Court 95Nu6151 (1996. 4. 23.)
111 Busan High Court 2013Na2146 (2014. 2. 11.) (judgment concluded for dismissal of appeal); Supreme Administrative Court 2013GuHap9373 (2014. 3. 20.)
112 Supreme Court 91Nu4164 (1991. 11. 12.); Supreme Administrative Court 2012GuHap21062 (2013. 10. 10.)
113 Supreme Court 95Nu6151 (1996. 4. 23.)

businesses that do not require strict dress codes, the act of wearing ribbons and union attire may be deemed as a justified union activity as long as it does not obstruct the normal operation of the business.

VI. Changes in Trade Unions

A. The Merger of Trade Unions

1) The Concept
A "merger" refers to an integration of two or more trade unions into a single trade union, pursuant to certain procedures, and is classified as a merger when only one party to the merger is dispersed and extinguished and the other party absorbs the extinguished trade union and becomes the sole surviving entity. Alternatively, it is seen as a consolidation when all parties to the merger are dispersed and extinguished, and at the same time a new trade union is established that brings together the extinguished entities.

Generally, the merger of trade unions is used to reorganize an existing enterprise union to a craft union, or to respond to the corresponding merger of more than one employer.[114]

2) The Procedure
The trade union party to a merger must pass resolutions regarding matters related to the merger through general or council delegates meetings.[115] The quorum for such a resolution requires the attendance of a majority of all union members (or council delegates) and a concurrent vote of two-thirds majority of the members (or council

---

114 The Judicial Research and Training Institute, *supra*, p. 134
115 Ibid., Articles 16(1)7 and 17(1)

delegates) present.[116] With consolidations, the members of the newly consolidated union must hold an establishment meeting and take the usual steps necessary to establish a trade union (e.g. the drafting of union bylaws, etc.). On the other hand, trade unions that have been dispersed and extinguished due to a merger or consolidation must report this fact through its representative to the relevant administrative agency.[117]

3) The Legal Effects

For mergers, the trade unions to the merger that are absorbed are dispersed and extinguished. For consolidations, all party trade unions are dispersed and extinguished.[118] The collective bargaining agreements that have been entered into by the trade union that will be extinguished as a result of the merger or consolidation as well as the rights and obligations of the workers with respect to the employer will be comprehensively transferred to the newly established or absorbing trade union and remain valid.[119] Also, the members of dispersed and extinguished trade unions automatically become qualified as members of the merged or consolidated trade union without going through a separate application process via the resolution authorizing the merger.

B. The Division of Trade Unions

1) The Concept

"Division" is an opposite concept from mergers, and refers to when a single trade union is dispersed and extinguished to be divided into two or more independent trade unions.

---

116 Ibid., Articles 16(2) proviso, 17(4)
117 Ibid., Article 28(2)
118 Ibid., Article 28(1)2
119 Im Jong-ryul, *supra*, p. 99; Ha Gab-rae, *supra*, p. 234

2) The Procedure

The trade union that wishes to undergo division must pass resolutions regarding matters related to the division through general or council delegates meetings.[120] The quorum for such a resolution requires the attendance of a majority of all union members (or council delegates) and a concurrent vote of two-thirds majority of the members (or council delegates) present.[121] The members of the newly divided union must hold an establishment meeting and take the usual steps necessary to establish a trade union (e.g. the drafting of union bylaws, etc.). Also, trade unions that have been dispersed and extinguished due to the division must report this fact through its representative to the relevant administrative agency.[122] The newly established trade union due to the division must report its establishment to the Ministry of Employment and Labor with the bylaws attached thereto.[123]

3) The Legal Effects

Upon division, the original trade union is dispersed and extinguished.[124] Members of the trade union that is dispersed and extinguished due to the division automatically become qualified as members of the divided trade unions without going through a separate application process due to the agreement regarding union membership contained in the resolution authorizing the division.

There are divided views over whether the collective bargaining agreement entered into by the original trade union is succeeded to the new trade union. According to the view that it is not succeeded, the agreement of the original trade union is extinguished and terminated, as the organization prior to and after the division is in substance not

---

120 Ibid., Articles 16(1)7 and 17(1)
121 Ibid., Articles 16(2) proviso, 17(4)
122 Ibid., Article 28(2)
123 Ibid., Article 10
124 Ibid., Article 28(1)2

the same.[125] On the other hand, the view that it is succeeded argues that the previous agreement is succeeded to the new trade union as the organization remains substantially the same after the division.[126]

There is no need to go through liquidation procedures for the dispersal of the trade union that is dispersed and extinguished, and the property management of the divided union is vested in the newly established trade union according to relevant agreements contained in the resolution authorizing the division.

C. Structural Reorganization of Trade Unions

1) The Concept

Structural reorganization of trade unions refers to when the trade union maintains its substantial identity while applying modifications to its organizational structure. The structural reorganization of trade unions is distinguished from the establishment of new trade unions through mergers or divisions in that the entity that results from the process maintains its substantial identity.

2) The Requirements

As a substantial requirement, the reorganization of trade unions is permitted to the extent that the union is recognized to have maintained its substantial identity throughout the process.[127] There are no stipulated regulations that clarify when substantive identity is deemed to be maintained. A representative characteristic case would be when a "trade union that is an associated organization of craft unions" that have enterprise unions as its members is reorganized into

125 Kim Hyung-bae, *supra*, p. 853; Ha Gab-rae, *supra*, p. 234
126 Im Jong-ryul, *supra*, p. 100
127 Supreme Court 95Nu4377 (1997. 7. 25.)

a single "unit craft union," or vice versa.[128]

As a procedural requirement, matters related to the structural reorganization of unions must be passed through resolutions in general or council delegates meetings.[129] The quorum for such a resolution requires the attendance of a majority of all union members (or council delegates) and a concurrent vote of two-thirds majority of the members (or council delegates) present.[130] If there are changes to the title of the union, the location of the main office, name of the representative, or the title of an associated organization to which it belongs due to the reorganization, the trade union must report these modifications to the relevant administrative agency,[131] as well as any modifications to the union bylaws.[132] If the structurally reorganized trade union is an incorporated entity, any modifications to the contents of its registration must undergo the process of registering the alterations.[133]

3) The Legal Effects

After the structural reorganization process, the resulting trade union assumes in its entirety the legal relations that it had prior to the structural reorganization (e.g. property relations, the union's status as the party to collective agreements that were entered into prior to the reorganization, etc.).

---

128 Im Jong-ryul, *supra*, p. 101; Ha Gab-rae, *supra*, p. 241; The Judicial Research and Training Institute, *supra*, p. 139

129 Union Act, Articles 16(1)8 and 17(1)

130 Ibid., Article 16(2) proviso, Article 17(4)

131 Ibid., Article 13(1)

132 Ibid.,.Article 13(2)1

133 Ibid., Article 6(2)

D. Dissolution of Trade Unions

1) The Concept

"Dissolution" refers to when a trade union ceases its activities and proceeds to take steps that lead to its dissolution. A trade union is first dispersed when reasons stipulated by the Union Act occur, at which point the union enters liquidation procedures while continuing to exist for the purpose of liquidation. The trade union is dissolved at the point of liquidation proceedings are concluded.[134]

2) The Requirements

According to Article 28(1) of the Union Act, a trade union is dissolved for any of the following reasons: ① When any cause for dissolution exists as prescribed by its bylaws; ②When it is extinguished due to merger or division; ③ When a general meeting or council of delegates has a resolution to dissolve it; ④ When it is deemed to have no officers and not to have carried out any activity as a trade union for not less than one year, and the administrative agencies obtains resolution of the Labor Relations Commission upon its dissolution. When a trade union is dissolved for reasons ① through ③, its representative must file a report on the fact of the dissolution to the relevant administrative agencies within 15 days from the date of the dissolution.[135] However, when a trade union is dissolved for reason ④, it is not necessary to file such a report.

3) The Legal Effects

When a trade union dissolves, the union ceases its activities and enters into the liquidation process through which the assets of the union are liquidated. The trade union is not dissolved at the point of dispersal,

---

134 Ha Gab-rae, *supra*, p. 231; Im Jong-ryul, *supra*, p. 102
135 Ibid., Article 28(2)

as it remains in existence within the purpose of the liquidation. Therefore, any existing collective agreements entered into between the trade union and the employer or employers' association remain valid to the extent that it advances the purpose of liquidation. Subsequently, as the dispersed trade union becomes extinguished upon the conclusion of the liquidation proceedings, the validity of the collective agreement is also finished at that point.[136]

---

136 Ha Gab-rae, *supra*, p. 237; Im Jong-ryul, *supra*, p. 103; The Judicial Research and Training Institute, *supra*, p. 1336

Chapter 2

Collective Bargaining and Collective Agreements

Part 1. Collective Bargaining

I. The Concept of Collective Bargaining

Collective bargaining refers to the series of processes in which the trade union or other labor organization negotiates with the employer through a representative bargaining trade union for the main purposes of ultimately arriving at an agreement with respect to labor conditions with the employer.[1]

The substance in general contracts is determined by negotiations between parties regarding how rights and obligations will be established in the resulting mutual agreement. The substance of working conditions is determined through bargaining between parties to the labor relationship. However, with respect to labor relationships it is possible for trade unions and the like to collectively determine the terms and conditions of the labor relationship through collective bargaining. This arrangement is largely due to the fact that having individual workers engage in separate bargaining with the employer

---

1 Im Jong-ryul, *Labor Law*, p. 111 (Pakyoungsa 2014)

would result in contracts where the working conditions reflect the unilateral interest of the latter, as workers are weaker than employers in terms of both economic and social power. In other words, collective bargaining ensures the right of workers to unify with each other so that they may stand on equal bargaining ground with the employer, and in so doing determine their labor relationship on the foundation of collective power (collective bargaining and the right to enter into collective agreements).

The following are highlights of statutes relevant to collective bargaining. Article 33(1) of the Constitution ensures the fundamental right of the worker to engage independently in collective bargaining with the employer through workers' organizations for the purpose of improving working conditions. Article 29 of the Union Act[2] stipulates that "[t]he representative of a trade union shall have the authority to bargain and make a collective agreement with the employer or employers' association for the trade union and its members,"[3] and that "the representative from a major trade union that is in the midst of bargaining . . . shall have the authority to bargain and make a collective agreement with an employer for all trade unions and members involved that are requesting bargaining,"[4] thereby determining the authority of the trade union representative or representative bargaining trade union to bargain and make collective agreements.

Furthermore, Article 30 of the Union Act stipulates that "[a] trade union and an employer or employers' association shall bargain and make a collective agreement with each other in good faith and sincerity and shall not abuse their authority,"[5] and also that "[a] trade union and an employer or employers' association shall not refuse or neglect, without any justifiable reason, to bargain or conclude a

---

2 Trade Union and Labor Relations Adjustment Act
3 Union Act, Article 29(1)
4 Ibid., Article 29(2)
5 Ibid., Article 30(1)

collective agreement,"[6] thereby designating the duty of the employer to engage in the collective bargaining and collective agreement process with sincerity.

Meanwhile, "[w]hen an employer has suffered damages due to collective bargaining or industrial action under this Act, he shall not claim damages against a trade union or workers,"[7] and "Article 20 of the Criminal Act [which stipulates the definition of justifiable acts] shall apply to justifiable... collective bargaining,"[8] such actions shall be given immunity from criminal liability.

II. Parties to Collective Bargaining

A. Employee Side

1) Proper Parties Possessing the Right to Request Collective Bargaining

i) Recognized Trade Unions

A trade union unit that is established while satisfying the formal and substantive requirements stipulated in the Union Act (i.e. "Recognized Trade Unions") may be a proper subject of the right to collectively bargain, whether its specific form is a union, craft, industrial, or regional union.

As long as a trade union's bylaws designate the engaging in collective bargaining and making collective agreements as its objective and it exerts control over company-level trade unions, this associated organization of trade unions may nevertheless be a party to collective bargaining.

---

6 Ibid., Article 30(2)

7 Ibid., Article 3

8 Ibid., Article 4

There are also instances where a chapter or branch is established under a company-level trade union, and such chapters or branches become an actively independent entity with separate bylaws and administrative organ. These chapters or branches may independently engage in collective bargaining or conclude collective agreements for matters concerning its own members or organization. Chapters or branches of company-level trade unions are not subject to Article 7 of the Enforcement Ordinance of the Union Act, and therefore are not impacted by whether or not they reported their establishment to relevant administrative agencies.[9]

Finally, "[r]efusal or delay of . . . collective bargaining with the representative of a trade union or with a person authorized by the trade union without any justifiable reason" is considered an unfair labor practice that may be dealt with through an order by the Labor Relations Commission by a request for remedy by Recognized Trade Unions.[10]

ii) Non-Recognized Trade Unions

Regarding whether non-recognized trade unions (trade unions that satisfy the substantive requirements of a union under the Union Act but are defective in that they failed to satisfy the formal requirement of reporting their establishment) are proper parties that may exercise the right to collective bargaining, the Supreme Court has ruled as follows: "While entities that do not satisfy the substantive requirements necessary to become a trade union may not be considered as such, thereby lacking the right to collective bargaining and not being subjects of proper industrial action, workers' organizations that are not trade unions under the Union Act cannot necessarily be said to lack rights such as collective bargaining."[11] Through this ruling, the

---

9 Supreme Court 2000Do4299 (2001. 2. 23.)

10 Union Act, Articles 7(1), (2), 81(3)

11 Supreme Court 96Nu2125 (1997. 2. 11.)

Supreme Court seems to be indirectly acknowledging that even non-recognized organizations may become proper subjects of the right to collective bargaining.[12]

According to Article 33(1) of the Constitution, the right to collective bargaining refers to the right of the worker to independently bargain, through workers' organizations, with the employer or employer's association and conclude collective agreements on matters that have been agreed upon. Therefore, an entity may become the subject of collective bargaining as defined in the Constitution by becoming a recognized workers' organization that satisfies the substantive requirements of worker identity, independence, purpose, and collectivity. Non-recognized trade unions may also become such a subject if they succeed in being recognized as a workers' organization.

Article 29 of the Union Act stipulates that the "trade union shall have the authority to bargain and make a collective agreement with the employer or employers' association for the trade union and its members."[13] Here, "trade union" refers to workers' organizations that satisfy the substantive requirements of a trade union as defined under Article 2(4) of the Union Act. This term cannot be said to be limited to trade unions as defined under Article 10 of the Union Act, which requires unions to have concluded the reporting process as well.

Also, the three fundamental labor rights as ensured by the Constitution, as well as the right to collective bargaining defined in Article 29 of the Union Act, mean that not only is the authority of workers' organizations to bargain legally recognized, but the authority of these organizations to conclude collective agreements regarding matters agreed upon through the bargaining process are as well. If workers' organizations were not given this recognition as proper

---

12 Nonetheless, administrative interpretations (Ministry of Labor, Guidance on Collective Bargaining and Collective Agreements) deem that non-recognized trade unions cannot be a party to collective bargaining.

13 Union Act, Article 29(1)

parties to conclude legally effective collective agreements, no extent of ensuring the right to organize, collectively bargain, or engage in collective action would be able to provide the leverage needed to regulate working conditions in a uniform and collective manner. Therefore, in light of the legislative intent behind the Constitution's protection of the three fundamental labor rights (which is to make possible the collective and uniform regulation of working conditions based on the strength of the worker's capacity to organize), workers' organizations are ensured the right to conclude collective agreements, as this is part-and-parcel to the right of collective bargaining. Put another way, as long as an entity satisfies the requirements to make it into a workers' organization, it becomes a proper party to conclude collective agreements.

In a relevant Supreme Court case, the court ruled, "A special collective bargaining steering committee, composed of a subset of the members from the already established trade union in the National Railroad Administration, does not possess the right to collective bargaining."[14] This ruling illustrates an instance when a special collective bargaining steering committee of a workplace that already has an established trade union attempted to start a strike.

Non-recognized trade unions cannot "make an application for adjustment of industrial disputes and for the remedy of unfair labor practices to the Labor Relations Commission"[15] when employers refuse or unduly delay engaging in collective bargaining.

iii) Temporary Strike Groups

The question of whether temporary strike groups formed to achieve a certain purpose could be proper subjects of collective bargaining is currently under dispute between the view that it cannot be a proper

---

14 Supreme Court 91Do324 (1991. 5. 24.). For similar cases, see Supreme Court 95Do1016 (1995. 10. 12.), Supreme Court 95Do748 (1997. 4. 22.).

15 Union Act, Article 7(1) and (2)

subject of collective bargaining on the grounds that it fails to possess the necessary substance to be recognized as a union, and the view that it can be a proper subject of collective bargaining on the grounds that it has appointed a representative, as temporary as it may be, and that trade unions are not the only parties that have the ability to exercise the right to association.

2) Representing Workers in Collective Bargaining

A trade union that has satisfied substantive requirements as a workers' organization may exercise its right to collective bargaining through its representative,[16] or by another person who is delegated authority by the trade union.[17] Article 29 of the Union Act stipulates that the trade union representative or the delegated authority be given the right to engage in collective bargaining and conclude collective agreements.

i) Whether Restrictions on the Right to Engage in Collective Bargaining Should Be Allowed

Regarding this question, court precedent suggests the following: If a collective agreement or trade union bylaw stipulates that a trade union representative or persons delegated authority by the trade union must, after reaching agreement with the employer as to the content of the collective agreement, depending on the results of the bargaining process, obtain approval from the trade union's general meeting via resolution in order to make the collective agreement effective, this would impose an overall and comprehensive restriction on the authority of the representative to conclude or delegate the conclusion of collective agreements. Such restrictions in effect reduce the previously mentioned right of the representative or delegate into a nominal one, and hence would be a violation of the provisions in the

---

16 Ibid., Article 29(1)
17 Ibid., Article 29(3)

Union Act that bestow this right and is therefore invalid.[18]

ii) Delegation of Authority of the Right to Collective Bargaining

A trade union may delegate authority to engage in collective bargaining or conclude collective agreements to a third person.[19] In such cases, the trade union must determine the bargaining items and the scope of authority to be given to the representative, and notify this fact to the opposing employer or employer's associations.[20]

There are no restrictions as to the scope of who may receive the delegated authority to engage in collective bargaining on behalf of the trade union. In practice, it is common to see company-level trade unions delegate this authority to their superordinate organization, the associated organization of labor unions. The issue of whether such company-level trade union's right to collective bargaining will be extinguished in such cases where the company-level trade union delegates its authority to engage in collective bargaining to a third party is still a matter of dispute. On this matter, relevant court precedent rules that if the above company-level trade union independently engages in collective bargaining and enters into a valid collective agreement before the associate organization that has been delegated the former's authority to do so, this collective agreement is recognized to be valid and effective.[21]

Therefore, if a collective agreement contains provisions that prohibit the trade union from delegating its collective bargaining authority to third parties, this would be considered invalid because it not only violates the Union Act above but it also infringes the

18 Supreme Court 91Nu12257 (1993. 4. 27.) (Consensus Decision), Supreme Court 91Nu10787 (1993. 5. 11.), Supreme Court 94Ma605 (1995. 3. 10.), Supreme Court 97Do588 (1998. 1. 20.), Supreme Court 2003Da27429 (2005. 3. 11.)

19 Union Act, Article 29(3)

20 Ibid., Article 29(3); Enforcement Decree of the Union Act, Article 14

21 Supreme Court 98Da20790 (1998. 11. 13.)

collective bargaining rights of other trade union organizations (e.g. associated organizations that the relevant union is a part of). The reason Article 29(3) of the Union Act allows trade unions to delegate collective bargaining authority to third parties is to make it possible for them to receive assistance from outside experts or superordinate associated organizations, and to compel employers or employer associations to engage in collective bargaining in a sincere manner. Through such measures, the trade union is ensured its right to collective bargaining.

3) Whether Provisions on Sole Collective Bargaining Should Be Allowed

If a collective agreement contains a collective agreement clause that recognizes the right of collective bargaining to only the designated trade union (the so-called sole bargaining body clause), the general agreement in the literature is that this clause cannot be enforced as it is an outright restriction on the right by a proper agent to collectively bargain.

4) Whether Prohibitions on Appointing Third Parties Should Be Allowed

There are situations where it is stipulated in the collective agreement that the right of collective bargaining can only be assigned to union members of the relevant trade unions. However, the question of whether such prohibition against appointing third parties to collectively bargain is valid is currently under dispute.

B. Employer Side

1) Parties under Duty to Engage in Collective Bargaining
i) The Employer

The Union Act defines "employer" as "a business owner, a person responsible for the management of a business, or a person who acts on behalf of a business owner with regard to matters concerning workers in the business."[22] In a Supreme Court case that ruled on the definition of "employer" in the context of him/her being a party under the duty to engage in collective bargaining as stipulated under Article 29 of the Union Act,[23] the Supreme Court defined "employer" as a person who has an employer-employee relationship with the worker, that is, a person who is under an explicit or implicit employment relationship with the worker, the purpose of which is to have the former direct and supervise the latter while paying wages for labor provided by the latter.

The Act on the Protection of Temporary Agency Workers stipulates under Article 34(1) that "The Labor Standards Act [(hereinafter referred to as "LSA")] shall apply to services provided by a temporary agency worker during his/her period of temporary employment as a temporary work agency, and a user company shall be deemed an employer defined in Article 2 of the same Act,"[24] but goes on to state that the term "employer" would mean "temporary work agencies" for certain provisions, and "employer" for other provisions in the LSA. Therefore, for a trade union that consists of temporary workers, it would have as its opposite party to the collective bargaining table (hence assuming the duty to engage in collective bargaining) not only the temporary work agency that the workers have signed employment contracts with (i.e. the employer that is under contractual relations with the temporary workers as defined under the LSA), but also the business owner that actually directs and supervises the temporary workers (as the business owner may make decisions regarding working conditions of

---

22 Union Act, Article 2(2)

23 Supreme Court 92Nu13011 (1993. 11. 23.), Supreme Court 95Nu3565 (1995. 12. 22.), Supreme Court 97Nu3644 (1997. 9. 5.)

24 Act on the Protection of Temporary Agency Workers, Article 34(1)

the temporary workers to the extent it is recognized as an employer under the LSA).

Meanwhile, court precedent views that the scope of who may be considered as an employer is different from the standard mentioned above (i.e. subjects of collective bargaining) for those who are the subjects of unfair labor practices such as dominating or interfering. That is, the courts consider that a business owner who is able to direct and supervise his/her workers in a substantial and specific manner to the extent that s/he may be considered to have authority over and duties for the basic working conditions of workers s/he employs must be considered an employer that may implement orders by the Labor Relations Commission to remedy unfair labor practices if s/he dominates or interferes with the organization or operation of the trade union.[25] Therefore, a person who would not be considered an employer under the LSA could still be considered an employer liable for unfair labor practices under the Union Act.

In cases where it has been decided that reorganization proceedings would commence, as the authority to manage and dispose of business operations and property of the corporation is given exclusively to the receiver according to the Debtor Rehabilitation and Bankruptcy Act, it is the receiver and not the chief executive officer of the corporation undergoing reorganization proceedings who shall be deemed to be the employer in the labor relationship. As such, the person representing the employer in collective bargaining for a corporation undergoing reorganization shall be the receiver of such corporation, not the chief executive officer.[26]

ii) Employer Associations
An employer association is a group of employers that has the authority

---

25 Supreme Court 2007Du8881 (2010. 3. 25.)

26 Supreme Court 99Da72422 (2001. 1. 19.)

to mediate or regulate among its member employers. The general understanding is that employer associations engage in collective bargaining and conclude collective agreements in a unified manner for member employers according to articles of association or bylaws, and possess substantive authority in regulating the labor management relationship of their member employers. In such cases, the employer association may become a party in the collective bargaining process.

2) The Person Representing the Employer Side in the Collective Bargaining Process

The employer or employer association, through its representative or through persons delegated with such authority, has the duty to engage in collective bargaining with workers' organizations such as the trade union.

Only those employer representatives who are delegated the authority to decide directly on matters related to working conditions (i.e. the subject of collective bargaining) may become the person representing the employer in the collective bargaining process. If this person delegated to represent the employer cannot properly refuse to engage in collective bargaining or conclude collective agreements by arguing s/he does not have the authority to make such decisions, such an attempt would be recognized as an unfair labor practice.[27]

C. Methods of Collective Bargaining

1) Types of Collective Bargaining Methods

If we were to classify types of collective bargaining methods depending on who the parties are, they would be divided as follows:

---

27 The Judicial Research and Training Institute, *Trade Union and Labor Relations Mediation Law*, p.169 (2014)

First is the company level collective bargaining method (company level bargaining), where the company-level trade union and employer engage in collective bargaining. Next would be the multi-union/employer bargaining method, where a superordinate organization that is delegated the right to collective bargaining from the company-level trade union bargains with the employer association. Third would be the diagonal bargaining method, where the associated union of the company-level unit that has been delegated the latter's right to collective bargaining independently negotiates with the company-level trade union's employer. Fourth would be the coordinated bargaining method, where the associated union and the company-level union both jointly and independently engage in collective bargaining with the employer at the same time. The last would be the multi-group bargaining method, where multiple company-level trade unions with shared interests engage in collective bargaining with a single employer.

2) The Method of Collective Bargaining in the Existence of Multiple Trade Unions

On July 1, 2011, the establishment of multiple trade unions became permissible. As such, in businesses or workplaces where multiple trade unions co-exist, a single bargaining window must be established[28] "where no fewer than two trade unions established or joined by workers exist in one business or one place of work regardless of the type of organization, trade unions shall determine a representative bargaining trade union and request the same to bargain on its behalf;"[29] "where the trade unions fail to determine a representative bargaining trade union, a labor union organized by the majority of all the members of the trade unions which participated in procedures for the simplification of bargaining windows shall be a representative

---

28 Union Act, Article 29-2, Addendum Article 7(1)
29 Ibid., Article 29-2(1)

bargaining trade union;"[30] and "where the trade unions fail to determine a representative bargaining trade union, all the trade unions which participate in procedures for the simplification of bargaining windows shall jointly organize a bargaining delegation (hereafter referred as "joint bargaining delegation") and bargain with an employer."[31]

III. Objects of Collective Bargaining

A. Significance of Matters for Collective Bargaining

The matters in which the workers may request bargaining on the grounds of their right to collective bargaining are deemed "Matters for Collective Bargaining."

Article 33(1) of the Constitution stipulates that a worker is entitled to three fundamental labor rights (including the right to collective bargaining) for "the purpose of improving working conditions," and Article 29(1) of the Union Act stipulates that "The representative of a trade union shall have the authority to bargain and make a collective agreement with the employer or employers' association for the trade union and its members." Objects of collective bargaining include "matters for trade union members" and "matters for trade unions," as they are part of the "improvement of working conditions." Also, the Union Act makes it clear that trade unions are established "for the purpose of maintaining and improving the working conditions of the workers and enhancing their economic and social status,"[32] and that "parties to labor relations ... [decide] matters as to working conditions and other labor-related matters through labor-management

---

30 Ibid., Article 29-2(3)

31 Ibid., Article 29-2(4)

32 Ibid., Article 2(4)

consultation or by collective bargaining,"[33] thereby placing priority on independent bargaining between parties. Towards this, the Union Act determines the duties of the parties to labor relations by stipulating "[t]he parties to labor relations shall make efforts to stipulate in their collective agreement procedures and methods for labor-management consultation and other collective bargaining to maintain reasonable labor relations, and shall make efforts to voluntarily resolve labor disputes, if any."[34]

In light of the above regulations, the subject matter for which the employer assumes the duty to engage in collective bargaining may be understood to include "matters related to the determination of working conditions;" activities of trade unions or procedures and methods of collective bargaining that are necessary for the enhancement of the economic and social status of workers; and "other matters related to labor relations that influence the determination of working conditions," such as the conclusion of collective agreements.

Matters that do not relate to the parties to the labor relations themselves, such as requests regarding the working conditions of non-union members, are generally deemed to be beyond the scope of matters considered as objects of collective bargaining.

B. Types and Scope of Matters for Collective Bargaining

As such, matters for which the employer is obligated to engage in collective bargaining (the so-called compulsory bargaining matters) are matters related to the determination of working conditions and matters related to other labor relations that influence working conditions. In principle, parties to labor relations are able to decide

---

33 Ibid., Article 47
34 Ibid., Article 48

what these matters will be, and are limited to matters related to the parties themselves. Furthermore, the employer may refuse to engage in bargaining on matters not related to the parties themselves. However, even if a bargaining item is not a compulsory bargaining matter, as long as the item does not violate one of the compulsory regulations under the Union Act (the so-called illegal bargaining matters), there is no reason to prohibit the employer from waiving his/her right to refuse to bargain and engage in collective bargaining and conclude collective agreements regarding this matter (the so-called voluntary bargaining matters).[35]

If continuous effort has been made through the collective bargaining process to reach an agreement on compulsory bargaining matters but such efforts failed to come to fruition, leading to the ceasing of negotiations, trade unions may resort to industrial action in order to accomplish their demands. For voluntary or illegal bargaining matters, however, the trade union may not resort to industrial action or other collective action even if they fail to achieve agreement with the employer independently through the collective bargaining process.

C. Scope of Matters for Collective Bargaining

1) Matters Related to the Determination of Working Conditions

Matters related to the determination of working and employment conditions regarding wage structure, working hours, welfare, dismissals, and other treatment that impact the entire union membership may become the subject matter of collective bargaining. Examples of such matters include the following: determination and calculation of wages and the method of payment; the method for paying wages and the timing of payment; promotions; severance pay

---

35 The Judicial Research and Training Institute, *supra*, p. 174

and bonuses; description and allocation of working hours (the start and end of regular working hours, break times), holidays, leaves, and shifts; retirement and resignation; the supplying of personal work equipment; welfare; educational facilities and educational training for workers; safety, sanitation and health; accident/disaster compensation and support; commendations and sanctions such as disciplinary action.

Matters related to working conditions that fall under the management authority of the employer may become objects of collective bargaining, but only to the extent that they are directly related or have a significant impact on working conditions and their negotiations would not fundamentally restrict the employer's management rights.

From this perspective, as matters relating to the standard of personnel decisions and procedure such as personnel movements and disciplinary action being carried out (e.g. dismissals, company and workplace transfers) are directly related to working conditions, there is no reason to treat these differently from other working conditions and hence must become objects of collective bargaining.

However, for dismissals where the employer establishes and executes employment adjustment plans (i.e. dismissal for managerial reasons, or layoffs), the Supreme Court ruled as follows: "decisions regarding whether to commence structural readjustments such as layoffs or the merging of divisions and units are an exercise of high-level managerial decision-making, and by principle are not objects of collective bargaining."[36] In another ruling the Supreme Court opined "the commencement of layoffs is a managerial action of the employer; therefore if the trade union's demand is that the employer should not implement the layoffs, this would be a fundamental restriction on the employer's management rights. Therefore, such a request cannot be an

---

36 Supreme Court 2001Do3380 (2003. 12. 26.), Supreme Court 2002Do5577 (2006. 5. 25.)

object of collective bargaining."[37]

According to court precedent, even if a certain matter is considered to be within the management rights of the employer, the parties to collective bargaining may nevertheless negotiate on the matter and conclude collective agreements, and such an agreement will be recognized to be effective so long as it does not violate any compulsory Acts or conflict with societal order. Therefore, the employer concluding a collective agreement where s/he agrees to restrict his/her right to conduct layoffs as a result of the collective bargaining process is not viewed as violating compulsory Acts or conflicting with societal order, assuming there are no special circumstances pointing to the contrary. Furthermore, as such an agreement is of such nature that determines the working conditions and other treatment of workers, layoffs that occurs subsequently in violation of this agreement is in principle an improper or unjustified dismissal. However, even when a collective agreement that restricts the use of layoffs exists, if subsequent to the agreement circumstances significantly change to the extent that compelling the employer to enforce this agreement would result in a clearly undue result, the employer is permitted to go beyond the restrictions imposed by the collective agreement and conduct layoffs.[38]

Another illustration would be a case where the trade union demanded the resignation of the director of the research institute (i.e. the employer), but in actuality the real purpose of the union was to reverse the expulsion of a portion of its members that the union considers a retaliatory measure against the members' leading of the movement to defend the ratio of researchers, which was a central agenda item of the trade union. The Supreme Court ruled that such a

---

37 Supreme Court 99Do4893 (2001. 4. 24.) (*but*, it is possible this ruling may have narrowed applicability, as the Supreme Court ruled that layoffs may not "in principle" be an object of collective bargaining in response to the party trade union's attempt to categorically reject the authority of the employer to conduct layoffs in accordance with the policy promoted by the Korean Confederation of Trade Unions and other union stakeholders.), Supreme Court 99Do5380 (2002. 2. 26)

38 Supreme Court 2011Du20406 (2014. 3. 27.)

purpose of the trade union may be recognized as a demand to improve the working conditions of its members, and hence is a proper purpose of collective bargaining, and in turn, a proper purpose of industrial action.[39] As such, court precedent seems to place a basic emphasis on the relationship that a potential subject matter of collective bargaining has with working conditions.

2) Matters Relating to Other Issues in Labor Relations

Other than matters concerning the determination of working conditions, there are other matters in labor relations that influence the determination of working conditions, such as trade union activities necessary for the enhancement of the economic and social status of the worker, the procedures and methods of collective bargaining, the conclusion of collective agreements, the procedure of initiating industrial action, and private mediation and arbitration. For matters of labor relations that relate to trade union activity, the union shop clause and the systems of checking off union fees and full-time union officers would be the most representative cases.

3) Issues with Respect to Matters for Collective Bargaining

i) Matters in Relation to Particular Workers

Whether a trade union may demand as an object of collective bargaining working conditions that apply only to specified individual union members is a matter of dispute (e.g. the trade union attempting to negotiate working conditions of individuals A and B, which would not have an impact on any other union members). Academic literature is of the position that such matters are meant for collective bargaining.

ii) Rights Disputes

Whether the trade union demands for the withdrawal of a dismissal

---

39 Supreme Court 91Da34523 (1992. 5. 12.)

or reinstatement of a particular worker could also be a matter for collective bargaining. Any matter concerning working conditions that are agreed upon in a collective agreement concluded through the collective bargaining process becomes binding,[40] and the provision containing this agreement functions to regulate working conditions in a collective and uniform manner. Therefore, since bargaining items that attempt to negotiate working conditions that apply only to specific workers are dispositions that cannot function as general regulations, demands that purport to withdraw dismissals or reinstate certain workers cannot become objects of collective bargaining as a matter of principle.[41]

However, in situations like the case reviewed above, where the trade union is seemingly demanding the withdrawal of dismissal or reinstatement of a particular dismissed worker but is actually attempting to use the present instance as an opportunity to clearly establish the employer's personnel standard or procedure vis-à-vis the entire union membership and thereby is actually attempting to improve working conditions or enhance the economic and social status of workers, such a demand advanced by the trade union may become a proper object of collective bargaining. Therefore, the employer cannot refuse to engage in collective bargaining by citing the surface-level demand of the trade union.[42]

Also, the above trade union's demand to withdraw the dismissal or reinstate a particular dismissed worker would be recognized as a proper purpose for industrial action as well, for the same reasons outlined in the previous paragraph.[43]

---

40 Union Act, Article 33(1)

41 Disputes between relevant parties as to interpretations, implementation and enforcement of existing laws, collective agreements, employment regulations and regulations of the like are commonly deemed "rights disputes."

42 Supreme Court of Japan (1960. 4. 26.), see Outline of Labor Law Cases, vol. 12, p. 123.

43 Supreme Court 91Da34523 (1992. 5. 12.)

IV. The Substance of the Duty to Engage in Collective Bargaining

A. The Duty of the Employer to Engage in Collective Bargaining

The substance of the duty of the employer to engage in collective bargaining may be divided into the duty to not refuse to engage in collective bargaining without justifiable reason (i.e. the duty to engage in collective bargaining); the duty to not delay or neglect the collective bargaining process without justifiable reasons (i.e. the duty to bargain in a sincere manner); and the duty to not refuse or neglect the concluding of the collective agreement to stipulate agreements reached during the collective bargaining process (i.e. the duty to conclude collective agreements).[44]

First, the employer or employer association refusing to engage in the collective bargaining process in the first place is a violation of the duty to engage in collective bargaining if the employer or employer association does not have justifiable reason to refuse. Not showing up at the bargaining venue without reasonable cause, insisting on negotiating only through documents and telephone, nominating a person who has not been verified to have the necessary authority to negotiate, delaying the bargaining by insisting on an impractical schedule or participants, leaving the bargaining table without justifiable reason all fall within the purview of violation of duty to engage in collective bargaining. There are instances where the employer refuses to engage in collective bargaining by arguing that the trade union demanding collective bargaining is not a proper party to engage in the process,[45] or that the employer him/herself or the

---

44 Union Act, Article 30

45 For an example in court precedent, *see* Supreme Court 97Nu8076 (1998. 5. 22.).

employer association itself is not a proper party subject to the duty to engage in collective bargaining. Another illustration would be the employer refusing to engage in collective bargaining by arguing that the matter demanded by the trade union is not a subject matter which the employer is under duty to engage in collective bargaining. In the above illustrations, whether the employer has violated his/her duty to engage in collective bargaining is determined by whether the reasons cited by the employer are justifiable.

If the employer seemingly agrees to engage in collective bargaining but in reality "insincerely engages" in the bargaining process, the employer is in violation of the duty to bargain in a sincere manner. The essence of the duty to bargain in a sincere manner is the obligation to collectively explore the possibility of arriving at an agreement. Examples of such insincere engagement in the bargaining process include: engaging in the collective bargaining process by entrusting the process to a person who does not hold the authority to make decisions regarding the matters demanded at the bargaining table; positioning as prerequisites to bargaining illegal requests or requests that do not have anything to do with matters being demanded through the bargaining process; delaying the collective bargaining process by citing reasons that are not justifiable in light of the former's procedure.

According to court precedent,[46] the employer is in violation of his/her duty to collectively bargain not only in cases where s/he refuses or neglects to engage in collective bargaining without justifiable reason, but also when s/he genuinely believes that s/he possessed justifiable reason to refuse collective bargaining or that s/he has engaged in the process with sincerity if it is objectively determined that the employer did not possess such justifiable reason or that s/he engaged in insincere collective bargaining. In such cases, whether the employer

---

46 Supreme Court 97Nu8076 (1998. 5. 22.), Supreme Court 2005Do8606 (2006. 2. 24.)

possesses justifiable reason to refuse collective bargaining depends on whether, in light of socially accepted norms, expecting the employer to perform his/her duty to collective bargaining would be justified when considering factors such as the bargaining representative of the union side, the bargaining time frame and location demanded by the union side, the matters to bargain, and the bargaining attitude of the union side.

The employer refusing or neglecting to conclude collective agreements even after final agreement has been reached through the collective bargaining process is also a violation of the employer's duty to engage in collective bargaining. The obligation to enter into such a collective agreement would be deemed to be included in the duty to bargain in a sincere manner. This means that in the event a collective bargaining is concluded in an agreement between the relevant parties, a collective agreement must be entered into immediately.

B. The Duty of the Union Side When Exercising the Right to Collective Bargaining

The trade union also has the duty to engage in the collective bargaining process with good faith and sincerity and conclude collective agreements, not abuse its right to collectively bargain, and not refuse or neglect to bargain or conclude collective agreements on demands made by the employer without justifiable reason.[47] If the trade union violates the above duties, the employer or employer organization would not be violating his/her duty to engage in collective bargaining with sincerity if s/he refuses or neglects the process of collective bargaining or agreement citing the above acts of the trade union.

Examples of how trade unions may violate their duty to engage

---

47 Union Act, Article 30

in collective bargaining with good faith and sincerity include reiterating bargaining demands that are objectively unacceptable to the employer's side despite being presented with compromise proposals from the latter without citing reasonable cause or proposing alternative proposals, or demanding the employer must produce explanations or material regarding bargaining matters that go beyond the scope of what they may reasonably request from the employer.

To take a couple of examples from court precedent, the Supreme Court ruled in the following cases that engaging in industrial action due to breakdowns in the collective bargaining effort would not be recognized as proper industrial action in terms of purpose, timing, and process. The first case is the trade union representative or delegated authority making clear that s/he will only conclude collective agreements with the employer after s/he has presented the results of the collective bargaining to the general meeting of the trade union and received approval to go ahead via resolution (depending on the results of the bargaining, that is).[48] The second case is when trade union members failed to alleviate the employer's doubts regarding the authority of the union side representative to conclude collective agreements due to the failure of union members to inform the employer of the fact that they had delegated authority to conclude collective agreements to the trade union head and the central executive committee despite being obligated, according to union bylaws, to notify the employer of any such matters.[49]

---

48 Supreme Court 97Do588 (1998. 1. 20.)
49 Supreme Court 98Do3299 (2000. 5. 12.)

V. Means to Remedy Violations of the Duty to Engage in Collective Bargaining

A. Administrative Remedies: Application for Remedies for Unfair Labor Practices

According to the Union Act, "Employers shall not conduct . . . refusal or delay of the execution of a collective agreement or other collective bargaining with the representative of a trade union, or with a person authorized by the trade union, without any justifiable reason."[50] A violation of this provision constitutes an unfair labor practice. Therefore, "[a] worker or trade union may make an application for remedy to the Labor Relations Commission on the grounds that his rights have been infringed upon by an unfair labor practice on the part of the employer"[51] after going through the designated administrative procedures.[52]

As an unfair labor practice for violations related to the duty to engage in collective bargaining occurs when the employer refuses or neglects to engage in collective bargaining without justifiable reason, and the employer still remains in violation of this duty even if the employer believed s/he had justifiable reason to refuse collective bargaining or that s/he has engaged with the process in a sincere manner yet objectively no such justifiable cause or sincere attitude existed,[53] the specific intent to engage in an unfair labor practice (reviewed above) does not become an issue when constituting an unfair labor practice due to a violation of the duty to engage in collective bargaining.

Again, "a worker or trade union may make an application for

---

50 Union Act, Article 81(3)
51 Ibid., Article 82(1)
52 Ibid., Articles 82(2) and 86
53 Supreme Court 97Nu8076 (1998. 5. 22.)

remedy to the Labor Relations Commission on the grounds that his rights have been infringed upon by an unfair labor practice on the part of the employer."[54] Therefore, only trade unions established in accordance with the Union Act may make such applications for remedy.[55]

B. Remedies under Private Law

1) Administrative Litigation: Litigation Requesting the Cancellation of the Decision on Review Made by the National Labor Relations Commission Regarding an Unfair Labor Practice

As was mentioned above, after the Local Labor Relations Commission makes its determination on an application for remedy for an unfair labor practice regarding the refusal or neglecting of collective bargaining and the National Labor Relations Commission issues its decision on review, "any of the parties concerned may institute an administrative appeal against a decision made by the National Labor Relations Commission within 15 days from the date of receiving the notice of the decision."[56]

In a relevant Supreme Court case,[57] the court ruled that "if during the litigation requesting the cancellation of the decision on review made by the National Labor Relations Commission (which, in this instance, dismissed the case) regarding an unfair labor practice in which the employer refused to conclude collective bargaining for certain matters, the parties to the dispute successfully reaches a settlement regarding the relevant collective bargaining item, the Supreme Court deems the purpose of the application for remedy as having been

54 Union Act, Article 82(1)
55 Ibid., Article 7(1)
56 Ibid., Article 85(2)
57 Supreme Court 94Nu3209 (1995. 4. 7.)

satisfied, and therefore the party bringing the appeal no longer has an interest in the litigation, making further proceedings regarding the appeal improper."

2) Provisional Dispositions to Have Parties Agree to Collective Bargaining

The right to collective bargaining has the nature of a claim under private law in which the trade union may request an action from the employer that would facilitate the latter's sincere engagement to the collective bargaining process. If the employer then refuses or neglects to engage in collective bargaining without justifiable reason, the trade union may request a provisional disposition (which, under the Civil Execution Act, prescribes a temporary status to be applied to the parties) to have the employer temporarily agree to engage in the collective bargaining process.[58]

3) Civil Litigation Concerning Merits

The duties of employers to engage in collective bargaining is characteristic of a liability under private law. Therefore, a trade union may initiate a civil suit to have the employer fulfill his/her legal obligation to engage in collective bargaining. Once such a suit results in an implementation order, the union may forcibly execute this order through indirect compulsory performance.

If the employer has violated his/her duty to engage in collective bargaining, the trade union may sue the employer for resulting damages under the legal theory that the employer's actions constitute default or intentional or negligent illegal actions.

The Supreme Court first laid out that an employer's act of refusing to engage in collective bargaining would constitute an illegal act (as a form of unfair labor practice) if its cause, purpose, method, form, and/

---

58 Civil Execution Act, Article 300(2)

or results are recognized to be such that it is unacceptable in light of socially accepted norms and rules, thereby derogating the right of workers to bargain collectively. Thus, if an employer that has refused to engage in collective bargaining without justifiable cause continues to do so despite receiving an order or provisional disposition from the court to engage in collective bargaining, this second refusal to engage in collective bargaining is an act unacceptable in light of socially accepted norms and rules. As such, the Supreme Court ruled that the employer's actions are an illegal act against the trade union and derogated the latter's right to collective bargaining.[59]

While the question of how to calculate the amount of damages to be paid by the employer to the trade union for defaulting or for committing an illegal act is difficult to answer definitively, at the very least compensation to victims for emotional pain suffered due to the illegal refusal and delay of the collective bargaining process by the employer has been recognized by case law.[60]

C. Violation of Obligation of Collective Bargaining by the Worker

In the event that workers violate their duty to bargain in a sincere manner, they will be subject to the disadvantage of not being able to request administrative or statutory remedy for the employer denying bargaining on the grounds of such violations.

---

59 Supreme Court 2004Da11070 (2006. 10. 26.)

60 *See* Busan High Court 2006Na19443 (2007. 2. 8.), which ruled after the Supreme Court had remanded the above case (Supreme Court 2004Da11070) back to the lower courts.

Part 2. Collective Agreements

I. Summarizing Collective Agreements

A. The Concept of Collective Agreements

Collective agreements are contracts that formalize the agreements reached regarding working conditions, other treatment of workers, and rights and obligations of workers and employers through the collective bargaining process.

Matters determined through collective agreements regulate and formulate the collective labor relations between the workers' organization and the employer as well as the individual labor relations between individual workers and the employer regarding the working conditions of individual workers.

B. The Legal Characteristics of Collective Agreements

Collective agreements were created through the revision and supplementation of the principles of contracts under civic law. On one hand, it exhibits characteristics similar to contracts in light of the fact that it is an agreement between workers and an employer. On the grounds of such special characteristics of the collective agreement, there are largely two opinions regarding how to understand the legal characteristics of collective agreements. The first opinion is that "collective agreements possess fundamentally different legal characteristics from contracts." The second opinion is that "collective agreements possess the same fundamental characteristics as contracts."

In terms of substance, the right of workers' organizations such as trade unions to conclude collective agreements that have the legal effect of collectively and uniformly regulating the labor relations of all their members is recognized. With respect to this right, the consensus in related literature is to view the legal characteristic of collective agreements as that of a collective normative contract.

C. Parties to Collective Agreements

A party to a collective agreement means a person who has the legal capability to enter into a collective agreement under his/her own name. As the collective agreement is the documentation of matters agreed upon in collective bargaining, in principle the parties to the collective bargaining are deemed the parties to the collective agreement.

II. The Execution and Filing of Collective Agreements

According to the Union Act, "[a] collective agreement shall be prepared in writing, and both of the parties shall affix their signatures or their seals thereto."[61] The reason why the collective agreement must be prepared in writing is to prevent disputes by clarifying the establishment of a collective agreement, and the reason why affixation of signatures or seals is required is to secure the authenticity of the collective agreement by expressing the conclusive intent of the parties. A Court precedent clearly rules that collective agreements which do not satisfy the stipulated methods in Article 31(1) of the Union Act are not legally effective against trade union members.[62] For example, if a collective agreement contains the written signature of the

---

61 Union Act, Article 31(1)
62 Supreme Court 99Da72422 (2001. 1. 19.), Supreme Court 2001Da15422, 15439 (2001. 5. 29.)

union chairperson but does not contain that of the employer's chief executive officer, the document would not be effective as a collective agreement.[63] An oral agreement between the union chairperson and the employer also would not in itself result in a validly concluded collective agreement.[64] As such, even if a party to the oral agreement argues the nullification of this collective agreement in violation of the above regulation, this would not be a violation of the duty of good faith.[65]

Also, according to the Union Act, "[p]arties to a collective agreement shall make a report of the collective agreement to the relevant administrative agencies within 15 days from the date of its conclusion."[66] The consensus interpretation of this provision is that it is not a compulsory regulation, and hence the violation of this requirement would not impact the legal effect of the collective agreement.

A final requirement of the Union Act regarding this topic is "[w]hen a collective agreement has any unlawful contents, the administrative agencies may, with a resolution from the Labor Relations Commission, order them to be corrected."[67] In other words, if an administrative agency determines that a provision in the collective agreement is illegal and orders its modification or cancellation, this order would not automatically cause the relevant provision to be modified or to lose its effectiveness. Even if the trade union refuses to accept the above corrective order, the administrative agency does not possess the power to enforce it.[68] However, the trade union does become subject to criminal liability under Article 93(2) of the Union Act.

---

63 Ibid.

64 Supreme Court 2001Da15422, 15439 (2001. 5. 29.)

65 Ibid.

66 Union Act, Article 31(2)

67 Ibid., Article 31(3)

68 Seoul High Court 92Gu12096 (1993. 3. 12.)

III. The Substance and Legal Effect of Collective Agreements

A. Overview

According to Article 33 of the Union Act, "Any part of the rules of employment or a labor contract that violate standards concerning working conditions and other treatment of workers as prescribed in a collective agreement shall be null and void,"[69] and "Matters not covered in a labor contract and the part which is null and void under paragraph (1) shall be governed by those standards of a collective agreement."[70] The portion of the collective agreement which the trade union has concluded as a party and that determines the "standards concerning working conditions and other treatment of workers" directly regulates on a compulsory and supplementary basis the contractual employment relationship between the worker and employer, taking precedence over similar provisions in the rules of employment or employment contracts. This is called the normative effect of collective agreements. The provisions within collective agreements that are recognized to have this normative effect possess a different legal effect than those which do not.

Parts of collective agreements that are not recognized to have the above normative effect determine the rights and obligations between the parties to the collective agreement (i.e. the trade union and the employer or employer association), and possess legal effects not different from that of regular contracts. This is the so-called contractual effect of the collective agreement.

---

69 Union Act, Article 33(1)
70 Ibid., Article 33(2)

B. The Normative Section and Its Legal Effect

1) The Normative Section

Sections of the collective agreement that determine standards regarding working conditions or other treatment of workers are given normative effect and are called normative sections.

Matters related to "working conditions or other treatment of workers" means "conditions and covenants under the employment agreement and treatment of the workers under the employment relationship" or "individual employment relationships (i.e. matters in relation to the maintenance and termination of an employment relationship)."

Determination of working and employment conditions regarding wage structure, working hours, welfare, dismissals, and other workers' treatment that impact the entire union membership, such as wage structure, method of payment of wages, the method for paying wages and the timing of payment; promotions; severance pay and bonuses; description and allocation of working hours (the start and end of regular working hours, break times), holidays, leaves, and shifts; retirement and resignation; the supplying of personal work equipment; welfare; educational facilities and educational training for workers; safety, sanitation and health; accident/disaster compensation and support; commendations and sanctions, including disciplinary action, are all included in the composition of an individual's employment relationship.

Matters that are not applicable between existing union members and the employer, such as matters related to the recruiting of a worker, are in principle not considered part of the normative section.

Also, as normative sections must regard matters related to the determination of specific rights and obligations of workers and employers in their individual labor relations, even if a provision determines matters in the parties' relationship, that provision would not be considered a normative section if it does not deal with the determination of specific rights and obligations.

In contrast, if a provision deals with the determination of rights and obligations between workers and employers, it will be considered part of the normative section irrespective of how and under what procedures it is generated. Therefore, procedural requirements for personnel dispositions such as dismissals would obviously be considered part of the normative section.

As the normative section of a collective agreement must determine "standards" regarding working conditions and other treatment of workers, matters determined under this section must be such that it may be applied to all union members in a uniform manner. Here, "apply to all union members in a uniform manner" does not necessarily mean that the matter must be able to be applied to all union members; it may also mean that the matter may apply to any union member that fulfills certain criteria.[71]

2) The Contractual Section
i) Subject Party
The contractual effect of collective agreements during its effective period extends to the regulation of "rights and obligations of the individual labor relationship" between "trade union members" that comprise the trade union (i.e. the party to the collective agreement) and "employers or employer associations of which the employer is a member of."[72] The contractual section of the collective agreement regulates the rights and obligations under individual labor relationships. Therefore, in principle the section is applies to and is enforceable by union members who were members at the time of the conclusion of the collective agreement and validly maintained his/her

---

71 The Judicial Research and Training Institute, *supra*, p. 203
72 Supreme Court 94Da49847 (1996. 6. 28.)

labor relationship since that point.[73]

In essence, the contractual effect of collective agreements do not reach non-union members, except for instances where Articles 35 and 36 of the Union Act allow for the binding application of the agreement on a general and regional basis. If a non-union member joins the trade union and becomes a union member after the collective agreement is concluded and before the agreement's expiration, s/he becomes subject to the contractual section of the collective agreement.

If a union member withdraws union membership, or is expelled from the trade union while the collective agreement remains valid, the normative section in the collective agreement that regulates individual labor relations remains in force. It is possible for the worker to modify his/her working conditions through subsequent individual employment contracts with the employer.

ii) The Substance of Contractual Sections and Their Compulsory Effectiveness and Supplementary (Direct) Effect

According to Article 33 of the Union Act, "Any part of the rules of employment or a labor contract that violate standards concerning working conditions and other treatment of workers as prescribed in a collective agreement shall be null and void."[74] As such, matters under the collective agreement that determine standards of working conditions and other treatment of workers take precedence over those determined under the rules of employment or employment contracts, and are recognized to have the effect of compulsory application. Furthermore, Article 33(2) of the Union Act stipulates "[m]atters not covered in a labor contract and the part which is null and void under paragraph (1) shall be governed by those standards of a collective agreement," and thereby recognizes that standards determined in

73 Supreme Court 91Da34073 (1992. 7. 24.)

74 Union Act, Article 33(1)

collective agreements may be applied on a supplemental and direct basis.

iii) Limitations of Contractual Sections
(1) Prohibition of Violations of Higher Laws and Regulations

If the working conditions and other treatment of workers determined by collective agreements violate compulsory laws stipulated in the LSA or are contrary to upright morals and other elements of strong social order as stipulated in the Civil Act,[75] these become nullified due to their conflict with the laws of a higher authority.[76]

(2) Internal Limitations
a. The Principles of Advantage (*Günstigkeitprinzip*)

Here, the question is whether provisions regarding working conditions determined under the rules of employment or individual employment contracts that are more advantageous to the worker yet nevertheless conflict with like provisions in the collective agreement should be nullified in their entirety along with the more disadvantageous provisions, or whether the more advantageous provisions should be allowed to remain valid while only the disadvantageous provisions are nullified. The Union Act does not have any stipulations clearly set forth with respect hereto. The answer to this question differs depending on which scenario is being considered.

The first scenario is when the collective agreement purports to determine the minimum standard of working conditions and other treatment of workers. In this case, the rules of employment or individual employment contracts entered into after the conclusion of the collective agreement that stipulate lower standards of working conditions would be considered a violation of the collective agreement,

---

75 Civil Act, Article 103
76 Supreme Court 90DaKa24496 (1990. 12. 21.), Supreme Court 92Nu15765 (1993. 4. 9.)

and hence declared nullified, while those that stipulate standards higher than contained in the collective agreement would be considered to be in compliance with the collective agreement and hence would be valid, irrespective of whether the principle of advantage is applied or not.

The second scenario is when the collective agreement purports to determine maximum standards of working conditions and other treatment of workers. This is in violation of the standards of public order and decency as recognized under the Constitutional principle of guaranteeing fundamental rights, and therefore is not permitted. In such cases, the stipulated standard functions only as an average, formal standard. Therefore, if a worker enters into an individual employment contract with the employer that determines the worker's working conditions (regardless of when this contract was made respective to the collective agreement), sections that are advantageous to the worker would not fall under the normative effect of the collective agreement as per the principle of autonomous regulation of collective agreements. Limitations of autonomous regulation of collective agreements are recognized within the scope of such situations.

However, in light of the basis of its recognition, the principle of advantage (*Günstigkeitprinzip*) related to collective agreements may only be applied to situations like the above where individual workers enter into separate employment contracts, and not to situations where subsidiary instruments (e.g. the rules of employment or labor practices) purport to collectively regulate workers.

Now, since an employer may modify the rules of employment in a manner unfavorable to workers, assuming the employer has the consent of a trade union composed of the majority of the workers in the business or workplace concerned,[77] the trade union is permitted under the LSA to modify working conditions as it stands under the

---

existing rules of employment in an unfavorable manner by concluding collective agreements that contain lower standards of working conditions. As such, the principle of advantage (*Günstigkeitprinzip*), as applied between the rules of employment and collective agreements, are limited by legislation to the extent detailed previously.[78]

There is a series of court precedents regarding the implementation of the standard of dismissal contained in the rules of employment, the logic of which goes as follows. Since implementing the rules of employment that are identical to the rules from before the revisions to the collective agreement would prevent the revised collective agreement from achieving its purpose, the revised collective agreement is assumed to contain an agreement between parties to exclude the implementation of advantageous provisions in the employment rules and replace them with the revised provisions in the collective agreement. Therefore, the Supreme Court has ruled that provisions within the rules of employment that stipulate the standard of dismissal must be excluded by the revised collective agreement.[79]

b. Matters Regarding the Disposition of Rights Originally Belonging to the Individual Worker

Parties to collective agreements may not stipulate binding regulations on matters regarding the disposition of rights originally attributed to the individual worker (i.e. individual freedom and rights), as such matters are not included in the scope of working conditions that may be regulated through the collective bargaining process.

---

78 The Judicial Research and Training Institute, *supra*, p. 210

79 Supreme Court 2002Du9063 (2002. 12. 27,). *See also*, Supreme Court 91Da34073 (1992. 7. 24.), Supreme Court 92Da51341 (1993. 3. 23.), Supreme Court 95Da34316 (1997. 6. 10.), Supreme Court 96Da6967 (1997. 8. 22.), Supreme Court 2000Da30516 (2001. 1. 19.), Supreme Court 2004Da4683 (2006. 4. 27.).

c. Matters Regarding the Disposition of Rights Already Belonging to the
   Individual Worker

Rights already obtained by individual union members are beyond the
scope of what parties to collective agreements may regulate. Collective
agreements that require union members to waive or defer payment
of part or whole of their right to demand wages or right to demand
severance pay that has already been generated are not effective unless
individual union member workers agree to such an agreement.[80]
Related to this, the specific timing of when the right to demand wages
or severance pay may become an issue.

Court precedent suggests the following. First, severance pay is a
form of deferred wages that is paid by the employer as compensation
for continuous employment to workers who have been employed over
a certain period. Therefore, the specific right to severance pay is only
generated once its factual requirement (i.e. the worker's resignation) is
satisfied. Consequently, even if the rate of severance pay (which forms
the basis of calculating the amount of severance payment) is unfavorably
modified through a collective agreement and is retroactively applied,
such a modification would be recognized to be normatively effective
due to the principle of autonomous agreement.[81]

d. Matters Related to Modifying the Status of the Worker under the
   Employment Contract

Matters that would modify the status of the worker under the
employment contract may not be determined as provisions that
have a normative effect on the trade union as well, when the latter
concludes the collective agreement. For example, even if a trade
union designates a certain group of workers to be subject to dismissal
via collective agreement, this serves merely as the standard to guide

---

80 Supreme Court 99Da67536 (2000. 9. 29.), Supreme Court 2001Da41384 (2002. 4. 12.)
81 Supreme Court 92Da17754 (1992. 9. 14.), Supreme Court 95Da19256 (1996. 5. 14.)

layoff proceedings, and does not in itself give effect to the layoff of any individual worker. Likewise, even if a trade union designates a certain group of workers to be subject to company transfers or redeployment, the designation in itself does not give effect to such dispositions.

e. Matters Related to the Establishment of Work Duties Requiring Consent from Individual Workers As Per Compulsory Regulations

For example, even if a provision in the collective agreement states that the trade union agrees to extended work, this would not give rise in individual workers the duty to conduct extended work; the employer would still need to obtain consent from the latter before ordering extended work.

According to court precedent, consent between parties to engage in extended work may be provided whenever the need arises or in advance through employment contracts, but in either case the consent must be provided through individual agreements between the employer and the individual worker.[82] Court precedent also acknowledges that this consent may be provided via collective agreement so long as it does not deprive or restrict the individual worker's right to provide consent for extended work. However, the substance of the consent via collective agreement would be limited to mean, for example, that there would be no need to deliberate with the trade union regarding extended work if individual consent from the worker has already been obtained. The consent via collective agreement may not give the employer permission to unilaterally order individual workers to engage in extended work despite the lack of consent.[83]

---

82 Supreme Court 93Nu5796 (1993. 12. 21.), Supreme Court 94Da19228 (1995. 2. 10.), Supreme Court 98Da54960 (2000. 6. 23.)

83 Supreme Court 93Nu5796 (1993. 12. 21.)

3) The Effect of Violating the Normative Section: Civil and Criminal Remedies

The normative section of the collective agreement is effective in the relations between individual union members and the employer. Therefore, if the employer violates his/her duties outlined in the normative section, the individual union member may directly bring suit against the employer to seek the latter's performance of his/her obligations, among other claims. For example, in the event that an allowance set forth in the collective agreement is not paid, the individual union member may initiate a lawsuit against the employer for the payment of said allowance, as stipulated under the collective agreement.

For trade unions, as parties to the collective agreement are under the obligation to comply with obligations that they have agreed upon regardless of whether the obligation is normative or contractual (this will be dealt with in more detail below), unions may claim compensation from damages against employers who have violated their obligation under the normative section. However, it is very difficult to calculate the damages arising therefrom.

Under Article 92(2), the Union Act stipulates that "A person who violates the matters falling under any of the following items from among the contents of a collective agreement concluded pursuant to Article 31(1): matters on wages, welfare costs and retirement allowances; matters on work, rest periods, holidays, and vacations; matters on causes for disciplinary measures, dismissals, and important procedures; matters on safety and health and disaster relief; matters on facilities, furnishing conveniences, and participation in meetings during on-duty hours; and matters on industrial actions."[84]

---

84 Union Act, Article 92(2)

C. The Contractual Section and Its Legal Effect

1) The Contractual Section

The section of the collective agreement that determines the rights and obligations applied to parties to the collective agreement (i.e. trade unions and employers or employer associations) is recognized to have the same legal effect as a general contract between the parties to the agreement, and is hence referred to as the contractual section.

The contractual section determines the rights and obligations between the trade union and employer or employer association regarding matters related to the subsistence, maintenance, and activities of the trade union. Representative matters include union activities during work hours or within the workplace, the full-time union officer, the use of the trade union office within the workplace and the installation of the union bulletin board, the Union Shop clause, the Union Dues Check-Off clause, collective bargaining, and industrial action. Among these, the following sections examine the matters of the Union Shop clause and the Union Due Check-Off clause.

i) The Union Shop Clause

(1) The Concept of the Union Shop Clause

The Union Shop clause refers to a clause under the collective agreement which stipulates that only workers who possess the status of union member are able to obtain and maintain their status as a "worker." In other words, organizational membership is mandated to enhance the solidarity of workers. The two main forms of the Union Shop clause are the "Closed Shop" clause and the "Union Shop" clause. The Closed Shop clause designates union membership as a condition for both gaining and maintaining employment. Under this scheme, the employer is under obligation to employ only union members and exclude non-union members.

The Union Shop clause does not require that the employer only hire those who are union members at the time of employment, but does require that the hired non-union worker join the trade union within a designated period. If the worker fails to do so, or withdraws his/her union membership after becoming a member, the employer is under obligation to dismiss the worker.

(2) Permitted Scope of the Union Shop Clause

The Union Shop clause has been struck down by the Supreme Court. The rationale of the Supreme Court was as such: the joining of and the withdrawal from trade unions is a matter of free choice of individual workers. As such, the Union Shop clause, which restricts the freedom of workers to choose whether to associate (which is part of the positive right to association) by stipulating as a condition of employment membership in a particular union and the condition of dismissal, withdrawal, or expulsion from the above union is not permissible.[85]

Article 81(2) of the Union Act also defines as an unfair labor practice the "[e]mployment of a worker on the condition that he should not join or should withdraw from a trade union, or on the condition that he should join a particular trade union"[86] under the Union Shop clause. While there are no such regulations prohibiting Closed Shop provisions that permit only trade union members to become employed, such a clause is not permitted as well. Yet the proviso to Article 81(2) provides "[t]hat where a trade union represents two-thirds or more of the workers working in the workplace concerned, a conclusion of a collective agreement under which a person is employed on condition that he should join the trade union shall be allowed as an exceptional case."[87] Even in such exceptions,

85 Supreme Court 87DaKa2646 (1989. 1. 17.)
86 Union Act, Article 81(2)
87 Ibid.

however "an employer may not carry out any disadvantageous acts against the status of a worker on the grounds that the worker has been expelled from the trade union in question."[88]

ii) The Union Dues Check-Off Clause

(1) The Concept

The Union Dues Check-Off clause refers to a provision in the collective agreement which authorizes the employer to make a blanket deduction from the wages to be paid to workers who are union members at an amount matching union-related expenses that the worker would have already paid, such as union dues and other monies to be collected, and then sends that money directly to the trade union. This clause is a form of assistance provided by the employer to the trade union for the latter's activities, and is generally seen to be an obligation assumed by the employer, hence making this part of the contractual section in the collective agreement.

As per the Check-Off clause in the collective agreement, the employer assumes the administrative duty originally held by trade unions to collect union dues from members, and to issue these funds to the trade union.

(2) Legality of the Clause

Article 43(1) of the LSA stipulates the principle of full payment of wages. Therefore, the Union Dues Check-Off clause is allowed only when a special clause authorizes the practice in the collective agreement, as per the proviso of Article 43(1).

2) The Contractual Effect

If a contractual section is stipulated among individual provisions of the collective agreement, the legal relationship between parties to the

---

88 Union Act, Article 81(2)

agreement is determined accordingly. Other than this, parties to the contract assume the duty of execution and the duty of peace towards the collective agreement. It is a generally recognized contractual effect that these duties are commonly assumed by all parties whenever collective agreements are concluded.

The duty of execution refers to the obligation assumed by parties to the collective agreement to observe the substance of the agreement, regardless of whether it is normative or contractual (the duty to observe agreement), as well as the obligation of the parties to endeavor not to violate the agreement.

The duty of peace refers to the obligation assumed by parties to a collective agreement to refrain from industrial action demanding the modification, insertion, or cancellation of provisions regarding working conditions that have been agreed upon in the existing agreement.[89] Court precedent acknowledges that the duty of peace includes the obligation of parties to prevent their members from engaging in industrial action as well.[90]

3) The Legal Effect of Violating the Contractual Section

Violations of the collective section would result in a similar legal effect as when a general contract has been violated. Considering the particularity of the collective agreement, however, it is oftentimes unfeasible for courts to recognize the right of the injured party to cancel the agreement or to protest by refusing simultaneous performance.

A method to remedy the violation would be to initiate a suit to compel execution of the collective agreement, which would result in the suing party receiving a title of debt, thereby resulting in the compulsory execution of the collective agreement. Here, the debt

---

89 Supreme Court 94Da4042 (1994. 9. 30.)

90 Supreme Court 92Nu7733 (1992. 9. 1.)

assumed by parties to collective agreements is mostly "debts of performance." Therefore, if the debt is "not entirely personal to the obligor for its subject" (i.e. substitutable debts of action),[91] alternative enforcement[92] would be possible. On the other hand, if the debt of performance cannot be substituted yet it is possible to compel performance, the method of indirect compulsory performance[93] may be used. Even indirect compulsory performance would not be allowed if the debt of performance may not be compelled.

It is possible to initiate a suit for compensation of damages if injury resulted from the nonperformance of debt by a party to the contract. Even in such cases, however, since the nature of the debt assumed by parties to collective agreements is that of performance, it would be difficult to assess a monetary value to the damages incurred due to the nonperformance. The norm in such cases, therefore, is to compensate for emotional damages.

IV. The Expanded Application of the Collective Agreement

A. Introduction

In principle, collective agreements are effective against the parties to the agreement, such as trade unions and employer or employer associations, as well as their members.

In addition to the above entities, the Union Act stipulates two mechanisms that allow collective agreements to be effective against non-union members or third-party employers. The first is the mechanism of "general binding force,"[94] which expands the

---

91 Civil Act, Article 389(2), second clause
92 Civil Execution Act, Article 260
93 Ibid., Article 261
94 Union Act, Article 35

effectiveness of the collective agreement at the workplace level. The second is the mechanism of "geographical binding force,"[95] which expands the effectiveness of the collective agreement at the geographical level.

B. General Binding Force

1) Definition
Article 35 of the Union Act lays out the definition of this concept: "When a collective agreement applies to a majority of workers of the same kind of job employed under ordinary circumstances in a business or workplace, it shall apply to the other workers of the same kind of job employed in the same business or workplace."[96]

2) Requirements
i) The general binding force is limited to collective agreements that apply to "a single business or workplace." It is not possible to recognize the general binding force of a collective agreement beyond a single business or workplace. According to court precedent, "business or workplace" refers to a single corporate organization that forms a management body that is operated in a continual and organic manner, while maintaining independence as a whole, such as a private business or a corporation that has a continuous legal identity.[97]

ii) The scope of workers subject to the collective agreement (i.e. union members) must be based on workers who are "regularly employed"

---

95 Ibid., Article 36
96 Ibid., Article 35
97 Supreme Court 89DaKa24445 (1990. 3. 13.), Supreme Court 90Nu9421 (1992. 5. 12.), Supreme Court 91Da21381 (1993. 2. 9.), Supreme Court 93Da18365 (1993. 10. 12.), Supreme Court 97Da24511 (1997. 11. 28.), Supreme Court 98Da765 (1999. 8. 20.)

within a single business or workplace. Generally, court precedent interprets the term "regularly" as being a status, which must be seen as the number of workers regularly present, as understood objectively, according to socially accepted norms. The term should not be viewed as the number of workers working every day without exception, nor should it be construed as the average number of workers that worked during a certain period. Court precedent also interprets the term "employ" to include not only workers regularly employed at the relevant workplace, but also day-to-day workers employed when the need arises.[98]

iii) The general binding force of the collective agreement is recognized between union members (subject to the collective agreement) and other workers (i.e. non-union members not subject to the collective agreement) only when both work in "the same kind of job." Here, workers who are eligible to join the trade union according to union bylaws yet elect not to do so are not included in the classification of workers working in the same kind of job.

iv) Among workers regularly employed in the same kind of job in a single business or workplace, the "majority of workers" must be subject to the collective agreement.

3) Legal Effects
Collective agreements that satisfy the above requirements are effective against workers working in the same kind of job in a single business or workplace, even if it did not originally apply to these workers.

It is important to note that, according to the Act, workers working in the same kind of job subject to the collective agreement are not

---

98 Supreme Court 87Do153 (1987. 4. 14.), Supreme Court 87DaKa831 (1987. 7. 21.), Supreme Court 93Da42238 (1995. 3. 14.), Supreme Court 97Da28971 (1997. 11. 28.), Supreme Court 99Do1243 (2000. 3. 14.), Supreme Court 99Da58433 (2000. 3. 23.)

restricted only to those workers employed "regularly." Therefore, the condition that workers must be "regularly" employed is excluded from the list of requirements for the general binding force of the collective agreement to become effective at a particular workplace. Once general binding force is recognized, these non-regular workers are included in those subject to the collective agreement.

The common view is that when the collective agreement's applicability is expanded due to the general binding force mechanism, this expansion is limited to the normative section of the collective agreement.

If the term of validity of the collective agreement expires, or other circumstances arise that prevent the general binding force from satisfying requisite conditions, the effect of the general binding force expires as well. For example, if the number of workers subject to the collective agreement falls below half of the total number of workers regularly employed in the same kind of job in a single workplace due to the withdrawal or retirement of existing union members and the hiring of new non-union members, the general binding force of the collective agreement is not recognized from that point onwards. In such cases, the working conditions of non-union members are considered to become what they would be upon the termination of the collective agreement. The working conditions of workers after the collective agreement terminates is examined in detail below.

C. Geographical Binding Force

"When two-thirds or more of the workers of the same kind of job employed in an area are subject to one collective agreement, the administrative agencies may, with a resolution issued by the Labor Relations Commission and at the request of either of the parties to the collective agreement or ex officio, make a decision that the said collective agreement shall apply to other workers of the same kind of job and their employers engaged in the same area."[99]

V. The Termination of the Collective Agreement

A. Grounds for Termination

1) The Expiration of the Effective Term
i) The Effective Term of Collective Agreements
If the collective agreement designates an effective term, it terminates upon the expiration of the term. Should a collective agreement designate an effective term, that period may not exceed two years.[100] Therefore, if the collective agreement determines the effective term to be a period within two years, that term is enforced as is. If the effective term is not specified in a collective agreement or it exceeds two years, the effective term will be considered to be two years.[101]

ii) The Extension or Renewal of the Effective Term
"When, even though both of the parties continued to conduct collective bargaining to make a new collective agreement before or after the expiry of the effective term of an existing agreement, they fail to make a new collective agreement, the existing collective agreement shall remain valid for three more months after its expiry, except as there exists a separate agreement to the contrary."[102]

In case a special arrangement exists to prepare for the situation where a new collective agreement is not concluded by the time the previous agreement expires, that arrangement is to be enforced.

If a collective agreement contains an "automatic renewal provision"

---

99 Union Act, Article 36(1)

100 Ibid., Article 32(1)

101 Ibid., Article 32(2)

102 Ibid., Article 33(3)

that automatically renews the agreement until a new collective agreement is concluded or a certain period of time has elapsed, the collective agreement is recognized to be automatically renewed until the above conditions have been satisfied even if a party to the agreement raises objections to the renewal, unless the provision is properly cancelled. Even if a collective agreement contains an automatic renewal provision, however, "[a]ny party to the agreement may . . . terminate the existing collective agreement by notifying the other party of such termination six months in advance of the date he intends to terminate it."[103]

In cases where a collective agreement contains an "automatic renewal provision," the legal effect is that a new collective agreement is concluded that contains the same substance as the previous collective agreement the moment the effective term of the previous agreement expires. Therefore, the effective term of the new collective agreement remains the same as in the previous one unless a special arrangement has been made,[104] and this new effective term is subject to the restrictions in Article 32(1) and (2).[105]

2) The Cancellation or Revocation of Collective Agreements

A collective agreement may be cancelled by communicating the intent to cancel to the other party in cases where grounds for cancellation as stipulated in the collective agreement itself or the Union Act (e.g. Article 32(3) proviso of the Union Act) arise. The effect of the cancellation is applied from that point onwards. Cancellation through mutual agreement of the parties to the collective agreement is always valid.

---

103 Ibid.

104 Unlike the perspective taken in this Supreme Court case, others cases argue that the effective term of the new collective agreement should be determined to be two years, regardless of the term stipulated in the previous collective agreement.

105 Supreme Court 92Da27102 (1993. 2. 9.)

3) The Extinction and Modification of Collective Agreements
i) The Extinction or Modification of the Employer
If an employer who is also a corporate entity is liquidated due to dissolution, the effectiveness of the collective agreement is extinguished upon the conclusion of liquidation procedures.

In cases where the corporation's organizational structure is modified,[106] while there may be changes in the identity of the employer, since the identity of the corporation common to the employers before and after the modification remains the same, the effectiveness of the collective agreement is maintained.

For corporate mergers,[107] it is stipulated in the Commercial Act that "[a] surviving company or a company newly consolidated as the result of a merger shall adopt the rights and obligations of the company which disappeared."[108] Both academic literature and court precedent[109] consider that the collective agreement concluded with the extinguished company remains effective as applied to the surviving or consolidated company after the merger. This is because the status of the worker under his/her employment contract with the extinguished corporation is comprehensively maintained with the surviving or consolidated company due to the Commercial Act provision cited above.

In the case of business transfers, by principle the labor relationship between the transferor business and its workers is comprehensively succeeded to the transferee, barring the existence of arrangements to the contrary.[110] Therefore, like corporate mergers, collective

---

106 Commercial Act, Articles 242, 269, 604, 607

107 Ibid., Articles 174, 175, 230, 240, 522, 529, 530(2), 598, 603

108 Ibid., Articles 235, 530(2), 603

109 Supreme Court 93Da1589 (1994. 3. 8.)

110 Supreme Court 84DaKa1409 (1987. 2. 24.), Supreme Court 90Da6545 (1991. 3. 22.), Supreme Court 91Da15225 (1991. 8. 9.), Supreme Court 91Da12806 (1991. 11. 12.), Supreme Court 91Da40276 (1992. 7. 14.), Supreme Court 92Da23834 (1994. 1. 25.), Supreme Court 93Da33173 (1994. 6. 28.), Supreme Court 93Da18938 (1994. 11. 18.)

agreements concluded with the transferor business maintain their effectiveness as applied to the transferee business.

Corporate mergers and transfers are not grounds for dispersing trade unions, and therefore the latter's survival is not impacted, nor are they required to undergo organizational change. Consequently, trade unions that existed prior to the merger or transfer may survive these proceedings, and it is possible to have multiple trade unions co-exist in a single workplace. In such cases, each existing collective agreement may be effective against members of trade unions that concluded them.

ii) The Extinction or Modification of the Trade Union

If a trade union is dissolved due to one of the grounds of dissolution outlined in Article 28(1) of the Union Act, the effectiveness of the collective agreement is terminated at the moment the procedure of liquidation is concluded.

While the merger of trade unions is stipulated as a grounds for the dissolution of previously existing trade unions,[111] the general agreement is that the property relations of the dispersed and extinguished trade union, as well as its status as the subject of collective agreements that it has concluded, is succeeded comprehensively by the merged or consolidated trade union.

When a trade union is divided, the pre-existing trade union is dispersed and extinguished.[112] Under the Union Act, however, "division" refers only to cases where a single trade union is dispersed and extinguished and is divided into two or more independent trade unions. It does not refer to cases where the original trade union maintains its existence while another trade union is newly established, resulting in two or more trade unions.

111 Union Act, Article 28(1)2
112 Ibid.

Trade unions dispersed and extinguished due to division do not need to undergo liquidation proceedings, and the property relations of the dispersed and extinguished union are vested in the newly established union according to the resolution that authorized the division.

Collective agreements that have been concluded by the trade union dispersed and extinguished due to division maintain their effectiveness regarding normative sections that regulate the rights and obligations of union members. However, most agree that the remaining sections of these collective agreements are not comprehensively succeeded if the actual identity between the dispersed trade union and the newly established union is not recognized to be the same.

Finally, court precedent and related literature generally agree that trade unions which have properly reorganized themselves maintain their status as being subjects to the collective agreement concluded by the union prior to the reorganization, as the identity of the trade union is considered to have been maintained throughout the reorganization process.[113]

B. Labor Relations after the Termination of the Collective Agreement

First off, it is rarely disputed that working conditions stipulated in the normative section of the terminated collective agreement retains its effectiveness and thereby regulates individual labor relations during the period where no agreements are in effect.[114] On the other hand, in principle contractual matters setting forth the rights and obligations of the parties during the effective period of the collective agreement are

---

113 Supreme Court 95Nu4377 (1997. 7. 25.)
114 Supreme Court 2007Da51758 (2007. 12. 27.)

terminated along with the lapse of the collective agreement.

The Supreme Court also interprets that the normative sections of collective agreements become incorporated into individual labor relations upon establishment, which remains in effect even after the collective agreement loses its effectiveness.[115]

The reason behind the above interpretation (that labor standards in normative sections remain effective after the termination of the collective agreement) is not that the collective agreement's effectiveness in itself is maintained, but that normative sections have already been incorporated into the text of employment contracts or in how parties interpret the substance of employment contracts. As such, modifications to the labor relationship determined by the collective agreement after the latter has been terminated are permitted through modifications in individual agreements (which is a form of employment contract) or the rules of employment.[116]

115 Supreme Court 98Da13747 (2000. 6. 9)
116 Ibid.

Chapter 3

Industrial Action

I. The Concept of Industrial Action

Under the Union Act,[1] industrial action is "actions or counteractions which obstruct the normal operation of a business, such as strikes, sabotage, lock-outs, and other activities through which the parties to labor relations[2] intend to accomplish their aims."[3] In other words, under the Union Act industrial action includes both (i) actions undertaken by trade unions, and (ii) actions undertaken by employers or employer organizations.

Article 33(1) of the Korean Constitution stipulates that the right to collective action is guaranteed. As such, industrial action undertaken by trade unions can be understood as an exercise of their constitutional right of collective action. On the other hand, industrial actions undertaken by employers or employer organizations are recognized by the Union Act, but not by the constitution. Therefore, its legal authority is based on fundamentally different legal foundations than industrial actions undertaken by trade unions. Throughout

---

1 Trade Union and Labor Relations Adjustment Act

2 "Parties to labor relations" is defined by the Union Act as trade unions, employers or employers' associations (Union Act, Article 2(5)).

3 Union Act, Article 2(6)

this chapter, the term "industrial action" will be used to indicate actions by trade unions, and industrial actions taken by employers or employer organizations will be dealt with separately in section five: "Counteracting Industrial Action."

II. Requirements for a Valid Industrial Action

Industrial action that is carried out by workers in a valid manner within the scope of legal protection (i.e. protecting the right of collective action) afforded to it by the Union Act and articles of the Constitution are exempt from prosecution.[4] Furthermore, dismissal of workers or other acts against their interests enforced on the grounds that workers have participated in justifiable collective activities are deemed impermissible as an unfair labor practice,[5] and may be subject to criminal liability.[6] The following examines four such requirements in turn: i) subject; ii) object; iii) timing and procedure; and iv) method.

A. Subjects of Industrial Action

Workers' associations are entitled to the right of collective action. Since industrial action is conditional on failure to execute collective agreement, both collective bargaining and industrial actions are conducted by workers' associations.[7] According to court precedent, a valid subject of industrial action must have the capacity to engage in collective bargaining and enter into collective agreements.[8]

---

4 Ibid., Articles 3 and 4

5 Ibid., Article 81(5)

6 Ibid., Article 90

7 Ha Gab-rae, *Collective Labor Relations Law*, p. 462 (Joongang Economy 2013); Kim Hyung-bae, *Labor Law*, p. 996 (Pakyoungsa 2014)

8 Supreme Court 99Da8377 (1999. 6. 25.)

1) Non-Recognized Trade Unions

It is still unclear whether trade unions that satisfy de facto requirements for a recognized trade union stipulated by Articles 2 and 4 of the Union Act but have failed to satisfy the formal requirement of reporting to the Labor Relations Commission of its foundation (i.e. non-recognized trade unions) are valid subjects of industrial action. The general agreement is that since such non-recognized trade unions fall under the legal definition of trade unions and have the capacity to engage in collective bargaining and collective agreements, they may also be valid subjects of industrial actions.[9]

2) Unauthorized Strikes (a.k.a. Wildcat Strikes)

Where there are established recognized or non-recognized trade unions, union members may organize temporary groups to conduct industrial actions in order to argue the implementation of certain working conditions. In such cases, it is questionable whether such groups may be valid subjects of industrial action. The Union Act stipulates that no member of a trade union shall take part in any industrial action that is not led by the trade union in such workplaces.[10]

3) Persons Who May Not Engage in Industrial Actions as a Matter of Law

Workers that fall within certain classifications cannot engage in industrial action as a matter of law. Examples would be: public officials, excluding those who are actually engaged in labor;[11] teachers;[12] and workers who are involved in the production of electricity, water, or

9 The Judicial Research and Training Institute, *Trade Union and Labor Relations Mediation Law*, p. 261 (2014)

10 Ibid., Article 37(2)

11 State Public Officials Act, Article 66(1); Local Public Officials Act, Article 58(1)

12 Act on the Establishment and Operation of Teacher's Trade Unions, Article 8

other workers that mainly produce national defense goods or those engaged in a major national defense industry business as designated by the Defense Acquisition Program Act.[13]

B. The Objects of Industrial Action

1) General Implications from Court Precedent
First off, the claims advanced through industrial action must be regarding items that are valid objects of collective bargaining. Specifically, these are items, such as working conditions, that must be negotiated through a collective bargaining process.[14]

Therefore, industrial actions cannot be taken for arbitrary or illegal negotiation items that cannot be negotiated in a collective bargaining process in the first place, items that have been excluded from collective bargaining at the collective agreement stage, and items that are regulated by a valid collective agreement at the time of the industrial action.

2) Specific Illustrations
i) Compulsory Negotiation Items
The following are instances where the issue of whether the object of industrial actions falls within the realm of compulsory negotiation and has been examined in court precedent.

① In principle, business decisions made by management entities (e.g. closing of a department or branch) cannot be an object of collective bargaining. Therefore, refusing to negotiate with the employer regarding how to rearrange working conditions due to the closing

---

13 Constitution, Article 33(3); Union Act, Article 41(2)
14 Supreme Court 94Da4042 (1994. 9. 30.)

of a department or a branch and instead engaging in industrial action for the purpose of overturning management's decision to close the department or branch is not valid; as such this object was determined to be invalid.[15]

② However, in a case involving a transportation company, while deciding how to allocate the order and schedule of union member drivers, it was determined that they do fall within the realm of business decisions. Furthermore, the nature of the items in question made them closely related to working conditions. Hence, they were deemed valid objects of collective bargaining.[16]

③ In the case of layoffs, the relevant prior decision suggests that such actions would also be considered as business decisions. As such, a trade union's request for management to refrain from conducting layoffs cannot be a valid object of collective bargaining, as that would result in fundamentally limiting the right of the employer to manage his/her business.[17]

ii) Items Not Falling under the Employer's Authority

It has been determined that engaging in industrial action for political purposes, promotion/restriction of legislation,[18] abolition of law,[19] or to request that a worker who has been arrested to be released from prison cannot be said to be a valid objective, as it is unrelated to the maintenance or improvement of working conditions.[20]

---

15 Supreme Court 93Da30242 (1994. 3. 25.)
16 Supreme Court 93Nu8993 (1994. 8. 26.)
17 Supreme Court 99Do4893 (2001. 4. 24.)
18 Supreme Court 99Do3865 (2000. 9. 5.)
19 Supreme Court 99Du4280 (2000. 11. 24.)
20 Supreme Court 90Do2852 (1991. 1. 29.)

iii) For Multiple Purposes
If industrial actions are taken for multiple purposes and if part or one of the reasons is not justifiable, the acceptability of purpose must be determined on the basis of the main or true purpose.[21] If it is determined that there would not have been any industrial actions had the request that cannot be a valid object of industrial actions was not part of the workers' requests, all parts of the industrial actions lack validity.[22]

iv) Items Regulated by a Valid Collective Agreement at the Time of the
   Industrial Action
Neither party shall induce an industrial action to modify the contents of the agreement during the effective period of a collective agreement. This is termed "the duty of peace." Any industrial action induced in violation of this duty of peace is considered invalid.[23]

C. Timing and Procedure of Industrial Action

1) Voting by Union Members
Trade unions shall not conduct industrial actions unless decided on by a majority of union members through direct, secret, and unsigned ballots.[24] In the case of multiple labor unions, where a representative bargaining trade union has been determined, industrial action shall not take place unless it is authorized with the consent of a majority of the total members of the trade unions which have participated in the procedure through a direct, secret, and unsigned ballot.[25]

21 Supreme Court 99Nu5204 (1992. 1. 21.)
22 Supreme Court 2000Do2871 (2001. 6. 26.)
23 Supreme Court 90Nu6620 (1991. 1. 15.)
24 Union Act, Article 41(1) first clause
25 Ibid., Article 41(1) second clause

Also, the trade union must incorporate into its bylaws matters concerning the publication of the results of the vote for and against the industrial actions, and not discard of the roll of voters and ballot papers.[26]

The Supreme Court used to rule that industrial action that did not undergo voting procedures could nevertheless regain validity. However, this interpretation has shifted and at present the Supreme Court tends to rule that such industrial actions cannot obtain validity.[27]

2) Mediation

According to Article 45(2) of the Union Act, "any industrial action shall not be conducted without completing adjustment procedures." However, "this shall not apply to cases where adjustment is not finished within the period as provided in Article 54 or where an arbitration award is not made within the period under Article 63.[28] In other words, it is possible to conduct industrial action if the stipulated period for mediation or arbitration has passed. On the other hand, industrial action conducted prior to the completion of the adjustment process subjects the entity to time in prison not exceeding one year or a fine not exceeding ten million won.[29]

3) Notification and Reporting Requirement to the Other Party

Upon the occurrence of a labor dispute, one party to labor relations shall notify thereof to the other party in writing.[30] When a trade union intends to conduct an industrial action, it shall report the date, place, the number of participants, and the method of the industrial action in

---

26 Ibid., Article 11(12)
27 Supreme Court 99Do4837 (2001. 10. 25.), unanimous decision
28 Union Act, Article 45(2)
29 Ibid., Article 91
30 Ibid., Article 45(1)

advance and in writing to the relevant administrative agencies and the competent Labor Relations Commission.[31]

D. The Methods of Industrial Action

1) Regulations as Stipulated by the Union Act

The Union Act stipulates the following regarding the methods of industrial action.

> **Article 38 (Guidance and Responsibility of Trade Unions):** ① An industrial action shall not be conducted in such a manner that it interferes with entry, work or other normal services by persons who are not related to it or persons who intend to provide work. Any attempt to follow through on acts of violence or threats to appeal for or persuade workers into participating in the industrial action shall not be carried out.
>
> ② Any work, the purpose of which is to prevent operational equipment from being damaged, or to prevent raw materials or products from being impaired or deteriorated shall be normally conducted during a period of industrial actions.

> **Article 42 (Prohibition of Acts of Violence):** ① Industrial actions shall not be conducted by resorting to violence or destruction or by occupying facilities related to production or other major work or other facilities equivalent thereto as prescribed by Presidential Decree.
>
> ② Industrial actions shall not be conducted to stop, close, or interrupt the normal maintenance and operation of facilities installed to protect the safety of workplaces.

---

31 Enforcement Decree of the Trade Union and Labor Relations Adjustment Act, Article 17

Article 42-2 (Restrictions on Industrial Actions Affecting Essential Business): ① The term "essential business" in this Act means the business whose suspension or discontinuance may seriously endanger the safety of people's lives, health or bodies and the daily life of the public, and which is prescribed by Presidential Decree from among the essential public service businesses provided for in Article 71(2).
② The acts of stopping, discontinuing or impeding the justifiable maintenance and operation of the essential business shall be prohibited industrial actions.

2) Specific Illustrations

i) Strikes

Strikes are the most common method used by trade unions to accomplish their aims by collectively refusing to provide labor in an organized way. The Union Act cites strikes as one example of industrial action.[32]

ii) Workplace Occupation

The term "workplace occupation" is used to describe the act of workers refusing to leave the workplace/factory facilities and occupying the premises. As mentioned above, Article 42(1) of the Union Act prohibits the occupation of "facilities related to production or other major work or other facilities equivalent thereto as prescribed by Presidential Decree." Therefore, the definitional scope of the facilities in which occupation is prohibited has significant meaning.

On this issue, the Ministry of Employment and Labor has determined that (i) hospital operation rooms and wards; (ii) hotel rooms, lounges, and banquet halls; (iii) stores and hallways of department stores; and (iv) display floors of car retailers are all facilities where occupation is prohibited. On the other hand, living

---

32 Union Act, Article 2(6)

facilities such as cafeterias, rest areas, playgrounds, dormitories were determined to be facilities where occupation is not prohibited.[33] Trade unions that occupy facilities that have been prohibited may be criminally charged with trespass in structure and business interference.

iii) Work-to-Rule

Work-to-rule is a method used by workers to deteriorate the company's operational efficiency by very strictly adhering to regulations and the rules of employment (e.g. taking breaks at the same time; collectively refusing to work overtime; strict observance of safety regulations, etc.). Many are split as to whether work-to-rule methods can be considered industrial action.

Both court precedent and the Ministry of Employment and Labor acknowledge that work-to-rule methods are industrial actions, given that the following conditions are satisfied.

Supreme Court 95Do2970 (1996. 2. 27.)

Even if overtime/holiday work is usually arranged by agreement of both parties, if the workers engaging in work-to-rule instigate other workers to collectively refuse overtime/holiday work that they have normally done and as a result undermine the regular functioning of the business, this would be deemed an industrial action.

Supreme Court 91Nu10473 (1992. 3. 13.)

If a worker uses his/her monthly paid holiday as a pretext for a purpose other than taking breaks, this cannot be a proper exercise to his/her right to take breaks. As such, workers collectively taking monthly paid vacations at the same time (an act of dispute via work-to-rule) are deemed to have engaged in industrial action.

---

33 Ministry of Employment and Labor Administrative Interpretation 68140-179 (1997. 5. 7.)

Ministry of Employment and Labor Administrative Interpretation 32281-11348 (1992. 6. 11.)
It is an industrial action to excessively observe regulations and rules of employment, thus causing deterioration to the company's operational efficiency.

III. Illegal Industrial Action and Liability for Damages/ Compensation

A. Generation of Liability

1) Conditions Where Liability Arises
Article 3 of the Union Act stipulates "when an employer has suffered damages due to collective bargaining or industrial action under this Act, he shall not claim damages against a trade union or workers." The general consensus within court precedent is that such "industrial action," as protected by the Act and with an exemption from damage liability, is one that has proper subject, objective, timing, and procedure.[34]

A logical extension to this interpretation would be that the employer may sue for damages against trade unions or workers for damages caused by industrial actions that failed to satisfy the requirements to make it proper. Therefore, it is common practice in Korea for an employer to resist industrial action by suing for damages against the trade union or worker that instigated the action, and by commencing a provisional seizure of their property at the same time.

2) Entities Assuming Liability
i) Trade Unions
When a trade union engages in industrial actions that are not proper

---

34 Ha Gab-rae, *supra*, p. 526

and hence illegal, the trade union assumes damage liability for its illegal acts.[35] In this case, approval for the invalid industrial action must have been handed down through the union's decision-making body (e.g. general assembly, board of representatives). The court precedent supporting this is Supreme Court 93Da32828 and 32835, which, through extrapolation of Article 35(1) of the Civil Act,[36] ruled that trade unions are liable for damages from invalid industrial actions if these actions were designed/directed/instructed by the union's representative or director.[37]

ii) Trade Unions Directors

Whether trade union directors who have instigated invalid industrial action become individually liable for damages incurred through industrial actions in addition to the trade union itself is still in dispute. The literature is divided on this issue.[38] That being said, court precedent suggests that directors do indeed assume individual liability for damages caused by illegal industrial actions.[39]

iii) Union Member Workers

Workers who participate in invalid industrial actions are in default of their obligations towards their employers.[40] Relevant court precedent suggests that due to the fact that (i) the regular union member's right to organize may be derogated if s/he is required to judge whether an industrial action is invalid or not every time s/he engages in one, and

---

35 The Judicial Research and Training Institute, *supra*, p. 287

36 Article 35 (Capacity of Juristic Person to Assume Responsibility for Unlawful Act) ① A juristic person shall be liable for any damages done to other persons by its directors or other representatives in the performance of their duties. This liability of a juristic person shall not relieve the directors or other representatives of their own liabilities for damages sustained thereby.

37 Supreme Court 93Da32828, 32835 (1994. 3. 25.)

38 Ha Gab-rae, *supra*, p. 529

39 Supreme Court 93Da32828, 32835 (1994. 3. 25.)

40 Ha Gab-rae, *supra*, p. 530

(ii) even if a regular union member has cause to doubt the validity of an industrial action it is difficult for him/her to not comply to the direction of the trade union and its executive members, a regular union member cannot assume joint liability with the trade union and its executive members for damages caused by an invalid industrial action for merely discontinuing his/her work. However, even regular union members may assume liability for damages arising from the cessation of work if s/he has received prior education related to the specialized aspects of his/her work as well as procedural steps to take prior to any work stoppage to prevent any danger or damages, yet s/he failed to do so as part of an invalid industrial action.[41]

B. Scope of Responsibility

1) Negative Damages
Negative damages incurred by the employer for ceased work are calculated by the amount of unearned revenue from not being able to sell the products that would have been produced but for the cessation of work.

2) Positive Damages
Regarding positive damages, a representative case ruled: "an example of damages that a manufacturing company incurs due to illegal cessation of work would be the fixed costs (e.g. rents, taxes, utilities, depreciation expenses, insurance premiums, etc.) that are expended regardless of whether work is conducted."[42]

Other examples of positive damages would be the cost to repair or replace corporate facilities damaged due to invalid industrial actions,

---

41 Supreme Court 2005Da30610 (2006. 9. 22.)
42 Supreme Court 93Da24735 (1993. 12. 10.)

and the expenses paid by the employer to devise countermeasures against the invalid industrial action.

3) Comparative Negligence

In determining the amount of damages attributable to an illegal act by the union the victim's (in this case the employer's) comparative negligence is used to offset the total amount due. Specific factors considered include the extent of intentionality or negligence of both parties and the extent that the victim's negligence contributed to the origination and aggravation of damages incurred.[43]

IV. Industrial Action and Labor Relations

A. Labor Relations during Industrial Action

Court precedent states that (i) workers are excused from their primary duty of providing labor, and (ii) employers lose their capacity to exert supervisory powers over workers during the period that industrial action is taking place. In other words, the major rights and duties applicable to workers and employers are placed at a standstill during industrial actions.[44]

B. The Right to Demand Wages during Industrial Action

Article 44(1) of the Union Act stipulates that "[a]n employer shall have no obligation to pay wages during a period of industrial actions to workers who did not provide labor because of their participation in

43 The Judicial Research and Training Institute, *supra*, p. 294

44 Supreme Court 94Da26721 (1995. 12. 21.), unanimous decision

industrial actions." This makes clear that a worker does not have the right to demand wages during period of industrial actions.

V. Counteracting Measures of the Employer against Industrial Actions

A. Restrictions on Hiring by the Employer during Industrial Actions

Since most work activities are put on hold during industrial actions in a business or a workplace, the employer typically attempts to minimize operational losses by continuing its business through alternative measures. The Union Act limits or allows such attempts to a certain extent through its provisions.

1) Prohibition of Recruitment of New Workers or Replacement of Existing

An employer shall not hire or substitute any person not related to the relevant business during a period of industrial actions in order to continue work which has been interrupted by industrial actions.[45] As the prohibition on hiring and replacing workers only applies to people not related to the relevant business, it is possible to hire or replace workers with those who are related to the relevant business. This makes it possible to have workers already working with the business fill in to complete the work ordinary done by those participating in the industrial action. Furthermore, it is permissible to hire a new recruit to fill the place of this worker (who has been working in the replaced position) if s/he subsequently resigns.[46] In principle, however, with the exception of the specific circumstances outlined above, it is not

---

45 Union Act, Article 43(1)
46 Supreme Court 2008Do4831 (2008. 11. 13.)

possible for an employer to recruit or replace workers to conduct the work of those workers who are taking part in an industrial action.

2) Prohibition of Outsourcing and Subcontracting

"An employer shall not, during a period of industrial action, contract or subcontract work which has been interrupted by the industrial action."[47]

3) Prohibition of Hiring Temp Agency Workers

No temporary work agency shall send workers to any workplace where industrial action is underway to perform business affairs interrupted by such industrial action.[48]

4) Allowance of Hiring Replacement Services to Maintain Minimum Services

An employer at an essential public service business may hire or replace any person who has nothing to do with the relevant business, as well as enter into contracts or subcontracts, in order to maintain essential public services. In such cases, the employer may hire, replace, outsource, or subcontract workers to the extent not exceeding 50/100 of the workers participating in a strike.[49] The term "public service businesses" refers to businesses whose interruption or discontinuation shall cause conspicuous threats to daily life of the public at large or the national economy, and whose replacement is not easy (e.g. passenger transport, airlines, utilities, medical services, banking, and the Korea Mint and Security Printing Corporation[50]).

---

47 Union Act, Article 43(2)
48 Act on the Protection of Temporary Agency Workers, Article 16(1)
49 Union Act, Article 43(4)
50 Ibid., 71(2)

B. Lock-outs

1) Definition of Lock-outs

A lock-out refers to an employer's act of expressing that s/he will refuse to accept work provided by his/her workers as a counteraction to the industrial action taken by trade unions, and subsequently refusing to pay wages. This method places economic pressure on workers and is used to bolster the employer's bargaining power so that equilibrium may be achieved vis-à-vis that of the trade union.

2) Conditions to Ensure the Validity of Lock-outs

i) Timing

"An employer may conduct a lock-out only after the trade union commences an industrial action."[51] This means that so-called pre-emptive lock-outs (i.e. lock-outs conducted prior to the initiation of industrial action) are not permitted under any circumstances.[52]

The requirement that lock-outs must be a counteraction to industrial actions applies not only when initiating the lock-out, but throughout the span of the exercise. Therefore, if a trade union terminates its industrial action, the employer must follow suit and discontinue its lock-out as well.[53] "When it comes to lock-outs, an employer shall report the lock-out in advance to the relevant administrative agencies and the Labor Relations Commission."[54]

ii) Purpose of Lock-outs

Court precedent recognizes that lock-outs may be recognized only if the following conditions are met: when the equilibrium of bargaining

---

51 Ibid., Article 46(1)
52 Im Jong-ryul, *supra*, p. 258
53 The Judicial Research and Training Institute, *supra*, p. 308
54 Union Act, Article 46(2)

power between the employer and the workers becomes disrupted due to the trade union's industrial action; this disruption results in substantially more pressure on the employer; and the counter-acting passive and defensive measure (i.e. the lock-out) implemented out of necessity remains within compliance of the principle of reciprocity.[55]

Therefore, the lock-outs are not allowed if it is determined that the purpose of a lock-out went beyond being defensive and strived to aggressively weaken the organizational power of the trade union.

3) Effect of Lock-outs

i) Exemption from Wage Payment Obligations

Should it be determined that the employer has satisfied the conditions for a valid lock-out, s/he may be exempt from the obligation to pay wages.

ii) Removal of Workplace Occupation by Trade Unions

As long as the lock-out is valid, the employer may exercise his/her right to manage corporate facilities without any limitations. As such, an employer may request that the trade union cease its industrial action.[56]

Again, the employer is permitted to conduct lock-outs to the extent that it is necessary to prevent the occupation of the workplace by workers due to industrial actions on production facilities, etc. As a result, the employer must allow access by workers to facilities in the workplace in which union or welfare activities regularly take place.[57]

---

55 Supreme Court 98Da34331 (2000. 5. 26.)

56 Kim Hyung-bae, *supra*, p. 1065

57 Ha Gab-rae, *supra*, p. 549

Chapter 4

Adjustment of Industrial Disputes

I. Industrial Disputes

A. Introduction

The term "industrial disputes" means any controversy or difference arising from disagreements between a trade union and an employer or employers' association with respect to the determination of terms and conditions of employment as wages, working hours, welfare, dismissal, and other treatments.[1]

In such cases, "disagreements" refers to situations in which the parties to labor relations are no longer likely to reach an agreement by means of voluntary bargaining even if they continue to make such an attempt, and includes situations when a party rejects or delays collective bargaining without just cause. The exact definition of other concepts of industrial disputes that go beyond disagreements regarding working conditions (e.g. disputes between parties of labor relations, disputes regarding determination of working conditions) has not been fully resolved in related literature as of yet.

---

1 Trade Union and Labor Relations Adjustment Act, Article 2(5); hereinafter referred to as the "Union Act"

B. The Concept of Industrial Disputes

1) Conflicts between Parties of Labor Relations

Conflicts that occur between an individual worker and his/her employer are excluded from the concept of industrial dispute; only conflicts that occur collectively may be regarded as an industrial dispute. Therefore, differences of opinion between an individual worker and employer regarding individual contracts or the interpretation/application of labor regulations with regards to the rights and duties of an individual worker are not the subject of industrial dispute adjustment (e.g. when an individual worker has a dispute with the employer that s/he has been discharged without just cause and demands reinstatement, or when an individual worker argues that the employer owes him/her unpaid wages and demands disbursement).

2) Conflicts Regarding Determination of New Working Conditions

With collective disputes, the Union Act considers only those where trade unions and employers or employer associations engage in collective bargaining to make decisions on new issues regarding working conditions as within the definition of industrial disputes.

3) Conflicts Regarding Determination of Union Members' Working Conditions

When conflicts arise from disagreements between employers and workers, only those regarding the determination of working conditions of union member workers are recognized as industrial disputes by the Union Act. The Supreme Court clearly ruled on this matter, stating: "in contractual relations between employers and workers, conflicts caused by matters not falling within the scope of working conditions cannot be said to be industrial disputes."[2] However, the exact scope of the concept of "working conditions" under the Union Act remains ambiguous and is a subject of debate.

Court precedent suggests that: (i) the standard of dismissal falls under the scope of working conditions as it determines the cause of termination and hence is a matter relating to retirement under the LSA,[3] and (ii) matters related to the establishment and composition of award/disciplinary action committees also fall under the scope of working conditions so long as it remains necessary to promote rational and fair human resource decisions (allowing for such activities to be considered activities that reward and penalize employees under the LSA).[4] Other instances where it has been ruled as not being a matter of working conditions are as follows:

In the context of a hospital workplace: "disputes regarding the streamlining of waiting periods and promoting the fairness of the hospitalization process is a problem that should be resolved through the cooperative efforts of members of management, and hence cannot be considered as a matter of industrial dispute."[5] The position of the full-time union officer is a type of accommodation provided by the employer for the benefit of the trade union which is recognized only if approved through the collective bargaining process. As such, it cannot be construed as a working condition issue to be dealt with through the labor relationship of the employer and worker. A more appropriate view of the full-time union is that it is an arbitrary subject of bargaining. Thus, conflicts arising from the position of the full-time union officer cannot be said to be industrial disputes.[6]

---

2 Supreme Court 94Nu9177 (1996. 2. 23.)

3 Labor Standards Act

4 Supreme Court 94Nu9177 (1996. 2. 23.)

5 Supreme Court 93Nu11883 (1994. 1. 11.)

6 Supreme Court 94Nu9177 (1996. 2. 23.)

II. The Concept of Industrial Dispute Adjustments

A. The Significance of Industrial Dispute Adjustments

Industrial dispute adjustments involve a conflict resolution process utilized to resolve industrial disputes, and may be used not only by workers and employers (i.e. the direct parties to labor relations), but also by third parties (e.g. private individuals, governmental organizations) to mediate discrepancies in opinions. Depending on the subjects of the adjustment, industrial dispute adjustments may be classified as "legal mediation" and "private mediation."

While resolving industrial disputes through self-help measures (i.e. industrial action) is a viable method of finding a solution, the reality is that exclusive reliance on such measures inevitably results in economic damages. Consequently, a system to adjust industrial disputes via pacific and supplementary measures is required in order to prevent any unnecessary damages.

B. The Conciliation-Prepositive Principle

According to the Union Act, "one party to labor relations shall notify thereof to the other party in writing ... upon the occurrence of a labor dispute,"[7] and "any industrial action shall not be conducted without completing adjustment procedures."[8] This is the conciliation-prepositive principle.

The reason the Union Act assumes the conciliation-prepositive principle is to ensure that parties to industrial disputes have an opportunity to resolve their differences in a peaceful manner before

---

7 Union Act, Article 45(1)

8 Ibid., Articles 45(2) and 52(3)

resorting to coercive measures such as industrial action, thereby ensuring industrial actions are taken only after exhausting all other means.[9] Related to this topic, the Supreme Court once ruled that "it is not the case that a final decision must be made in the adjustment process in order for an industrial action to be valid. A trade union may legitimately initiate industrial action if the adjustment procedure is terminated due to the fact that the union has submitted a mediation request to the Labor Relations Commission, or if the adjustment period has expired."[10]

III. Types of Industrial Disputes and Their Procedural Adjustments

A. Legal Mediation and Arbitration

1) Mediation

Mediation is a conflict resolution process in which a mediation committee (established once one party unilaterally files for relief with the Labor Relations Commission) hears each interested party's opinion on the issue and presents a mediation plan for the parties to accept. In principle, mediation is a voluntary process that the parties enter into freely without enforcement from third parties, such as administrative agencies. Furthermore, acceptance of the mediation plan is voluntary. However, an exception to this principle would be when initiation of the mediation process is enforced through an emergency adjustment process.

---

9 Kim Hyung-bae, *Labor Law*, p.1007 (Pakyoungsa 2014)
10 Supreme Court 2000Do2871 (2001. 6. 26.)

2) Arbitration

Arbitration is also a form of conflict resolution process that resolves conflicts through the following process. First, the Labor Relations Commission establishes an arbitration committee (established when both parties agree to enter into arbitration or when utilization of the arbitration process is stipulated in the collective agreement) and hears the opinions of both parties. Next, the arbitration committee decides on an arbitration settlement regarding the matter of industrial dispute put forth before it. Finally, the committee enforces the content of this settlement to the parties and ultimately resolves the dispute. Although initiation of the arbitration process is voluntary, the find decision is binding. However, an exception to the principle of voluntary entry into arbitration procedures is recognized when an administrative agency directs the parties to enter into such proceedings mandatorily.

B. Private Mediation and Arbitration

As examined above, the Union Act designates adjustment procedures via the Labor Relations Commission for the resolution of industrial disputes. However, Article 52(1) of the Union Act also allows for other (i.e. private) methods of mediation or arbitration that do not go through the Labor Relations Commission and which parties may utilize via mutual or collective agreements. As such, parties to labor relations have the freedom to determine for themselves the following: whether to utilize mediation, arbitration, or both procedures in resolving the dispute; how to frame the issues when initiating the adjustment procedure; which institution to appoint as the provider, or whether to take advantage of arbitration or mediation services; and the procedure through which the mediation or arbitration proceedings will take place. One condition to this is that when the parties to labor relations decide to resolve a labor dispute through such private means, they must notify this fact to the Labor Relations Commission.[11]

As there are no limitations as to when private adjustment settlements may take place, the parties may report a settlement agreement to the Labor Relations Commission even when a legal mediation or arbitration is in process with the Labor Relation Commission.[12]

Should parties to the labor relations decide to resolve an industrial dispute through the private mediation process, that process must observe the following time limitations: the mediation process must conclude within 10 days for regular businesses and 15 days for public service businesses, subject to a 10-day (for regular businesses) and 15-day (for public service businesses) extension if there is mutual agreement by both parties to grant such an extension. Industrial action is prohibited during this period of active mediation, but is allowed again should the mediation procedure fail to conclude within the previously mentioned time limitations.[13] In cases where private mediation is followed by a private arbitration process, industrial action is prohibited for 15 days from the date that the private arbitration has been initiated. This period of limitation stands irrespective of the bar on industrial action imposed during the previous mediation process. However, should the arbitration process fail to conclude within the above time limitation, industrial action may nevertheless be commenced.[14] When the parties to labor relations mutually agree to resolve matters of industrial disputes through the private mediation adjustment process, the results of the mediation or arbitration shall have the same effect as that of a collective agreement.[15]

---

11 Union Act, Article 52(2)

12 Enforcement Decree of the Trade Union and Labor Relations Adjustment Act, Article 23(2)

13 Union Act, Articles 53(3)(1), 45(2), 54

14 Ibid., Articles 52(3)(2), 63, 45(2)

15 "These disputes are placed in the same priority category with state, local governments, state or local government-run enterprises, and national defense businesses." (Union Act, Article 52(4))

C. Special Provisions Concerning Adjustment Procedures

1) Public Service Adjustment Procedures

Adjustment of industrial disputes in public service businesses, as prescribed by the Union Act,[16] shall be treated with priority and processed in a prompt manner.[17] For arbitration of public service businesses, there are special provisions in place (e.g. establishment of a Special Arbitration Committee) to facilitate this process.[18]

2) Emergency Adjustment Procedures

The Minister of Employment and Labor may carry out an emergency adjustment of any industrial action when it is related to a public service business or is likely to impair the national economy or endanger people's daily lives because of its large scale and specific nature.[19]

When a decision to conduct an emergency adjustment is publicly announced, the parties concerned shall immediately suspend any industrial action, and no industrial action shall resume until 30 days have passed from the announcement date of that decision.[20]

The National Labor Relations Commission shall commence the procedure of mediation upon notification,[21] and the chairman of the National Labor Relations Commission shall, if s/he deems that the mediation is unlikely to be successful, decide whether or not to refer the case in question to arbitration.[22]

The National Labor Relations Commission also conducts arbitration if one or both of the parties concerned request to do so or

---

16 Union Act, Article 71(1)
17 Ibid., Article 51
18 For more information, see Articles 72 and 73 of the Union Act.
19 Union Act, Article 76
20 Ibid., Article 77
21 Ibid., Article 78
22 Ibid., Article 79

if the Nation Labor Relations Commission has decided to refer the case to arbitration.[23]

---

23 Ibid., Article 80

Chapter 5

Unfair Labor Practices

I. What Constitutes Unfair Labor Practices

A. The Meaning of Unfair Labor Practices

"Unfair labor practices" refer to acts of the employer that obstruct or interfere with the worker or workers' organization from independently exercising their three fundamental labor rights ensured by the Constitution.[1]

Article 81 of the Union Act[2] prohibits employers from engaging in unfair labor practices.[3] Here, the term "employer" includes not only the business owner, but also the person responsible for the management of the business or a person who acts on behalf of a business owner with regard to matters concerning workers at the business (i.e. managers).[4]

Article 81 of the Union Act stipulates the following five types of acts as unfair labor practices: ① unfavorable treatment; ② entering into unfair employment contracts ("Yellow Dog" contracts); ③ refusal

---

1 The Judicial Research and Training Institute, *Trade Union and Labor Relations Mediation Law*, p. 365 (2014)

2 Trade Union and Labor Relations Adjustment Act

3 Union Act, Article 81

4 Ha Gab-rae, *Collective Labor Relations Law*, p. 547 (Joongang Economy 2013)

of collective bargaining; ④ domination of, interference or provision of financial support for operations; and ⑤ unfavorable treatment as retribution.

The following sections will examine the conditions identified by case law in which each of the above types of unfair labor practices has been or would be recognized.

B. Types of Unfair Labor Practices Prescribed by Article 81 of the Union Act

1) Justifiable Unified Activities of the Worker

The first type of unfair labor practice is when the employer dismisses or otherwise unfavorably treats a worker for reasons of joining or engaging in other justified union activities,[5] or for participation in justifiable collective actions, or for reporting to or testifying before the Labor Relations Commission of the fact that the employer has violated the provisions of Article 81 of the Union Act, or for presenting other evidence to relevant administrative agencies.[6][7]

i) Justifiable Union Activity or Collective Action

The actual grounds for an unfair labor practice must be one from those stipulated above. The usual issues that come under dispute are ① whether the union activity or collective action that the worker argues is justified actually can be considered a union activity or collective action in the first place, and ② whether these activities are justified.

---

5 Union Act, Article 81(1)

6 Ibid., Article 81(5)

7 The Judicial Research and Training Institute, *supra*, p. 366

(1) The Standard Used in Determining Whether an Act Is for the
Operation of the Trade Union

Generally, as an act for the operation of the trade union refers
to ordinary union activities, it shall include not only collective
bargaining and industrial action, but also such activities as election of
union officers and union members' union operation activities as well.[8]
However, even if an act is not one organized by the trade union *per
se*, if the nature of the act may be construed to be an act by the union
or with tacit or implied union authorization/approval, this act may be
considered an act for the operation of the trade union.[9]

The act of running for chairperson of the union is considered
an act of the trade union due to its nature.[10] Exposing or charging
an executive of wrongdoing, such as gambling, or posting notices
concerning the wages of on-call drivers on the break room bulletin
board are considered justifiable union activity.[11]

Generally, it would be difficult for acts that run counter to the
intent of the trade union to be considered acts for the operation of the
trade union.[12] However, case law has recognized an exception, which
is when a worker who is also the financial auditor of the union led a
movement for a non-confidence motion of the union representative
for having agreed to a wage agreement that provides lower wages than
other companies. The aforementioned representative later convened a
special general meeting to officially hand in his resignation. Here, the
act of non-confidence considered a justifiable act for the operation of
the trade union.[13]

8 Kim Hyung-bae, *Labor Law*, p. 1127 (Pakyoungsa 2014)

9 Supreme Court 89Nu2837 (1990. 10. 23.), Supreme Court 91Nu4164 (1991. 11. 12.), Supreme Court 95Da1323 (1995. 6. 13.)

10 Supreme Court 89Nu8217 (1990. 8. 10.)

11 Supreme Court 89Nu8217 (1980. 8. 10.)

12 The Judicial Research and Training Institute, *supra*, p. 366

13 Supreme Court 89Nu2837 (1990. 10. 23.)

On the other hand, case law also identified another case in which a worker's actions were not considered an act for the operation of the trade union. In this case, a worker who was merely a union member (i.e. not an officer) submitted a petition against the CEO of the company arguing that the collective agreement had been violated regarding issues related to car wash expenses and personnel and bus schedule matters. The Supreme Court ruled that this petition could not be seen as an act of the trade union due to its nature.[14] Other cases where acts were not recognized as acts for the operation of the trade union include: i) the posting of printed material that criticized the concluded collective agreement in a manner contrary to the trade union's intent and through means that disregarded stipulated procedures;[15] and ii) the organizing of an emergency planning committee immediately after the conclusion of a new collective agreement, arguing for the agreement's nullification without specifying the grounds that made it invalid, while engaging in industrial action that violated the duty of peace.[16]

(2) The Standard Used in Determining Justification

This topic will be examined in further detail in Section "C. 2)" of the present chapter.

ii) Unfavorable Treatment

The types and manner of unfavorable treatment are very diverse. Examples of unfavorable treatment include anything regarding status (including dismissal, coercing resignation, and workplace transfers), economic matters (including discriminatory payment of various allowances, and discriminatory rejection to extended work), emotional/psychological matters or living conditions (including suspension, requiring a written explanation and apology, and discrimination in the

---

14 Supreme Court 94Nu3001 (1994. 12. 23.)

15 Supreme Court 90Nu6927 (1991. 5. 28.)

16 Supreme Court 94Da4092 (1994. 9. 30.)

use of welfare facilities), and uniform activity (transfer redeployment, or promotion to a work position that is inappropriate for union activity).[17]

(1) Unfavorable Treatment towards Union Activity
Prohibiting or restricting union activity through means of promotion or transfer is deemed to be unfavorable treatment.[18] Ordering a full-time union officer to return to his/her original work duties for the purpose of hindering union activity is also considered an unfair labor practice.[19] In addition, while an order of job transfer is not unfavorable *per se*, transferring workers (who have just attempted to join a company-dominated union and transform it into a functioning trade union) to departments where it is difficult to conduct union activities would be considered an unfair labor practice.[20] Furthermore, transferring union officers in succession to a small makeshift office that used to be a locker room in a different factory would be considered an unfair labor practice as well.[21]

(2) Promotions
In the event a promotion would have the worker relinquish his/her eligibility as a union member to the extent that it restricts union activities, such promotion may be deemed as unfavorable treatment.[22] The decision whether to promote a worker is within the authority and discretion of the employer. Whether a promotion constitutes unfavorable treatment is determined by considering the following factors: i) the timing of the promotion and whether it is related to union activity; ii) the status and actual influence of the worker who

17 The Judicial Research and Training Institute, *supra*, p. 369, Im Jong-ryul, *Labor Law*, p. 275 (Pakyoungsa 2014)
18 Ha Gab-rae, *supra*, p. 593
19 Supreme Court 90Nu6392 (1991. 5. 28.)
20 Supreme Court 92Nu9425 (1992. 11. 13.)
21 Supreme Court 97Nu18035 (1998. 12. 23.)
22 Ha Gab-rae, *supra*, p. 593

has been promoted within the trade union; iii) the maintenance of equality vis-à-vis other related personnel; iv) operational necessity; v) the eligibility of the worker's competencies; vi) the reasonableness of the personnel decision; and vii) the impact of the promotion on trade union activities.[23] Even if, as taken as a whole, there is a demonstrable discrepancy in the promotion of union and non-union workers, this is not grounds sufficient in and of itself to indicate that an unfair labor practice has occurred.[24]

2) Unfair Employment Contracts

The Union Act prohibits the act of making it an employment condition for the worker to not join a trade union, withdraw from a trade union or join a particular trade union, as such conditions are deemed unfair labor practices. Contracts that set forth such conditions are unfair employment contracts (Yellow Dog Contracts, Anti-Union Contracts).[25] Unfair employment contracts are invalid under private law as a violation of Article 33(1) of the Constitution and Article 81 of the Union Act.

Unfair employment contracts are rarely found in practice in the Republic of Korea. However, the proviso of Article 81(2) of the Union Act provides that in the event a trade union represents more than two-thirds of the workers working in a workplace, it is possible to enter into collective agreements that make it a condition for the relevant worker to be a member of such trade union (i.e. a limited "union shop" agreement).[26] However, as this kind of clause may infringe upon the worker's right to uniform selection, the second sentence of this proviso also stipulates, "in such cases, an employer may not commit any disadvantageous act against the status of a worker on the grounds

---

23 Supreme Court 97Nu18035 (1998. 12. 23.)
24 Supreme Court 96Nu10188 (1998. 2. 10.)
25 Ha Gab-rae, *supra*, p. 602
26 Ha Gab-rae, *supra*, p. 604

that the worker is expelled from the trade union concerned," thereby weakening the actual strength of union shop agreements.[27]

In a case related to the union shop clause, a group of workers in a workplace governed by the union shop clause withdrew from the trade union but subsequently recanted their intent to withdraw and attempted to rejoin the union. The trade union refused membership to these workers, and asked the employer to dismiss these workers as per the collective agreement, to which the latter obliged. In this case, the Supreme Court ruled that this dismissal was invalid. The court's rationale was that the trade union effectively expelled a group of workers that had recanted their intention to withdraw and wished to join the union, thereby betraying the spirit of solidarity. Such action, according to the Supreme Court, went beyond the purpose of dismissals under the union shop clause.[28]

3) Refusal to Engage in Collective Bargaining

Article 81(3) of the Union Act provides that refusal to engage in collective bargaining occurs constituted "when the employer refuses or delays to engage in the collective bargaining process with the trade union representative, or the person commissioned by the trade union, without justifiable cause."[29] [30]

Whether a justifiable cause exists cannot be determined generally or in the abstract by merely looking at the unilateral actions of the employer, as it is an issue with respect to the relationship with the worker as a bargaining party. In other words, the bargaining attitude of both parties must be comprehensively reviewed.[31]

According to case law, the fact that the union was conducting

27 Kim Hyung-bae, *supra*, p. 1744, The Judicial Research and Training Institute, *supra*, p. 372

28 Supreme Court 94Da15363 (1995. 2. 28.)

29 Im Jong-ryul, *supra*, p. 281

30 Supreme Court 2003Du11834 (2001. 3. 12.)

31 Kim Hyung-bae, *supra*, p. 1149, Ha Gab-rae, *supra*, p. 609

industrial action cannot be a justifiable cause for the employer to refuse to enter into collective bargaining.[32] This is because industrial actions are, by their very nature, a means to promote the collective bargaining process. Of course, there are cases where the employer may successfully argue that the cause for refusing to engage in collective bargaining is justified. This would be when the parties to the process have reached a stalemate despite sincere negotiation on the part of both parties and no further progress seems feasible, leading to the employer refusing further participation in the process. However, even in such scenarios the employer is still required to come back to the bargaining table if the trade union proposes a new compromise package and makes the re-commencement of the bargaining process meaningful. If the employer still continues to refuse to engage in the collective bargaining process despite this change in circumstances, his/her actions would be presumed to lack justifiable cause.[33]

Meanwhile, in order for an employer organization (in which the relevant employer is a member) to become a party that may engage in collective bargaining with the trade union, the organization must possess the authority to adjust or regulate the labor relations of the employer. To obtain this authority, the employer organization must have as its purpose to engage in collective bargaining with the trade union and conclude collective agreements, and at the same time possess control over its member employers.[34] In the case of a trade union that has commissioned its right to collective bargaining to an individual, the trade union maintains its right to collective bargaining, which competitively overlaps with that which it granted to the commissioned person. This is true even if there were no separate expressions of intent that decommissioned the above individual.[35]

---

32 Supreme Court 2005Do8606 (2006. 2. 24.)

33 Ibid.

34 Supreme Court 98Du137 (1999. 6. 22.)

35 Supreme Court 98Da20790 (1998. 11. 13.)

This type of unfair labor practice (i.e. "refusal to engage in collective bargaining") is expected to increase significantly in the future. This is due to the rising movement within trade unions of large conglomerates to request collective bargaining on matters that have the properties of management, as they increasingly move beyond bargaining for working conditions related to matters of livelihood. Responding to this movement, employers argue that such matters are not subject to collective agreement and refuse to engage in collective bargaining, giving rise to claims of unfair labor practices.[36]

4) Domination, Interference, and Financial Support

The Union Act, in order to protect the independence and autonomy of trade unions, prohibits the domination of or interference in the organization or operation of a trade union, the payment of wages to the full-time union officer, or the provision of financial support for its operation on the grounds that they are unfair labor practices.[37] Case law regarding this matter is as follow.

In a case where the employer refused to issue proof of employment to a portion of his/her employees despite the fact that the trade union bylaws require the submission of such documentation to register as a council delegate, the Supreme Court ruled that this is a form of unfair labor practice due to the domination and interference of the employer on the operation of the trade union.[38]

In another case, the Supreme Court ruled that unfair labor practices due to dominance or interference do not necessarily require infringement on a worker's right to organize. Specifically, in a case where an employer is disputing the dismissal of a trade union representative, if the employer returns the notification to reinstate

---

36 The Judicial Research and Training Institute, *supra*, p. 375
37 Ha Gab-rae, *supra*, p. 616
38 Supreme Court 92Nu3496 (1992. 6. 23.)

a union representative and requests the union to submit a blanket deduction request (for union dues, etc.) under the name of a union member other than the union representative, the Supreme Court has determined that the employer has interfered with the union activities of the trade union representative, and has therefore engaged in a form of unfair labor practice.[39]

Furthermore, case law suggests in cases where the employer expressed his/her opinion through speeches, corporate broadcasts, bulletins, or letters; the circumstances, location, content, and method of communication, and the impact that the expression had on the operation and activities of the trade union will be comprehensively evaluated to determine whether there was intent by the employer to dominate or interfere with the organization or operation of the trade union. If such intent is recognized, the courts will consider the employer to have engaged in an unfair labor practice.[40]

In relation to this subject, issues that become especially contentious are ① payment of wages to the full-time union officer, and ② financial support.

The Union Act completely bans the payment of wages to a full-time union officer, and allows workers to conduct affairs prescribed by the Union Act or other laws as well as to maintain and manage a trade union for the healthy development of labor-management relations without loss of wages, such as consultation or bargaining with an employer, grievance settlements, or industrial safety activities, within the maximum time-off limit.[41] Therefore, if the employer pays wages to the full-time union officer, to time-off workers for hours spent on union activities that exceed the prescribed maximum time-off limit, or for work that does not fall under the time-off scheme, this may be considered an unfair labor practice through domination or

39 Supreme Court 96Nu2057 (1997. 5. 7.)
40 Supreme Court 97Nu8076 (1998. 5. 22.)
41 Union Act, Articles 24 and 81(4)

interference.[42]

Case law decided prior to the recent amendment to the Union Act[43] that financial support to trade unions does not necessarily constitute an unfair labor practice in certain situations. Specifically, considering that the purpose of prohibiting financial support is to ensure the independence of the trade union, the determination of whether such support is an unfair labor practice should turn not on formal requirements alone but also on the risk of the trade union to lose its independence. In circumstances where financial support is a result reaped via active solicitation and struggle on the part of the trade union, the Supreme Court determined that the risk of the union losing its independence is nominal, and hence such support does not constitute an unfair labor practice. However, circumstances changed with the amendment to the Union Act, which categorically prohibits the payment of wages to full-time union officers. Whether the above precedent will hold in light of this amendment is yet to be determined.

However, the proviso of Article 81(4) of the Union Act does stipulate that "it may be justified that the employer allows workers to consult or bargain with him during working hours, and it shall be allowed as an exception that the employer contributes funds for the welfare of workers, or for prevention and relief of economic misfortunes or other disasters, or that the employer provide a trade union office of a minimum size." A recent decision of the Supreme Court clarified that while the employer paying for the electricity bills of the trade union office would in principle be considered as financial support by the employer to the trade union and hence would constitute an unfair labor practice, an exception to this principle would be recognized if the practice of the employer supporting the electricity bills of the union office is clearly approved as a normative

---

42 Kim Hyung-bae, *supra*, p. 1158; The Judicial Research and Training Institute, *supra*, p. 377
43 Supreme Court 90Nu6392 (1991. 5. 28.)

fact that regulates labor relations, or the practice is accepted by all parties as a de facto institution.[44]

C. Unfair Labor Practices Prescribed by Articles 81(1) through 81(5) of the Union Act

1) Prerequisites

In order for an unfair labor practice as prescribed by Articles 81(1) through 81(5) of the Union Act to be established, the worker must first receive unfavorable treatment from the employer for engaging in justified union activities or participating in collective activities (hereinafter referred to as "justified trade union activities"). Therefore, even if the employer dismisses or otherwise unfavorably treats the worker for union activities, this would not be considered an unfair labor practice if the worker's actions are not recognized as justified trade union activities.[45] That only justified union activities that may be protected are not only set forth in the foregoing provisions of the Union Act, but are also clearly set forth in Articles 2 and 4 of the Union Act with respect to civil and criminal indemnification.[46]

2) The Standard of Determining Justified Trade Union Activities

The Supreme Court limits the scope of justified trade union activities to the extent that it is reasonably balanced with the legal rights of the employer to manage facilities, and is proper in light of socially accepted norms.[47] The following are quotes from relevant Supreme Court cases that provide some insight into the matter: "Unless there are separate provisions in the rules of employment or collective

---

44 Supreme Court 2011Da109531 (2014. 2. 27.)

45 Supreme Court 94Nu11583 (1995. 4. 28.)

46 Kim Hyung-bae, *supra*, p. 1128

47 Kim Hyung-bae, *supra*, p. 1129; The Judicial Research and Training Institute, *supra*, p. 379

agreements that provide otherwise, or the worker or union has obtained the employer's consent, any trade union activity within the workplace must be subject to reasonable regulations and restrictions based on the employer's right to manage facilities."[48] "Determination of whether a certain action is a justified activity for the trade union's work must be made by comprehensively assessing, in light of socially accepted norms, the following factors: the attitude of labor and management regarding the act in question, and the extent, form, and pattern of the unfavorable treatment.[49] The Supreme Court has ruled that "even if the unpermitted assembly has taken place during the lunch hour, due to the fact that the particularities of this case indicate that the action had taken place within the workplace (where the right of the employer to manage facilities extends), and despite the fact that the rules of employment specifically prohibit such actions, the assembly is subject to disciplinary action." As a result, this is another decision in line with the above rulings.[50] Regarding trade union activities during work hours, the Supreme Court ruled that "in order for such trade union activity to be justified, there must exist separate provisions in the rules of employment or collective agreements that permit this act, or the act must be established in practice or obtain the employer's consent. Otherwise, trade union activities must take place outside of work hours.[51] The Supreme Court in these cases ruled that, other than in cases where it was customary practice or there was consent by the employer, union activities in the workplace must comply with reasonable rules and regulations based on the employer's right to maintain the facility.[52]

Regarding the distribution of printed material, the Supreme

---

48 Supreme Court 92Da18542 (1992. 9. 25.)

49 Supreme Court 98Da54960 (2000. 6. 23.)

50 Supreme Court 93Da32002 (1994. 5. 13.)

51 Supreme Court 90Do357 (1990. 5. 15.)

52 Kim Hyung-bae, *supra*, p. 1129

Court ruled that even in a system that requires the permission of the employer for the distribution of printed material (as the employer cannot prohibit activities for justified trade union work), whether the act of distribution is justified or not should not be determined based on whether permission was given, but on the content of the printed material, the number of pages, the timing/target/method of distribution, and the impact the material makes on the corporation and its work.[53] Therefore, even when the printed material is distributed as part of trade union activities, if the material infringes on the corporation's business profits or an individual's physical, psychological, and personal freedom through injury to the reputation or honor of the corporation and/or its executives, the justification of this act is denied as a matter of principle.[54]

Other cases where the act of distribution of printed material was denied as well as the justification thereof are as follows: i) when printed material was distributed during the night (at approximately 12:40 AM) without the corporation's approval or the authorization or approval of the trade union, justification was denied by the Supreme Court;[55] ii) when a trade union covertly distributed printed material without the approval of the employer (thereby infringing on the latter's right to manage facilities) and contained false facts that slandered the company and thereby led to concerns over corporate disorder the Supreme Court ruled that the distribution lacked justification even if it took place during the council of delegates election campaign period.[56]

On the other hand, the Supreme Court ruled that distribution of material during break periods in the work week does not lose its justification merely because it failed to receive approval from the employer, as long as it does not negatively influence the work of

---

53 Supreme Court 98Da54960 (2000. 6. 23.)
54 Supreme Court 91Nu5020 (1992. 3. 13.)
55 Supreme Court 94Nu3001 (1994. 12. 23.)
56 Supreme Court 92Nu4253 (1992. 6. 23.)

other workers, hinder their ability to freely use their break time, or otherwise cause specific instances of corporate disorder.[57]

As such, even if the content of the printed material causes injury to another person's character, credibility, or honor, or risk causing injury, and a part of the facts contained in the material is false or somewhat exaggerated or distorted, as long as the content of the material is true overall and the purpose of the distribution is not to infringe upon the rights or interests of other people, but to maintain and improve working conditions as well as promote the welfare and improve the economic and social status of the worker, the Supreme Court has acknowledged the distribution to be within the justifiable activities of workers.[58]

A series of Supreme Court cases outlined the following requirements for the justification of another important form of collective action (i.e. industrial action): ① The purpose of the industrial action must be justified in that it purports to maintain and improve working conditions through the process of collective bargaining; ② the timing and process of industrial action must be justified and in compliance with regulations contained in the Union Act; ③ the method and form of the industrial action must stay within the limits of justification and must not involve acts of violence or destruction nor may it demonstrate a high degree of anti-social behavior; ④ even if an industrial action violated certain procedural rules (i.e. those stipulated in the Union Act), this does not necessarily mean that the action has lost justification; the determination of justification must examine specific circumstances, such as whether the violation has caused unexpected disorder or injury to the stability of society or the employer's business operations.[59]

---

57 Supreme Court 91Nu4164 (1991. 11. 12.)

58 Supreme Court 2008Da29123 (2011. 2. 24.)

59 Supreme Court 90Nu4006 (1991. 5. 14.)

The Supreme Court further reviewed the exact definition of what constitutes justifiable purpose of an industrial action, ruling that such a purpose must be to create an environment of autonomous bargaining between labor and management to improve working conditions, and this would mean that the demands for which an industrial action is conducted must be items that are permitted to be collectively bargained.[60]

Regarding the process of industrial action, the Supreme Court ruled that the following cases are not justifiable acts for the work of the trade union, and hence dismissing workers who have engaged in them would not constitute an unfair labor practice: the act of conducting a sit-in within the office (while sitting on a straw bag) for 12 days without going through legally mandated mediation;[61] and the act of organizing an emergency planning committee immediately after the conclusion of a new collective agreement, arguing for the agreement's nullification without specifying the grounds that make it invalid, while engaging in industrial action that violates the duty of peace.[62] [63]

3) Intent to Engage in Unfair Labor Practice

An active debate in the literature involves whether intent to engage in unfair labor practices (i.e. anti-union intentions or motivations) is necessary for the constitution of an unfair labor practice. The Supreme Court has clearly ruled that it is, and that this intent of the employer to engage in an unfair labor practice is assumed from objective facts that are revealed externally.[64] Specific instances are as follows:

---

60 Supreme Court 94Da4042 (1994. 9. 30.)

61 Supreme Court 82Nu334 (1983. 12. 13)

62 Supreme Court 92Nu7733 (1992. 9. 1.)

63 The Judicial Research and Training Institute, *supra*, p. 382

64 Supreme Court 90Nu7685 (1991. 4. 23.)

i) Unreasonableness in the Severity of Disciplinary Disposition, and
   Defects in the Disciplinary Action Procedure
Whether a dismissal has cited justifiable trade union activity as
grounds for dismissal is determined by considering and comparing
the following circumstances in their totality: the grounds of dismissal
advanced by the employer; the substance of the justified trade union
action that the worker has conducted; the timing of the disciplinary
dismissal; the relationship between the employer and the trade union;
any discriminatory application of sanctions for similar instances;
and other circumstances that may suggest the existence of intent
by the employer to engage in an unfair labor practice. Therefore,
while the fact that there exists unreasonableness in the severity of
the disciplinary action or other defects in the disciplinary action
procedure may serve as material for consideration when determining
whether an employer has engaged in an unfair labor practice, they are
not in and of themselves sufficient to indicate that the employer has
done as such.[65]

This is true for layoffs (or dismissals for managerial reasons) that lack
justifiable cause or are based on unreasonable standards. Irrespective
of whether the layoff is in fact valid, such facts do not automatically
make the employer's action an unfair labor practice.[66]

This is the same for violations of the disciplinary action procedures
as well. Such violations are not directly related to the constitution of
an unfair labor practice, regardless of whether it may ultimately be a
cause for the invalidation of dismissal.[67]

ii) Disparate Treatment
Whether an employer treats union members and workers that actively

---

65 Supreme Court 94Nu3940 (1994. 8. 26.), 94Nu3001 (1994. 12. 23.), 96Nu4220 (1997. 3. 28.)
66 Supreme Court 89Nu336 (1990. 10. 23.)
67 Supreme Court 92Nu11176 (1994. 2. 22.)

participate in union activities different from those who do not in a discriminatory fashion is an important indicator of the existence of the intent to engage in an unfair labor practice.[68] Regarding this, case law has recognized that intent of the employer to engage in an unfair labor practice exists in the following cases:

① Where an employer disciplines workers who are actively engaged in trade union activities in a manner more severe (i.e. adding an extra charge of non-compliance to disciplinary action) compared to those who are non-members or have withdrawn from union membership (the latter only receiving the penalty of a decrease in wages) for being involved in traffic accidents of a similar nature. Taking this together with the fact that the employer has usually expressed his/her disapproval of the trade union, the Supreme Court recognized the existence of intent of the employer to engage in an unfair labor practice.[69] ② Where an employer suddenly orders union officers preparing to establish a trade union to go on a business trip, subsequently dismisses them all without going through the proper process, and reemploys only those workers who agree to comply with company policy, the Supreme Court also recognized the existence of intent of the employer to engage in an unfair labor practice.[70] ③ Where an employer disciplinarily dismisses a worker (who happened to be active in trade union activities) for failing to satisfy requisite work days despite the fact that the worker has never previously received disciplinary action for failing to do so, and that there were four other workers who had fewer work days logged than the dismissed worker, the Supreme Court recognized the existence of intent of the employer to engage in an unfair labor practice.[71]

---

68 The Judicial Research and Training Institute, *supra*, p. 382

69 Supreme Court 90Nu6132 (1991. 2. 22.)

70 Supreme Court 88Nu7729 (1990. 10. 23.)

71 Supreme Court 89Nu1193 (1990. 1. 12.)

iii) Time Difference between the Union Activity and Dismissal

The temporal proximity between the worker's trade union activity that became the cause of dismissal and the actual dismissal is an important basis in determining the existence of intent to engage in an unfair labor practice.[72] For example, in one Supreme Court case, a worker who gained employment while misrepresenting his education in 1982 and has since been active as a member of the council of delegates and the steering committee was disciplinarily dismissed on March 2, 1985, less than a month after he made a comment conflicting with the employer in a council of delegates meeting on February 5, 1985, and shortly after he was elected to be the trade union's education and promotion officer on February 25, 1985. The Supreme Court recognized the existence of intent of the employer to engage in an unfair labor practice in this case as well.[73]

iv) Business Necessity for the Personnel Disposition or the Reasonability of the Personnel Disposition

The Supreme Court ruled that it is an unfair labor practice for an employer to transfer a worker who has worked in the production division for over 20 years to a remote branch far away from headquarters where only three or four employees are employed and subsequently request the worker to serve as the president of the staff council. The rationale behind this determination is that the Supreme Court failed to discern a business need that would require the worker to be transferred to such a remote location.[74]

In another case, the Supreme Court ruled that a workplace transfer order of a worker who is active as a member of the collective bargaining committee during the bargaining period is not an unfair

---

72 The Judicial Research and Training Institute, *supra*, p. 385

73 Supreme Court 85Nu851 (1986. 10. 28.)

74 Supreme Court 91Nu3789 (1991. 12. 10.)

labor practice, due to the fact that the transfer occurred while complying with the procedures outlined in the employee workplace transfer regulations and personnel movement standards in light of the worker's experience, capabilities, and city of origin.[75]

v) Relationship between the Employer and the Trade Union
In a Supreme Court case relevant to this topic, dismissing a worker who has enthusiastically engaged in activities to advance the interests of the trade union (to the extent that the worker came into conflict with the union itself), and to whom the employer had demonstrated caution against, was not ruled to be an unfair labor practice. The Supreme Court ruled that this was because neither particular conflict nor communication existed between the employer and the trade union at the time regarding union activity, and also because the employer had a separate justifiable cause to dismiss the worker.[76]

Related to this, the Supreme Court stated in a separate case that another consideration in making the above determination would be whether the activities of the trade union had suffered a decline.[77]

4) When Justifiable Cause and Intent to Engage in an Unfair Labor Practice Conflict
i) Opposing Views in Related Literature
In cases where the intent to engage in an unfair labor practice co-exists with justifiable cause, there are multiple views in related literature as to whether the action would constitute an unfair labor practice. Such views include ① those that reject the constitution of unfair labor practices (the so-called "justifiable cause theory"); ② those that acknowledge that an unfair labor practice has occurred; ③ those

75 Supreme Court 91Nu11025 (1992. 12. 8.)
76 Supreme Court 91Nu2571 (1992. 1. 17.)
77 Supreme Court 91Nu11025 (1992. 12. 8.)

that acknowledge an unfair labor practice if the decisive cause of the disposition was the justifiable trade union activities of the worker (the so-called "decisive cause theory"); and ④ those that observe that the unfair labor practice would not have taken place if not for the worker's trade union activities (the so-called "proximate-cause relationship theory").[78]

ii) Implications from Case Law

The majority of Supreme Court cases relevant to this issue use the following expression: "If the actual cause of the dismissal of a worker is his/her justified union activity instead of the ostensible cause cited by the employer, such a disposition must be construed as an unfair labor practice."[79] However, the Supreme Court has also stated that if the employer has dismissed a worker under the intent to do so, and that the cause for this intent is justified, even if it is estimated that the dismissal is due to the employer's disgust of the worker's trade union activity (the intent to engage in an unfair labor practice is internal to the employer, and hence may only be estimated from various external circumstances), it cannot be said that the cause of dismissal at hand is only an ostensible justification formally given to dismiss the worker, and therefore an unfair labor practice cannot be recognized for the above reasons.

Here are some examples of specific rulings: "As long as facts exist that satisfy the requirements for disciplinary dismissal, and the employer has dismissed the worker due to his/her determination that the employment relationship cannot continue based on these facts, this dismissal cannot be said to be illegal merely because it is possible to assume the existence of anti-trade union intent."[80] "As long as an

78 Kim Hyung-bae, *supra*, p. 1141

79 Supreme Court 89Nu4659 (1989. 10. 24.), Supreme Court 96Nu6431 (1997. 7. 8.)

80 Supreme Court 87DaKa3196 (1989. 3. 14.)

employer has disciplinarily dismissed a worker based on a valid cause, even if there exists circumstances that suggest the employer did not approve of the worker's trade union activities, such circumstances in and of themselves cannot lead us to conclude that an unfair labor practice has taken place."[81] Consequently, these rulings seem to be direct expressions of the justifiable cause theory.

iii) Actual Judgments in Practice

In actual litigation practice, it is difficult to find cases where the Supreme Court has affirmed the existence of an unfair labor practice where the employer is recognized to have justifiable cause for his/her unfavorable treatment of the worker. Almost all of the cases where the Supreme Court has affirmed the constitution of an unfair labor practice are when the employer had failed to establish such justifiable cause for the dismissal.

Therefore, it is possible to conclude that the Supreme Court would deny the constitution of an unfair labor a practice, even in light of the existence of intent to engage in such a practice, if the employer is recognized to have had justifiable cause for dismissing the worker.

Based on this trend in case law, one may conclude that as long as the employer's dismissal or other unfavorable disposition against the worker is determined to be justified, the disposition would not be considered as merely an ostensible justification. As a result, the justified union activity of the worker would not be considered the actual cause of the dismissal, and consequently the unfair labor practice charge would be unlikely to succeed.[82]

---

81 Supreme Court 94Nu3001 (1994. 12. 23.)

82 The Judicial Research and Training Institute, *supra*, p. 385

II. Application for Remedy from Unfair Labor Practices

A. Outline of the Application for Remedy from Unfair Labor Practices

"A worker or trade union may make an application for remedy to the Labor Relations Commission (Local or Special Labor Relations Commission) concerned on the grounds that his/her rights have been infringed upon by an unfair labor practice on the part of the employer."[83] "In cases (the above commission judge) where the employer has committed an unfair labor practice after completing the (above) inquiry, the Labor Relations Commission shall issue an order of remedy to the employer, otherwise it shall make a decision to dismiss the application for remedy."[84]

"When any of the parties challenge an order of remedy or dismissal decision by the Regional Labor Relations Commission or by the Special Labor Relations Commission, s/he may file an application for review of said order or decision to the National Labor Relations Commission,"[85] which in turn conducts the necessary investigation for the review.

"When an employer has instituted an administrative suit (against a decision for review made by the National Labor Relations Commission), the relevant court may, by its decision at the request of the National Labor Relations Commission, order the employer to perform all or part of the remedy ordered by the National Labor Relations Commission until a court judgment is rendered."[86]

---

83 Union Act, Article 82(1)
84 Ibid., Article 84
85 Ibid., Article 85
86 Ibid., Article 85(5)

B. Entities Eligible to Apply for Remedy from Unfair Labor Practices

According to Article 82(1) of the Union Act, "A worker or trade union may make an application for remedy to the Labor Relations Commission concerned on the grounds that his/her rights have been infringed upon by an unfair labor practice on the part of the employer." As the unfair labor practice against a union member in his/her personal capacity may be deemed as an infringement on the trade union itself, the trade union that such union member is a part of may make an application for remedy as well. Interested stakeholders (i.e. not the party subject to the unfair labor practice) maintain an independent right to apply for remedy from unfair labor practices, so trade unions established after the unfair labor practice has occurred may still exercise this right after the fact, such as in the case when the employer has committed an unfair labor practice against workers who have attempted to organize a trade union.[87]

For situations falling under Articles 81(1), (2), and (5) of the Union Act, even members of non-recognized unions may directly apply for remedy from an unfair labor practice. For other situations, however, only recognized unions and their members possess the right to do so. Also, the majority opinion is that individual workers, and not just trade union officers, must be given the right to apply for remedy.

Labor Relations Commission regulations require that the application for Remedy from an Unfair Labor Practice must contain the following entries: "specific facts that constitute an unfair labor practice or dismissal without justifiable cause," and "the description of the relief to be requested." For the latter requirement, details sufficient for the reader to understand what kind of relief is being sought in light of the overall purpose of the application will suffice. According to case

---

87 Supreme Court 90Nu4952 (1991. 1. 25.)

law, since the Labor Relations Commission has the discretion to order relief that is appropriate and reasonable according to the specific facts of the petitioned case, even when a particular application for remedy does not contain the details of the remedy sought for, if the application nevertheless contains specific factual assertions that, if true, would constitute an unfair labor practice or dismissal without justifiable cause, the Labor Relations Commission must construe the applicant to be requesting remedy for such acts of the employer as well.[88]

C. The Application Period for Remedy from Unfair Labor Practice Applications

"Application for remedy (from unfair labor practices) shall be made within three months from the date of occurrence of the unfair labor practice concerned (where any such practice is in progress, from the date of its termination)."[89] For indefinite suspensions, the three-month period above starts from the day that the disposition was made.[90] These three months are an exclusionary period in order to ensure that the process maintains its function as an expedited and simple administrative remedial procedure. Therefore, once this period expires, the worker's right to request administrative remedy of his/her rights expires as well. This is still the case even if the applicant is able to demonstrate justifiable reasons for the failure to meet the period requirements, such as delays due to circumstances not attributable to the worker.

Also, even in cases where the rules of employment or other such instruments stipulate a process to review disciplinary action, such

---

88 Supreme Court 98Du9233 (1999. 5. 11.)

89 Union Act, Article 82(2)

90 Supreme Court 92Nu15406 (1993. 3. 23.)

as dismissal for the worker's benefit, as a principle the three-month application period for remedy from unfair labor practices under the Union Act starts from the day of the original disciplinary action has been taken, and not from the day the review procedure is concluded (through rejection or other means).[91] This is because the disciplinary action becomes effective from the moment the disposition is made, so long as it is not cancelled or modified during the review process.

D. Interests in Remedy and Litigation: The Question of Mootness

1) Interest in Remedy
Even if there were grounds to apply for remedy at the time the application for remedy was made, in the event that there is no such necessity or interest (i.e. an interest in remedy) to make an application for remedy at the point in time the Local or National Labor Relations Commission reviews the same such application is denied without a review on its merits as to whether an unfair labor practice was established.[92] Therefore, there is no longer a need to make such an order of remedy.

2) Interest in Litigation
An administrative suit may be advanced against a decision in review made by the National Labor Relations Commission to request its cancellation.[93] Yet just as with the case of an administrative suit up for cancellation, the plaintiff must possess an interest in the litigation (i.e. the legal interest to request the cancellation of the relevant order or

91 Supreme Court 95Nu11238 (1996. 8. 23.)
92 Im Jong-ryul, *supra*, p. 299
93 Union Act, Article 85(2)

disposition).

Whether interest in litigation exists becomes an issue mostly after the National Labor Relations Commission has made its decision and issued its order of relief does actual interest under legal dispute no longer exist due to a change in circumstance.

3) Point in Time to Determine the Existence of Interests in Remedy and Litigation

As disputes regarding administrative cases regarding the valid application of administrative regulations generally have to work around constantly changing circumstances of its subject after the disposition in question has been made, a determination as to whether the administrative disposition remains illegal, or whether the interest in remedy or litigation still exists, must be made. Here, the exact point in time where such determination needs to be made becomes an issue.

i) Point in Time to Determine the Existence of an Interest in Remedy

With respect to suits requesting the cancellation of the decision on review made by the National Labor Relations Commission regarding an unfair labor practice, "the moment of disposition" refers not to the moment when the employer has committed an "unfair labor practice," but to when the Labor Relations Commission issued its "order of remedy" or decided to "dismiss the application for remedy." Therefore, the Labor Relations Commission uses the moment when it decides on whether to issue the order of remedy (i.e. the moment of disposition) as the standard of time when determining whether "an interest in remedy" exists.[94]

A Supreme Court case illustrates this point, in which it ruled that when a worker no longer has a workplace to return to work for due to the actual closure of the employer's business, s/he no longer has "an

---

94 The Judicial Research and Training Institute, *supra*, p. 400

interest in requesting remedy from an unfair labor practice."[95]

If an order of remedy is issued by a Local Labor Relations Commission, the interest in remedy must exist at the time of the Commission's decision to issue such order. If the Local Labor Relations Commission dismisses the worker's application for an order of remedy, but this is subsequently reversed by the National Labor Relations Commission as a result of the worker's appeal, the worker's interest in remedy must exist at the time of the National Labor Relations Commission decision.

ii) Point in Time to Determine the Existence of an Interest in Litigation

Regarding the issue of point in time to determine the existence of an interest in litigation, case law mostly follows the argument that the moment of determining the existence of an interest in litigation should be at the point fact-finding proceedings have been concluded, and that the suit must be dismissed if such an interest is deemed lacking at such point in time. This is because the occurrence of circumstances that would render the implementation or execution of the order of remedy impossible would nullify the plaintiff's legal interest to request the cancellation of the problematic disposition.[96]

A case that illustrates this point ruled the following: If the National Labor Relations Commission affirms the Unfair Labor Practice Commission's dismissal of a particular request for remedy and the worker initiates an administrative suit requesting the cancellation of the decision on review made by the National Labor Relations Commission, but the worker loses his/her interest in the remedy prior to the conclusion of the fact-finding proceedings due to a change in circumstances, the Supreme Court ruled that since the worker has lost his/her interest in the litigation, the court has no choice but to

---

95 Supreme Court 91Nu2762 (1991. 12. 24.)

96 Supreme Court 91Nu11131 (1992. 4. 24.)

dismiss the case due the court's lack of capacity to render a substantive judgment regarding the validity of the decision on review made by the National Labor Relations Commission.[97]

4) The Relationship between the Interest in Remedy and the Interest in Litigation

If the worker is advancing a suit requesting the cancellation of the decision on review made by the National Labor Relations Commission regarding an unfair labor practice, the worker's interest in litigation and remedy is substantially identical. If the issue of mootness is brought up during remedial procedures, the issue becomes that of an interest in remedy, while the interest in litigation comes into play during litigation proceedings.

For example, if a worker has applied for an order of relief from an unfair labor practice due to relocation, but subsequently reaches retirement age and retires prior to the conclusion of the remedial process, the worker's application must be withdrawn due to a lack of interest in remedy.

If the worker overlooks this lack of remedial interest during the remedial process and his/her application is ultimately dismissed, or the worker reached retirement age and subsequently retired only after initiating the litigation phase, the worker lacks the necessary interest in litigation. In such cases, there is no need for the courts to make a judgment regarding the substantive matter at hand; in fact, courts must dismiss the suit requesting the cancellation of the decision on review.[98]

However, if the employer is the one advancing the suit requesting the cancellation of the decision on review made by the National Labor Relations Commission regarding an unfair labor practice,

---

97 Supreme Court 94Nu3209 (1995. 4. 7.)

98 The Judicial Research and Training Institute, *supra*, p. 402

the extinguishment of the employer's interest in remedy does not necessarily mean the extinguishment of his/her interest in litigation. Let's say, for example, that an order of remedy (reinstatement and payment of wages until the point of reinstatement) is issued as a result of the worker applying for remedy from an unfair labor practice, and the employer initiates a suit requesting the cancellation of this decision on review by the National Labor Relations Commission (assuming the process progressed this far). If the workplace is shut down after the initiation of this suit, even if the order for reinstatement is valid, the employer may seek the cancellation of the entire decision of the National Labor Relations Commission in order to avoid its duty to pay wages. In other words, the employer maintains it legal interest in the litigation despite extinguishment of his/her interest in the litigation.[99]

5) Whether Interests in Remedy and Litigation Exists: A Detailed Examination

i) Interest in Litigation (The Capacity to Initiate Administrative Litigation) When Decisions or Final Judgments Are Reached in the Remedial Process

The matter to be dealt with in the remedial process is determining whether the Labor Relations Commission will issue an order of remedy to the employer, or, in other words, whether to burden the employer with the public law duties to comply with the order of remedy. Therefore, orders of remedy do not directly generate or modify any private law relationship between the employer and the worker.

Even if the National Labor Relations Commission finalizes the commission's decision to dismiss the worker's application for remedy, the Supreme Court ruled that the worker retains his/her capacity to initiate a separate civil suit.[100]

---

99 Supreme Court 92Nu13196 (1993. 4. 27.)
100 Supreme Court 90Da9353 (1991. 7. 12.)

Even when a worker initiates an administrative suit after receiving a decision to dismiss his/her application for remedy, but subsequently receives a decision from the administrative court that his/her suit to cancel the dismissal has been dismissed, this worker is still considered to retain his/her interest in litigation for further civil suits, such as litigation to confirm the invalidity of his/her dismissal.

Likewise, workers who have secured orders for remedy against wrongful dismissals or unfair labor practices through remedial proceedings or administrative litigation also retain their interest in litigation for further civil suits, including litigation to confirm the invalidity of his/her dismissal in order to secure their status under private law and obtain relief according to their rights.[101]

ii) Interest in Litigation (The Capacity to Initiate Administrative Litigation) Upon Final Judgment of Litigation to Confirm the Invalidity of Dismissal and the Application for Relief

In situations where the judgment to dismiss the litigation for the purpose of confirming the invalidity of the dismissal brought about by the worker is finalized, the fact that the wrongful dismissal is not invalid is already determined, so there is no further need to continue with remedial proceedings. Therefore, the interest of the worker for remedy is deemed to be extinguished.[102]

There is debate, however, as to whether a worker maintains his/her interest in litigation for a suit requesting the cancellation of the decision on review made by the National Labor Relations Commission regarding an unfair labor practice that dismisses his/her request for remedy.

Case law generally denies the worker his/her interest in litigation in such cases. For instance, in a Supreme Court case that dealt with

---

101 Supreme Court 90DaKa27389 (1991. 2. 22.)
102 Supreme Court 92Nu6099 (1992. 7. 28.)

this issue, a worker argued that his dismissal and other unfavorable treatment by the employer constituted an unfair labor practice and applied for relief. At the same time, the worker also initiated separate litigation to confirm the invalidity of his dismissal against the employer, which the court ultimately dismissed. At the time the worker's suit was dismissed, the justification of the employer's unfavorable treatment of the worker had been finalized, and hence the Labor Relations Committee was barred from issuing an order for relief by determining the employer had engaged in an unfair labor practice. Thus, the Supreme Court ruled that the interest of the worker in litigation had been extinguished. As such, if the worker had initiated a suit to cancel the National Labor Relations Commission's upholding of the Local Labor Relations Commission's decision to dismiss the worker's application for relief by dismissing the worker's petition for appeal, or cancel the Local Labor Relations Commission's order for remedy, the worker would not have been able to do this due to a lack of interest in litigation.[103]

iii) Interest in Litigation (The Capacity to Initiate Administrative Litigation) Towards Relief from Wrongful Dismissal upon the Final Judgment of an Application for Relief from an Unfair Labor Practice and Vice Versa

Even if the final judgment of the application for relief from an unfair labor practice is a dismissal, it cannot be said that the worker's interest in relief (for an application for relief) and in litigation (regarding administrative litigation) for wrongful dismissal is extinguished. This is because the purpose and requirements for wrongful dismissal[104] are different from those for an unfair labor practice.[105] On the other

---

103 Supreme Court 95Nu6151 (1996. 4. 23.)

104 LSA, Article 28(1): "When a worker is subjected by the employer to any unfair dismissal, (lay-offs, suspensions, or transfers)."

105 The Judicial Research and Training Institute, *supra*, p. 407

hand, if the final judgment on the application for relief from wrongful dismissal is the dismissal itself, the worker's interest in relief and in litigation for an unfair labor practice is deemed extinguished.

If an application for relief for wrongful dismissal or an unfair labor practice is dismissed without a final decision on its merits (the same holds true for dismissals of litigation to confirm the invalidity of a discharge), the dismissal cannot be said to be "justified" at that point because no determination has been rendered on the subject.

Another matter of dispute is whether the worker's interest in relief and in litigation for wrongful dismissal still exists if an order of remedy for an unfair labor practice is finalized. However, the two regulations are separate in both legislative purpose and required elements, as they are viewed in terms of form and content. Therefore, the consensus is that orders of relief for wrongful dismissal need to be recognized separately from those for unfair labor practices, and vice versa.

E. Other Related Issues

1) Burden of Presentation and Proof
The burden of presenting and proving facts that satisfy the requirements to constitute an unfair labor practice (i.e. the worker has engaged in justifiable trade union actions and the employer has dismissed the worker on these grounds) is on the worker.

2) Reasons for Insubordination That May Be Argued
While the legality of the decision on review made by the National Labor Relations Commission regarding the application of remedy from an unfair labor practice must be made based on the point in time when the decision has been made, this does not necessarily mean that the parties involved in this administrative suit are limited to the reasons for insubordination (and other issues) already presented

during the Labor Relations Commission proceedings. As such, reasons for insubordination that were not argued during the Labor Relations Commission proceedings may be argued during the administrative litigation process, as long as these new reasons did not occur after the National Labor Relations Commission issued its decision or directive.[106]

3) Partial Cancellation of Orders for Remedy

There is a Supreme Court case[107] that cancelled the entire order of remedy for an unfair labor practice because a portion of the many remedies ordered was determined to be illegal. The court is believed to have done this due to the policy consideration that it is difficult to cancel only a part of a network of remedial measures that are all interconnected, as this would make it hard for the Labor Relations Commission to devise an appropriate overall remedial package due to the fact that it may only modify the cancelled portions and unable to modify the non-cancelled portions. If no such risks exist, however, it would be possible to cancel a portion of an order of remedy issued by the Labor Relations Commission.

4) The Legal Effect of Violating Orders for Remedy

According to the Union Act, "When the (order of remedy to the employer regarding an unfair labor practice) is issued, the (employer must) comply with it."[108] "The effect of an order of remedy . . . made by the Labor Relations Commission shall not be suspended by an application for review to the National Labor Relations Commission or by the institution of an administrative suit."[109] However, while complying with such an order of remedy means that the employer

---

106 Supreme Court 92Nu13196 (1980. 8. 10.)
107 Supreme Court 92Nu13196 (1993. 4. 27.)
108 Union Act, Article 84(3)
109 Ibid., Article 86

assumes a duty of public law regarding his/her relationship with the employer, it does not mean that any relationship in private law is directly generated or modified between labor and management.[110] "When a dismissal decision or decision on review (regarding the order of remedy) is final and decisive, the parties concerned (including the employer) shall comply with it."[111] While an employer who violates an order of remedy that has not been finalized is not subject to criminal liability, an employer who violates an order of remedy that has been finalized "shall be punished by imprisonment for not more than three years or by a fine not exceeding thirty million won."[112]

5) Order to Perform

As can be seen above, while an order for remedy assumes a legal effect the moment it is issued, the employer may violate the order without assuming criminal liability until the order is subsequently finalized. In other words, its effectiveness is limited prior to the finalization. Because this finalization by the court system may be significantly delayed, the Union Act provides for the institution of "order to perform" to secure actual effectiveness of an order for remedy before the legal process has run its course. According to Article 85(5) of the Union Act, "When an employer has instituted an administrative suit, the court may, by its decision at the request of the National Labor Relations Commission, order the employer to perform all or part of the order of remedy made by the National Labor Relations Commission until the judgment of the court is rendered." In this way, the Union Act stipulates that an employer that does not follow the court's order would be punishable by fine.[113]

---

110 Supreme Court 95Da53102 (1996. 4. 23.)
111 Union Act, Article 85(4)
112 Ibid., Article 89(2)
113 Ibid., Article 95

Appendix

Appendix 1

LABOR STANDARDS ACT

[Enforcement Date 02. Aug, 2012.] [Act No.11270, 01. Feb, 2012., Partial Amendment]

Chapter I GENERAL PROVISIONS

Article 1 (Purpose)

The purpose of this Act is to establish the standards for terms and conditions of employment in conformity with the Constitution, thereby securing and improving the fundamental living standards of workers and achieving a well-balanced development of the national economy.

Article 2 (Definitions)

(1) The definitions of terms used in this Act shall be as follows:

1. The term "worker" means a person, regardless of being engaged in whatever occupation, who offers work to a business or workplace for the purpose of earning wages;
2. The term "employer" means a business owner, or a person responsible for the management of a business or a person who acts on behalf of a business owner with respect to matters relating to workers;
3. The term "work" means both mental work and physical work;
4. The term "labor contract" means a contract which is entered into in order that a worker offers work for which the employer pays its corresponding wages;
5. The term "wages" means wages, salary and any other kind of money or valuables, regardless of their titles, which the employer pays to a worker as remuneration for work;
6. The term "average wages" means the amount calculated by dividing

the total amount of wages paid to a relevant worker during three calendar months immediately before the day on which a cause for calculating his/her average wages occurred by the total number of calendar days during those three months. This shall apply mutatis mutandis to the employment of less than three months;

7. The term "contractual work hours" means work hours on which workers and their employer have made an agreement within the limit of work hours under Article 50 or the main sentence of Article 69 of this Act, or under Article 46 of the Occupational Safety and Health Act; and

8. The term "part-time worker" means a worker whose contractual work hours per week are shorter than those of a full-time worker engaged in the same kind of work at the workplace concerned.

(2) When the amount calculated pursuant to the provisions of paragraph (1) 6 is lower than that of the ordinary wages of the worker concerned, the amount of the ordinary wages shall be deemed his/her average wages.

Article 3 (Standards of Terms and Conditions of Employment)

The terms and conditions of employment prescribed by this Act shall be the minimum standards for employment, and the parties to labor relations shall not lower the terms and conditions of employment under the pretext of compliance with this Act.

Article 4 (Establishment of Terms and Conditions of Employment)

Terms and conditions of employment shall be freely established on the basis of equality, as agreed between workers and their employer.

Article 5 (Observance of Terms and Conditions of Employment)

Both workers and employers shall comply with collective agreements, rules of employment, and terms of labor contracts and be obliged to fulfill them in good faith.

Article 6 (Equal Treatment)

An employer shall neither discriminate against workers on the basis of gender, nor take discriminatory treatment in relation to terms and conditions of employment on the ground of nationality, religion, or social status.

Article 7 (Prohibition of Forced Labor)

An employer shall not force a worker to work against his/her own free will through the use of violence, intimidation, confinement, or any other means by which the mental or physical freedom of the worker might be unduly restricted.

Article 8 (Prohibition of Violence)

An employer shall not do violence to a worker for the occurrence of accidents or for any other reason.

Article 9 (Elimination of Intermediary Exploitation)

No person shall intervene in the employment of another person for making a profit or gain benefit as an intermediary, unless otherwise prescribed by any Act.

Article 10 (Guarantee of Exercise of Civil Rights)

An employer shall not reject a request from a worker to grant time necessary to exercise the franchise or other civil rights, or to perform official duties, during work hours: Provided, That the time requested may be changed, unless such change impedes the exercise of those rights or performance of those official duties.

Article 11 (Scope of Application)

(1) This Act shall apply to all businesses or workplaces in which not less than five workers are ordinarily employed: Provided, That this Act shall neither apply to any business or workplace in which only the employer's blood relatives living together are engaged, nor to servants hired for the employer's domestic works.

(2) With respect to a business or workplace in which not more than four workers are ordinarily employed, some provisions of this Act may apply as prescribed by Presidential Decree.

(3) When this Act applies, the method of calculation of the number of workers ordinarily employed shall be prescribed by Presidential Decree.
<Newly Inserted by Act No. 8960, Mar. 21, 2008>

Article 12 (Scope of Application)

This Act and Presidential Decree promulgated in accordance with this Act shall apply to the State, Special Metropolitan City, Metropolitan City, Do, Si, Gun, Gu, Eup, Myeon, Dong or other equivalents.

Article 13 (Obligations to Report and Appear)

An employer or a worker shall report on, or attend meetings relating to, necessary matters without delay, whenever the Minister of Employment and Labor, a Labor Relations Commission under the Labor Relations Commission Act (hereinafter referred to as "Labor Relations Commission"), or a labor inspector requests to do so with respect to the enforcement of this Act. <Amended by Act No. 10339, Jun. 4, 2010>

Article 14 (Publicity of Purport, etc. of Acts and Subordinate Statutes)

(1) An employer shall acquaint workers with the purport of this Act and Presidential Decree promulgated pursuant hereto, and the rules of employment, by posting or keeping them at a place readily accessible to workers at all times.

(2) An employer shall post or keep the provisions relating to dormitories of Presidential Decree as referred to in paragraph (1) and the dormitory rules as provided for in Article 99 (1), in the dormitories, to acquaint workers accommodated therein with them.

Chapter II LABOR CONTRACTS

Article 15 (Labor Contracts in Violation of This Act)

(1) A labor contract which has established terms and conditions of employment which do not meet the standards as prescribed by this Act shall be null and void to that extent.

(2) Those parts which are null and void in accordance with paragraph (1) shall be governed by the standards as prescribed by this Act.

Article 16 (Term of Contract)

The term of a labor contract shall not exceed one year, except in case where there is no fixed term or where there is an otherwise fixed term as necessary for the completion of a certain project.

<The amended provisions of this Article shall be effective until June 30, 2007 pursuant to Article 3 of the Addenda of Act No. 8372 of April 11, 2007>

Article 17 (Clear Statement of Terms and Conditions of Employment)

(1) An employer shall state the following matters clearly. The same shall also apply to the changes of the following matters after entering into a labor contract. <Amended by Act No. 10319, May 25, 2010>

1. Wages;
2. Contractual work hours;
3. Holidays under Article 55;
4. Annual paid leaves under Article 50;
5. Other terms and conditions prescribed by Presidential Decree.

(2) An employer shall deliver the written statement specifying constituent items, calculation methods and payment methods of wages with respect to the wages under paragraph (1) 1 and the matters prescribed in subparagraphs 2 through 4 to workers: Provided, That where the matters under the main sentence is modified due to reasons prescribed by Presidential Decree, such as changes, etc. of collective agreements or rules of employment, such matters shall be delivered to the relevant workers at their request. <Newly Inserted by Act No. 10319, May 25, 2010>

Article 18 (Terms and Conditions of Employment of Part-Time Workers)

(1) The terms and conditions of employment of part-time workers shall be determined on the basis of relative ratio computed in comparison to those work hours of full-time workers engaged in the same kind of work at the pertinent workplace.

(2) Criteria and other necessary matters to be considered for the determination of terms and conditions of employment under paragraph (1) shall be prescribed by Presidential Decree.

(3) Articles 55 and 60 shall not apply to workers whose contractual

working hours per week on an average of four weeks (in cases where their working periods are less than four weeks, such period of working) are less than 15 hours. <Amended by Act No. 8960, Mar. 21, 2008>

Article 19 (Breach of Terms and Conditions of Employment)

(1) When any of the terms and conditions of employment as expressly set forth pursuant to Article 17 is not observed, the worker concerned shall be entitled to claim damages on the ground of the breach of the terms and conditions of employment and may terminate the labor contract forthwith.

(2) When a worker intends to claim damages in accordance with paragraph (1), he/she may file a claim with the Labor Relations Commission, and, if the labor contract has been terminated, the employer concerned shall provide travel expenses for returning home to the worker who changes his/her residence for the purpose of taking up a new job.

Article 20 (Prohibition of Predetermination of Penalty for Breach-of Contract)

An employer shall not enter into any contract in which a penalty or indemnity for possible damages caused by the breach of a labor contract is predetermined.

Article 21 (Prohibition of Offsetting Wages with Advances)

An employer shall not offset wages with an advance or other credits given in advance on the condition that a worker offers work.

Article 22 (Prohibition of Compulsory Savings)

(1) An employer shall not enter into any contract incidental to a labor contract, which provides for compulsory savings or savings deposits management.

(2) Where an employer manages savings deposits entrusted by a worker, the following shall be observed:

1. Types and periods of deposits, and financial institutions shall be determined by the worker, and the deposit shall be made under the worker's name;

2. The employer shall immediately comply with the worker's request for the inspection or return of the certificate of deposit or other related documents.

Article 23 (Restriction on Dismissal, etc.)

(1) An employer shall not, without justifiable cause, dismiss, lay off, suspend, or transfer a worker, reduce his/her wages, or take other punitive measures (hereinafter referred to as "unfair dismissal, etc.") against him/her.

(2) An employer shall not dismiss a worker during a period of suspension of work for medical treatment of an occupational injury or disease and within 30 days immediately thereafter, and any woman before and after childbirth shall not be dismissed during a period of suspension of work as prescribed by this Act and for 30 days immediately thereafter: Provided, That this shall not apply where the employer has paid a lump sum compensation as provided for under Article 84 or where the employer may not continue to conduct his/her business.

Article 24 (Restrictions on Dismissal for Managerial Reasons)

(1) Where an employer intends to dismiss a worker for managerial reasons, there must be an urgent managerial necessity. In this case, it shall be deemed that there is an urgent managerial necessity for the transfer, merger, or acquisition of the business in order to prevent managerial deterioration.

(2) In case of paragraph (1), an employer shall make every effort to avoid dismissal and shall establish and follow reasonable and fair criteria for the selection of those persons subject to dismissal. In this case, there shall be no discrimination on the basis of gender.

(3) Where there is an organized labor union that represents more than half of the workers at the business or workplace, the employer shall inform at least 50 days before the intended date of dismissal and consult in good faith with the labor union (where there is no such organized labor union, this shall refer to a person who represents more than half of the workers; hereinafter referred to as "labor representative") regarding the methods for avoiding dismissals, the criteria for dismissal, etc. under paragraph (2).

(4) When an employer intends to dismiss personnel under paragraph (1) above the fixed limit prescribed by Presidential Decree, he/she shall report to the Minister of Employment and Labor as determined by Presidential Decree. <Amended by Act No. 10339, Jun. 4, 2010>
(5) When an employer dismisses workers in accordance with the conditions prescribed in paragraphs (1) through (3), it shall be deemed a dismissal with proper cause under Article 23 (1).

Article 25 (Preferential Reemployment, etc.)
(1) When an employer who has dismissed a worker under the provisions of Article 24 wishes to hire, within three years of the date of the dismissal, any worker who will perform the same duty as the dismissed worker did at the time of such dismissal, he/she shall preferentially rehire the worker dismissed under Article 24, if the worker so desires.
(2) The Government shall take necessary measures for the dismissed workers under the provisions of Article 24, such as stabilization of livelihood, reemployment and vocational training, on a priority basis.

Article 26 (Advance Notice of Dismissal)
When an employer intends to dismiss a worker (including dismissal for managerial reason), he/she shall give the worker a notice of dismissal at least 30 days in advance of such dismissal, and, if the employer fails to give such advance notice, he/she shall pay that worker ordinary wages for not less than 30 days: Provided, That this shall not apply where a natural disaster, calamity or other unavoidable circumstances prevent the continuance of the business or where the worker has caused a considerable hindrance to the business or inflicted any damage to the property on purpose and it falls under any cause determined by Ordinance of the Ministry of Employment and Labor. <Amended by Act No. 10339, Jun. 4, 2010>

Article 27 (Written Notice of Reasons, etc. for Dismissal)
(1) When an employer intends to dismiss a worker, he/she shall notify the worker in writing of the reasons for and time of the dismissal.
(2) The dismissal of a worker shall become effective only upon written notice pursuant to paragraph (1).

Article 28 (Request for Remedy from Unfair Dismissal, etc.)

(1) When a worker is subjected by the employer to any unfair dismissal, etc., he/she may request a remedy therefor from a labor relations commission.

(2) A request for remedy under paragraph (1) shall be made within three months from the date of the unfair dismissal, etc.

Article 29 (Investigation, etc.)

(1) The Labor Relations Commission shall, upon receipt of a request for remedy pursuant to Article 28, immediately conduct necessary investigation and examine the parties concerned.

(2) In making an examination pursuant to paragraph (1), the labor relations commission may, upon a request by the party concerned or ex officio, have a witness present himself/herself to make necessary inquiries.

(3) The Labor Relations Commission shall, in making an examination pursuant to paragraph (1), give the parties concerned sufficient opportunity to produce evidence and to cross-examine the witness.

(4) The detailed procedures for the investigation and examination by the Labor Relations Commission under paragraph (1) shall be as prescribed by the Central Labor Relations Commission under the Labor Relations Commission Act (hereinafter referred to as the "Central Labor Relations Commission").

Article 30 (Order, etc. for Remedy)

(1) If a dismissal, etc. is judged to be unfair in consequence of the examination under Article 29, the Labor Relations Commission shall issue to the employer an order for remedy, and, if the dismissal, etc. is judged not to be unfair, make a decision to reject the request for remedy.

(2) The judgment, order for remedy and decision of rejection under paragraph (1) shall be notified in writing to the employer and worker, respectively.

(3) In issuing an order for remedy (only referring to an order for remedy following dismissal) under paragraph (1), if a worker does not desire to be reinstated in his/her former office, the Labor Relations Commission may, instead of issuing an order to reinstate him/her in his/her former

office, order the employer to pay such worker the amount of money or other valuables equivalent to or higher than the amount of wages which he/she would have been paid if he/she had offered work during the period of dismissal.

Article 31 (Confirmation of Order, etc. for Remedy)

(1) An employer or worker who is dissatisfied with an order for remedy or a decision of rejection made by a local Labor Relations Commission under the Labor Relations Commission Act may apply for reexamination to the Central Labor Relations Commission within ten days from the date when he/she has received a written notice of such order or decision.

(2) With respect to a decision made by reexamination of the Central Labor Relations Commission's reexamination under paragraph (1), the employer or worker may institute a lawsuit pursuant to the Administrative Litigation Act within 15 days from the date when he/she is served with the written decision made by reexamination.

(3) If neither application for reexamination nor administrative litigation is filed within the period referred to in paragraph (1) or (2), the order for remedy, the decision of rejection or the decision made by reexamination shall become final and conclusive.

Article 32 (Effect of Order for Remedy, etc.)

The effect of the order for remedy, decision of rejection or decision made by reexamination of the Labor Relations Commission shall not be suspended even if an application for reexamination or administrative litigation is filed with or against the Central Labor Relations Commission pursuant to Article 31.

Article 33 (Compulsory Performance Money)

(1) The Labor Relations Commission shall impose compulsory performance money of not exceeding 20 million won on an employer who fails to comply with an order for remedy (including the decision made by reexamination in which an order for remedy is contained; hereafter in this Article, the same shall apply) within the specified deadline for executing the order after such order is issued.

(2) The Labor Relations Commission shall give the employer a prior

notice in writing to the effect that the compulsory performance money shall be imposed and collected, by not later than 30 days before it is imposed pursuant to paragraph (1).

(3) The imposition of compulsory performance money pursuant to paragraph (1) shall be made in writing specifying the amount of the compulsory performance money, grounds for imposition, payment deadline, receiving institutions, methods of raising an objection, agency to which an objection may be raised, etc.

(4) The kinds of violation subject to the imposition of the compulsory performance money under paragraph (1), amounts of imposition by the extent of violation, procedures for return of the compulsory performance money imposed and collected, and other necessary matters shall be prescribed by Presidential Decree.

(5) The Labor Relations Commission may impose and collect the compulsory performance money provided for in paragraph (1) repeatedly within the limit of two times per year from the date when it issues the first order for remedy, until the order for remedy is complied with by the person subject to the order for remedy. In this case, the compulsory performance money shall not be imposed and collected for more than two years.

(6) The Labor Relations Commission shall not impose an additional compulsory performance money if the order for remedy is complied with, but shall collect the compulsory performance money already imposed before the order for remedy is complied with.

(7) If the person liable to pay the compulsory performance money fails to pay it by the time limit for payment, the Labor Relations Commission may urge him/her to pay it within a fixed period, and, if the compulsory performance money provided for in paragraph (1) is not paid within the fixed period, collect it in the same manner as delinquent national taxes are collected.

(8) When the employer subject to the order for remedy fails to comply with it by the deadline for execution thereof, the worker concerned may inform the Labor Relations Commission thereof within 15 days after such deadline has expired.

Article 34 (Retirement Allowance System)

The retirement allowance system under which an employer pays retiring workers retirement allowances shall comply with the Guarantee of Workers' Retirement Benefits Act.

Article 35 (Exception of Advance Notice of Dismissal)

The provisions of Article 26 shall not apply to a worker falling under any one of the following subparagraphs:

1. A daily employed worker who has been employed for less than three consecutive months;
2. A worker who has been employed for a fixed period of not exceeding two months;
3. A worker who has been employed for less than six months as a monthly paid worker;
4. A worker who has been employed for any seasonal work for a fixed period of not exceeding six months;
5. A worker in a probationary period.

Article 36 (Settlement of Payments)

When a worker dies or retires, the employer shall pay the wages, compensations, and other money or valuables within 14 days after the cause for such payment occurred: Provided, That the period may, under special circumstances, be extended by mutual agreement between the parties concerned.

Article 37 (Interest for Delayed Payment of Wages)

(1) When an employer fails to pay the whole or a part of the wages and the allowances (referring to only lump-sum allowances) provided for in subparagraph 5 of Article 2 of the Guarantee of Workers' Retirement Benefits Act which he/she is liable to pay under Article 36 within 14 days after the cause for such payment occurred, he/she shall pay interest accrued for the delayed days from the following day to the day of the payment in accordance with the interest rate prescribed by Presidential Decree by taking account of the economic situations such as overdue interest rates etc. applied by the banks established under the Banking Act within the limit of 40/100 per year. <Amended by Act No. 10303, May

17, 2010>

(2) The provisions of paragraph (1) shall not apply where an employer delays the payment of wages for natural disasters, calamities, or other reasons prescribed by Presidential Decree, for the period in which the said reasons exist.

Article 38 (Preferential Payment for Claims for Wages)

(1) Wages, accident compensations, and other claims arising from labor relations shall be paid in preference to taxes, public charges, or other claims except for claims secured by pledges, mortgages or the security rights under the Act on Security over Movable Property, Claims, Etc. on the whole property of the employer concerned: Provided, That this shall not apply to taxes and public charges which take precedence over the said pledges, mortgages or the security rights under the Act on Security over Movable Property, Claims, Etc. <Amended by Act No. 10366, Jun. 10, 2010>

(2) Notwithstanding paragraph (1), any of the following claims shall be paid in preference to any claims secured by pledges, mortgages or the security rights under the Act on Security over Movable Property, Claims, Etc. on the whole property of the employer, taxes, public charges and other claims: <Amended by Act No. 10366, Jun. 10, 2010>

1. The wages of the last three months;
2. Accident compensations.

Article 39 (Certificate of Employment)

(1) Whenever an employer is requested by a worker to issue a certificate specifying the term of employment, kinds of work performed, positions taken, wages received, and other necessary information, he/she shall immediately prepare and deliver a certificate based on facts, even after the retirement of the worker.

(2) The certificate referred to in paragraph (1) shall contain nothing other than what has been requested by the worker.

Article 40 (Prohibition of Interference with Employment)

No person shall prepare and use secret signs or lists, or have communications, for the purpose of interfering with the employment of a worker.

Article 41 (Register of Workers)

(1) An employer shall prepare a register of workers by workplace, containing each worker's name, birth date, personal history, and other items as prescribed by Presidential Decree.

(2) When there is any change in the items stated on the register of workers pursuant to paragraph (1), correction shall be made without delay.

Article 42 (Preservation of Documents in Relation to Contract)

An employer shall, for three years, preserve a register of workers and other important documents related to labor contracts as prescribed by Presidential Decree.

Chapter III WAGES

Article 43 (Payment of Wages)

(1) Payment of wages shall be directly made in full to workers in currency: Provided, That if otherwise prescribed by Acts and subordinate statutes or by a collective agreement, wages may partially be deducted or may be paid by means other than currency.

(2) Wages shall be paid at least once per month on a fixed day: Provided, That this shall not apply to extraordinary wages, allowances, or other similar payments, or those wages prescribed by Presidential Decree.

Article 43-2 (Disclosure of Name of Business Owners who Delayed Payment of Wages)

(1) Where at least twice of conviction against the business owner (including the representative person in cases of a corporation; hereinafter referred to as "business owner in arrear") who fails to pay wages, compensations, allowances or any other money or valuable pursuant to Articles 36, 43, 56 (hereinafter referred to as "wages, etc.") are upheld due to his/her failure to pay the wages, etc. within three years prior to the date of disclosure of name and the total amount of money in arrear

with the wages, etc. during the period of one year prior to the date of the said disclosure is at least 30 million won, the Minister of Employment and Labor may disclose his/her personal information, etc.: Provided, That this shall not apply where the aforementioned disclosure of name is meaningless due to death or closure of business of the business owner in arrear or where other reasons as prescribed by Presidential Decree exist.

(2) Upon disclosing the name pursuant to paragraph (1), the Minister of Employment and Labor shall provide the business owner in arrear with an opportunity to explain and grant him/her a period of at least three months for such explanation.

(3) In order to review whether or not the personal information, etc. of the business owner in arrear should be disclosed pursuant to paragraph (1), the Committee for Review of Information on Overdue Wages (hereinafter referred to as the "Committee" in this Article) shall be established within the Ministry of Employment and Labor. In such cases, necessary matters, such as structure and operation, etc. of the Committee, shall be determined by Ordinance of the Ministry of Employment and Labor.

(4) Details, period and method, etc. of disclosure of name under paragraph (1) and other necessary matters for the disclosure shall be determined by Presidential Decree.

[This Article Newly Inserted by Act No. 11270, Feb. 1, 2012]

Article 43-3 (Provision of Data on Delayed Payment of Wages, etc.)

(1) Where the centralized credit information collection agency under Article 25 (2) 1 of the Use and Protection of Credit Information Act requests personal information and the data on the amount of arrears, etc. (hereinafter referred to as "data on delayed payment of wages, etc.") of the business owner in arrear against whom at least twice of conviction are upheld due to his/her failure to pay the wages, etc. within three years prior to the date of provision of the data on delayed wages. etc. and the total amount of money in arrear with the wages, etc. during the period of one year prior to the date of such provision of the data is at least 20 million won, the Minister of Employment and Labor may provide the aforementioned data if deemed necessary to prevent delay in payment of wages, etc.: Provided, That this shall not apply where the aforementioned provision of data is meaningless due to death of the business owner in

arrear or closure of the business or where other reasons prescribed by Presidential Decree exist.

(2) A person who has received the data on delayed payment of wages, etc. pursuant to paragraph (1) shall not use or disclose such data for the purposes other than those for determining credit rating and ability to deal on credit of the business owner in arrear.

(3) Procedure for and method, etc. of providing the data on delayed payment of wages, etc. pursuant to paragraph (1) and other necessary matters for such provision shall be determined by Presidential Decree.

[This Article Newly Inserted by Act No. 11270, Feb. 1, 2012]

Article 44 (Payment of Wages for Contract Work)

(1) When a project is executed based on several tiers of contracts and a subcontractor fails to pay wages to workers because of a cause attributable to the immediate upper tier contractor, the immediate upper tier contractor shall be liable for the wages jointly and severally with the subcontractor concerned: Provided, That where a cause attributable to the immediate upper tier contractor is caused by that of his/her upper tier contractor, such upper tier contractor shall also be jointly and severally responsible. <Amended by Act No. 11270, Feb. 1, 2012>

(2) The scope of the attributable causes referred to in paragraph (1) shall be determined by Presidential Decree. <Amended by Act No. 11270, Feb. 1, 2012>

Article 44-2 (Joint and Several Responsibility for Payment of Wages in Construction Business)

(1) When a construction project is being carried out through two or more tiers of contracts under subparagraph 11 of Article 2 of the Framework Act on the Construction Industry (hereinafter referred to as "contract for construction work"), if a subcontractor that is not a constructor under subparagraph 7 of Article 2 of the same Act fails to pay wages (limited to wages arising from the construction works concerned) to workers he/she has employed, an immediate upper tier contractor shall have joint and several responsibility for payment of wages to workers employed by the subcontractor. <Amended by Act No. 10719, May 24, 2011>

(2) When the immediate upper tier contractor under paragraph (1) is not

a constructor under subparagraph 7 of Article 2 of the Framework Act on the Construction Industry, the lowest tier contractor among the upper tier contractors who are constructors under the same subparagraph shall be deemed the immediate upper tier contractor. <Amended by Act No. 10719, May 24, 2011>
[This Article Newly Inserted by Act No. 8561, Jul. 27, 2007]

Article 44-3 (Special Case concerning Wages under Contract for Construction Works)

(1) In cases of falling under any of the following subparagraphs where a contract for construction work has been concluded, an immediate upper tier contractor shall directly pay the workers employed by a subcontractor an amount of money equivalent to wages (limited to wages arising from the construction works concerned) that the subcontractor shall pay at the request of workers employed by such subcontractor, within the obligation extent of the subcontract cost the immediate upper tier contractor shall pay to the subcontractor:

1. Where the immediate upper tier contractor has agreed with the subcontractor with respect to the intention that the immediate upper tier contractor may directly pay wages that the subcontractor is liable to pay to workers employed by the subcontractor and the method of and procedure for such payment;

2. Where there is an order for payment decided under subparagraph 3 of Article 56 of the Civil Execution Act, an execution deed proving that workers have a claim for wages to a subcontractor under subparagraph 4 of Article 56 of the same Act, a decision of advice of performance made pursuant to Article 5-7 of the Trial of Small Claims Act, or other title of debt corresponding to such items as above;

3. Where the subcontractor informs the immediate upper tier contractor that he/she has obligation to pay wages to his/her workers and the immediate upper tier contractor recognizes that the subcontractor has evident reasons to be unable to pay wages due to such reasons as bankruptcy, etc.

(2) When a contract for construction work has been subcontracted down two or more levels from a contractor (hereinafter referred to as "prime

contractor") of a person awarding a contract under subparagraph 10 of Article 2 of the Framework Act on the Construction Industry, where workers employed by a subcontractor (including any subcontractor who has been awarded a sub-subcontract by a subcontractor who has been awarded a contract; hereafter the same shall apply in this paragraph) have a title of debt under paragraph (1) 2 to such subcontractor, workers may request the prime contractor to pay directly an amount of money equivalent to wages (limited to wages arising from the construction works concerned) which a subcontractor is to pay. The prime contractor shall comply with such request to the extent of the amount of money for which workers are entitled to exercise the subrogation right of a creditor under Article 404 of the Civil Act to themselves. <Amended by Act No. 10719, May 24, 2011>

(3) Where an immediate upper tier contractor or a prime contractor has paid the amount of money equivalent to wages to workers employed by a subcontractor pursuant to paragraphs (1) and (2), it shall be deemed that the obligation to pay the subcontract price to a subcontractor has expired within such extent.

[This Article Newly Inserted by Act No. 8561, Jul. 27, 2007]

Article 45 (Emergency Payment)

An employer shall pay wages corresponding to work already offered even prior to the payday, if a worker requests the employer to do so in order to meet expenses for childbirth, diseases, disasters, or other cases of emergency as prescribed by Presidential Decree.

Article 46 (Shutdown Allowances)

(1) When a business shuts down due to a cause attributable to the employer, he/she shall pay the workers concerned allowances of not less than 70 percent of their average wages during the period of shutdown: Provided, That if the amount equivalent to the 70 percent of their average wages exceeds that of their ordinary wages, their ordinary wages may be paid as their shutdown allowances.

(2) Notwithstanding the provisions of paragraph (1), the employer who is unable to continue to carry on the business for any unavoidable reason may, with the approval of the Labor Relations Commission concerned,

pay the workers shutdown allowances lower than the standards as prescribed in paragraph (1).

Article 47 (Pieceworkers)

For those workers who are employed on a piece work or other similar basis, the employer shall guarantee certain amount of wages in proportion to their work hours.

Article 48 (Wage Ledger)

An employer shall prepare a wage ledger for each workplace and shall enter therein the matters which serve as a basis for determining wages and family allowances, the amount of wages, and other matters as prescribed by Presidential Decree, at each time of paying wages.

Article 49 (Prescription of Wages)

A claim for wages under this Act shall be extinguished by prescription, unless exercised within three years.

Chapter IV WORK HOURS AND RECESS

Article 50 (Work Hours)

(1) Work hours shall not exceed 40 hours a week, excluding hours of recess.

(2) Work hours shall not exceed eight hours a day, excluding hours of recess.

(3) Upon calculating the work hours under paragraphs (1) and (2), any waiting time, etc. spent by workers under the direction and supervision of their employers that is necessary for the relevant work shall be deemed work hours. <Newly Inserted by Act No. 11270, Feb. 1, 2012>

Article 51 (Flexible Work Hours System)

(1) An employer may, as prescribed by the rules of employment (including other rules equivalent thereto), extend work hours in excess of those as referred to in Article 50 (1) in a particular week, or extend work hours in excess of those as referred to in Article 50 (2) in a particular day, to the

extent that average work hours per week during a certain unit period of not more than two weeks do not exceed the work hours as referred to in Article 50 (1): Provided, That work hours in any particular week shall not exceed 48 hours.

(2) When an employer has determined matters falling under the following subparagraphs by a written agreement with the labor representative, he/she may extend work hours in excess of those as referred to in Article 50 (1) in a particular week, or may extend work hours in excess of those as referred to in Article 50 (2) in a particular day, to the extent that average work hours per week during a certain unit period of not more than three months do not exceed the work hours referred to in Article 50 (1): Provided, That work hours in any particular week or in any particular day shall not exceed 52 hours or 12 hours respectively:

1. Scope of workers subject to this paragraph;
2. Unit period (determined to be a certain period of not exceeding three months);
3. Working days in the unit period, and work hours for each working day;
4. Other matters prescribed by Presidential Decree.

(3) The provisions of paragraphs (1) and (2) shall not apply to workers who are not less than 15 years and less than 18 years of age and to pregnant female workers.

(4) When an employer needs to have a worker work in accordance with paragraphs (1) and (2), the employer shall take measures to supplement his/her wages so that the existing level of wages may not be lowered.

Article 52 (Selective Work Hours System)

When an employer has determined the matters falling under the following subparagraphs by a written agreement with the labor representative with regard to workers who are allowed to decide on their own beginning and finishing time of work pursuant to the rules of employment (including other rules equivalent thereto), he/she may extend weekly work hours beyond those referred to in Article 50 (1) and daily work hours beyond those referred to in Article 50 (2), to the extent that average work hours per week during the period of adjustment set within the limit of a month do not exceed the work hours referred to in Article 50 (1):

1. Scope of workers to whom the above provisions shall apply (excluding those workers at the age of not less than 15 and less than 18);
2. Adjustment period (determined to be a specified period of not exceeding one month);
3. Total work hours during the adjustment period;
4. Beginning and finishing time of work hours during which work must be provided, if so required;
5. Starting and ending time of work hours which workers are allowed to determine;
6. Other matters prescribed by Presidential Decree.

Article 53 (Restrictions on Extended Work)

(1) Where there exists an agreement between the parties, work hours referred to in Article 50 may be extended up to 12 hours per week.

(2) Where there exists an agreement between the parties, work hours referred to in Article 51 may be extended up to 12 hours per week, and work hours referred to in Article 52 may be extended up to 12 hours per week averaged during the adjustment period as referred to in subparagraph 2 of Article 52.

(3) Under special circumstances, an employer may extend work hours referred to in paragraphs (1) and (2) with the authorization of the Minister of Employment and Labor and the consent of the workers: Provided, That where a situation is urgent that the employer does not have enough time to obtain authorization of the Minister of Employment and Labor, he/she shall immediately obtain ex post facto approval of the Minister of Employment and Labor. <Amended by Act No. 10339, Jun. 4, 2010>

(4) Where the Minister of Employment and Labor deems that the extension of work hours referred to in paragraph (3) is not appropriate, he/she may order the employer to allow the workers recess hours or days off equivalent to the extended work hours. <Amended by Act No. 10339, Jun. 4, 2010>

Article 54 (Recess)

(1) An employer shall allow workers a recess of not less than thirty minutes if working for four hours or a recess of not less than one hour if working for eight hours, during work hours.

(2) Recess hours may be freely used by workers.

Article 55 (Holidays)

An employer shall allow workers at least one paid holiday per week on average.

Article 56 (Extended, Night or Holiday Work)

An employer shall, in addition to the ordinary wages, pay 50 percent or more thereof for extended work (work during the hours as extended pursuant to Articles 53 and 59 and the proviso of Article 69), night work (work between 10:00 p.m. and 6:00 a.m.), or holiday work.

Article 57 (Compensatory Leave System)

An employer may grant workers leaves in lieu of wage payments for extended work, night work, or holiday work pursuant to Article 56 according to a written agreement that is concluded between him/her and the labor representative.

Article 58 (Special Provisions for Calculation of Work Hours)

(1) When it is difficult to calculate work hours provided by a worker because he/she carries out his/her duty in whole or in part outside the workplace owing to a business trip or any other reason, it shall be deemed that he/she has worked for contractual working hours: Provided, That where it is ordinarily necessary for the worker to work in excess of contractual working hours in order to carry out the said duty, it shall be deemed that he/she has worked for the hours ordinarily required to carry out that duty.

(2) Notwithstanding the proviso of paragraph (1), in case where there exists a written agreement between an employer and the labor representative in regard to the work concerned, the hours as determined by such a written agreement shall be regarded as those ordinarily required to carry out the relevant duty.

(3) In case of works designated by Presidential Decree as those works which, in the light of their characteristics, require leaving the methods of performance to a worker' discretion, it shall be deemed that the works have been provided for such work hours as determined by a written agreement between the employer and the labor representative. In this case, such written agreement shall specify the matters falling under the following subparagraphs:

1. Work to be provided subject to such written agreement;
2. Statement that the employer would not give specific directions to the worker regarding how to perform the work, how to allocate work hours, etc.;
3. Statement that the calculation of work hours shall be governed by the written agreement concerned.

(4) Matters necessary for implementing paragraphs (1) and (3) shall be determined by Presidential Decree.

Article 59 (Special Provisions as to Work and Recess Hours)

An employer who runs a business which falls under any one of the following subparagraphs may, if any written agreement between him/her and the labor representative exists, have workers work in excess of 12 hours per week as referred to in Article 53 (1) or change recess hours as referred to in Article 54:

1. Transportation business, goods sales and storage business, finance and insurance business;
2. Movie production and entertainment business, communications business, educational study and research business, advertisement business;
3. Medical and sanitation business, hotel and restaurant business, incineration and cleaning business, barber and beauty parlor business;
4. Other businesses determined by Presidential Decree, which are necessary for the convenience of the public at large or in consideration of the characteristics of business.

Article 60 (Annual Paid Leave)

(1) Every employer shall grant any worker who has worked not less than

80 percent of one year a paid leave of 15 days. <Amended by Act No. 11270, Feb. 1, 2012>

(2) Every employer shall grant any worker who has continuously worked for less than one year or who has worked less than 80 percentage of one year one paid-leave day for each month during which he/she has continuously worked. <Amended by Act No. 11270, Feb. 1, 2012>

(3) Where an employer grants any worker a paid leave for the latter's first year of work, the former shall grant the latter a paid leave of 15 days, including the paid-leave referred to in paragraph (2), and, if the latter has already taken the paid-leave provided for in paragraph (2), deduct the number of days of such paid-leave from the said 15 days.

(4) Every employer shall grant any worker who has continuously worked for not less than three years paid-leave days that are calculated by adding one day for every two continuously working years not including the first one year to the 15 paid-leave days referred to in paragraph (1). In this case, the total number of paid-leave days, including the additional paid-leave days, shall not exceed 25 days.

(5) Every employer shall grant the paid leave referred to in paragraphs (1) through (4) at the time when a worker files a claim therefor and pay the worker an ordinary wage or an average wage during the period of paid leave as prescribed by the rules of employment, etc.: Provided, That in the event that granting the worker a paid leave at the time when such worker wants to take the paid leave greatly impedes the business operation, the relevant employer may change the time of the paid leave.

(6) In applying paragraphs (1) through (3), any of the following periods shall be deemed the period of attendance at work: <Amended by Act No. 11270, Feb. 1, 2012>

1. Period during which a worker takes time off due to any injury or sickness arising out of duty;
2. Period during which a woman in pregnancy takes time off due to the leave under the provisions of Article 74 (1) through (3).

(7) The paid leave referred to in paragraphs (1) through (4) shall, if it is not taken for one year, be terminated by time limitation: Provided, That the same shall not apply where the paid leave is not taken for reasons attributable to the employer.

Article 61 (Measures to Urge Workers to Take Annual Paid Leave)

Where any worker's paid leave is terminated by time limitation pursuant to the main sentence of Article 60 (7) after the worker fails to take his/her paid leave although the relevant employer has taken the measures falling under each of the following subparagraphs to urge workers to take their respective annual leave pursuant to Article 60 (1), (3) and (4), the relevant employer is not liable to indemnify the worker for his/her failure to take the paid leave and his/her failure to take the paid leave shall be deemed not to fall under the reasons attributable to the employer provided for in the proviso to Article 60 (7): <Amended by Act No. 11270, Feb. 1, 2012>

1. Any employer shall notify in writing every worker of the number of days of his/her paid leave that has not been taken and to urge every worker to notify the former of a period during which he/she intends to take his/her paid leave after deciding on such period within ten days as of six months before the period provided for in the main sentence of Article 60 (7) expires;

2. An employer shall notify in writing any worker who does not take his/her paid leave after setting a period during which the latter may take his/her paid leave by not later than two months before the period provided for in the main sentence of Article 60 (7) expires, in the event that the worker fails to notify the employer of a period during which the former intends to take, in whole or in part, his/her paid leave which has not been taken, within ten days from the date on which he/she is urged to take his/her paid leave, notwithstanding the urge referred to in subparagraph 1.

Article 62 (Substitution of Paid Leave)

An employer may, by a written agreement with the labor representative, get workers to take a paid leave on a particular working day in substitution of an annual paid leave provided for in Article 60.

Article 63 (Exclusion from Application)

The provisions pertaining to work hours, recess and holidays referred to in this Chapter and Chapter V shall not apply to a worker who falls under any one of the following subparagraphs: <Amended by Act No. 10339,

Jun. 4, 2010>

1. A worker engaged in cultivation or reclamation of land, seeding, cultivation or collection of plants, or other agricultural and forestry work;

2. A worker engaged in breeding of animals, collection or catching of marine animals and plants, cultivation of marine products, or other cattle breeding, sericulture and fishery business;

3. A worker engaged in surveillance or intermittent work, whose employer has obtained the approval of the Minister of Employment and Labor;

4. A worker engaged in such business as prescribed by Presidential Decree.

Chapter V WOMEN AND MINORS

Article 64 (Minimum Age and Employment Permit Certificate)

(1) A minor under the age of 15 (including any minor under the age of 18 who attends a middle school under the Elementary and Secondary Education Act) shall not be employed at any work: Provided, That this shall not apply to a person with an employment permit certificate issued by the Minister of Employment and Labor according to the standards prescribed by Presidential Decree. <Amended by Act No. 10339, Jun. 4, 2010>

(2) An employment permit certificate referred to in paragraph (1) may be issued only by designating the kind of work at the request of the relevant minor himself/herself, to the extent that the compulsory education is not impeded.

(3) If a person obtains the employment permit certificate provided for in the proviso to paragraph (1) in any false or other wrongful manner, the Minister of Employment and Labor shall revoke the permit. <Amended by Act No. 10339, Jun. 4, 2010>

Article 65 (Prohibition of Employment)

(1) An employer shall not employ women in pregnancy or women for whom one year has not passed after childbirth (hereinafter referred to as

the "pregnant women and nursing mothers") and those under the age of 18 in any work detrimental to morality or health or any dangerous work.

(2) An employer shall not employ women of 18 years or over who are not pregnant women and nursing mothers in any work harmful and dangerous to the function of pregnancy or delivery from among those detrimental or dangerous to health under paragraph (1).

(3) The prohibited kinds of work under paragraphs (1) and (2) shall be prescribed by Presidential Decree.

Article 66 (Minor Certificate)

For each minor worker under the age of 18, the employer shall keep at his/her workplace a certificate of family relationships records verifying the minor's age and a written consent of the person with parent authority or the guardian. <Amended by Act No. 8435, May 17, 2007>

Article 67 (Labor Contract)

(1) Neither a person with parent authority nor a guardian may enter into a labor contract on behalf of a minor.

(2) A person with parent authority or guardian of a minor, or the Minister of Employment and Labor may terminate a labor contract henceforward, if deemed disadvantageous to the minor. <Amended by Act No. 10339, Jun. 4, 2010>

(3) Where an employer enters into a labor contract with a person under 18 years of age, he/she shall deliver a document to such person, specifying the terms and conditions of employment under Article 17. <Newly Inserted by Act No. 8561, Jul. 27, 2007>

Article 68 (Claim for Wages)

A minor may claim his/her wages in his/her own right.

Article 69 (Work Hours)

Work hours of a person at the age of not less than 15 and less than 18 shall not exceed seven hours per day and 40 hours per week: Provided, That the work hours may be extended only for one more hour per day and six more hours per week by an agreement between the parties concerned.

Article 70 (Restrictions on Night Work and Holiday Work)

(1) Where an employer intends to have the women of 18 years or over work during the time from 10:00 p.m. to 6:00 a.m. and on holidays, he/she shall obtain the workers' consent.

(2) An employer shall not have pregnant women and nursing mothers and those under 18 years old work during the time from 10:00 p.m. to 6:00 a.m. and on holidays: Provided, That this shall not apply to any of the following cases where approval of the Minister of Employment and Labor is obtained: <Amended by Act No. 10339, Jun. 4, 2010>

  1. Where there exists a consent of those under 18 years old;
  2. Where there exists a consent of the women for whom one year has not passed after childbirth;
  3. Where a woman in pregnancy makes a clear request.

(3) Before obtaining the approval of the Minister of Employment and Labor in the case of paragraph (2), an employer shall make a faithful consultation with the labor representative of the relevant business or workplace on whether to execute it, its methods, etc., in order to protect the workers' health and maternity. <Amended by Act No. 10339, Jun. 4, 2010>

Article 71 (Overtime Work)

An employer shall be forbidden to have any women for whom one year has not passed after childbirth do overtime work exceeding two hours per day, six hours per week, or 150 hours per year, even if provided for in a collective agreement thereon.

Article 72 (Prohibition of Work Inside Pit)

An employer shall not have a woman or a minor under the age of 18 do any work inside a pit: Provided, That this shall not apply where it is temporarily required for carrying out the affairs as prescribed by Presidential Decree, such as health and medical treatment, the gathering and report of news, etc.

Article 73 (Monthly Physiologic Leave)

Every employer shall, when any female worker files a claim for a physiologic leave, grant her one day of physiologic leave per month.

Article 74 (Protection of Pregnant Women and Nursing Mothers)

(1) An employer shall grant a pregnant woman a 90-day maternity leave before and after childbirth. In such case, after the childbirth, 45 days or more of the leave period shall be allotted. <Amended by Act No. 11270, Feb. 1, 2012>

(2) Where a pregnant female worker requests the leave under paragraph (1) due to her experience of miscarriage or other reasons prescribed by Presidential Decree, an employer shall allow her to use the leave at multiple times any time before her childbirth. In such cases, the period of leave after the childbirth shall be at least 45 days consecutively. <Newly Inserted by Act No. 11270, Feb. 1, 2012>

(3) Where a pregnant woman has a miscarriage or a stillbirth, an employer shall, upon the relevant worker's request, grant her a miscarriage/stillbirth leave as prescribed by Presidential Decree: Provided, That the same shall not apply to an abortion carried out by an operation for an artificial abortion (excluding the cases under Article 14 (1) of the Mother and Child Health Act). <Amended by Act No. 11270, Feb. 1, 2012>

(4) The first 60 days in the period of leave under paragraphs (1) and (3) shall be stipendiary: Provided, That when the leave allowances before and after childbirth, etc. have been paid under Article 18 of the Equal Employment Opportunity and Work-Family Balance Assistance Act, the payment responsibility shall be exempted within the limit of the relevant amount. <Amended by Act No. 8781, Dec. 21, 2007; Act No. 11270, Feb. 1, 2012>

(5) The employer shall not have a female worker in pregnancy assigned to an overtime work, and, if there exists a request from the relevant worker, he/she shall transfer her to an easy type work. <Amended by Act No. 11270, Feb. 1, 2012>

(6) The business owner shall reinstate her to the same work or to the work for which wages of the same level as before leave are paid after the end of a maternity leave under paragraph (1). <Newly Inserted by Act No. 9038, Mar. 28, 2008; Act No. 11270, Feb. 1, 2012>

Article 74-2 (Permission, etc. for Time for Medical Examination of Unborn Child)

(1) Where a pregnant worker claims time necessary for a periodical medical examination of pregnant women under Article 10 of the Mother and Child Health Act, an employer shall grant permission for such time.

(2) The employer shall not cut wages of such worker by reason of time for medical examination under paragraph (1).

[This Article Newly Inserted by Act No. 8960, Mar. 21, 2008]

Article 75 (Nursing Hours)

An employer shall grant thirty-minute or longer paid nursing time twice a day to those female workers who have infants under the age of one, upon request.

Chapter VI SAFETY AND HEALTH

Article 76 (Safety and Health)

Safety and health of workers shall be subject to the conditions as prescribed by the Industrial Safety and Health Act.

Chapter VII APPRENTICESHIP

Article 77 (Protection of Apprentices)

An employer shall neither maltreat training workers, probational workers, or other workers, regardless of their titles, whose objective is to acquire technical skills, nor have them do his/her own domestic works or other works not related to the acquisition of technical skills.

Chapter VIII ACCIDENT COMPENSATION

Article 78 (Compensation for Medical Treatment)

(1) An employer shall provide necessary medical treatment at his/her expense or bear corresponding expenses for a worker who suffers from

an occupational injury or disease.

(2) The scope and period of a compensation for medical treatment of occupational diseases as referred to in paragraph (1) shall be prescribed by Presidential Decree. <Amended by Act No. 8960, Mar. 21, 2008>

Article 79 (Compensation for Suspension of Work)

(1) An employer shall pay a worker who is under medical treatment pursuant to Article 78 a compensation for suspension of work equivalent to 60 percent of his/her average wages during the period of his/her medical treatment. <Amended by Act NO. 8960, Mar. 21, 2008>

(2) Where, during the period of receiving a compensation for suspension of work under paragraph (1), a person who is to receive such compensation has received part of his/her wages, an employer shall pay the compensation for suspension of work equivalent to 60/100 of the difference between the paid amount and his/her average wages. <Newly Inserted by Act No. 8960, Mar. 21, 2008>

(3) Period of a compensation for suspension of work shall be prescribed by Presidential Decree. <Newly Inserted by Act No. 8960, Mar. 21, 2008>

Article 80 (Compensation for Disability)

(1) When a worker suffers from a physical disability remaining even after finishing treatment for an occupational injury or disease, the employer shall provide him/her, in accordance with the grade of disability, with a compensation for disability calculated by multiplying the average wages by the number of days as provided for in attached Table. <Amended by Act No. 8960, Mar. 21, 2008>

(2) In cases where a person who already has a physical disability suffers from more serious disability of the same part of body due to injury or disease, an amount of a compensation for such disability shall be the amount calculated by multiplying the number of days, which is the difference between the number of days of a compensation for disability falling under the previous grade of disability and the number of days of a compensation for disability falling under the grade of disability which has become more serious, by average wages at the time when a ground for claim for compensation arises. <Newly Inserted by Act No. 8960, Mar. 21, 2008>

(3) Criteria for determination of the grade of physical disability eligible for a compensation for disability and period of a compensation for disability shall be prescribed by Presidential Decree. <Newly Inserted by Act No. 8960, Mar. 21, 2008>

Article 81 (Exception to Compensation for Suspension of Work and Compensation for Disability)

If a worker suffers from an occupational injury or disease due to his/her own gross negligence and the employer obtains admission for said negligence from the Labor Relations Commission concerned, the employer shall not be required to provide a compensation for suspension of work or a compensation for disability.

Article 82 (Compensation for Survivors)

(1) An employer shall provide a compensation equivalent to the average wages of 1,000 days to surviving family members of a worker who has deceased during the performance of his/her duties immediately after the worker has deceased. <Amended by Act No. 8960, Mar. 21, 2008>

(2) The scope of surviving family under paragraph (1), order of a compensation for surviving family and order of a compensation for surviving family in case of death of a person determined to receive a compensation shall be prescribed by Presidential Decree. <Newly Inserted by Act No. 8960, Mar. 21, 2008>

Article 83 (Funeral Expenses)

When a worker has deceased during the performance of his/her duties or as a result thereof, the employer shall, immediately after the relevant worker has deceased, provide funeral expenses equivalent to the average wages of 90 days. <Amended by Act No. 8960, Mar. 21, 2008>

Article 84 (Lump Sum Compensation)

When a worker who receives a compensation in accordance with Article 78 does not completely recover from the occupational injury or disease even after two years have passed since the medical treatment began, the employer may be exempted from any further liability for compensation under this Act by providing a lump sum compensation in an amount equivalent to the average wages of 1,340 days.

Article 85 (Installment Compensation)

When an employer proves his/her ability to pay compensation and obtains the consent of the recipient concerned, he/she may pay any such compensation as referred to in Article 80, 82 or 84 in installments over one year.

Article 86 (Claim for Compensation)

A claim for compensation shall not be affected by the retirement of the worker concerned and may not be transferred or confiscated.

Article 87 (Relationships with other Damage Claims)

When a person eligible to receive compensation has received money or other valuables corresponding to an accident compensation as prescribed by this Act for the same cause in accordance with the Civil Act or any other Acts and subordinate statutes, the employer shall be exempted from the obligation of compensation to the extent of the said value received.

Article 88 (Review and Arbitration by Minister of Employment and Labor)

(1) When a person has an objection to the admission of occupational injury, disease or death, methods of medical treatment, determination of compensation amount, or any other matter pertaining to the implementation of compensation, he/she may request the Minister of Employment and Labor to review or arbitrate the case in question. <Amended by Act No. 10339, Jun. 4, 2010>

(2) When a request referred to in paragraph (1) is filed, the Minister of Employment and Labor shall review or arbitrate the case within one month. <Amended by Act No. 10339, Jun. 4, 2010>

(3) The Minister of Employment and Labor may review or arbitrate the case ex officio, if deemed necessary. <Amended by Act No. 10339, Jun. 4, 2010>

(4) The Minister of Employment and Labor may have a doctor diagnose or examine a worker, if deemed necessary for a review or arbitration. <Amended by Act No. 10339, Jun. 4, 2010>

(5) With regard to the interruption of prescription, the request for review or arbitration referred to in paragraph (1) and the commencement of the review or arbitration referred to in paragraph (2) shall be regarded as a claim by way of judicial proceedings.

Article 89 (Review and Arbitration by Labor Relations Commission)

(1) If a review or arbitration is not made by the Minister of Employment and Labor within the period specified under Article 88 (2) or if a person is dissatisfied with the result of a review or arbitration, the person may file a request for a review or arbitration with the Labor Relations Commission. <Amended by Act No. 10339, Jun. 4, 2010>

(2) When the request referred to in paragraph (1) is filed, the Labor Relations Commission shall review or arbitrate the case within one month.

Article 90 (Exceptional Cases related to Contract Work)

(1) If a project is executed based on several tiers of contracts, the prime contractor shall be regarded as an employer with regard to accident compensation.

(2) In cases of paragraph (1), if the prime contractor makes his/her subcontractor liable for compensation by a written agreement, the subcontractor shall be also regarded as an employer: Provided, That the prime contractor shall not have two or more subcontractors bear overlapping compensation with regard to the same project.

(3) In cases of paragraph (2), if the prime contractor has been requested to pay compensation, he/she may ask the requesting person to demand compensation first from the subcontractor who has agreed to be liable for such compensation: Provided, That this shall not apply where the said subcontractor is declared bankrupt or his/her whereabout is unknown.

Article 91 (Preservation of Documents)

An employer shall not abandon important documents related to accident compensation unless an accident compensation is finished or before a claim for accident compensation expires by prescription pursuant to Article 92. <Amended by Act No. 8960, Mar. 21, 2008>

Article 92 (Prescription)

A claim for accident compensation as referred to in this Act shall be extinguished by prescription, unless exercised within three years.

Chapter IX RULES OF EMPLOYMENT

Article 93 (Preparation and Reporting of Rules of Employment)

An employer who ordinarily employs ten or more workers shall prepare the rules of employment regarding the matters falling under each of the following subparagraphs and report such rules to the Minister of Employment and Labor. The same shall also apply where he/she amends such rules: <Amended by Act No. 9038, Mar. 28, 2008; Act No. 10339, Jun. 4, 2010; Act No. 11270, Feb. 1, 2012>

1. Matters pertaining to the beginning and ending time of work, recess hours, holidays, leaves, and shifts;
2. Matters pertaining to the determination, calculation and payment method of wages, the period for which wages are calculated, the period for paying wages, and pay raises;
3. Matters pertaining to the methods of calculation and payment of family allowances;
4. Matters pertaining to retirement;
5. Matters pertaining to retirement allowances under Article 4 of the Guarantee of Workers' Retirement Benefits Act, bonuses, and minimum wages;
6. Matters pertaining to the burden of workers' meal allowances, expenses of operational tools or necessities and so forth;
7. Matters pertaining to educational facilities for workers;
8. Matters pertaining to the protection of workers' maternity and work family balance assistance, such as leaves before and after childbirth and child-care leaves;
9. Matters pertaining to safety and health;
9-2. Matters pertaining to the improvement of environment of a place of work according to characteristics of workers, such as sex, ages or physical conditions, etc.;
10. Matters pertaining to assistance with respect to occupational and

non-occupational accidents;
11. Matters pertaining to award and punishment;
12. Other matters applicable to all workers within the business or workplace concerned.

Article 94 (Procedures for Preparation and Amendment of Rules)

(1) An employer shall, with regard to the preparation or alteration of the rules of employment, hear the opinion of a trade union if there is such a trade union composed of the majority of the workers in the business or workplace concerned, or otherwise hear the opinion of the majority of the said workers if there is no trade union composed of the majority of the workers: Provided, That in case of amending the rules of employment unfavorably to workers, the employer shall obtain their consent thereto.

(2) When an employer reports the rules of employment pursuant to Article 93, he/she shall attach a document containing the opinion as referred to in paragraph (1).

Article 95 (Restrictions on Punishment Regulations)

When a punitive wage cut for workers must be contained in the rules of employment, the amount of reduced wage for each infraction shall not exceed half of one day's average wages of the relevant worker and the total amount of reduction shall not exceed one-tenth of the total amount of wages at each time of wages payment.

Article 96 (Observance of Collective Agreement)

(1) Rules of employment shall not conflict with any Acts and subordinate statutes, or a collective agreement applicable to the business or workplace concerned.

(2) The Minister of Employment and Labor may give an order to modify any part of the rules of employment which conflict with any Acts and subordinate statutes or the collective agreement concerned. <Amended by Act No. 10339, Jun. 4, 2010>

Article 97 (Effect of Violation)

If a labor contract includes any term or condition of employment which fails to meet the standards of labor as provided for in the rules of employment, such part shall be null and void. In this case, the invalidated part shall be governed by the standards provided for in the rules of employment.

Chapter X DORMITORY

Article 98 (Protection of Dormitory Life)
(1) An employer shall not interfere in the private life of workers lodging in a dormitory annexed to the business or workplace concerned.
(2) An employer shall not interfere with the election of staff required for the autonomous management of a dormitory.

Article 99 (Preparation of and Amendment to Dormitory Rules)
(1) An employer who intends to lodge his/her workers in a dormitory annexed to a business or workplace shall prepare dormitory rules concerning the following matters:
1. Matters pertaining to getting-up and sleeping, and going-out and overnight stay;
2. Matters pertaining to events;
3. Matters pertaining to meals;
4. Matters pertaining to safety and health;
5. Matters pertaining to the maintenance of buildings and facilities;
6. Other matters to be applicable to all workers lodging in the dormitory.
(2) The employer shall obtain the consent of the representative of the majority of the lodging workers with regard to the preparation of or amendment to the dormitory rules stipulated in paragraph (1).
(3) Both the employer and the workers lodging in the dormitory concerned shall comply with the dormitory rules.

Article 100 (Facilities, and Safety Sanitation)
(1) An employer shall take measures necessary for the maintenance of health, public morals and lives of the workers lodging in a dormitory annexed to the business or workplace.
(2) The standards for the measures to be taken pursuant to paragraph (1) shall be prescribed by Presidential Decree.

Chapter XI LABOR INSPECTOR, ETC.

Article 101 (Supervisory Authorities)

(1) The Ministry of Employment and Labor and its subordinate offices shall have a labor inspector to ensure the standards of the terms and conditions of employment. <Amended by Act No. 10339, Jun. 4, 2010>

(2) Matters concerning the qualifications, appointment and dismissal, and placement of the labor inspector shall be prescribed by Presidential Decree.

Article 102 (Authority of Labor Inspector)

(1) A labor inspector shall have the authority to inspect workplaces, dormitories and other annexed buildings, to request the submission of books and documents, and to interrogate both an employer and workers.

(2) A labor inspector who is a medical doctor or a medical doctor entrusted by a labor inspector shall have the authority to conduct a medical examination of workers who seem vulnerable to those diseases due to which their continuous employment should be precluded.

(3) In cases of paragraphs (1) and (2), the labor inspector or a medical doctor entrusted by the labor inspector shall show his/her identification card and a letter of order of inspection or medical examination issued by the Minister of Employment and Labor. <Amended by Act No. 10339, Jun. 4, 2010>

(4) In a letter of order of inspection or medical examination order referred to in paragraph (3), its date and time, place, and scope shall be specified clearly.

(5) A labor inspector shall have the authority to perform the official duties of judiciary police officials as prescribed by the Act on the Persons Performing the Duties of Judicial Police Officials and the Scope of Their Duties with regard to the crimes in violation of this Act or other labor-related Acts and subordinate statutes.

Article 103 (Duty of Labor Inspector)

A labor inspector shall keep strictly any confidential matter which comes to his/her knowledge in the course of performing his/her duties. This shall also apply after he/she is retired from the position.

Article 104 (Reporting to Supervisory Authorities)

(1) Workers may report to the Minister of Employment and Labor or a labor inspector if any violation of the provisions of this Act or Presidential Decree under this Act occurs at a business or workplace. <Amended by Act No. 10339, Jun. 4, 2010>

(2) An employer shall not dismiss or treat a worker unfairly for making such a report referred to in paragraph (1).

Article 105 (Restrictions on Person Having Authority to Exercise Judicial Police Power)

Only public prosecutors and labor inspectors shall have the authority to conduct inspections, request the submission of documents, and interrogate employers and workers as prescribed by this Act and any other labor-related Acts and subordinate statutes: Provided, That this shall not apply to the investigation of crimes related to the duties of labor inspectors.

Article 106 (Delegation of Authority)

The authority of the Minister of Employment and Labor under this Act may be delegated partly to the head of a regional employment and labor authority as prescribed by Presidential Decree. <Amended by Act No. 10339, Jun. 4, 2010>

Chapter XII PENAL PROVISIONS

Article 107 (Penal Provisions)

A person who has violated Article 7, 8, 9, 23 (2) or 40 shall be punished by imprisonment for not more than five years or by a fine of not exceeding 30 million won.

Article 108 (Penal Provisions)

A labor inspector who has connived, on purpose, at violations of this Act shall be punished by imprisonment for not more than three years or by a suspension of qualification for not more than five years.

Article 109 (Penal Provisions)

(1) A person who has violated Articles 36, 43, 44, 44-2, 46, 56, 65 or 72 shall be punished by imprisonment for not more than three years or by a fine of not exceeding 20 million won. <Amended by Act No. 8561, Jul. 27, 2007>

(2) A public prosecution against a person who has violated Articles 36, 43, 44, 44-2, 46 or 56 may not be raised against the clearly expressed will of the person who has suffered the loss concerned. <Amended by Act No. 8561, Jul. 27, 2007>

Article 110 (Penal Provisions)

Any of the following persons shall be punished by imprisonment for not more than two years or by a fine of not exceeding ten million won: <Amended by Act No. 9699, May 21, 2009; Act No. 11270, Feb. 1, 2012>

1. A person who violates Articles 10, 22 (1), 26, 50, 53 (1), (2) and (3) (main sentence), 54, 55, 60 (1), (2), (4) and (5), 64 (1), 69, 70 (1) and (2), 71, 74 (1) through (5), 75, 78 through 80, 82, 83 and 104 (2);
2. A person who fails to comply with the order issued under Article 53 (4).

Article 111 (Penal Provisions)

A person who has failed to comply with an order for remedy or the decision made by reexamination in which an order for remedy is contained, which became final and conclusive pursuant to Article 31 (3) or through an administrative litigation, shall be punished by imprisonment for not more than one year or by a fine of not exceeding ten million won.

Article 112 (Accusation)

(1) The offense provided for in Article 111 may be prosecuted only upon the Labor Relations Commission's accusation.

(2) A public prosecutor may notify the Labor Relations Commission of a violation which falls under the offense under paragraph (1) to ask it for the accusation thereof.

Article 113 (Penal Provisions)

A person who has violated Article 45 shall be punished by a fine of not exceeding ten million won.

Article 114 (Penal Provisions)

Any of the following persons shall be punished by a fine of not exceeding five million won: <Amended by Act No. 8561, Jul. 27, 2007; Act No. 9038, Mar. 28, 2008; Act No. 9699, May 21, 2009; Act No. 11270, Feb. 1, 2012>

1. A person who violates Articles 6, 16, 17, 20, 21, 22 (2), 47, 53 (3) (proviso), 67 (1) and (3), 70 (3), 73, 74 (6), 77, 94, 95, 100 and 103;
2. A person who violates an order referred to in Article 96 (2).

Article 115 (Joint Penal Provisions)

If an agent, employee or any other worker of a business owner commits an offense prescribed in Articles 107, 109 through 111, 113 or 114 with respect to the affairs of the workers of the relevant business, not only the offender shall be punished, but the business owner shall also be punished by a fine pursuant to the relevant Article: Provided, That this shall not apply where such business owner has not been negligent in giving due attention and supervision concerning the relevant duties to prevent such violation.

[This Article Wholly Amended by Act No. 9699, May 21, 2009]

Article 116 (Fines for Negligence)

(1) A person who falls under any one of the following subparagraphs shall be punished by a fine for negligence of not exceeding five million won: <Amended by Act No. 9699, May 21, 2009; Act No. 10339, Jun. 4, 2010>

1. A person who has failed to make a report, or who has made a fraudulent report, or who has failed to attend, at the request of the Minister of Employment and Labor, the Labor Relations Commission, or a labor inspector as referred to in Article 13;
2. A person who has violated Articles 14, 39, 41, 42, 48, 66, 91, 93, 98 (2) or 99;
3. A person who has refused, obstructed or evaded inspections or

examinations by a labor inspector under Article 102 or a medical doctor entrusted by him/her, who has not made any of the required statements to his/her official questioning or has made false statements, or who has failed to present books or documents or has presented false books or documents.

(2) The fine for negligence under paragraph (1) shall be imposed and collected by the Minister of Employment and Labor as prescribed by Presidential Decree. <Amended by Act No. 10339, Jun. 4, 2010>

(3) through (5) Deleted. <by Act No. 9699, May 21, 2009>

ADDENDA <No. 8435, 17. May, 2007>
Article 1 (Enforcement Date)
This Act shall enter into force on January 1, 2008. (Proviso Omitted.)
Articles 2 through 9 Omitted.

ADDENDA <No. 8781, 21. Dec, 2007>
Article 1 (Enforcement Date)
This Act shall enter into force six months after the date of its promulgation. (Proviso Omitted.)
Articles 2 and 3 Omitted.

ADDENDA <No. 8960, 21. Mar, 2008>
Article 1 (Enforcement Date)
This Act shall enter into force on July 1, 2008.
Article 2 (Applicability concerning Permission for Time for Medical Examination of Unborn Child)
The amended provisions of Article 74-2 shall apply starting from a pregnant worker at the time when this Act enters into force.
Article 3 (Applicability concerning Special Case in Application of Working Hours)
The amended provisions of Article 5-2 of the Addenda of the wholly amended Labor Standards Act (Act No. 8372) shall apply starting from workers employed for the related work a contract of which is entered into on or after the date when this Act enters into force.

ADDENDA <No. 9038, 28. Mar, 2008>

(1) (Enforcement Date) This Act shall enter into force on the date of its promulgation: Provided, That the amended provisions of subparagraphs 8 and 9-2 of Article 93 shall enter into force three months after the date of its promulgation.

(2) (Applicability concerning Return to Work, etc. after Completion of Leave before and after Childbirth) The amended provisions of Article 74 (5) shall apply starting from a worker on her leave before and after childbirth at the time when this Act enters into force.

(3) (Applicability concerning Preparation and Report of Employment Regulations) The amended provisions of subparagraphs 8 and 9-2 of Article 93 shall apply beginning with the first employment regulations reported after this Act enters into force.

ADDENDA <No. 9699, 21. May, 2009>

(1) (Enforcement Date) This Act shall enter into force three months after the date of its promulgation.

(2) (Transitional Measures) The application of penal provisions of acts committed before this Act enters into force shall be subject to the previous provisions.

ADDENDA <No. 10303, 17. May, 2010>

Article 1 (Enforcement Date)

This Act shall enter into force six months after the date of its promulgation. (Proviso Omitted.)

Articles 2 through 10 Omitted.

ADDENDA <No. 10319, 25. May, 2010>

This Act shall enter into force on January 1, 2012.

ADDENDA <No. 10719, 24. May, 2011>

Article 1 (Enforcement Date)

This Act shall enter into force six months after the date of its promulgation. (Proviso Omitted.)

Articles 2 through 6 Omitted.

ADDENDA <No. 11270, 01. Feb, 2012>

Article 1 (Enforcement Date)

This Act shall enter into force six months after the date of its promulgation.

Article 2 (Applicability to Disclosure of Name of Business Owners who Delayed Payment of Wages)

Among the amended provisions of Article 43-2 (1), where the total amount of money in arrear with the wages, etc. during the period of one year prior to the date of disclosure of name is at least 30 million won, the amended provisions shall apply starting from the first case where the Minister of Employment and Labor confirms a delayed payment of wages, etc. after this Act enters into force.

Article 3 (Applicability to Provision of Data on Delayed Payment of Wages, etc.)

Among the amended provisions of Article 43-3 (1), where the total amount of money in arrear with the wages, etc. during the period of one year prior to the date of provision of data on delayed wages, etc. is at least 20 million won, the amended provisions shall apply starting from the first case where the Minister of Employment and Labor confirms a delayed payment of wages, etc. after this Act enters into force.

Article 4 (Applicability to Annual Paid Leave)

The amended provisions of Article 60 (2) shall apply starting from the worker whose period of working becomes one year for the first time after this Act enters into force and his/her period of reporting to work during the said one year is less than 80 percentage.

Article 5 (Applicability to Use of Maternity Leave at Multiple Times)

The amended provisions of Article 74 (2) shall apply starting from the worker who applies, for the first time after this Act enters into force, for use of the maternity leave at multiple times.

Article 6 (Applicability to Miscarriage/Stillbirth Leave)

The amended provisions of Article 74 (3) shall apply starting from the first worker who applies for a miscarriage/stillbirth leave after this Act enters into force.

Article 7 Omitted.

Appendix 2

TRADE UNION AND LABOR RELATIONS ADJUSTMENT ACT

[Enforcement Date 05. Jul, 2010.] [Act No.10339, 04. Jun, 2010., Other Laws and Regulations Amended]

Chapter I GENERAL PROVISIONS

Article 1 (Purpose)

The purpose of this Act is to maintain and improve the working conditions and the economic and social status of workers by securing the their rights of association, right to collective bargaining and collective action pursuant to the Constitution, and to contribute to the maintenance of industrial peace and to the development of the national economy by preventing and resolving labor disputes through the fair adjustment of labor relations.

Article 2 (Definition)

The definitions of terms used in this Act shall be as follows:

1. The term "worker" means a person who lives on wages, salary, or other equivalent form of income earned in pursuit of any type of job;
2. The term "employer" means a business owner, a person who is responsible for the management of a business, or a person who works on behalf of a business owner with respect to matters relating to workers in the business;
3. The term "employers' association" means an organization of employers which has an authority to adjust and control its constituent members with regard to labor relations.
4. The term "trade union" means an organization or associated organization of workers that is formed in a voluntary and collective

manner upon the workers initiative for the purpose of maintaining and improving working conditions, or improving the economic and social status of workers. In cases where an organization falls into one of the following categories, it shall not be regarded as a trade union.

(a) Where an employer or other persons who always act in their employers interests are allowed to join the organization;

(b) In cases where most of the organization's expenditure is supported by the employer;

(c) Where activities of an organization are only aimed at mutual benefits, moral culture and other welfare undertakings;

(d) Where those who are not workers are allowed to join the organization, Provided that a dismissed person shall not be regarded as a person who is not a worker, until a review decision is made by the National Labor Relations Commission when he/she has made an application to the Labor Relations Commission for remedies for unfair labor practices; or

(e) Where the aims of the organization are mainly directed at political movements.

5. The term "labor disputes" means any controversy or difference arising from disagreement between the trade union and employer or employers association (hereinafter referred to as "parties to labor relations") concerning the terms and conditions of employment such as wages, working hours, welfare, dismissal, other treatment, etc. In this case, "disagreement" is referred to as situations in which no agreement is likely to be reached by the parties even though they attempted to reach an agreement.

6. The term "industrial action" means actions or counter-actions which obstruct the normal operation of a business, such as strikes, sabotage, lock-outs, or other activities through which the parties to labor relations intend to achieve their claims.

Article 3 (Restriction on Claims for Damages)

No employer shall claim damages against a trade union or workers in cases where he/she has suffered damage because of collective bargaining or industrial action under this Act.

Article 4 (Justifiable Activities)

The provisions of Article 20 of the Criminal Code shall apply to justifiable activities undertaken to achieve the purpose of Article 1 as collective bargaining, industrial action, or other activities by trade unions. However no act of violence or destruction shall be construed as justifiable for any ground.

Chapter II TRADE UNION

Section 1 GENERAL PROVISIONS

Article 5 (Organization and Membership of Trade Union)

Workers are free to organize a trade union or to join it, except for public servants or teachers who are subject to other enactments.

Article 6 (Incorporation of Trade Union)

(1) A trade union shall be incorporated according to its by-laws.

(2) The trade union shall be registered in accordance with the Presidential Decree.

(3) Except for such matters prescribed by this Act, the provisions on incorporated associations in the Civil Code shall apply to incorporated trade union.

Article 7 (Requirements for the Protection of Trade Union)

(1) Trade unions that are not established by this Act shall not make an application for the adjustment of labor disputes and for the remedy for unfair labor practices to the Labor Relations Commission.

(2) The provisions of paragraph (1) shall not be construed as excluding the protection of workers under subparagraphs 1, 2 and 5 of Article 81.

(3) Except specifically for the trade unions formed under this Act, the term "trade union" shall not be used.

Article 8 (Exemption from Taxation)

No tax shall be imposed on a trade union except for its affiliated businesses.

Article 9 (Prohibition of Discrimination)

No member of a trade union shall be discriminated on the basis of race, religion, sex, age, physical condition, employment type, political party, or social status. <Amended by Act No. 9041, Mar. 28, 2008>

Section 2 ESTABLISHMENT OF TRADE UNION

Article 10 (Report on Establishment of Trade Union)

(1) A person who intends to establish a trade union shall prepare a report containing the matters described in the following subparagraphs, attached in the by-laws under Article 11 and submit it to the Minister of Employment and Labor, in case the trade union takes the form of an associated organization or is a unit trade union spanning not less than two (2) areas out of the Special City, Metropolitan Cities, Provinces and Special Self-Governing Provinces; to the Special City Mayor, relevant Metropolitan City Mayors and relevant Provincial Governors, in case the trade union is a unit trade union spanning not less than two (2) areas out of Sis/Guns/Gus (referring to autonomous Gus); and to relevant Governors of Special Self-Governing Provinces and relevant heads of Sis/Guns/Gus (referring to heads of autonomous Gus; hereinafter the same shall apply in Article 12 (1) in the case of other trade unions: <Amended by Act No. 10339, Jun. 4, 2010>

1. Name of a trade union;
2. Location of main office/headquarters;
3. Number of union members;
4. Name and address of union officials;
5. Name of an associated organization to which it belongs; and
6. In the case of a trade union in the form of an associated organization, the name of its constituent organizations, the number of union members, the address of its main office/headquarters, and the name and address of its officials.

(2) A trade union which is an associated organization under paragraph (1) means an industrial-level organization comprised of unit trade unions in the same industry and a federation comprised of industry-level organizations or nationwide industry-level unit trade unions.

Article 11 (By-laws)

In order to guarantee an autonomous and democratic operation of the organization, a trade union shall include the following matters in its by-laws: <Amended by Act No. 8158, Dec. 30, 2006>

1. Name of a trade union;
2. Purposes and activities;
3. Location of main office/headquarters;
4. Matters relevant to union members (matters regarding its constituent organizations in the case of a trade union in the form of an associated organization);
5. Name of the associated organization which it belongs to;
6. Matters on a council of delegates if such council of delegates has been established;
7. Matters concerning meetings;
8. Matters concerning representatives or officials;
9. Matters concerning accounting, including union dues and others;
10. Matters concerning modification of the union by-laws;
11. Matters concerning dissolution;
12. Matters concerning disclosure of the result of a vote on industrial action, the keeping of and access to voters' roll and ballot papers;
13. Matters concerning impeachment of representatives or officials for violation of the by-laws;
14. Matters concerning election of officials and delegates; and
15. Matters concerning discipline and control.

Article 12 (Issuance of Certificate)

(1) The Minister of Employment and Labor, the Mayor of Special City, the Mayor of Metropolitan City, the Provincial Governor, the Governor of Special Self-Governing Province or the head of Si/Gun/Gu (hereinafter referred to as the "Administrative Authorities") shall issue a certificate within three (3) days after receiving the report on establishment under paragraph (1) of Article 10, except for cases prescribed in paragraphs (2) and (3). <Amended by Act No. 10339, Jun. 4, 2010>

(2) In cases where a report or by-laws need to be supplemented because of any omission or other reasons, the Administrative Authorities shall order a supplement thereof by designating a submission period up to

twenty (20) days in accordance with the Presidential Decree. Upon receiving the supplemented report or by-laws, a certificate shall be issued within three (3) days.

(3) The Administrative Authorities shall return a report filed in cases where a trade union which made the report falls under the purview of any of the following subparagraphs: 1.Where a trade union falls within the categories of each subparagraph 4 of Article 2; 2.Where supplements are not submitted within the designated period in spite of the order to supplement a report in accordance with the provisions of paragraph (2).

(4) With regard to the issuance of a certificate, a trade union shall be construed to have been established at the time when a report of the establishment of the trade union was submitted.

Article 13 (Notification of Modifications)

(1) A trade union shall notify modifications of the contents of its by-laws to the Administrative Authorities within thirty (30) days from the date when changes occur in any of the following subparagraphs from among those which have been filed in accordance with paragraph (1) of Article 10: <Amended by Act No. 6456, Mar. 28, 2001>

1. Name;
2. Location of its main office/headquarters;
3. Name of representatives; or
4. Name of the associated organization which it belongs to.

(2) A trade union shall give notice as to matters which fall within each of the following subparagraphs to the Administrative Authorities by January 31st of each year. However, this shall not apply to matters whose modification was notified in the previous year pursuant to the paragraph (1). <Newly inserted by Act No. 6456, Mar. 28, 2001>

1. Where by-laws were modified in the previous year, and the contents thereof is the modification of the by-laws;
2. Where union officials were replaced in the previous year, and the name of union officials are replaced; or
3. The number of union members as of December 31st of the previous year (the number of union members in each constituent organization in the case of a trade union in the form of an associated organization).

Section 3 MANAGEMENT OF TRADE UNION

Article 14 (Documents to be kept)

(1) A trade union shall prepare each of the following documents within thirty (30) days from the date of its establishment, and keep them at its headquarters or main offices:

1. Registration of union members (the name of its constituent organizations in the case of a trade union in the form of an associated organization);
2. Union by-laws;
3. Name and address of union officials;
4. Minutes of meetings; and
5. Financial records and documents.

(2) Documents stipulated in subparagraphs 4 and 5 of paragraph (1) shall be retained for three (3) years.

Article 15 (Holding of General Meetings)

(1) A trade union shall hold one (1) or more general meetings each year.

(2) The representative of a trade union shall preside over general meetings.

Article 16 (Matters for Resolution by General Meeting)

(1) Each of the following matters shall require a resolution adopted by the general meeting:

1. Adoption and modification of by-laws;
2. Election or discharge of union officials;
3. Collective bargaining;
4. Budgets or closing;
5. Establishment, operation, and disposition of funds;
6. Establishment, admission, and withdrawal of an associated organization;
7. Merger, division, or dissolution;
8. Structural changes; or
9. Other important matters.

(2) The general meeting shall adopt resolutions by the affirmative vote of a majority of the members present at a general meeting where a majority

of all members are present. However, resolutions as to the introduction and modification of by-laws, discharge of union officials, and merger, division, dissolution and structural change of a trade union shall be passed by the affirmative vote of at least two-thirds (2/3) of members present at a general meeting where a majority of all members are present.
(3) Notwithstanding the provisions of paragraph (2), in an election in which no candidate running for union official has obtained the consent of a majority of the union members present, a run-off election may be held and a candidate with the highest votes may be elected in accordance with the by-laws.
(4) Resolutions as to the adoption and modification of union by-laws, or the election and discharge of union officials shall be made by a direct, secret, and unsigned ballot.

Article 17 (Council of Delegates)
(1) A trade union may, in accordance with its by-laws, establish a council of delegates in lieu of a general meeting of its union members.
(2) Delegates shall be elected in a direct, secret, and unsigned ballot by union members.
(3) The tenure of delegates shall be specified in the by-laws of the trade union and shall not exceed three (3) years.
(4) Where a council of delegates has been established, the provisions on general meetings shall be applied mutatis mutandis.

Article 18 (Calling of Extraordinary General Meetings)
(1) The representative of a trade union may, if he/she deems necessary, convene an extraordinary general meeting of the union members or a meeting of the council of delegates.
(2) The representative of a trade union shall convene, without delay, an extraordinary general meeting of the union members or a meeting of the council of delegates in cases where more than one-third (1/3) of the union members or of the delegates bring matters that need to be referred to the union members or the delegates and require a call of meetings (in the case of a trade union in the form of an associated organization, more than one-third (1/3) of its constituent organizations).
(3) Where a representative of a trade union deliberately neglects or

avoids the convening of a general meeting provided in paragraph (2), and a request is made by one-third (1/3) or more of the union members to appoint a convener of the meeting, the Administrative Authorities shall ask the Labor Relations Commission to adopt a resolution within fifteen (15) days, and upon the adoption of such resolution, immediately appoint a person to convene the meeting.

(4) Where there is no person entitled to convene a general meeting of the union members or of the council of delegates, if at least one-third (1/3) of the union members or delegates bring matters that need to be referred to the union members or to the delegates, and submit a request to appoint a person to convene the meeting, the Administrative Authorities shall appoint a person within fifteen (15) days of such request.

Article 19 (Procedure of Calling a Meeting)

At least seven (7) days before a general meeting of the trade union members or of the council of delegates, a public notice of matters to be discussed shall be made and the meeting shall be convened according to the method prescribed in the bylaws.

Article 20 (Special Provision as to Voting Rights)

In cases where a trade union is to make resolve matters regarding a particular union member, that union member shall have no right to partake in the vote.

Article 21 (Correction of By-laws, Resolution and Measures)

(1) The Administrative Authorities may, with the resolution of the Labor Relations Commission, order the correction of the union by-laws when it conflicts with the Labor-related Laws.

(2) The Administrative Authorities may, with the resolution of the Labor Relations Commission, order the correction of resolutions or measures made by a trade union, when it is in conflict with the Labor-related Laws and union by-laws. An order for the correction of by-laws shall be made only by the application of the interested party.

(3) In the case of orders for correction under paragraph (1) or (2), a trade union shall implement such orders within thirty (30) days, except that the period may be extended for a reasonable cause.

Article 22 (Rights and Duties of Union Members)

Every union member has equal rights and duties to participate in all affairs of the trade union. However, a trade union may restrict, under union by-laws, the rights of those members who do not pay union dues.

Article 23 (Election of Union Officials)

(1) Union officials shall be elected from among the union members.

(2) The tenure of union officials shall be determined by the union by-laws, and shall not exceed three (3) years.

Article 24 (Full-time Official of Trade Union)

(1) A worker may perform duties only for a trade union, without providing the services specified in his/her employment contract, if it is stipulated in the collective bargaining agreement or with the employer's consent.

(2) A person who is engaged in duties only for a trade union in accordance with paragraph (1) (hereinafter referred to as "full-time official") shall not be remunerated in any way by the employer for the duration of his/her tenure.

(3) An employer shall not restrict legitimate union activities of a full-time union official. <Amended by Act No. 9930, Jan. 1, 2010>

(4) Notwithstanding paragraph (2), a worker may take time off from work to carry out the functions prescribed by this Act or other applicable acts, including consulting and bargaining with the employer, handling of grievance and occupational safety activities, and the functions of maintaining and managing the trade union for the sound development of industrial relations without any loss of wages as long as he/she does not exceed the maximum time-off limit (hereinafter referred to as "the maximum time-off limit") set in consideration of the number of union members, in each business or workplace in accordance with Article 24-2, if it is stipulated in the collective agreement or consented by the employer. <Amended by Act No. 9930, Jan. 1, 2010>

(5) A trade union shall not demand the payment of wages in violation of paragraphs (2) and (4) and take industrial action to achieve such a goal. <Amended by Act No. 9930, Jan. 1, 2010>

Article 24-2 (Time-off System Deliberation Committee)

(1) In order to set the maximum time-off limit, the Time-off System Deliberation Committee (hereinafter referred to as "the Committee" in this Article) shall be set up by the Ministry of Employment and Labor. <Amended by Act No. 10339, Jun. 4, 2010>

(2) The maximum time-off limit shall be announced by the Minister of Employment and Labor according to the results of deliberation and decision by the Committee, and may be decided anew every three (3) years after a re-deliberation on whether it is adequate or not. <Amended by Act No. 10339, Jun. 4, 2010>

(3) The Committee shall be composed of five (5) members recommended by labor circles, five (5) members recommended by business circles, and five (5) public interest members recommended by the government.

(4) The chairperson shall be elected by the Committee from among the public interest members.

(5) Decisions of the Committee shall require the attendance of a majority of all members and the approval of a majority of the members present.

(6) Necessary matters concerning the qualifications and appointment of members, the operation of the Committee, etc., shall be prescribed by the Presidential Decree.

[This Article Newly Inserted by Act No. 9930, Jan. 1, 2010]

Article 25 (Auditing of Account Records)

(1) The representative of a trade union shall have an auditor conduct, at least once every six (6) months, an audit of all of financial resources of a trade union, purposes of the financial resources, names of major contributors and current financial and accounting status, and shall disclose the results of the audit to all the union members.

(2) The auditor of a trade union may, if necessary, conduct an audit of the trade union, and disclose the results of the audit.

Article 26 (Disclosure of Status of Operation)

The representative of a trade union shall notify union members of the financial closing and the status of operation each fiscal year, and have them available for inspection when union members so request.

Article 27 (Presentation of Materials)
A trade union shall report the outcome of the financial closing and the status of its operation upon request of the Administrative Authorities.

Section 4 DISSOLUTION OF TRADE UNION

Article 28 (Cause for Dissolution)
(1) A trade union shall be dissolved if it falls within the purview of any of the following subparagraphs:
1. Occurrence of causes for dissolution as prescribed by its by-laws;
2. Dissolution due to merger or division;
3. Dissolution by a resolution adopted by a general meeting or by a meeting of the council of delegates; or
4. Dissolution by the Administrative Authorities with the resolution of the Labor Relations Commission when the trade union has no officials and has not carried out any activity for more than one (1) year.

(2) If a trade union is dissolved on the grounds specified in subparagraphs 1 to 3 of paragraph (1), the representative of the trade union shall report it to the Administrative Authorities within fifteen (15) days of the date of the dissolution.

Chapter III COLLECTIVE BARGAINING AND COLLECTIVE AGREEMENTS

Article 29 (Authority of Bargaining and Making Agreements)
(1) The representative of a trade union has the authority to bargain with employers or employers association, and to make collective agreements for the trade union and union members.

(2) The bargaining representative trade union (hereinafter referred to as "the bargaining representative union") determined pursuant to Article 29-2 shall have the authority to conduct bargaining and conclude a collective agreement with the employer on behalf of all trade unions or its members demanding bargaining. <Amended by Act No. 9930, Jan. 1, 2010>

(3) Any person who has been authorized by a trade union or by an employer or an employers' association to bargain and to make a collective agreement may exercise his/her power within the scope of the authority which the trade union, or employer or employers' association has granted. <Amended by Act No. 9930, Jan. 1, 2010>

(4) In cases where a trade union, or an employer or an employers' association delegates the authority to conduct bargaining or to conclude a collective agreement in accordance with paragraph (3), it shall notify the other party. <Amended by Act No. 9930, Jan. 1, 2010>

Article 29-2 (Procedure for Determining the Bargaining Representative Union)

(1) If there are two (2) trade unions or more which are established or joined by workers in a business or workplace regardless of the type of organization, the trade unions shall determine the bargaining representative union (including the bargaining representative body composed of members of two (2) different trade unions or more; hereinafter the same shall apply) and then demand bargaining. Provided, that this shall not apply where the employer consents not to undergo the procedure for determining the bargaining representative union channel prescribed in this Article within the period during which the bargaining representative union can be determined autonomously.

(2) All trade unions participating in the procedure for determining the bargaining representative union shall autonomously determine the bargaining representative union within the period prescribed by the Presidential Decree.

(3) Where the bargaining representative union is undetermined within the period referred to in paragraph (2) and the consent of the employer as referred to in paragraph (1) is not obtained from the employer, the trade union (including the case where two (2) trade unions or more, between them, have a majority of the members of all trade unions participating in the procedure for determining the bargaining representative union by delegating authority, uniting themselves together, etc.) composed of a majority of the members of all trade unions participating in the procedure for determining the bargaining representative union shall become the bargaining representative union.

(4) Where all trade unions participating in the procedure for determining the bargaining representative union, fails to determine such pursuant to paragraphs (2) and (3), shall jointly organize a bargaining representative team (hereinafter referred to as "the joint bargaining representative team") and then conduct bargaining with the employer. In this case, a trade union eligible to participate in the joint bargaining representative team shall be the one whose members make up not less than 10/100 (tenth of a hundred) of the members of all trade unions participating in the procedure for determining the bargaining representative union.

(5) If no agreement is reached on the organization of the joint bargaining representative team, the Labor Relations Commission may decide in consideration of the proportions of union members at the request of the concerned trade union.

(6) Where an objection is raised to the demand for bargaining, the number of union members, etc., in relation to the determination of the bargaining representative union pursuant to paragraphs (1) through (4), the Labor Relations Commission may decide on such objection at the request of the trade union under the conditions prescribed by the Presidential Decree.

(7) Article 69 and Article 70 (2) shall apply mutatis mutandis to the procedure for appeal against a decision made by the Labor Relations Commission pursuant to paragraphs (5) and (6) and to the effect of such decision.

(8) Necessary matters concerning the procedure for determining the bargaining representative union, including the method by which a trade union demands and participates in bargaining and the standards for calculating the number of union members to determine the bargaining representative union, the prevention of an increase in bargaining costs, and so on shall be prescribed by the Presidential Decree.

[This Article Newly Inserted by Act No. 9930, Jan. 1, 2010]

Article 29-3 (Decision on Bargaining Unit)

(1) The unit (hereinafter referred to as "the bargaining unit") at which the bargaining representative union shall be determined pursuant to Article 29-2 shall be a business or workplace.

(2) Notwithstanding paragraph (1), if it is deemed necessary to divide

the bargaining unit given the considerable disparity in working conditions, employment status, bargaining practices, etc., in a business or workplace, the Labor Relations Commission may decide to divide the bargaining unit at the request of either or both of the parties to the labor relationship.

(3) Article 69 and Article 70 (2) shall apply mutatis mutandis to the procedure for appeal against a decision made by the Labor Relations Commission pursuant to paragraph (2) and the effect of such a decision.

(4) Necessary matters concerning requests to divide the bargaining unit, the standards and procedure for decision-making by the Labor Relations Commission and other related matters shall be prescribed by the Presidential Decree.

[This Article Newly Inserted by Act No. 9930, Jan. 1, 2010]

Article 29-4 (Duty of Fair Representation)

(1) The bargaining representative union and employer shall not discriminate against trade unions participating in the procedure for determining the bargaining representative union or their members without any reasonable grounds.

(2) If the bargaining representative union and employer engage in discrimination in violation of paragraph (1), the trade union may request the Labor Relations Commission to redress such discrimination within three (3) months from the date the act was committed (referring to the date of the signing of the collective agreement, in case all or part of the collective agreement violates paragraph (1)) in accordance with the method and procedure prescribed by the Presidential Decree.

(3) With regard to the request referred to in paragraph (2), if the Labor Relations Commission recognizes that there has been discrimination without any reasonable grounds, it shall issue an order necessary for redressing such discrimination.

(4) Article 85 and Article 86 shall apply mutatis mutandis to the procedure for appeal against an order or decision rendered by the Labor Relations Commission pursuant to paragraph (3), and so on.

[This Article Newly Inserted by Act No. 9930, Jan. 1, 2010]

Article 29-5 (Other Matters Relating to the Determination of the Bargaining Representative Union)

If the bargaining representative union exists, the "trade union" in subparagraph 5 of Article 2, Article 29 (3) and (4), Article 30, Article 37 (2), Article 38 (3), Article 42-6 (1), Article 44 (2), Article 46 (1), Article 55 (3), Article 72 (3) and subparagraph 3 of Article 81 shall be deemed as the "bargaining representative union."

[This Article Newly Inserted by Act No. 9930, Jan. 1, 2010]

Article 30 (Principle of Bargaining)

(1) A trade union and an employer or an employers' association shall bargain with each other in good faith and sincerity and make a collective agreement, and shall not abuse their authority.

(2) A trade union and an employer or an employers' association shall not refuse or delay, without just causes, bargaining or concluding collective agreements.

Article 31 (Drawing up of Collective Agreements)

(1) Collective agreements shall be in writing, and both parties concerned shall sign or affix their seals thereto. <Amended by Act No. 8158, Dec. 30, 2006>

(2) The parties to collective agreements shall report the conclusion of the collective agreements to the Administrative Authorities within fifteen (15) days of the date of conclusion.

(3) If any provision of a collective agreement is determined to be unlawful, the Administrative Authorities may, with the resolution of the Labor Relations Commission, order the amendment of said collective agreement.

Article 32 (Valid Term of Collective Agreement)

(1) No collective agreement shall have a valid term exceeding two (2) years.

(2) In cases where a collective agreement does not specify a valid term nor has a valid term exceeding the period stipulated in paragraph (1), the valid term shall be deemed to be for two (2) years.

(3) Unless otherwise provided in a separate agreement, if no new

collective agreement is concluded by the expiry date of the existing agreement even though the parties have continuously engaged in collective bargaining before and after the expiry date, the existing collective agreement shall remain effective for up to three (3) months after its expiry date. If no conclusion is made on a new collective agreement after the expiration of the extended effective term, the existing agreement shall be applicable only if the existing agreement specifically provides that it shall remain in effect until a new collective agreement is concluded, provided, however, that any party concerned may terminate the collective agreement by giving notice to the other party six (6) months in advance. <Amended by Act No. 5511, Feb. 20, 1998>

Article 33 (Validity of Terms and Conditions)

(1) Part of the rules of employment or contract of employment which violates the standards concerning working conditions and other treatment of workers specified in collective agreement shall be null and void.

(2) Matters which are not stipulated by a contract of employment, and what has been invalidated by paragraph (1), shall be governed by the terms and conditions of collective agreement.

Article 34 (Interpretation of Collective Agreement)

(1) In cases where the parties do not reach an agreement on interpretation or implementation of the collective agreement, one or both of the parties to the collective agreement may ask the Labor Relations Commission for its opinion about the disputed interpretation or implementation.

(2) The Labor Relations Commission shall give its clear view on the requested matter under paragraph (1) within thirty (30) days from receipt of such request.

(3) The opinion of the Labor Relations Commission regarding the interpretation or implementation rendered under paragraph (2) shall have the same effect as that of an arbitrated judgment.

Article 35 (General Binding Force)

Where a collective agreement applies to at least half of the ordinary number of workers performing the same kind of job and employed in a single business or a workplace, it shall also apply to other workers performing the same kind of job and employed in the same business or workplace.

Article 36 (Geographical Binding Force)

(1) Where more than two-thirds (2/3) of the workers performing the same kind of job and employed in the same area are subject to the application of one collective agreement, the Administrative Authorities may, with the resolution of the Labor Relations Commission, and upon the request of one or both parties to the collective agreement or by its own authority, make a decision that such collective agreement shall apply to other workers performing the same kind of job and employed in the same area, as well as to their employers.

(2) The Administrative Authorities shall notify, without delay, the decision made under paragraph (1).

Chapter IV INDUSTRIAL ACTION

Article 37 (Basic Principles of Industrial Action)

(1) No industrial action, in its purposes, methods, and processes, shall violate legislations and public order.

(2) Union members shall not take part in any industrial action which is not led by a trade union.

Article 38 (Guidance and Responsibility of Trade Union)

(1) No industrial action shall be conducted by way of obstructing or interrupting entry to the premises, or the work itself or other normal services by individuals who are not related to the dispute or would want to provide work; no violence or threat shall be used to induce workers and individuals into participating in industrial action.

(2) During a period of industrial action, work to prevent damage to operational equipments or to prevent impairment or deterioration of raw materials or manufactured goods, shall be performed normally.

(3) A trade union shall have the responsibility to direct, manage, and

supervise industrial action in compliance with the related laws.

Article 39 (Restriction on Detention of Workers)

Except when caught in the act of committing a crime, no worker shall be detained for violation of this Act during a period of industrial action.

Article 40 <Deleted, Dec. 30, 2006> <Effective Jul. 1, 2007>

Article 41 (Restriction on and Prohibition of Industrial Action)

(1) No industrial action by a trade union shall be conducted unless a majority of its union members have decided in favor of taking industrial action by a direct, secret, and unsigned ballot. If the bargaining representative union has been determined, no industrial action shall be taken unless a majority of the members of all the trade unions (limited to union members belonging to the business or workplace concerned) involved in the process have decided in favor of taking industrial action by a direct, secret and unsigned ballot. <Amended by Act No. 9930, Jan. 1, 2010>

(2) No industrial action shall be taken by workers who are engaged in major defense businesses subject to the Defense Business Act, and by those who are involved in electricity, water or in the production of defense goods. The scope of workers who are engaged in a business which produces mainly defense goods shall be determined by the Presidential Decree. <Amended by Act No. 7845, Jan. 2, 2006>

Article 42 (Prohibition of Acts of Violence)

(1) No industrial action shall take the form of violence or destruction, or occupation of facilities related to production or other important businesses or such equivalent facilities as determined by the Presidential Decree.

(2) No industrial action shall be conducted to stop, close, or interrupt the normal maintenance and operation of security facilities of a workplace.

(3) If the Administrative Authorities determines that any industrial action falls under the purview of paragraph (2), it shall serve notice that such action must cease and desist, upon the resolution of the Labor Relations Commission. If, however, there is not enough time to seek

such resolution, it may service notice to immediately cease and desist without waiting for the resolution of the Labor Relations Commission. <Amended by Act No. 8158, Dec. 30, 2006>

(4) In the case of the proviso of paragraph (3), the Administrative Authorities shall immediately obtain approval from the Labor Relations Commission, ex post facto. If the Administrative Authorities fail to obtain such approval, the notice to cease and desist shall lose its effect at that moment. <Amended by Act No. 8158, Dec. 30, 2006>

Article 42-2 (Restrictions on Industrial Action in Minimum Services to Be Maintained)

(1) The term "minimum services to be maintained" in this Act refers to those services among essential public services prescribed in Article 71 (2), which, if suspended or discontinued, could remarkably endanger the lives, health, physical safety or daily life of the public and are prescribed by the Presidential Decree.

(2) No act of stopping, discontinuing or obstructing the proper maintenance and operation of the minimum services to be maintained shall be carried out as legitimate industrial action. <Newly inserted by Act No. 8158, Dec. 30, 2006>

Article 42-3 (Agreement on Minimum Services to Be Maintained)

The parties in labor relations shall conclude an agreement (hereinafter referred to as the "agreement on minimum services to be maintained") in writing that stipulates the levels of minimum services to be maintained and provided, the specific work designated as minimum services, the necessary number of workers, etc., in order to ensure the proper maintenance and operation of the minimum services during a period of industrial action. In this case, both parties shall sign or seal the agreement on minimum services to be maintained. <Newly inserted by Act No. 8158, Dec. 30, 2006>

Article 42-4 (Decision on Maintenance and Levels of Operation of Minimum Services to Be Maintained)

(1) If an agreement on minimum services to be maintained is not concluded, both or either of the parties in labor relations shall make an

application for the Labor Relations Commission to decide the levels of minimum services to be maintained and operated, the specific work designated as minimum services, the necessary number of workers, etc.

(2) The Labor Relations Commission, receiving the application under paragraph (1), may decide the levels of minimum services to be maintained and operated, the specific work designated as minimum services, the necessary number of workers, etc., taking into account the characteristics, contents, etc., of the minimum services according to business or workplace.

(3) The Special Mediation Committee under Article 72 shall take charge of implementing the decision made by the Labor Relations Commission pursuant to paragraph (2).

(4) If there is a difference of opinion between the parties concerned over interpretation or implementation of the decision made by the Labor Relations Commission pursuant to paragraph 2, the parties shall follow the interpretation of the Special Mediation Committee. In this case, the interpretation of the Special Mediation Committee shall have the same effect as the decision made by the Labor Relations Commission pursuant to paragraph 2.

(5) With regard to the procedure to raise an objection to the decision of the Labor Relations Commission under paragraph (2) and the effect of the decision, the provisions of Articles 69 and 70 (2) shall apply mutatis mutandis thereto. <Newly inserted by Act No. 8158, Dec. 31, 2006>

Article 42-5 (Industrial Action by a Decision of the Labor Relations Commission)

If the Labor Relations Commission makes a decision pursuant to Article 42-4 (2) and industrial action is done in accordance with that decision, the industrial action shall be deemed to have been done while duly maintaining and operating the minimum services to be maintained. <Newly inserted by Act No. 8158, Dec. 31, 2006>

Article 42-6 (Designation of Workers For Minimum Services to Be Maintained)

(1) If an agreement on minimum services to be maintained is in place or a decision is made by the Labor Relations Commission pursuant to

Article 42-4 (2), the trade union shall notify the employer of its members, among those engaged in minimum services, who will work during a period of industrial action, and the employer shall designate workers accordingly and notify the trade union and the designated workers of this fact. However, in case the trade union fails to make such notification prior to the commencement of the industrial action, the employer shall designate workers who will work to provide minimum services to be maintained and shall notify the trade union and the workers of the same. <Newly inserted by Act No. 8158, Dec. 31, 2006>

(2) In making a notification and designation pursuant to paragraph (1), the trade union and employer, if there are two (2) trade unions or more which are composed of workers engaged in minimum services to be maintained, shall give consideration to the proportion of members of each trade union, who are engaged in such minimum services. <Newly Inserted by Act No. 9930, Jan. 1, 2006>

Article 43 (Restriction on Hiring by Employer)

(1) No employer shall hire persons who are not related to their business operations, or use replacements during a period of industrial action so as to continue work which has been stopped by an industrial action.

(2) No employer shall, during a period of industrial action, contract or subcontract out work which has been suspended because of the industrial action concerned.

(3) The provisions of paragraphs (1) and (2) shall not apply to the employer of essential public services who hires persons unrelated to the business concerned or use replacements, or contract or subcontract out the work only during a period of industrial action. <Newly inserted by Act No. 8158, Dec. 31, 2006>

(4) In the case of paragraph (3), an employer may hire or use replacements or contract or subcontract out the work as long as the proportion of the replacement workers do not exceed 50/100 of strike participants of the business or workplace concerned. In this case, the method to compute the number of strike participants, shall be prescribed in the Presidential Decree. <Newly inserted by Act No. 8158, Dec. 30, 2006>

Article 44 (Prohibition of Demands for Wage Payment during Industrial Action)

(1) Employers shall have no obligation to pay wages during a period of industrial action to workers who did not provide labor because of their participation in industrial action.

(2) No trade unions shall commit industrial action with the intention of demanding wage payment during the period of industrial action.

Article 45 (Mediation before Industrial Action)

(1) Upon the occurrence of a labor dispute, one of the parties in the labor relations shall notify the other in writing.

(2) No industrial action shall be taken without first undergoing mediation procedures (excluding mediation procedures that come after the decision to end the mediation is made pursuant to Article 61-2) under the provisions of Sections Two to Four of Chapter V. This paragraph shall not apply when mediation procedures do not finish within the period prescribed in Article 54, or when the arbitration ruling is not made within the period prescribed in Article 63. <Amended by Act No. 8158, Dec. 30, 2006>

Article 46 (Requirements for Lock-out of Workplace)

(1) An employer may execute a lock-out of the workplace only after its trade union commences industrial action.

(2) In the case of a lock-out under paragraph (1), an employer shall report it in advance to the Administrative Authorities and the Labor Relations Commission.

Chapter V MEDIATION OF LABOR DISPUTES

Section 1 GENERAL PROVISIONS

Article 47 (Efforts for Voluntary Adjustment)

No provisions of this Act shall be construed to prevent parties to labor relations from taking part in deciding labor related matters including, but not limited to, working conditions, or from making every effort to resolve disputes or differences arising from labor relations, through labor-management consultation or by collective bargaining.

Article 48 (Obligation of the Parties)

The parties to labor relations shall stipulate in their collective agreement the procedures and methods for labor-management consultation or other collective bargaining means to maintain the reasonable labor relations, and shall make every effort to resolve labor disputes by themselves when such disputes arise.

Article 49 (Obligation of the Government)

The Government and local self-governing bodies, when the parties are unable to reach an agreement on their labor relations, shall make every effort to prevent industrial actions from taking place and to resolve labor disputes rapidly and fairly by helping the relevant parties to industrial relations settle differences on their own.

Article 50 (Expedient Proceedings)

The parties to labor relations, the Labor Relations Commission and other relevant institutions shall make best efforts to provide expeditious means for the settlement when the labor disputes need to be mediated pursuant to this Act.

Article 51 (Priority Given to Public Services)

Labor disputes related to the Government, local self- governing bodies, state or public corporations, defense industries, and public services shall be given priority and dealt with expeditiously.

Article 52 (Private Mediation or Arbitration)

(1) The provisions of Sections 2 and 3 shall not be construed to prevent the parties to labor relations from settling labor disputes through other means of mediation or arbitration (hereinafter referred to as "private mediation") pursuant to mutual agreements or collective agreements. <Amended by Act No. 8158, Dec. 30, 2006>

(2) When the parties to labor relations have agreed to resolve labor disputes pursuant to paragraph (1), they shall notify the Labor Relations

Commission.

(3) When labor disputes are to be resolved in accordance with paragraph (1), each of the following subparagraphs shall apply:

1. With respect to resolutions by means of mediation, the provisions of Articles 45 (2) and 54 shall apply. In this case, a period of mediation shall begin with the date of the commencement of such mediation; or

2. With respect to resolutions by means of arbitration, the provisions of Article 63 shall apply. In this case, a prohibition period of industrial actions shall begin with the date of commencement of the arbitration.

(4) An agreement made by means of mediation or arbitration under paragraph (1) shall have the same effect as that of a collective agreement.

(5) Persons who conduct private mediation, shall be those who meet the qualification requirements described in each item of Article 8 (2) 2 of the Labor Relations Commission Act. In this case, the person who conducts private mediation, may receive service fees, allowances and travel expenses from the parties concerned. <Newly inserted by Act No. 8158, Dec. 30, 2006>

Section 2 MEDIATION

Article 53 (Commencement of Mediation)

(1) The Labor Relations Commission shall conduct the proceedings of mediation, without any delay, when one of the parties to labor relations submits a request for mediation to the Labor Relations Commission. The parties concerned shall undertake the proceedings of mediation in good faith.

(2) The Labor Relations Commission may assist the parties concerned to settle their dispute autonomously and efficiently by, among other things, arranging negotiation prior to the request for mediation made pursuant to paragraph (1). <Newly inserted by Act No. 8158, Dec. 31, 2006>

Article 54 (Period of Mediation)

(1) Mediation shall be completed within ten (10) days in the case of general businesses, and fifteen (15) days in the case of public services, after the request is made for mediation pursuant to Article 53.

(2) The parties concerned may agree to extend a period of mediation

under paragraph (1) up to ten (10) days in the case of general businesses, and fifteen (15) days in the case of public services.

Article 55 (Composition of Mediation Committee)

(1) A Mediation Committee shall be established within the Labor Relations Commission for purpose of mediation of labor disputes.

(2) The Mediation Committee under paragraph (1) shall be composed of three (3) mediation members.

(3) The mediation members under paragraph (2) shall be designated by the Chairman of the Labor Relations Commission from among the members of the Labor Relations Commission concerned so that each member can represent employers, workers, and the public interest. The member representing workers shall be designated from the members recommended by the employer, and the member representing employers shall be designated from the members recommended by the trade union. However, in cases where a list of members who have been recommended by the parties concerned is not submitted within three (3) days prior to a meeting of the Mediation Committee, the Chairman may designate the members.

(4) Where undue hardship is present in organizing the Mediation Committee pursuant to paragraph (3), due to the fact that either the member representing workers or the member representing employers fails to participate, the Chairman of the Labor Relations Commission may designate three (3) members, from among the members of the Commission who represent public interest, as the mediation members, except where there is a member of the Labor Relations Commission, selected based on agreement between both parties, the selected member shall be designated as a mediation member. <Newly inserted by Act No. 8158, Dec. 30, 2006>

Article 56 (Chairman of Mediation Committee)

(1) There shall be a chairman in the Mediation Committee.

(2) The Chairman shall be the mediation member representing public interest, except that the Chairman of the Mediation Committee organized pursuant to Article 55 (4) shall be elected by mutual voting of the Mediation Committee. <Amended by Act No. 8158, Dec. 30, 2006>

Article 57 (Mediation by a Single Mediator)

(1) The Labor Relations Commission may authorize a single mediator to conduct mediation proceedings in lieu of the Mediation Committee at the request or with the agreement of both of the parties concerned.

(2) The single mediator under paragraph (1) shall be designated by the Chairman of the Labor Relations Commission from among the members of the Labor Relations Commission who have been agreed upon by the parties involved.

Article 58 (Verification of Claims)

The Mediation Committee or the single mediator, as the case may be, shall designate a specific date for the parties concerned to appear before the said committee or the single mediator to verify the main points of their respective claims.

Article 59 (Restriction on Attendance)

The Chairman of the Mediation Committee or the single mediator, as the case may be, may restrict the attendance of persons other than the parties concerned and witnesses for the hearing.

Article 60 (Preparation of a Mediation Proposal)

(1) The Mediation Committee or the single mediator, as the case may be, shall prepare a mediation proposal to be presented to the parties concerned, with recommendation for their acceptance, and may simultaneously publish it along with its reasons, and if necessary, may request cooperation of the press or broadcasting media for reporting.

(2) If the Mediation Committee or the single mediator, as the case may be, determines that further proceedings of the mediation is not warranted due to the parties' refusal to accept the mediation proposal, it shall decide to terminate the mediation procedure and notify the decision to the parties concerned.

(3) If the parties concerned, after accepting the mediation proposal in accordance with paragraph (1), do not agree on any of the interpretation or implementation measures of the proposal, they shall request the Mediation Committee or the single mediator, as the case may be, to provide a clear opinion on the interpretation or implementation

measures.

(4) Upon receipt of the request made pursuant to paragraph (3), the Mediation Committee or the single mediator, as the case may be, shall render a clear opinion within seven days from date of receipt of such request.

(5) No parties concerned shall conduct industrial actions with regard to the interpretation or implementation of the mediation proposal concerned, until the opinion on the interpretation or implementation measures is rendered in accordance with paragraphs (3) and (4).

Article 61 (Effect of Mediation)

(1) If the parties have accepted the mediation proposal referred to in paragraph (1) of Article 60, all members of the Mediation Committee or the single mediator, as the case may be, shall prepare a mediated agreement in writing, signed or sealed by the parties concerned. <Amended by Act No. 8158, Dec. 30, 2006>

(2) The contents of the mediated agreement shall have the same effect as a collective agreement.

(3) The opinion on the interpretation and implementation measures which have been rendered by the Mediation Committee or the single mediator, as the case may be, in accordance with paragraph (4) of Article 60 shall have the same effect as an arbitration ruling.

Article 61-2 (Mediation after Decision Made to End Mediation)

(1) The Labor Relations Commission may conduct mediation to settle a labor dispute even after the decision to end mediation is made pursuant to Article 60 (2).

(2) The provisions of Articles 55 through 61 shall apply mutatis mutandis to the mediation prescribed in paragraph (1). <Newly inserted by Act No. 8518, Dec. 30, 2006>

Section 3 ARBITRATION

Article 62 (Commencement of Arbitration)

The Labor Relations Commission shall conduct arbitration in any of the following cases:

1. Where a request for arbitration is made by both of the parties concerned; or
2. Where a request for arbitration is made by one of the parties in accordance with the provisions of a collective agreement.
3. Deleted. <Act No. 8158, Dec. 30, 2006>

Article 63 (Prohibition of Industrial Action during Period of Arbitration)

Industrial actions shall not be conducted for fifteen (15) days from the date when labor disputes have been referred to arbitration.

Article 64 (Composition of Arbitration Committee)

(1) An Arbitration Committee shall be established within the Labor Relations Commission for the arbitration or review of labor disputes.
(2) The Arbitration Committee under paragraph (1) shall be composed of three (3) members.
(3) The arbitration members under paragraph (2) shall be designated by the Chairman of the Labor Relations Commission from among those who represent public interest in the Labor Relations Commission and are mutually agreed upon by both parties. In cases where the parties do not reach an agreement, the arbitration members shall be designated from members of the Labor Relations Commission who represent public interest.

Article 65 (Chairman of Arbitration Committee)

(1) There shall be a chairman in the Arbitration Committee.
(2) The Chairman shall be elected by mutual voting among members of the Arbitration Committee.

Article 66 (Verification of Claims)

(1) The Arbitration Committee shall designate a specific date for one or both of the parties concerned to appear before the said committee to verify the main points of their respective claims.
(2) With the consent of the Arbitration Committee, members of the Labor Relations Commission representing employers or workers who are

designated by the parties concerned may attend an arbitration meeting to present their opinion.

Article 67 (Restriction on Attendance)

The Chairman of the Arbitration Committee may restrict the attendance of persons other than the parties concerned and witnesses for the hearing.

Article 68 (Arbitration Ruling)

(1) The arbitration ruling shall be made in writing and the effective date shall be clearly stated therein.

(2) If the parties concerned do not agree on the interpretation or implementation measures of the arbitration ruling under paragraph (1), the interpretation by the Arbitration Committee concerned shall prevail and have the same effect as that of an arbitration ruling.

Article 69 (Completion of Arbitration Ruling)

(1) If the party concerned considers that an arbitration ruling rendered by the Regional Labor Relations Commission or Special Labor Relations Commission violates law or is an act beyond its authority, he/she may apply for review of the case to the National Labor Relations Commission within ten (10) days from the date of receipt of the arbitration ruling.

(2) Notwithstanding the provisions of Article 20 of the Administrative Litigation Act, if the party concerned considers that an arbitration ruling rendered by the National Labor Relations Commission or a decision on review in accordance with paragraph (1) violates law or is an act beyond its authority, he/she may bring an administrative suit within fifteen (15) days from the date of receipt of an arbitration ruling or decision on review.

(3) When a request for review has not been made, or an administrative suit has not been brought within the designated period under paragraphs (1) and (2), the arbitration ruling or decision on review shall be final.

(4) When an arbitration ruling or a decision on review has been finalized in accordance with the provisions of paragraph (3), the parties concerned shall comply therewith.

Article 70 (Effect of Arbitration Ruling)

(1) The contents of the arbitration ruling rendered pursuant to Article 68 (1) shall have the same effect as a collective agreement.

(2) The effect of the arbitration ruling or review decision rendered by the Labor Relations Commission shall not be suspended by any application for review or any administrative lawsuit filed with the National Labor Relations Commission pursuant to Article 69 (1) and (2). <Amended in its entirety by Act No. 8158, Dec. 30, 2006>

Section 4 SPECIAL PROVISIONS FOR THE MEDIATION OF LABOR DISPUTES IN PUBLIC SERVICES

Article 71 (Scope of Public Services)

(1) "Public service" under this Act means a service described in each of the following subparagraphs, which is indispensable to daily lives of the general public or has great influence on the national economy: <Amended by Act No. 8158, Dec. 30, 2006>

1. Regular line public transportation services;
2. Water, electricity, gas supply, oil refinery and supply services;
3. Public health and medical services and blood supply services;
4. Banking and mint services; and
5. Broadcasting and telecommunication services.

(2) "Essential public service" under this Act means each service described in the following subparagraphs, which falls within the category of public services under paragraph (1) and whose stoppages and discontinuance may endanger daily lives of the general public, or may undermine the national economy considerably, and whose replacement presents a hardship: <Amended by Act No. 8158, Dec. 30, 2006>

1. Railroad services, inter-city railroad services, and aviation services;
2. Water, electricity, gas supply, oil refinery and supply services;
3. Hospital and blood supply services;
4. Bank of Korea; and
5. Telecommunication services.

Article 72 (Composition of Special Mediation Committee)

(1) A Special Mediation Committee shall be established within the Labor

Relations Commission for the mediation of labor disputes in public services.

(2) The Special Mediation Committee under paragraph (1) shall be composed of three (3) members.

(3) The members of the Special Mediation Committee under paragraph (2) shall be designated by the Chairman of the Labor Relations Commission from four (4) to six (6) members of the Labor Relations Commission who represent public interest and have not been excluded by the trade union or by the employer, after completion of rounds of selection by exclusion. However, in cases where the parties concerned agree to recommend those who are not members of the Labor Relations Commission concerned, those non-members shall be designated. <Amended by Act No. 8158, Dec. 30, 2006>

Article 73 (Chairman of Special Mediation Committee)

(1) There shall be a chairman in the Special Mediation Committee.

(2) The Chairman shall be elected by mutual voting among the members of the Special Mediation Committee who are the members of the Labor Relations Commission representing public interest. If the Special Mediation Committee is composed solely of members not from the Labor Relations Commission, then the Chairman shall be elected by mutual voting among the members. However, in cases where there is only one member representing public interest in the Special Mediation Committee, that member shall be the Chairman.

Article 74 Deleted. <Act No. 8158, Dec. 30, 2006>

Article 75 Deleted. <Act No. 8158, Dec. 30, 2006>

Section 5 EMERGENCY ADJUSTMENT

Article 76 (Decision of Emergency Adjustment)

(1) The Minister of Employment and Labor may make a decision to conduct an emergency adjustment when a labor dispute is related to public services, of vast extent or of specific character, and there is danger of impairing the national economy or the daily lives of the general public.

<Amended by Act No. 10339, Jun. 4, 2010>
(2) The Minister of Employment and Labor shall consult with the Chairman of the National Labor Relations Commission prior to making a decision for an emergency adjustment. <Amended by Act No. 10339, Jun. 4, 2010>
(3) When the Minister of Employment and Labor decides to conduct the emergency adjustment under paragraphs (1) and (2), he shall publicize, without any delay, his decision along with reasons and shall simultaneously notify the decision to each of the parties concerned as well as the National Labor Relations Commission. <Amended by Act No. 10339, Jun. 4, 2010>

Article 77 (Suspension of Industrial Action during Emergency Adjustment)

The parties concerned shall immediately suspend any industrial action when the decision of emergency adjustment is publicized in accordance with paragraph (3) of Article 76, and shall not resume industrial action within thirty (30) days from the date of publication of the decision.

Article 78 (Mediation by National Labor Relations Commission)

The National Labor Relations Commission shall commence, without delay, the procedure of mediation, when it has been notified in accordance with paragraph (3) of Article 76.

Article 79 (National Labor Relations Commission's Right to Refer Disputes to Arbitration)

(1) The Chairman of the National Labor Relations Commission shall, in consultation with its members representing public interest, determine whether the case shall be referred to arbitration, if the mediation provided in Article 78 is not likely to be concluded.
(2) The decision under paragraph (1) shall be made within fifteen (15) days from the date of receipt of the notification made in accordance with paragraph (3) of Article 76.

Article 80 (Arbitration by National Labor Relations Commission)

The National Labor Relations Commission shall conduct, without delay, an arbitration if one or both of the parties concerned have made a request for arbitration, or if it has made a decision to refer the case to arbitration in accordance with Article 79.

Chapter VI UNFAIR LABOR PRACTICES

Article 81 (Unfair Labor Practices)

No employer shall commit an act which falls within the purview of any of the following subparagraphs (hereinafter referred to as "unfair labor practices"): <Amended by Act No. 8158, Dec. 30, 2006>

1. Dismissal of or discrimination against a worker on the grounds that the worker has joined or intended to join a trade union, intended to establish a trade union, or performed a lawful act for the operation of a trade union;

2. Making it a condition of employment that the worker abstain from joining or withdrawing from a trade union, or join a particular trade union. However, in cases where a trade union represents more than two-thirds (2/3) of workers employed in the same business, the conclusion of a collective agreement under which a person is employed on condition that he/she becomes a member of the trade union shall be allowed as an exception. In this case, the employer shall not put the worker in any disadvantageous position in terms of status, on the ground that the worker has been expelled from the trade union, or has withdrawn from the trade union to organize a new trade union or to join another trade union;

3. Refusal or delay of concluding a collective agreement or conducting collective bargaining, without justifiable reasons, with the representative of a trade union or a person who has been authorized by a trade union;

4. Domination of or interference with the formation or operation of a trade union by workers and wage payment for full-time officials of a trade union or financial support for the operation of a trade union. However, the employers may allow the workers to carry out the activities referred to in Article 24 (4) during the working hours and may provide subsidies for the welfare of the workers or for the

prevention and relief of financial difficulties and other disasters and may also provide union office in minimum size; or <Amended by Act No. 9930, Jan. 1, 2010>

5. Dismissal of or discrimination against a worker on the grounds that the worker has taken part in lawful collective activities, has reported the violation of the provisions of this Article by the employer to the Labor Relations Commission, or has testified about such violations or presented evidences to administrative authorities.

Article 82 (Application for Remedy)

(1) A worker or trade union whose rights have been infringed by unfair labor practices may make an application for remedy to the Labor Relations Commission.

(2) Application for remedy under paragraph (1) shall be made within three (3) months from the date when such unfair labor practices have been committed (or from the date of termination in cases where such activities continue).

Article 83 (Investigation)

(1) The Labor Relations Commission shall, without delay, conduct necessary investigation and inquiry of the parties concerned, upon receipt of an application for remedy in accordance with Article 82.

(2) When conducting the inquiry in accordance with paragraph (1), the Labor Relations Commission may, at the request of the parties or by its own authority, have witnesses appear before the Commission, and conduct examinations on the pertinent matters.

(3) When conducting the inquiry in accordance with paragraph (1), the Labor Relations Commission shall provide sufficient opportunities for the parties concerned to present evidence and to cross-examine witnesses.

(4) The procedures concerning the investigation and inquiry by the Labor Relations Commission under paragraph (1) shall be specified by separate rules promulgated by the National Labor Relations Commission.

Article 84 (Order of Remedy)

(1) The Labor Relations Commission, after completing the inquiry

under Article 83 and finding that the employer has committed unfair labor practices, shall issue an order for remedy to the employer. When the Commission determines that unfair labor practice has not been committed, it shall enter a decision to dismiss the application for remedy.

(2) Judgments, orders and decisions under paragraph (1) shall be made in writing, and shall be issued to the pertinent employer and the applicant.

(3) Each of the parties shall comply with the order issued pursuant to paragraph (1).

Article 85 (Finalization of Remedy Order)

(1) Where one of the parties disagrees with any remedy order or dismissal decision by the Regional Labor Relations Commission or by the Special Labor Relations Commission, he/she may make an application for review of such order to the National Labor Relations Commission within ten (10) days from the date of receipt of notice of the order or decision.

(2) The party concerned may bring an administrative suit in accordance with the Administrative Litigation Act against a decision on review made by the National Labor Relations Commission under paragraph (1) within fifteen (15) days from the date of receipt of notice of the decision on review.

(3) Unless an application for review or an administrative suit has been made within the period specified in paragraphs (1) and (2), remedy orders, dismissal decisions or review decisions shall be final.

(4) When dismissal decisions or review decisions have been finalized in accordance with paragraph (3), the parties concerned shall comply with those decisions.

(5) When an employer has initiated an administrative suit in accordance with paragraph (2), the competent court may, at the request of the National Labor Relations Commission, order to enforce the whole or part of the remedy order made by the Central Labor Relations Commission until the judgment of the court is rendered, and may, at the request of the parties or by its own authority, revoke such decision.

Article 86 (Effect of Remedy Order)

The effect of remedy orders, dismissal decisions or review decisions made by the Labor Relations Commission shall not be suspended by an application for review to the National Labor Relations Commission or by the initiation of an administrative suit in accordance with Article 85.

Chapter VII SUPPLEMENTARY PROVISIONS

Article 87 (Delegation of Authority)
The authority of the Minister of Employment and Labor under this act may be partially delegated to a chief of regional labor authorities in accordance with the Presidential Decree. <Amended by Act No. 10339, Jun. 4, 2010>

Chapter VIII PENAL PROVISIONS

Article 88 (Penal Provision)
A person who violates the provisions of Article 41 (2) shall be punished by imprisonment up to five (5) years, or by a fine up to Fifty Million Won.

Article 89 (Penal Provision)
A person who falls under the purview of any of the following subparagraphs shall be punished by imprisonment up to three (3) years, or by a fine up to Thirty Million Won: <Amended by Act No. 8158, Dec. 30, 2006>

1. A person who violates the provisions of Article 37 (2), 38 (1), 42 (1), or 42-2 (2); or
2. A person who violates remedy orders which were finalized pursuant to Article 85 (3) (including the case of applying mutatis mutandis under Article 29-4 (4)), or by an administrative court ruling. <Amended by Act No. 9930, Jan. 1, 2010>

Article 90 (Penal Provision)
A person who violates the provisions of Article 44(2), 69(4), 77, or 81 shall be punished by imprisonment up to two (2) years, or by a fine up to Twenty Million Won.

Article 91 (Penal Provision)
A person who violates the provisions of Article 38 (2), Article 41 (1), Article 42 (2), Article 43 (1), (2) and (4), Article 45 (2), Article 46 (1) or Article 63 shall be punished by imprisonment of up to one year or a fine not exceeding Ten Million Won. <Wholly amended by Act No. 8158, Dec. 30, 2006>

Article 92 (Penal Provision)
A person who falls under the purview of any of the following subparagraphs shall be punished by a fine up to Ten Million Won:
1. A person who violates Article 24 (5); <Newly Inserted by Act No. 9930, Jan. 1, 2010>
2. A person who violates any of the items below among the contents of the collective agreements pursuant to Article 31(1):
   (a) Matters relating to wages, welfare costs, and severance pay;
   (b) Matters relating to working hours and recess hours, holidays and leave;
   (c) Matters relating to the reasons and the major procedures concerning disciplinary actions and dismissal;
   (d) Matters relating to safety and health and assistance in industrial accident;
   (e) Matters relating to provision of facilities and accommodations, and participation in meetings during working hours; and
   (f) Matters relating to industrial action. <Amended by Act No. 6456, Mar. 28, 2001>
3. A person who fails to comply with the contents of the mediated agreement under Article 61(1), or the arbitration ruling under Article 68(1).

Article 93 (Penal Provision)
A person who falls under the purview of any of the following subparagraphs shall be punished by a fine up to Five Million Won:
1. A person who violates the provisions of Article 7(3); or
2. A person who violates orders under Article 21(1), (2), or 31(3).

Article 94 (Joint Penal Provision)

When a representative of a corporation or organization, or agent, worker or other hired persons of a corporation, organization, or individual has committed actions in violation of Articles 88 through 93 in connection with the business of the corporation, organization or individual, a fine prescribed in each of the pertinent Articles shall be imposed on the corporation, organization or individual, as well as on the offender.

Article 95 (Fine for Negligence)

A person who violates a court order under Article 85(5) shall be punished by a fine for negligence up to Five Million Won (in cases where the order is a performance order, an amount computed by a rate of less than half a million won per day multiplied by the number of days during which the order has not been complied).

Article 96 (Fine for Negligence)

(1) A person who falls under purview of any of the following subparagraphs shall be punished by a fine for negligence up to Five Million Won:

1. A person who fails to place or keep documents in accordance with Article 14;
2. A person who fails to report or make a fraudulent report under Article 27;
3. A person who fails to make a report under Article 46(2).

(2) A person who fails to make a report or notification under Articles 13, 28(2), or 31(2) shall be punished by a fine for negligence up to Three Million Won.

(3) The Administrative Authorities shall impose and collect fines for offense under paragraphs (1) and (2) in accordance with the Presidential Decree.

(4) A person who is not satisfied with the imposition of a fine for negligence under paragraph (3) may file complaints to the Administrative Authorities within thirty (30) days from the date of notice of fine for negligence.

(5) When a person subject to a fine for negligence under paragraph (3) files complaints in accordance with paragraph (4), the Administrative

Authorities shall give, without delay, notice of such a complaint to a competent court. The court so notified shall adjudicate on the fine for negligence in accordance with the Summary Proceedings Act.

(6) When the complaint has not been made and the fine for negligence has not been paid within the period stipulated in paragraph (4), the fine for negligence shall be collected according to the process for the recovery of the national taxes in arrears.

ADDENDA <No. 10339, 04. Jun, 2010>

Article 1 (Enforcement Date)
This Act shall enter into force one month from the date of its promulgation. (proviso omitted)

Article 2 Omitted.

Article 3 Omitted.

Article 4 Omitted.

Article 5 Omitted.